A CONCORDANCE TO THE POEMS
OF
OLIVER GOLDSMITH

A CONCORDANCE TO THE POEMS
OF
OLIVER GOLDSMITH

Compiled and Edited
by
WILLIAM DOREMUS PADEN
and
CLYDE KENNETH HYDER

THE UNIVERSITY OF KANSAS

GLOUCESTER, MASS.
PETER SMITH
1966

CONTENTS

INTRODUCTION

This concordance is based exclusively upon The Poetical Works of Oliver Goldsmith edited by Austin Dobson and published by the Oxford University Press in 1906. The copies used had been made from the plates, on India paper, in 1927. Today, more than a decade later, the edition is still the standard collection of Goldsmith's verse. Thirty-five years of usefulness, in these days of vigorous research, may be taken as proof--if anyone need proof--that the edition has merit.

Yet Dobson, when dealing with a major work, pursued the plan of printing the text of a late edition published during Goldsmith's life, and recording "the more important" variants. He seems to have recorded all verbal changes; but he did not describe his practice in so many words. He did not always say what editions he had, and what editions he had not, seen. When dealing with a minor work, he could remark that it was "unnecessary to specify the variations" between texts a half-century apart, and then print the later of the two. Though he does not say so, it is probable that the later text was printed from the original manuscript. A systematic treatment would inspire more complete confidence in students of our day; still, we need not suppose that Dobson missed much that is significant.

The editors of this concordance have not attempted to glean where Dobson harvested. They have possessed neither the materials nor the time for such a task. And since the basis of the concordance is admittedly not exhaustive, the editors have not attempted to deal with the texts of Goldsmith's verse which have been discovered since Dobson's day--with one exception, explained below. They have, however, for the convenience of the student, listed those new texts which are available and the announcements of texts which are as yet unpublished, so far as they are aware of them.

The editors have received permission to publish the following paragraph from a letter by Professor R. S. Crane: "I doubt very much whether any verses ascribed to Goldsmith not included in Dobson's edition have any serious claims to authenticity. On the other hand, I am inclined to suspect the genuineness of several poems which Dobson included. Among these are 'The Logicians Refuted' and 'An Epigram, Addressed to the Gentlemen Reflected on in The Rosciad': I know of no clear positive evidence for accepting these late ascriptions. And I feel even more strongly convinced that the translation of Vida's Game of Chess should henceforth be excluded from the canon. The sole ground of its ascription to Goldsmith in the middle of the nineteenth century was the belief that the manuscript in which it appears (originally in the possession of Bolton Corney) was in Goldsmith's hand. I have compared a photograph of the manuscript with the rather extensive collection of Goldsmith autographs in the British Museum and can assure you that there is no resemblance between the hand in which the Game of Chess is written and Goldsmith's hand at any period of his life from 1757 to 1774." In compliance with Professor Crane's opinion, and in order to save expense, we have dealt with the translation of Vida in a summary manner which will be explained below. The two shorter poems mentioned by Professor Crane have been fully treated. Concerning "The Logicians Refuted," Mr. Harold Williams has remarked that "There can hardly be a doubt ... that the poem was written by Goldsmith ... in imitation of Swift" (The Poems of Jonathan Swift, 1937, p. 1141). Among the verses attributed to Goldsmith by editors previous to Dobson, only "The Fair Thief" has found a recent champion, and he was half-hearted (Notes and Queries, CLXIV, 1933, 438-440). Incidentally, the manuscript of the Game of Chess reappeared in 1928 (TLS, March 15, 1928, p. 192).

We have not indicated verses which are said to have been written by Dr. Johnson, or which were borrowed by Goldsmith from other poets. We have excluded the stage-directions in prologues and epilogues and in "The Captivity," and the couplet supposed to have been made by Goldsmith at the age of nine.

We have taken account of one text discovered since Dobson's time. This is the earliest text of "The Double Transformation," which Mr. Arthur Friedman discovered (under the title of "The Double Metamorphosis") in The Weekly Magazine: or, Gentleman and Lady's Polite Companion (#2, January 5, 1760). Only one copy, in the Henry E. Huntington Library, is known. Dobson printed the text which he found in the second edition of Essays: by Mr. Goldsmith (1766), and noted the variants in the first edition (1765). All these variants appear, with others, in the text of 1760. In the circumstances, we have considered that special treatment was necessary. We have therefore given the 1760 text completely, and have added a concordance of the verbal variants. The variants of 1765, noted by Dobson, do not appear in the main concordance. We have included all other variants noted by Dobson which involve a verbal change, and the fragmentary translations collected by Dobson in his Appendix D.

The editors wish to thank Miss Martha Tillman and Miss Velma Wilson, successively directors of the College Aid Project of the National Youth Administration at the University of Kansas, and the students whom they assigned to help us; Mr. C. M. Baker, Director of Libraries, who provided space where the work might be carried on; and the Committee on Graduate Research, which made a grant for necessary materials. Professor Lane Cooper of Cornell, Professor R. S. Crane of Chicago, and Professor C. B. Tinker of Yale have written us letters of counsel--not all of which we have been able to follow. Mr. Leslie E. Bliss, the librarian of the Henry E. Huntington Library, has allowed us to reproduce material from photostats.

EXPLANATION OF METHOD

Each poem is referred to by an easily translated symbol. Thus, the "Elegy on the Death of a Mad Dog" is referred to as "MDog." An alphabetical list of symbols appears below.

Each occurrence of a word (with the exceptions listed below) is indicated by a line such as the following:

Both mongrel, puppy, whelp, and hound, ... 15 MDog 65

--which shows that, for example, the word "mongrel" appears in the fifteenth line of the "Elegy on the Death of a Mad Dog," on page 65 of Dobson's edition.

When two lines are identical, the reference for any word in them is illustrated by

Tremble, ye mortals, at my rage! . . . . . 79,83 Thrn 76, 77

But when a line appears in two different poems, it is entered twice.

References to the second act of "The Captivity" are illustrated by the form "II:5 Capt 118"; and similarly with the first and third acts.

Line-numbers have been carried on consecutively throughout "Threnodia Augustalis."

A word which occurs twice in one line is given only one entry for that line.

All words are listed alphabetically, in their modern spelling; cross-references indicate the occurrence of unorthodox or unusual spellings.

Homonyms and different parts of speech are separated, and differentiated by subscripts.

A hyphenated word is listed--by an indented entry--after the independent occurrences of each of its elements. A few words, not now thought of as compounds, are treated as such: thus "to-day" is entered under "today," but has cross-references under "to-" and "-day."

Formations which are the result of metrical elision are usually disregarded; thus, "t'advance" is entered only under "advance."

LIST OF WORDS OMITTED

a	have	on	to
am	he	or	too
an	her	our	up
and	hers	ours	us
are	him	out	was
at	his	shall	we
be	if	she	were
been	in	that	which
but	is	the	will (verb)
by	it	their	with
for	its	them	you
from	no	these	your
had	not	they	yours
has	of	this	

LIST OF WORDS CITED BY SYMBOL AND LINE-NUMBER

about	behind	down	I
above	below	each	I'd
after	beneath	e'en	I'll
again	beside	e'er	I'm
against	between	'em	into
all	beyond	even	it's
along	both	ever	I've
around	can	every	may
away	cannot-can't	here	me
before	could	how	might (the verb)

more	so	those	what
my	some	thou	when
ne'er	still	though	where
never	such	through	while (conjunction)
nor	than	thus	who
o'er	that's	thy	whom
off	thee	till	whose
oft	then	'tis	within
often	there	'twas	without
once	there's	until	would
over	they're	upon	ye
should	thine	we'll	yet
			you'll

The occurrences of the word "as" are listed partly in the full form, partly by symbol and line-number only.

Words occurring in the translation of Vida's Game of Chess are listed by symbol and line-number only, after the other entries.

TREATMENT OF VARIANTS

Obvious typographical errors, noted as such by Dobson, have been disregarded.

Variants in punctuation have been disregarded.

A single variant line placed by Dobson in his "Notes" is indicated by the letter v placed before its line number.

Variants of more than one line placed by Dobson in his "Notes" have been given line-numbers, for the sake of simplicity, in an illogical manner: the first line of the variant has been given the line-number of the first line in the equivalent passage in the text--or a line-number following that of the last line in the passage in the text which it should succeed; later lines of the variant have been given succeeding line-numbers. All such line-numbers are preceded by the letter v and enclosed in parentheses. Thus the entry,

And patriotic boasting reason's shame! . . . . . v(82) Trav 168

is not a variant of the eighty-second line of "The Traveller," but the eighth line in a variant of the passage which begins with the seventy-fifth line in Dobson's text of "The Traveller."

RECENTLY DISCOVERED TEXTS OF GOLDSMITH'S VERSE

The texts of Goldsmith's verse which have been discovered since Dobson's time are as follows:

(a) Professor Pottle has printed (Boswell Papers, IX, 1930, 114) the MS from which Dobson's text of the "Song intended for She Stoops to Conquer" ultimately descends. There are no variants.

(b) Miss Katharine C. Balderston has printed (Collected Letters of Oliver Goldsmith, 1928, xliv-xlvi, 64-65, 131-135) the original MSS of the second "Epilogue written for She Stoops to Conquer," "Description of an Author's Bedchamber," and the "Letter to Mrs. Bunbury." To Dobson's text of the first, she adds sixteen verses suppressed by Bishop Percy; to his text of the third, she adds a hitherto unknown final couplet. Miss Balderston has also provided the only authoritative version of the couplet supposed to have been made by Goldsmith at the age of nine (p. 166); and she gives some verses which he is said to have composed at the age of seven (pp. 163-164).

(c) Mr. Arthur Friedman has discovered the earliest text of "The Double Transformation," and has attributed to Goldsmith an "Epitaph for the Rev. Dr. Milner." His article is in Modern Philology, XXXII (1935), 281-299.

(d) Professor Crane has attributed to Goldsmith nine lines of a parody, which may be found in his New Essays by Oliver Goldsmith (1927), p. 115.

(e) Mr. Philip Magnus has announced his discovery of holograph MSS of some additional lines of "Retaliation" and of a hitherto unknown poem written by Goldsmith to Reynolds (TLS, December 11, 1937, p. 947).

(f) Miss Balderston has recorded (A Census of the Manuscripts of Oliver Goldsmith, 1926) the existence of two MS copies of "The Captivity," and has located the MS (published in 1801) of the first epilogue written for She Stoops to Conquer. She has also announced the existence of a licencer's MS copy of the play (MLN, XLV, 1930, 84-85).

(g) A MS of "The Haunch of Venison," said to contain variants "from the last printed version." was sold at Sotheby's in 1929 (TLS, October 24, 1929, p. 852).

SYMBOLS USED IN THIS CONCORDANCE

"Amw	Song ("Ah, me! when shall I marry me?")
Byth	On a Beautiful Youth struck Blind with Lightning
Capt	The Captivity
Cati	Translation ("Chaste are their instincts")
ClRp	The Clown's Reply
DABd	Description of an Author's Bedchamber
DRtH	On the Death of the Right Hon. ***
DTrn	The Double Transformation
DVil	The Deserted Village
Ed&A	Edwin and Angelina
eGNM	Epilogue to The Good Natured Man
epEP	Epitaph on Edward Purdon
epLL	Epilogue for Mr. Lee Lewes
epTP	Epitaph on Thomas Parnell
eSis	Epilogue to The Sister
$eSSC_1$	(First) Epilogue written for She Stoops to Conquer
$eSSC_2$	(Second) Epilogue written for She Stoops to Conquer
$eSSC_3$	Epilogue to She Stoops to Conquer
GCRL	To G. C. and R. L.
Gift	The Gift
GRos	An Epigram. Addressed to the Gentlemen reflected on in The Rosciad...
HofV	The Haunch of Venison
Invt	Verses in Reply to an Invitation to Dinner
LetB	Letter ... to Mrs. Bunbury
LogR	The Logicians Refuted
"LSm	Song ("Let school-masters puzzle their brain")
MBlz	An Elegy on Mrs. Mary Blaize
MDog	Elegy on the Death of a Mad Dog
MrsX	On seeing Mrs. *** perform in the Character of ****
NSim	A New Simile, in the Manner of Swift
pLab	Prologue of Laberius
pZob	Prologue to Zobeide
Queb	Stanzas on the Taking of Quebec
Rtal	Retaliation
Sonn	A Sonnet ("Weeping, murmuring, complaining")
Thrn	Threnodia Augustalis...
Tr	Fragments of translations in Dobson's Appendix D
Trav	The Traveller
TrSA	Translation of a South American Ode
Vida	Vida's Game of Chess
"Wlw	Song ("When lovely woman stoops to folly")

From The Weekly Magazine: or, Gentleman and Lady's Polite Companion, No. 2 (January 5, 1760), pp. 47-50:

We know not whom to thank for the following exquisite piece of humour; all we can say is, that every future favour of our anonymous correspondent will meet with as much gratitude from us, as it will esteem from the public.

The DOUBLE METAMORPHOSIS: A TALE:

Secluded from domestic strife
Jack Book wit liv'd a college life;
A fellowship at twenty five
Made him the happiest man alive,
He drank his glass, and crack'd his joke,
And Freshmen wonder'd as he spoke;
He rak'd and toasted, dived or shone:
And even was thought a knowing one.
Without politeness aim'd at breeding,
And laugh'd at pedantry and reading;
Thus sad or sober, gay or mellow,
Jack was a college pretty fellow.
Such pleasures unallay'd with care,
Could any accident impair?
Could Cupid's shaft at length transfix,
Poor Jack arriv'd at thirty six?
O had the archer ne'er come down
To ravage in a country town!
Or Hetty been content to stop,
At triumphs in a Fleet-street shop.
O had her eyes forgot to blaze!
Or Jack had wanted eyes to gaze:
O——but let exclamation cease,
Her presence banish'd all his peace.
Our altered Parson now began,
To be a perfect ladies man;
Made sonnets, lisp'd his sermons o'er,
And told the tales he told before,
Of bailiffs pump'd, and proctors bit,
At college how he shew'd his wit;
And as the fair one still approv'd,
He fell in love-- or thought he lov'd.
They laugh'd, they talk'd with giddy glee,
Miss had her jokes well as he:
In short, their love was passing wonder,
They tallied as if torn assunder;
So with decorum all things carried,
Miss psha'd and frown'd, and then was married.
Need we expose to vulgar sight,
The raptures of the bridal night?
Need we intrude on hallow'd ground,
And draw the curtains clos'd around:
Suffice to say that each had charms,
Jack clasp'd a goddess in his arms;
And tho' she felt his visage rough,
Yet in a man 'twas well enough.
And here direction might prevail,
To interrupt the tedious tale;
Poetic justice bids it rest,
And leave 'em both completely blest:
Yet more importunate than they,
Truth bids me on, and I obey.
The honey month like lightening flew,
The second brought its transports too.
A third, a fourth were not amiss,
The fifth was friendship mix'd with bliss:
But when a twelvemonth pass'd away
Jack found his goddess made of clay:
Found half the charms that deck'd her face,
Arose from powder shreds or lace;
But still the worst remain'd behind,
That very face had rob'd her mind.
Skill'd in no other arts was she,
But dressing, patching, repartee;
And just as humour rose or fell,
By turns a slattern or a belle:
'Tis true she dress'd with modern grace,
Half naked at a ball or race;
But when at home, at board or bed,
Five greasy nightcaps wrap'd her head:
Could so much beauty condescend,
To be a dull domestic friend?
Could any courtain lectures bring,
To decency so fine a thing?
In short by night 'twas fits or fretting,
By day 'twas gadding or coquetting.
Now tawdry Madam kept a bevy,
Of powder'd coxcombs at her levy;
The squire and captain took their stations,
And twenty other near relations;
Jack suck'd his pipe and often broke
A sigh in suffocating smoke;
She in her turn became perplexing,
And found substantial bliss in vexing.
Thus every hour was pass'd between,
Insulting repartee or spleen:
Each day the more her faults are known,
He thinks her features coarser grown;
He fancies every vice she shews,
Or thins her lip, or points her nose:
Whenever rage or envy rise,
How wide her mouth, how wild her eyes!
He knows not how, but so it is,
Her face is grown a knowing phyz;
And tho' her fops are wondrous civil,
He thinks her ugly as the Devil.
Thus to perplex the ravell'd nooze,
While each a different way pursues,
While sulky or loquacious strife,
Promis'd to hold them on for life.
That dire disease whose ruthless power
Withers the beauty's transient flower:
Lo! the small pox with horrid glare,
Levell'd its terrors at the fair;
And rifling every youthful grace,
Left but the remnant of a face.
The glass grown hateful to her sight,
Reflected now a perfect fright:
Each former art she vainly tries
To bring back lustre to her eyes.
In vain she tries her pastes and creams,
To smooth her skin, or hide its seams;
Her country beaux and city cousins,
Lovers no more; flew off by dozens:
The squire himself was seen to yield,
And even the captain quit the field.

Poor Madam now condemn'd to hack
The rest of life with anxious jack,
Perceiving others fairly flown
Attempted pleasing him alone.
Jack soon was dazzl'd to behold
Her present face surpass the old;
With modesty her cheeks are dy'd,
Humility displaces pride;
For tawdry finery is seen,
A person ever neatly clean:
No more perfuming on her sway
She learns good nature every day,
Serenely gay, and strict in duty,
Jack finds his wife a perfect beauty.

VARIANTS IN "THE DOUBLE METAMORPHOSIS"

The following is a concordance of the verbal variants for the lines given above. All words not variant from Dobson's text, as well as all words systematically omitted from the main concordance, are of course omitted here. Numbers indicate lines in this text (1760).

aimed 9
altered 25
approved 31
as 31, 34, 36
assunder (sic) 36

bailiffs 29
became 83
before 28
began 25
bids 49, 52
bit 29
blest 50
bliss 84
book 2
book(-)wit 2
both 50
breeding 9

college 12, 30
completely 50

dived (dined?) 7
direction 47

'em 50
even 8, 116
every 85

fair 31
fell 32
fellow 12
found 84

gay 11
giddy 33
glee 33

here 47
Hetty 19
hour 85
how 30

I 52
importunate 51
interrupt 48

Jack 12, 16, 44
jokes 34
justice 49

knowing 8

ladies 26
laughed 10, 33
leave 50
lisped 27
lived 2
love 32, 35
loved 32

Madam 77
made 27
man 26
mellow 11
might 47
Miss 34
more 51, 87

now 25, 77

obey 52
o'er 27
one 8, 31

parson 25
passing 35
pastes 111
pedantry 10
perfect 26
perplexing 83
poetic 49
politeness 9
pretty 12
prevail 47
proctors 29
psha'd 38
pumped 29

raked 7
reading 10
rest 49

sad 11
say 43
sermons 27
shewed 30
shone 7
short 35
sober 11
sonnets 27
still 31
substantial 84
suffice 43
sulky 99

tale 48
tales 28
talked 33
tallied 36
tawdry 77
tedious 48
than 51
thought 8, 32
thus 11, 85, 97
toasted 7
told 28
torn 36
truth 52
turn 83

unallayed 13

vexing 84
visage (usage?) 45

well 34
while 98
wit 2, 30
without 9
wonder 35

yet 51

A- A-preaching that drinking is
sinful ....11 "LSm 84
ABIDE See also 'BIDE.
Yet, though to fortune lost, here
still abide ....v145 Trav 170
ABLE Here, waiter! more wine, let
me sit while I'm able, ...19 Rtal 87
ABODE Bless'd that abode, where want
and pain repair, ...15 Trav 5
ABOUND Bless'd be those feasts where
mirth and peace abound, ...v17 Trav 167
Hoards, e'en beyond the miser's
wish abound, ...271 DVil 32
Here ill-condition'd oranges
abound-- ....21 pZob 72
ABOUT NSim, 45; eGNM, 7, 10; "LSm, 19; eSSC$_3$,
15; HofV, 106; LetB, 8
ABOVE Trav, 33, 332, 417; DVil, 405; Thrn, 111;
Rtal, 124; epLL, 16; Vida, 167
ABRIDGMENT An abridgment of all
that was pleasant in man; ....94 Rtal 90
ABSTAIN Vida, 169
ACCENTS And his last falt'ring
accents whisper'd praise. ....176 DVil 29
His gentle accents fell: ....34 Ed&A 60
ACCIDENT Could any accident impair? 8 DTrn 52
ACCORD Good people all, with one
accord, ...1 MBlz 47
ACCORDANT And now his voice, accord-
ant to the string, ...II:69 Capt 121
ACCUMULATES Where wealth accumu-
lates, and men decay: ....52 DVil 25
ACCUSE His very worst foe can't
accuse him of that: ....132 Rtal 91
ACQUAINTANCE An acquaintance, a
friend as he call'd himself, enter'd;36 HofV 96
'Some lords, my acquaintance, that
settle the nation, ...43 HofV 96
My acquaintance is slight, or I'd ask
my Lord Clare. ....50 HofV 96
ACQUAINTED His well acquainted tints,
and kindred hues. ....6 Cati 94
ACT$_1$ The First Act shows the simple
country maid, ...9 eSSC$_3$ 85
Her Second Act displays a livelier
scene-- ....13 eSSC$_3$ 85
The Fourth Act shows her wedded to
the 'Squire, ...23 eSSC$_3$ 85
The Fifth and Last Act still remains
for me. ....33 eSSC$_3$ 86
ACT$_2$ Vida, 229
ACT$_3$ And footmen, lords and dukes
can act. ....56 LogR 45
To act as an angel, and mix with the
skies: ....120 Rtal 91
No--I will act. I'll vindicate the
stage: ....19 epLL 101
ACTED Here Cumberland lies, having
acted his parts, ...61 Rtal 89
ACTING 'Twas only that when he was off
he was acting. ....102 Rtal 90
ACTION Bring action for assault and
battery, ...21 LogR 44
Blushes when hir'd, and, with unmean-
ing action, ...11 eSSC$_3$ 85
ACTOR As an actor, confess'd without
rival to shine: ....95 Rtal 90
ACTS What! five long acts--and all to
make us wiser! ....1 eSis 70
ADD Add too, what certain writers
tell, ...41 NSim 57
ADDED Ev'ry added pang she suffers 40,48 Thrn 75
And every added weight of woe .....I:9 Capt 113
Vida, 171
ADDRESS For you, bright fair, the
nine address their lays, ...1 MrsX 49
Still thus address the fair with voice
beguiling:-- ....22 eSSC$_1$ 104
ADDRESSED With fond complaint ad-
dressed the listening Jove, ...10 MrsX 49
ADMIRE Vida, 677
ADMIT Merry Whitefoord, farewell!
for thy sake I admit ....171 Rtal 93
ADMITS Here, richly deck'd, admits the
gorgeous train; ....320 DVil 33
ADOPTING Adopting his portraits, are
pleas'd with their own. ....72 Rtal 89
ADOPTS The soul adopts, and owns their
first-born sway; ....256 DVil 31
ADORN Her modest looks the cottage
might adorn, ...329 DVil 34
'No more shall my crook or my temples
adorn, ...240 Thrn 83
No more will her crook or her temples
adorn; ....252 Thrn 83
ADORNED His looks adorn'd the vener-
able place; ....178 DVil 29
While thus the land adorn'd for
pleasure, all ....285 DVil 32
ADORNS Adorns and cheers our way; II:38 Capt 119
Adorns and chears the way; .....vII:38 Capt 250
ADVANCE At sports like these, while
foreign arms advance, ...v(155) Trav 170
Vida, 187, 220, 325, 458, 504
ADVANCES When time advances, and
when lovers fail, ...292 DVil 33
First Sir Charles advances with
phrases well strung, ...55 LetB 133
ADVANCING Hither the affected city dame
advancing, ...19 eSSC$_2$ 108
ADVENTURE This is his first adven-
ture; lend him aid, ...33 pZob 73
All smirking, and pleasant, and big
with adventure, ...3 LetB 131
ADVENTURES And fits his little frigate
for adventures: ....10 pZob 72
ADVENTUROUS Vida, 496
ADVERSE Vida, 4, 32, 52, 198, 271, 585
ADVERTISER When both have been spoil'd
in to-day's Advertiser? ....44 Invt 129
ADVICE I ask for advice from the lady
that's next: ....28 LetB 132
'Pray, Ma'am, be so good as to give
your advice; ....29 LetB 132
For giving advice that is not worth
a straw, ...37 LetB 132
ADVISE 'I advise,' cries the lady,
'to try it, I own.-- ....31 LetB 132
ADVISER Our authoress sure has wanted
an adviser. ....2 eSis 70
Of all the tribe here wanting an adviser ....33 eSSC$_2$ 109
AESOP'S 'Twas thus that Aesop's stag,
a creature blameless, ...27 epLL 102

AFAR Such be her fate. But listen!
from afar ....III:83 Capt 126
AFFECTATION 'Twere affectation all,
and school-taught pride, ...v39 Trav 168
AFFECTED Hither the affected city
dame advancing, ...19 eSSC$_2$ 108
AFFECTING On the stage he was nat-
ural, simple, affecting; ....101 Rtal 90
AFFIRM The Moon, says he:-- but I
affirm the Stage: ....6 eSSC$_2$ 108
AFFLICTED Vida, 465
AFFLICTION Affliction still is vir-
tue's opportunity! ....35 Thrn 75
Affliction o'er each feature reign-
ing, ...233 Thrn 82
AFFORD No product here the barren
hills afford, ...169 Trav 10
AFFRIGHT A visage so sad, and so
pale with affright, ...109 HofV 98
Vida, 514
AFFRONTS Goes out, affronts his man,
and takes a beating. ....30 eSSC$_1$ 109
AFRAID Looking, as who should say,
D-- --! who's afraid? ....30 eSis 71
Harmless and young, of ev'ry thing
afraid; ....10 eSSC$_3$ 85
AFRIC'S O'er Afric's sandy plain, ..214 Thrn 82
O'er Afric's sandy plain, ...II:16 Capt 118
AFTER Trav, 53; LogR, 49; Thrn, 207; eSSC$_1$, 65; Vida, 27, 47, 666
AGAIN Trav, 136; NSim, 24; Thrn, 118, 229; Rtal, 60; HofV, 25; LetB, 57; Ed&A, v(168); Vida, 105, 352, 399, 408, 415, 559
AGAINST Trav, 4, 284; Vida, 88, 155, 234, 301, 330, 333, 527, 648
AGE$_1$ For talking age and whisp'ring
lovers made; ....14 DVil 23
A youth of labour with an age of
ease; ....100 DVil 26
She, wretched matron, forc'd, in age,
for bread, ...131 DVil 27
And save from infamy my sinking age! 2 pLab 41
For grief had seized his early age, v59 Ed&A 208
Bending at once with sorrow and with
age, ...169 Thrn 80
Or how shall age support its feeble
fire? ....172 Thrn 80
'Till having lost in age the power to
kill, ...30 eSSC$_3$ 86
AGE$_2$ But where's this place, this
storehouse of the age? ....5 eSSC$_2$ 108
AGED Whose beard descending swept his
aged breast; ....152 DVil 28
AGES Alike all ages. Dames of an-
cient days ....251 Trav 13
AGO That a few days ago, ...24 Invt 128
AGONISING The lifted axe, the ago-
nising wheel, ...435 Trav 19
AGREE When I behold a factious band
agree ....383 Trav 18
In which all modern bards agree, ...59 NSim 58
In which our scribling bards agree, v59 NSim 206
The base bestow them: but the good
agree ....10 Thrn 74
Truth, Fortitude, and Friendship shall
agree ....136 Thrn 78
Let us, let all the world agree, ...138 Thrn 79
Oil, vinegar, sugar, and saltness
agree: ....12 Rtal 87
And first I hope, you'll readily
agree. ....13 eSSC$_1$ 104
We both agree, like friends, to end
our jarring? ....66 eSSC$_1$ 106
His lunar, and our mimic world
agree. ....8 eSSC$_2$ 108
This moves:--so at last I agree to
relent, ...65 LetB 134
Vida, 182
AGREEABLE But, missing his mirth and
agreeable vein, ...59 Rtal 89
AGREED What if we leave it to the
House? The House!-- Agreed. A-
greed. ....11 eSSC$_1$ 104
Agreed. Agreed. And now with late
repentance, ...69 eSSC$_1$ 106-7
AH Where then, ah! where, shall
poverty reside, ...303 DVil 33
Are these thy serious thoughts?--
Ah, turn thine eyes ....325 DVil 34
Ah, no. To distant climes, a dreary
scene, ...341 DVil 34
For ah! too partial to my life's
decline, ...11 pLab 41
I'll give thee--Ah! too charming
maid, ...19 Gift 43
'And, ah! forgive a stranger rude, 93 Ed&A 62
Yet, ah! what terrors frowned upon
her fate-- ....52 Thrn 76
And ah! bless'd spirit, wheresoe'er
thy flight, ...106 Thrn 77
'And ah!' she cries, all woe-begone,187 Thrn 81
And so was too foolishly honest?
Ah no! ....134 Rtal 91
Ah, me! when shall I marry me? ......1 "Amw 94
Where are the chiels? Ah! Ah, I
well discern ....39 eSSC$_1$ 105
Ah, me! what angry terrors round
us grow; ....II:25 Capt 119
'Well done!' cry the ladies; 'Ah,
Doctor, that's good! ....25 LetB 132
The pool's very rich--ah! the
Doctor is loo'd!' ....26 LetB 132
Ah! the Doctor is loo'd! Come, Doc-
tor, put down.' ....32 LetB 132
AID$_1$ This is his first adventure;
lend him aid, ...33 pZob 73
From China borrows aid to deck the
scene-- ....150 Thrn 79
Kindly came in beauty's aid; ....234 Thrn 82
And gain'd a husband without aid
from dress, ...2 eSSC$_3$ 85
Celestial themes confess'd his
tuneful aid; ....5 epTP 100
Who without your aid must die. ...26 eSSC$_1$ 104
Vida, 379, 616
The soul rejects the aid of art, ...15 Tr 267
AID$_2$ Aid slighted truth; with thy
persuasive strain ....423 DVil 37
But aid the power of doing good-- ..16 Thrn 74
Come, end the contest here, and aid
my party. ....56 eSSC$_1$ 106
AIM$_1$ Each nobler aim, repress'd
by long control, ...155 Trav 10
And the brown Indian marks with
murd'rous aim; ....416 Trav 19
And the brown Indian takes a

deadly aim; ....v416 Trav 175
My wealth perhaps their aim. .....v108 Ed&A 209
Vida, 113, 228, 343, 506, 527, 553
AIM$_2$ Yet still they sit snug, not
a creature will aim ....11 LetB 132
Vida, 120
AIMING Still aiming at honour, yet
fearing to roam, ...47 Rtal 88
AIMS$_1$ With daring aims irregularly
great; ....326 Trav 16
And all that freedom's highest aims
can reach, ...373 Trav 17
Far other aims his heart had learned
to prize, ...147 DVil 28
When noble aims have suffer'd long
controul, ...v155 Trav 171
AIMS$_2$ And spurns the plan that
aims at other ends; ....96 Trav 8
In vain rebellion aims her secret
blow; ....III:4 Capt 122
AIR$_1$ Breasts the keen air, and
carols as he goes; ....186 Trav 11
And waft his godship through the air; 26 NSim 56
But of all the birds in the air, ...25 "LSm 84
Vida, 178, 433, 503, 605
AIR$_2$ He promises with equal air, ...51 LogR 45
ALARMED Vida, 589
ALARMS Alternate spread alarms: .....90 Ed&A 62
Vida, 331, 409
ALAS 'Alas! the joys that fortune
brings ....69 Ed&A 61
'Alas, young man, my writing days are
over; ....12 eGNM 68
Alas! they never had thy hate: ......24 Thrn 75
But alas! that return I never shall
see, ...243 Thrn 83
Would you ask for his merits? alas!
he had none; ....49 Rtal 88
Alas, that such frolic should now be
so quiet! ....52 Rtal 88
What pity, alas! that so lib'ral a
mind ....157 Rtal 93
Alas! too well mine eyes indignant
trace ....III:19 Capt 123
But, alas! your good worships, how
could they be wiser, ...43 Invt 129
Vida, 430
ALE And news much older than their
ale went round. ....224 DVil 30
ALIKE Nature, a mother kind alike
to all, ...81 Trav 8
Alike all ages. Dames of ancient
days ....251 Trav 13
And thou, fair Freedom, taught alike
to feel ....365 Trav 17
Thou transitory flower, alike undone 367 Trav 17
Behave alike--for all ape all. ......58 LogR 45
Alike too both conduce to sleep. ....50 NSim 57
And coxcombs, alike in their failings
alone, ...71 Rtal 89
Thus we, O Lord, alike distrest, III:43 Capt 124
Alike of Heaven and man the foe; III:74 Capt 125
Vida, 25, 106, 394
ALIVE Scarce half alive, oppress'd
with many a year, ...3 pLab 41
Alive, the foe thy dreadful vigour
fled, ...9 Queb 46
Made him the happiest man alive; ....4 DTrn 52
ALL Trav, 18, 30, v39, 41, 44, 64, 72, 78, 81,
v(81), 124, 127, 131, 141, 153, 176, 178, 210,
235, 242, 248, 251, 264, 270, 272, 301, 302,
307, 321, 342, 353, 355, 373, 376, 377, 399,
418, 429, 438; DVil, 17, 34, 36, 38, 47, 72,
81, 83, 84, 92, 111, 123, 128, 129, 135, 141,
149, 166, 188, 202, 207, 216, 217, 237, 254,
260, 272, 284, 285, 294, 331, 345, 384, v384,
402, 413; pLab, 9, 10; LogR, 12, 58; MBlz, 1,
7, 22; DABd, 20; MrsX, 7, 11; GCRL, 1, 4;
TrSA, 1; DTrn, 18, 19, 59; NSim, 13, 59;
Ed&A, 30, 92, 103, 115, v115, 116, v116, 156,
v156, v(165); MDog, 1, 21; eSis, 1, 6, 25,
38; pZob, 5, 27; Thrn, 17, 57, 74, 85, 101,
138, 153, 154, 165, 176, 187, 195, 248; "LSm,
8, 16, 25; eSSC$_3$, 5, 7, 27, 31; Rtal, 20, 33,
37, 56, 65, 81, 94, 169; "Amw, 7; HofV, 49,
67, 98, 105, 106, 122; epLL, 11; eSSC$_1$, 14,
29, 48, 65; eSSC$_2$, 17, 23, 33; Capt, I:5, 6,
7, 26, 61, 67, 85; II:4, 46, 74, 75, 85, 93;
III:10, 11, 14, 37, 47, 49, 59, 75, 104, 106;
Invt, 2; LetB, 3, 8, 10, 15, 23, 27, 43, 45,
53, 58; Vida, 35, 74, 85, 106, 116, 192, 200,
279, 293, 304, 310, 368, 402, 423, 426, 440,
454, 459, 486, 497, 533, 579, 590, 602, 622,
625, 634, 635, 636, 655, 677, 678; Tr, 11
ALL- **MrsX**, 4; Capt, III:67
ALLAY A heart's distress allay; ..v98 Ed&A 209
ALLIED And every want to opulence
allied, ...67 DVil 25
And every want to luxury allied, **v67 DVil 181**
ALLOW And slander itself must allow
him good nature: ....126 Rtal 91
Vida, 570
ALLOWED Claim'd kindred there, and
had his claims allow'd; ....154 DVil 28
Vida, 121
ALLOY Too bless'd, indeed, were such
without alloy, ...337 Trav 16
ALLURED Allur'd to brighter worlds,
and led the way. ....170 DVil 28
ALLURES Allures from far, yet, as I
follow, flies; ....28 Trav 6
ALMIGHTY How long, how long, Almighty
God of all, ...III:37 Capt 124
Vida, 168
ALMOST And here my simile almost
tript, ...55 NSim 57
Till his relish grown callous, almost
to disease, ...111 Rtal 90
That a Scot may have humour, I had
almost said wit: ....172 Rtal 93
ALOFT He bounds aloft, outstrips the
fleeting wind: ....40 epLL 102
ALONE My fortune leads to traverse
realms alone, ...29 Trav 6
Conforms and models life to that
alone. ....94 Trav 8
But small the bliss that sense alone
bestows, ...123 Trav 9
But not their joys alone thus coarsely
flow: ....227 Trav 12
The self-dependent lordlings stand
alone, ...341 Trav 16
Hence all obedience bows to these
alone, ...353 Trav 17

Attempted pleasing him alone. ......94 DTrn 55
And coxcombs, alike in their failings alone, ...71 Rtal 89
Thinks black alone is beauty's favourite hue. ....10 Cati 94
There's my countryman H--gg--ns--Oh! let him alone, ...29 HofV 96
Left alone to reflect, having emptied my shelf, ...59 HofV 97
Both shine at night, for, but at Foote's alone, ...9 $eSSC_2$ 108
Our God alone is all we boast below.I:6 Capt 113
Ourselves alone from idol-worship free? ....I:34 Capt 114
Vida, 104, 179, 416

ALONG Trav, 245; DVil, 43, 65; MrsX, 5; Thrn, 216; Rtal, 45; Capt, I:53, 81; II:18, 50; III: 16, 51, 61; Vida, 230, 314; Tr, 10

ALOUD Vida, 322

ALPINE E'en now, where Alpine solitudes ascend, ...31 Trav 6
Vida, 78

ALREADY Vida, 488

ALSO It gives their follies also room to rise; ....268 Trav 14

ALTAMA Where wild Altama murmurs to their woe. ....344 DVil 34

ALTERED But times are alter'd; trade's unfeeling train ....63 DVil 25

ALTERNATE Thus to my breast alternate passions rise, ...55 Trav 7
Alternate spread alarms: ....90 Ed&A 62
Vida, 26, 367, 494

ALWAYS And always found her kind; ....6 MBlz 47
'Tis Nature's kind retreat, that's always open ....97 Thrn 77
They always preach best with a skinful. ....13 "LSm 84
I answer, no, no, for he always was wiser: ....130 Rtal 91
For you're always polite and attentive, ...61 $eSSC_1$ 106
Vida, 647

AMAIN Vida, 597

AMAZED Amazed the gazing rustics rang'd around, ...214 DVil 30

AMAZEMENT But, whence that shout? Good heavens! amazement all! ...III:47 Capt 124

AMAZONS Vida, 393

AMBITION Repress'd ambition struggles round her shore, ...346 Trav 16
When first ambition struck at regal power; ....394 Trav 18

AMBITIOUS When idly first, ambitious of the town, ...335 DVil 34

AMIDST Amidst the store, should thankless pride repine? ....38 Trav 6
Amidst the store, 'twere thankless to repine. ....v38 Trav 168
And oft I wish, amidst the scene, to find ....59 Trav 7
Spreads its long arms amidst the wat'ry roar, ...289 Trav 14
Amidst thy bowers the tyrant's hand is seen, ...37 DVil 24
Amidst thy desert walks the lapwing flies, ...45 DVil 24
Amidst thy tangling walks, and ruin'd grounds, ...78 DVil 25
Amidst these humble bowers to lay me down; ....86 DVil 26
Amidst the swains to show my booklearn'd skill, ...90 DVil 26
Amidst the clamour of exulting joys, 1 Queb 46
Amidst profusion still I pine; ......2 TrSA 51
Whene'er he spoke amidst the train,v121 Ed&A 210
Here amidst sylvan bowers we'll rove, ...v(161) Ed&A 211
Vida, 475

AMISS A third, a fourth, were not amiss, ...31 DTrn 53
So, perhaps, in your habits of thinking amiss, ...123 HofV 99

AMONG Among the rest young Edwin bow'd, ...v111 Ed&A 209
'What, plant my thistle, Sir, among his roses! ....16 eGNM 68
Still stoops among the low to copy nature. ....40 $eSSC_2$ 109
Vida, 172

AMONGST Amongst the rest young Edwin bow'd, ...111 Ed&A 63

AMPHIBIOUS Sees an amphibious world beneath him smile; ....292 Trav 15

AMPLE What! no reply to promises so ample? ....37 pZob 73

AMUSE I'll sing to amuse you by night and by day, ...41 $eSSC_1$ 105
Still to amuse us inventive, ...62 $eSSC_1$ 106

AMUSED Vida, 679

ANCHORING Down where yon anchoring vessel spreads the sail, ...399 DVil 36

ANCHOVY That Ridge is anchovy, and Reynolds is lamb; ....14 Rtal 87

ANCIENT Alike all ages. Dames of ancient days ....251 Trav 13

ANEW And e'en in penance planning sins anew.. ....130 Trav 9

ANGEL To act as an angel, and mix with the skies: ....120 Rtal 91

ANGELIC O peace of mind, angelic guest! ....II:1 Capt 118

ANGELICA'S And Angelica's whim ....41 Invt 129

ANGELINA 'Turn, Angelina, ever dear,149 Ed&A 64

ANGELS Angels around befriending Virtue's friend; ....108 DVil 26

ANGLE With patient angle trolls the finny deep, ...187 Trav 11

ANGRILY But the judge bids them, angrily, take off their hat. ......46 LetB 133

ANGRY The rabble's rage, and tyrant's angry steel; ....366 Trav 17
Say, would the angry fair one prize 7 Gift 43
Let not the <u>hungry</u> Bavius' angry stroke ....1 GRos 51
Yon broad, bold, angry spark, I fix my eye on, ...27 eSis 71
The Mohawk too--with angry phrases stored, ...27 $eSSC_2$ 109
The whips and angry tortures shall prevail. ....I:94 Capt 117
Than angry monarch's raging. ...II:24 Capt 119
Ah, me! what angry terrors round us grow; ....II:25 Capt 119

Vida, 265, 304
ANGUISH Despair and anguish fled the
struggling soul; ....174 DVil 29
ANIMA Deus est anima brutorum. ......18 LogR 44
ANNOY But foster'd e'en by Freedom,
ills annoy: ....338 Trav 16
With secret course, which no loud
storms annoy, ...433 Trav 19
Sure scenes like these no troubles
e'er annoy! ....323 DVil 34
ANNUAL What annual offering shall I
make, ...3 Gift 43
ANOTHER$_1$ Vida, 351
ANOTHER$_2$ O! had he liv'd another
year!-- ....3 DRtH 50
'Give me another horse! bind up my
wounds!--soft--'twas but a dream,'24 epLL 101
ANOTHER'S Leans for all pleasure on
another's breast. ....272 Trav 14
ANSWER I answer, no, no, for he
always was wiser: ....130 Rtal 91
They, I am sure, will answer my
commands: ....15 eSSC$_1$ 104
Doctors, who cough and answer every
misfortuner, ...53 eSSC$_1$ 106
ANSWERING With answ'ring care
oppress'd; ....62 Ed&A 61
AN'T 'An't please you,' quoth John,
'I'm not given to letters, ...3 ClRp 100
ANXIOUS My anxious day to husband near
the close, ...v87 DVil 182
The rest of life with anxious Jack, 92 DTrn 55
Vida, 145
ANY A courtier any ape surpasses. ..46 LogR 45
Could any accident impair? ....8 DTrn 52
Could any curtain-lectures bring ...49 DTrn 53
If he had any faults, he has left us
in doubt, ...25 Rtal 87
Whose talents to fill any station were
fit, ...161 Rtal 93
APACE Vida, 99
APE$_1$ Of beasts, it is confess'd, the
ape ....41 LogR 45
A courtier any ape surpasses. ....46 LogR 45
APE$_2$ Behave alike--for all ape all. 58 LogR 45
Vida, 39
APENNINE Far to the right where
Apennine ascends, ...105 Trav 8
APING Aping the conduct of superiors; 50 LogR 45
APOLLO Vida, 177, 238, 268, 288, 601, 657
APOLLO'S Vida, 454
APPARENTLY I lay down my stake, ap-
parently cool, ...7 LetB 131
APPEAR Look downward where a hundred
realms appear; ....34 Trav 6
Whatever blooms in torrid tracts
appear, ...115 Trav 9
In florid beauty groves and fields
appear, ...125 Trav 9
But view them closer, craft and fraud
appear, ...305 Trav 15
How sad the groves and plains appear, 9 DRtH 50
Lovely, lasting Peace, appear; .....116 Thrn 78
Vida, 82, 144, 156, 578
APPEARED Next appear'd a lovely maid,232 Thrn 82
Vida, 42, 210
APPEARS If, shrinking thus, when
frowning power appears, ...II:29 Capt 119
Vida, 7
APPETITES These in their turn,
with appetites as keen, ...19 eSis 70
APPLAUDED If dunces applauded, he
paid them in kind. ....114 Rtal 91
APPLAUSE Shall offer up unfeign'd
applause. ....II:96 Capt 122
Vida, 655
-APPLAUSE Nor weighs the solid
worth of self-applause. ....280 Trav 14
APPLES And apples, bitter apples
strew the ground. ....22 pZob 73
APPLY Now to apply, begin we then; ..43 NSim 57
APPROACH So next day, in due splendour
to make my approach, ...65 HofV 97
The growing sound their swift approach
declares;-- ....I:55 Capt 115
APPROACHED Vida, 647
APPROACHING Fears th' approaching
bridal night. ....4 Sonn 46
-APPROACHING Except when fast-
approaching danger warms: ....380 Trav 17
APPROVED Vida, 655
APT Calm is my soul, nor apt to rise
in arms, ...379 Trav 17
ARCADIAN Where lawns extend that
scorn Arcadian pride, ...319 Trav 15
ARCH Like some well-fashion'd arch
thy patience stood, ...32 Thrn 75
ARCHER O had the archer ne'er come
down ....11 DTrn 52
Vida, 280, 313, 324, 332, 342, 350, 370, 385,
442, 447, 554
ARCHERS Vida, 48, 61, 353
ARGUE For e'en though vanquish'd, he
could argue still; ....212 DVil 30
ARGUING In arguing too, the parson
own'd his skill, ...211 DVil 30
ARGUMENT His conduct still right,
with his argument wrong; ....46 Rtal 88
ARIOSTO There is a place, so Ariosto
sings, ...1 eSSC$_2$ 108
ARISE Ferments arise, imprison'd
factions roar, ...345 Trav 16
And all around distressful yells
arise, ...418 Trav 19
Arise, ye sons of worth, arise, ...1 Thrn 74
Arise, all potent ruler, rise, ..II:93 Capt 122
Vida, 275
ARISTOTLE Wise Aristotle and Smig-
lecius, ...5 LogR 44
ARM And while he sinks, without one
arm to save, ...301 DVil 33
ARMED Vida, 115
ARMIES Vida, 1, 31, 435
ARMOUR Vida, 59, 67, 207
ARMS$_1$ Spreads its long arms amidst the
wat'ry roar, ...289 Trav 14
And left a lover's for a father's
arms. ....378 DVil 35
And left a lover's for her father's
arms. ....v378 DVil 190
He clasp'd a goddess in his arms; ...26 DTrn 52
'To win me from his tender arms ....105 Ed&A 62
In Sleep's refreshing arms, ...v126 Ed&A 210
ARMS$_2$ At sports like these, while

foreign arms advance, ...v(155) Trav 170
The land of scholars, and the nurse
of arms, ...356 Trav 17
Calm is my soul, nor apt to rise in
arms, ...379 Trav 17
Vida, 4, 46, 84, 107, 147, 201, 225, 277, 330,
338, 374, 381, 399, 407, 461, 474, 483, 513,
579

ARMY See where an army covers all the
ground, ...III:49 Capt 124
All, all is lost. The Syrian army
fails, ...III:59 Capt 125
Vida, 69, 77, 189, 376, 453
The shouting army cry'd with joy
extreme, ...1 Tr 267

ARNO'S On Idra's cliffs as Arno's
shelvy side; ....84 Trav 8

AROMATIC As aromatic plants bestow I:47 Capt 115

AROSE Arose from powder, shreds, or
lace; ....36 DTrn 53

AROUND Trav, 18, 37, 297, 321, 411, 418; DVil,
91, 108, 181, 214, 272, 283, 352; MrsX, 11;
DTrn, 24; Ed&A, 53; MDog, 21; Rtal, 153, 169;
Capt, I:20, 50; II:75; Vida, 17, 151, 219,
224, 254, 289, 305, 500, 577, 655

ARRAY No vernal blooms their torpid
rocks array, ...171 Trav 11

ARRAYED Here may be seen, in bloodless
pomp array'd, ...149 Trav 10
With all the freaks of wanton wealth
array'd, ...260 DVil 31
In nature's simplest charms at first
array'd; ....296 DVil 33

ARREARS With beer and milk arrears
the frieze was scor'd, ...17 DABd 48

ARRIVED Our swain, arriv'd at thirty-
six? ....10 DTrn 52

ARROW Vida, 281, 346

ART$_1$ As different good, by Art or Nature
given, ...79 Trav 8
Find that each good, by Art or Nature
given, ...v79 Trav 168
From Art more various are the blessings sent; ....87 Trav 8
But while this softer art their bliss
supplies, ...267 Trav 14
Hence ostentation here, with tawdry
art, ...273 Trav 14
And sleights of art and feats of
strength went round; ....22 DVil 24
He tried each art, reprov'd each dull
delay, ...169 DVil 28
One native charm, than all the gloss
of art; ....254 DVil 31
Nor shares with art the triumph of
her eyes: ....290 DVil 32
Each former art she vainly tries ....83 DTrn 54
'For still I tried each fickle art, 129 Ed&A 63
What art can wash her guilt away? ....4 "wlw 67
The only art her guilt to cover, ...5 "wlw 67
Who knows each art of coaxing up the
town, ...5 eGNM 68
And art exhausts profusion round, ..129 Thrn 78
The man had his failings, a dupe to
his art. ....98 Rtal 90
Taught by our art her ridicule to
pause on, ...21 $eSSC_2$ 108
No, never! May this hand forget each
art ....I:89 Capt 117
Mark where he sits, with executing
art, ...II:65 Capt 120
Skilled in every peaceful art; III:100 Capt 127
Vida, 538
The soul rejects the aid of art, ...15 Tr 267

ART$_2$ This world itself, if thou art
here; ....117 Thrn 78
Whence, and what art thou, visionary
birth? ....7 epLL 101
O Babylon, how art thou fallen! III:78 Capt 126

ARTIFICIAL Lift the tall rampire's
artificial pride. ....286 Trav 14
Ogles and leers with artificial
skill, ...29 $eSSC_3$ 86

ARTIST There the pale artist plies
the sickly trade; ....316 DVil 33

ARTS By arts, the splendid wrecks of
former pride; ....146 Trav 10
Some splendid arts, the wrecks of former
pride; ....v146 Trav 170
Theirs are those arts that mind to
mind endear, ...257 Trav 13
Convenience, plenty, elegance, and
arts; ....304 Trav 15
And, e'en while fashion's brightest
arts decoy, ...263 DVil 32
To see ten thousand baneful arts
combin'd ....311 DVil 33
Thou guide by which the nobler arts
excel, ...415 DVil 37
Skill'd in no other arts was she ...39 DTrn 53
On 'Squires and Cits she there dis-
plays her arts, ...19 $eSSC_3$ 85

AS (partial list)
As some lone miser visiting his store,51 Trav 7
As different good, by Art or Nature
given, ...79 Trav 8
Bright as the summer, Italy extends; 106 Trav 8
As in those domes, where Caesars once
bore sway, ...159 Trav 10
And as a child, when scaring sounds
molest, ...205 Trav 12
Dull as their lakes that slumber in
the storm. ....312 Trav 15
And, as a hare, whom hounds and horns
pursue, ...93 DVil 26
And, as a bird each fond endearment
tries ....167 DVil 28
As some tall cliff, that lifts its
awful form, ...189 DVil 29
As some fair female unadorn'd and
plain, ...287 DVil 32
Sweet as the primrose peeps beneath
the thorn; ....330 DVil 34
As ocean sweeps the labour'd mole
away; ....428 DVil 37
As rocks resist the billows and the
sky. ....430 DVil 37
As when in Paphian groves the Queen
of Love ....9 MrsX 49
He thinks her ugly as the devil. ...70 DTrn 54
Soft as the dew from heav'n descends,33 Ed&A 60
Blest as the songsters of the
grove, ...v(163) Ed&A 211
As puffing quacks some caitiff wretch

procure ....1 eGNM 68
As some unhappy wight, at some new
play, ...23 eGNM 68
As a safe inn, where weary travel-
lers, ...87 Thrn 77
Where, splendid as the youthful poet's
dream, ...142 Thrn 79
Awful as clouds that nurse the growing
storm; ....II:68 Capt 121
As panting flies the hunted hind,III:39 Capt 124
Trav, 28, 83, 84, 100, 186, 229, 235, 334, 349,
v349, 350, 400, 413; DVil, 20, 23, 54, 77,
v(81), 115, 117, 397; pLab, 18; LogR, 2, 28;
DRtH, 19, 20; GRos, 5; DTrn, 6, 41, 61, 72;
NSim, 21, 30, 51, 60; Ed&A, 8, 88, 103,
v103, v(164); MDog, 14; eGNM, 28; eSis, 19,
30; Thrn, 11, 65, 66, 86, 95, 160, 180;
eSSC$_3$, 3, 4, 12, 21; Rtal, 60, 64, 95, 96,
107, 120, 133; HofV, 8, 9, 12, 19, 22, 36,
38, v38, 51, 74, 80, 85, 121; ClRp, 6;
eSSC$_2$, 28; Capt, I:42, 47; II:6, 39, 55, 58,
81; III:57; Invt, 5; LetB, 22, 24, 29, 36;
Vida, 27, 43, 62, 77, 99, 166, 176, 177,
235, 261, 323, 362, 363, 370, 371, 373, 401,
423, 434, 435, 439, 562, 563, 568, 583, 624,
629, 648, 668, 671; Tr, 10
'AS Yet ere he lands he 'as ordered
me before, ...13 pZob 72
ASCEND E'en now, where Alpine solitudes
ascend, ...31 Trav 6
ASCENDING Vida, 624
ASCENDS Far to the right where Apennine
ascends, ...105 Trav 8
ASIDE Nor force nor fraud could turn
my steps aside; ....6 pLab 41
Vida, 135, 213, 306
ASK Nor ask luxuriance from the
planter's toil; ....120 Trav 9
At proud men's doors they ask a little
bread! ....340 DVil 34
Go, ask your manager.' 'Who, me?
Your pardon; ....19 eGNM 68
To ask for charity? ....190 Thrn 81
Too late in life for me to ask, ...191 Thrn 81
Would you ask for his merits? alas!
he had none; ....49 Rtal 88
Perhaps you may ask if the man was a
miser? ....129 Rtal 91
It's a truth--and your Lordship may
ask Mr. Byrne. ....18 HofV 95
It's a truth--and your Lordship may
ask Mr. Burn. ....v18 HofV 238
My acquaintance is slight, or I'd ask
my Lord Clare. ....50 HofV 96
I ask for advice from the lady that's
next: ....28 LetB 132
Now, ladies, I ask, if law-matters
you're skill'd in, ...35 LetB 132
ASKED Those calm desires that ask'd
but little room, ...70 DVil 25
ASKS The heart distrusting asks, if
this be joy. ....264 DVil 32
ASLANT Vida, 212
ASLEEP Vida, 36
ASPECT In thy black aspect every
passion sleeps, ...9 epLL 101
ASPEN With aspen boughs, and flowers,
and fennel gay; ....234 DVil 31
ASPIRE Ye powers of truth, that bid
my soul aspire, ...363 Trav 17
ASPIRES Who think it freedom when a
part aspires! ....378 Trav 17
ASS All play their own way, and they
think me an ass,-- ....15 LetB 132
ASSAIL Vida, 203, 418
ASSAULT Bring action for assault and
battery, ...21 LogR 44
ASSERTS Boldly asserts that country
for his own, ...v66 Trav 168
ASSES To tell them the reason why
asses had ears? ....2 ClRp 100
As I hope to be saved! without think-
ing on asses.' ....6 ClRp 100
ASSIGNED Such are the charms to barren
states assign'd; ....209 Trav 12
Lost human wits have places there
assign'd them, ...3 eSSC$_2$ 108
ASSIST Not to assist, but to bewail 70 Thrn 76
Assist my cause with hands and voices
hearty; ....55 eSSC$_1$ 106
Assist me, I pray, in this woful
attack; ....58 eSSC$_1$ 106
Vida, 5
ASSISTANCE Shall lend my simile
assistance. ....62 NSim 58
Give him good words indeed, but no
assistance. ....22 eGNM 68
Good Savages, our Captain craves
assistance; ....30 pZob 73
Vida, 204
ASSOCIATES Vida, 489
ASSUAGE But nothing mirthful could
assuage ....v57 Ed&A 208
Vida, 437
ASSUME Yet, when he deigns his real
shape t' assume, ...35 eSis 71
ASSUMES Here vanity assumes her pert
grimace, ...275 Trav 14
ASTONISHED The astonish'd fair one
turned to chide,-- ....v147 Ed&A 211
Whilst thus he spoke, astonish'd,
to his view, ...37 epLL 102
ASTRAY And strangers led astray. ...40 Ed&A 60
ASTRONOMERS When wise Astronomers to
India steer, ...3 pZob 72
ATLANTIC Vida, 365
ATTACK$_1$ Assist me, I pray, in this
woful attack; ....58 eSSC$_1$ 106
ATTACK$_2$ If with a bribe his candour
you attack, ...39 eSis 71
ATTEMPT Vida, 180, 228
ATTEMPTED Attempted pleasing him
alone. ....94 DTrn 55
ATTEMPTS$_1$ Vida, 598
ATTEMPTS$_2$ Vida, 580
ATTEND And round his dwelling guardian
saints attend: ....12 Trav 5
How would my heart attend! ......v122 Ed&A 210
The triumphs that on vice attend I:43 Capt 115
ATTENDANTS Vida, 471
ATTENDING The praise attending pomp
and power, ...6 Thrn 74
ATTENDS Each to the favourite happiness
attends, ...95 Trav 8

I still had hopes, for pride attends
us still, ...89 DVil 26
ATTENTION Vida, 20
ATTENTIVE For you're always polite
and attentive, ...61 eSSC$_1$ 106
ATTORNEY He was, could he help it?--
a special attorney. ....136 Rtal 91
AUBURN Sweet Auburn! loveliest village
of the plain, ...1 DVil 23
Sweet Auburn! parent of the blissful
hour, ...75 DVil 25
Do thine, sweet AUBURN, thine, the
loveliest train, ...337 DVil 34
AUGHT Yet he was kind; or if severe
in aught, ...205 DVil 30
AUGUSTA On the grave of Augusta
these garlands be plac'd, ...255 Thrn 83
On the grave of Augusta this garland
be plac'd, ...259 Thrn 83
AUGUSTA'S$_1$ All whom Augusta's bounty
fed, ...153 Thrn 79
Augusta's care had well supplied. ..186 Thrn 81
AUGUSTA'S$_2$ I'll not wear a garland--
Augusta's away, ...241 Thrn 83
AUTHOR Excuse me, Ma'am. The Author
bid me sing it. ....4 eSSC$_1$ 103
AUTHORESS Our authoress sure has
wanted an adviser. ....2 eSis 70
AUTHOR'S$_1$ His wand's a modern author's
pen; ....44 NSim 57
Our Author's friends, thus plac'd
at happy distance, ...21 eGNM 68
AUTHOR'S$_2$ Our Author's the least
likely to grow wiser; ....34 eSSC$_2$ 109
AUTHORS By classic authors term'd
caduceus, ...33 NSim 57
They('re) both of them merry and
authors like you; ....76 HofV 97
AVARICE And all are taught an avarice
of praise; ....264 Trav 14
One sink of level avarice shall lie, 359 Trav 17
I venture at all,--while my avarice
regards ....23 LetB 132
AVENGING And wish the avenging fight.230 Thrn 82
Vida, 101
AVER Her love was sought, I do aver, 17 MBlz 47
AVERSE To coxcombs averse, yet most
civilly steering, ...143 Rtal 92
AVERSION Now, my Lord, as for tripe,
it's my utter aversion, ...85 HofV 98
AWAKE$_1$ Though ne'er so much awake
before, ...39 NSim 57
AWAKE$_2$ Awake resentment, or your rage
provoke; ....2 GRos 51
AWAY Trav, 256; DVil, 50, 156, 364, 428; DRtH,
3, 16; DTrn, 33; "wlw, 4; Thrn, 241, 253; eSSC$_1$,
44, 57; eSSC$_2$, 18; Capt, II:32; Vida, 187,
387, 449, 586, 661
AWE Still gather strength, and force
unwilling awe. ....352 Trav 17
AWFUL As some tall cliff, that lifts
its awful form, ...189 DVil 29
Awful as clouds that nurse the grow-
ing storm; ....II:68 Capt 121
Vida, 420
AWFULLY Vida, 160
AWHILE Suspend awhile the task, the
tear suspend, ...I:3 Capt 113
Awhile the bliss suspend; ......III:28 Capt 123
Vida, 192, 208
AWKWARD To dress, and look like
awkward Frenchmen here, ...34 eSSC$_1$ 105
AXE The lifted axe, the agonising
wheel, ...435 Trav 19
AXLE The parting surface leaves his
brazen axle dry. ....6 Tr 267
AY But how? ay, there's the rub!--I've
got my cue: ....11 eSis 70
Ay, take your travellers, travellers
indeed! ....37 eSSC$_1$ 105
AYE Aye, 'twas but a dream, for now
there's no retreating: ....25 epLL 101

B--B Nor draw the quill to write for
B--b. ....32 LogR 45
BABES And kiss'd her thoughtless babes
with many a tear, ...381 DVil 36
'And where,' he cried, 'shall now my
babes have bread, ...171 Thrn 80
BABYLON On Babylon it lies; .....II:76 Capt 121
Then shall Babylon fall. ....III:12 Capt 122
O Babylon, how art thou fallen! III:78 Capt 126
BACK To bring back lustre to her
eyes. ....84 DTrn 54
I'd best step back--and order up a
sample. ....38 pZob 73
As often we wish'd to have Dick back
again. ....60 Rtal 89
For he knew when he pleas'd he could
whistle them back. ....108 Rtal 90
I don't think he'll wish to come back.4 epEP 100
When the ladies are calling, to blush
and hang back; ....60 eSSC$_1$ 106
BACKS Vida, 28, 49, 114
BACKWARD Vida, 117
BACON One gammon of bacon hangs up
for a show: ....10 HofV 95
This tale of the bacon a damnable
bounce? ....14 HofV 95
At the top a fried liver and bacon
were seen, ...81 HofV 97
And your bacon I hate like a Turk or
a Persian; ....86 HofV 98
While the bacon and liver went merri-
ly round. ....88 HofV 98
BAD Each case, however bad, he'll new
japan; ....6 GRos 51
BADE Those gentle hours that plenty
bade to bloom, ...69 DVil 25
The broken soldier, kindly bade to
stay, ...155 DVil 28
My friend bade me welcome, but struck
me quite dumb, ...69 HofV 97
BAGPIPES When you with your bagpipes
are ready to play, ...43 eSSC$_1$ 105
BAILEY What justice, when both to the
Old Bailey brought! ....41 LetB 133
BAILIFFS There in a lonely room,
from bailiffs snug, ...5 DABd 48
BAIRN The smiling looks of each
bewitching bairn. ....40 eSSC$_1$ 105
BAKER$_1$ That she came with some terrible
news from the baker: ....112 HofV 98
BAKER$_2$ And Baker and his bit, ...12 Invt 128

Vida, 86, 193
BEARD Whose beard descending swept
his aged breast; ....152 DVil 28
-BEARD Where grey-beard mirth and
smiling toil retir'd, ...222 DVil 30
BEAST Vida, 237, 551
BEASTS Where beasts with man divided
empire claim, ...415 Trav 19
And that brute beasts are far before
'em, ...17 LogR 44
Of beasts, it is confess'd, the ape 41 LogR 45
Vida, 114
BEATEN He quits the woods, and tries
the beaten ways; ....41 epLL 102
BEATING Goes out, affronts his man,
and takes a beating. ....30 $eSSC_2$ 109
BEAUMONTS And Beaumonts and Bens be
his Kellys above. ....124 Rtal 91
BEAUTIES In all my Enna's beauties
blest, ...1 TrSA 51
Surpris'd, he sees new beauties rise,85 Ed&A 62
He sees unnumber'd beauties rise, v85 Ed&A 209
Unite to stamp the beauties of the
place, ...**145 Thrn 79**
That she who form'd your beauties is
no more. ....166 Thrn 80
BEAUTY In florid beauty groves and
fields appear, ...125 Trav 9
Dear mercenary beauty, ...2 Gift 43
Or dim thy beauty with a tear? ......6 Sonn 46
Why dim thy beauty with a tear? ...v6 Sonn 196
Could so much beauty condescend ....47 DTrn 53
Jack finds his wife a perfect
beauty. ....104 DTrn 55
Truth, beauty, worth, and all that
most engage, ...74 Thrn 76
'The garland of beauty'--'tis thus
she would say-- ....239 Thrn 83
With garlands of beauty the queen of
the May ....251 Thrn 83
Like an ill-judging beauty, his
colours he spread, ...99 Rtal 90
No foreign beauty tempts to false
desire; ....2 Cati 94
Wine and beauty thus inviting, ..I:71 Capt 116
BEAUTY'S Withers the beauty's
transient flower: ....76 DTrn 54
Kindly came in beauty's aid; ......234 Thrn 82
Thinks black alone is beauty's
favourite hue. ....10 Cati 94
BEAUX By twenty beaux and more; ....18 MBlz 47
Her country beaux and city cousins, 87 DTrn 55
Ye beaux and belles, that form this
splendid ring, ...5 $eSSC_1$ 103
BECOMES Becomes a source of pleasure
when redrest. ....214 Trav 12
-BECOMING Those ill-becoming rags--
that matted hair! ....III:34 Capt 123
BED With many a tale repays the
nightly bed. ....198 Trav 11
Luke's iron crown, and Damiens' bed
of steel, ...436 Trav 19
Beside the bed where parting life
was laid, ...171 DVil 29
A bed by night, a chest of drawers
by day; ....230 DVil 30
But when at home, at board or bed, 45 DTrn 53

There, sorrowing by the river's glassy
bed, ...151 Thrn 79
Vida, 466
BEDS These rocks, by custom, turn to
beds of down. ....86 Trav 8
BEEF If our landlord supplies us with
beef, and with fish, ...3 Rtal 87
I think they love venison--I know they
love beef; ....28 HofV 96
BEER With beer and milk arrears the
frieze was scor'd, ...17 DABd 48
BEFORE Trav, 283; DVil, 345; LogR, 17; **MBlz**,
20; DRtH, 8; **NSim**, 39; pZob, 13; Thrn, 195,
217; epLL, 1, 43; Capt, III:68, 71; Invt, 4;
LetB, 36, 44; **Vida**, 6, 135, 195, 490; Tr, 5
BEFRIENDING Angels around befriending
Virtue's friend; ....108 DVil 26
BEG No stirring--I beg--my dear
friend--my dear friend! ....56 HofV 97
Vida, 522
BEGAN A time there was, ere England's
griefs began, ...57 DVil 25
His pity gave ere charity began. ..162 DVil 28
Then pull'd his breeches tight, and
thus began, ...v(22) DABd 200
And tears began to flow. ....60 Ed&A 61
But when a pique began, ...18 MDog 65
Our empire began, ...III:8 Capt 122
Like yours, his life began in
pride, ...III:29 Capt 123
BEGETS This favourite good begets
peculiar pain. ....98 Trav 8
And industry begets a love of gain. 300 Trav 15
BEGGAR Here beggar pride defrauds her
daily cheer. ....277 Trav 14
The long-remember'd beggar was his
guest, ...151 DVil 28
And so bold, and so bold, I'm at last
a bold beggar. ....34 LetB 132
BEGGAR'S The beggar's pouch and
prince's purple lie, ...104 Thrn 77
BEGGED Vida, 379
BEGIN That quickly they begin to
snore. ....40 NSim 57
Now to apply, begin we then; ....43 NSim 57
Begin, ye captive bands, and strike
the lyre, ...II:45 Capt 120
Let us, and all, begin and end, in
Thee! ....III:106 Capt 127
Vida, 194
Begin, ye daughters of immortal
verse; ....8 Tr 267
BEGINNING A hopeful end indeed to such
a blest beginning. ....8 $eSSC_1$ 103
O Thou, without beginning, without
end, ...III:105 Capt 127
BEGINS And Madam now begins to hold
it higher; ....24 $eSSC_3$ 85
-BEGONE 'And ah!' she cries, all
woe-begone, ...187 Thrn 81
BEGUILE Or friend beguile with lies
and flattery? ....22 LogR 44
BEGUILED By sports like these are all
their cares beguil'd, ...153 Trav 10
The lingering hours beguil'd. ......52 Ed&A 60
BEGUILING Still thus address the fair
with voice beguiling:-- ....22 $eSSC_1$ 104

Hear the grove to bliss be-
guiling; ....II:48 Capt 120
BEGUN E'en now the devastation is
begun, ...395 DVil 36
Are not this very morn those feasts
begun, ...I:35 Capt 114
Thy vengeance be begun: ....III:56 Capt 124
BEHAVE Behave alike--for all ape
all. ....58 LogR 45
BEHELD Beheld the duteous son, the
sire decay'd, ...407 Trav 18
Beheld each hour ....63 Thrn 76
Beheld our power in Zedekiah's
fall? ....II:86 Capt 121
BEHIND Trav, 132, 157; DVil, 228; MBlz, 8; DRtH, 7; DTrn, 37; Rtal, 138; HofV, 58; epLL, 39; Capt, II:13, 91; Vida, 135, 525
BEHOLD When I behold a factious band
agree ....383 Trav 18
Behold him humbly cringing wait .....47 LogR 45
Jack soon was dazzl'd to behold .....95 DTrn 55
Behold his wretched corse with sorrow
worn, ...III:31 Capt 123
BEING Being each as great a thief as
he: ....60 NSim 58
In the hopes of being blest. .....39,47 Thrn 75
And comedy wonders at being so fine; 66 Rtal 89
I put off being shaved; ....6 Invt 128
Vida, 540, 553
BELGIC Heavens! how unlike their Belgic
sires of old! ....313 Trav 15
BELIEVE This, I believe, between us
great or small, ...3 GCRL 51
BELLE By turns a slattern or a belle: 42 DTrn 53
BELLES Ye beaux and belles, that form
this splendid ring, ...5 $eSSC_1$ 103
BELONGS Reason, they say, belongs to
man, ...3 LogR 44
BELOW Trav, 63, 376; DVil, 116; Ed&A, 31; Thrn, 4, 112; epTP, 8; epLL, 15; Capt, I:6, 7, 64; II: 23; Vida, 247, 606
BEND That this way slowly bend along
the plain? ....III:16 Capt 123
Vida, 62, 122, 402
BENDING Ye bending swains, that dress
the flow'ry vale, ...48 Trav 6
The pensive exile, bending with his
woe, ...419 Trav 19
**Bending at once with sorrow and with
age, ...169 Thrn 80**
BENDS Bends at his treasure, counts,
re-counts it o'er; ....52 Trav 7
Bends to the grave with unperceiv'd
decay, ...109 DVil 26
That feebly bends beside the plashy
spring; ....130 DVil 27
The modest stranger lowly bends .....35 Ed&A 60
The grateful stranger lowly bends. v35 Ed&A 208
BENEATH Trav, 254, 292; DVil, 13, 18, 330; DABd, 6, 9; Ed&A, 41; Vida, 609; Tr, 11
BENEFACTOR And hail the benefactor
of mankind: ....III:88 Capt 126
BENS And Beaumonts and Bens be his
Kellys above. ....124 Rtal 91
BENT And calmly bent, to servitude
conform, ...311 Trav 15
**More bent to raise the wretched
than to rise. ....v148 DVil 84**
Vida, 90, 333, 459, 639
BEPLASTERED And beplaster'd with
rouge his own natural red. ....100 Rtal 90
BESIDE Trav, 244; DVil, 130, 171, 193, 318; Ed&A, 101, v102, 117; eSis, 15; Thrn, 159; $eSSC_1$, 7; Invt, 13
BESIDES Besides, a singer in a comic
set!-- ....9 $eSSC_1$ 104
BESIEGE Vida, 91
BESIEGED Vida, 253, 588
BESPOKE Vida, 296
BEST His first, best country ever is,
at home. ....74 Trav 7
His best companions, innocence and
health; ....61 DVil 25
And his best riches, ignorance of
wealth. ....62 DVil 25
'Tis best, however, keeping at a
distance. ....29 pZob 73
I'd best step back--and order up a
sample. ....38 pZob 73
Let us prize death as the best gift
of nature-- ....86 Thrn 77
They always preach best with a
skinful. ....13 "LSm 84
Let each guest bring himself, and he
brings the best dish: ....4 Rtal 87
Those poets, who owe their best fame
to his skill, ...121 Rtal 91
'Thou best humour'd man with the worst
humour'd muse.' ....174 Rtal 93
To paint it, or eat it, just as he
lik'd best. ....22 HofV 95
But in this parallel my best pretence
is, ...13 $eSSC_2$ 108
Don't you think the best way is to
venture for't twice? ....30 LetB 132
Vida, 477, 582, 614
BESTOW The base bestow them: but the
good agree ....10 Thrn 74
And copious libations bestow on his
shrine: ....168 Rtal 93
Needless to him the tribute we
bestow-- ....7 epTP 100
As aromatic plants bestow ....I:47 Capt 115
Both similar blessings bestow; ..I:62 Capt 116
To Heaven their praise bestow, III:66 Capt 125
BESTOWS But small the bliss that
sense alone bestows, ...123 Trav 9
To seek a good each government
bestows? ....426 Trav 19
Whate'er my cell bestows; ....18 Ed&A 59
Some increasing good bestows, ...41,49 Thrn 75
BESTRIDES Perhaps, to vulgar eyes,
bestrides the state; ....34 eSis 71
He turns old woman, and bestrides a
broom. ....36 eSis 71
BETIDE Yet still (and woe betide the
hour!) ....v129 Ed&A 210
BETRAY And finds too late that men
betray, ...2 "wlw 67
BETRAYED Thus fares the land, by
luxury betray'd, ...295 DVil 33
His love-lorn guest betray'd. ......84 Ed&A 62
The bashful guest betray'd. ......v84 Ed&A 209
Vida, 378

BETRAYER'S Near her betrayer's door
she lays her head, ...332 DVil 34
BETS Comes here to saunter, having
made his bets, ...25 eSSC$_2$ 108
BETTER 'From better habitations
spurn'd, ...65 Ed&A 61
Gives <u>genus</u> a better discerning. ....4 "LSm 84
He has not left a better or wiser
behind: ....138 Rtal 91
Nature, a better guide than you. II:54 Capt 120
BETTERS Nor dare I pretend to know
more than my betters; ....4 ClRp 100
BETWEEN Trav, 109; DVil, 268, 342; GCRL, 3;
DTrn, 59; Thrn, 170; Vida, 364, 530, 549, 592,
630, 647
BEVY Fond to be seen, she kept a
bevy ....53 DTrn 53
BEWAIL Not to assist, but to bewail 70 Thrn 76
Vida, 465
BEWITCHING The smiling looks of each
bewitching bairn. ....40 eSSC$_1$ 105
BEYOND Trav, 137, 410; DVil, 271, 368, 374;
pLab, 19; Thrn, 143
BID Ye powers of truth, that bid my
soul aspire, ...363 Trav 17
Excuse me, Ma'am. The Author bid
<u>me</u> sing it. ....4 eSSC$_1$ 103
Is this a time to bid us raise the
strain, ...I:87 Capt 117
Come on, and bid the warbling
rapture rise, ...II:43 Capt 119
Vida, 182, 199, 314, 325, 422
'BIDE 'To 'bide the pelting of this
pitiless storm'-- ....32 eGNM 69
BIDS And bids his bosom sympathise
with mine. ....422 Trav 19
That strain once more; it bids re-
membrance rise, ...I:15 Capt 114
Bids expectation rise. ....II:36 Capt 119
But the judge bids them, angrily,
take off their hat. ....46 LetB 133
Vida, 8, 479.
BIG Yon ill foreboding cloud seems
big with thunder. ....18 pZob 72
All smirking, and pleasant, and big
with adventure, ...3 LetB 131
Vida, 367, 570
BILL A bill, a jewel, watch, or toy, 9 Gift 43
BILLOWED Along the billow'd main: 216 Thrn 81
BILLOWS As rocks resist the billows and
the sky. ....430 DVil 37
BIND But bind him to his native
mountains more. ....208 Trav 12
All claims that bind and sweeten life
unknown; ....342 Trav 16
'Give me another horse! bind up my
wounds!--soft--'twas but a dream,'24 epLL 101
BINDS Only binds the willing
heart. ....III:102 Capt 127
BIRD And, as a bird each fond en-
dearment tries ....167 DVil 28
Prompt not their loves:--the patriot
bird pursues ....5 Cati 94
BIRDS Those matted woods where birds
forget to sing, ...349 DVil 34
But of all the birds in the air, ...25 "LSm 84
BIRTH Whence, and what art thou,
visionary birth? ....7 epLL 101
Ere I forget the land that gave me
birth, ...I:91 Capt 117
BIT$_1$ And, 'Madam,' quoth he, 'may
this bit be my poison, ...**91 HofV 98**
And Baker and his bit, ...12 Invt 128
BIT$_2$ Went mad and bit the man. .....20 MDog 65
Vida, 350
BITE$_1$ The man recover'd of the bite, 31 MDog 66
BITE$_2$ To bite so good a man. ....24 MDog 65
BITES His frothy slaver, venom'd
bites; ....48 NSim 57
BITTER And make full many a bitter
pill go down. ....6 eGNM 68
And apples, bitter apples strew
the ground. ....22 pZob 73
BITTERN The hollow-sounding bittern
guards its nest; ....44 DVil 24
BLACK$_1$ He bows, turns round, and
whip--the man's a black! ....40 eSis 71
BLACK$_2$ Thinks black alone is beauty's
favourite hue. ....10 Cati 94
Vida, 27, 475, 501
-BLACK And brave prince William
show'd his lamp-black face: ....14 DABd 48
And Prussia's monarch shew'd his
lamp-black face ....v14 DABd 200
BLACK$_3$ There the black gibbet
glooms beside the way. ....318 DVil 33
Where Calvert's butt, and Parsons'
black champagne, ...3 DABd 48
In thy black aspect every passion
sleeps, ...9 epLL 101
Vida, 62, 87, 125, 131, 197, 303,
565, 640
BLACKBIRD But the chaste blackbird,
to its partner true, ...9 Cati 94
BLADE He drives his flock to pick
the scanty blade, ...306 DVil 33
BLAIZE Lament for Madam Blaize, ...2 MBlz 47
BLAME Blame where you must, be
candid where you can; ....33 eGNM 69
We scarcely can praise it, or blame
it too much; ....30 Rtal 88
Vida, 543
BLAMELESS 'Twas thus that Aesop's
stag, a creature blameless, ...27 epLL 102
BLAMES Vida, 540
BLAND His manners were gentle,
complying, and bland; ....140 Rtal 91
BLASPHEMERS Blasphemers, all be
dumb. ....II:74 Capt 121
BLAST$_1$ That shades the steep, and
sighs at every blast. ....104 Trav 8
Vida, 438
BLAST$_2$ May rosined lightning blast
me, if I do! ....18 epLL 101
Vida, 582
BLAZE$_1$ His children's looks, that
brighten at the blaze; ....194 Trav 11
BLAZE$_2$ O had her eyes forgot to
blaze! ....15 DTrn 52
BLAZING Tumultuous grandeur crowds
the blazing square, ...321 DVil 34
Those blazing suns that dart a
downward ray, ...347 DVil 34
BLEAK Where the bleak Swiss their

stormy mansións tread, ...167 Trav 10
BLEED Vida, 382
BLEND To blend their virtues while
they think of thee. ....137 Thrn 78
BLENDING While sweetly blending
still are seen ....146 Thrn 79
BLESS She then shines forth,
solicitous to bless, ...293 DVil 33
O! were he born to bless mankind, ...5 DRtH 50
To bless the tomb that wraps thy
clay; ....133 Thrn 78
But ev'ry day her name I'll bless, .199 Thrn 81
Each day, each hour, her name I'll
bless-- ....203 Thrn 81
Wine shall bless the brave and
free. ....I:70 Capt 116
And learn to bless your own. ..III:26 Capt 123
BLESSED See also BLEST
Bless'd be that spot, where
cheerful guests retire ....13 Trav 5
Bless'd that abode, where want and
pain repair, ...15 Trav 5
Bless'd be those feasts with simple
plenty crown'd, ...17 Trav 5
Bless'd be those feasts where mirth
and peace abound, ...v17 Trav 167
May gather bliss to see my fellows
bless'd ....62 Trav 7
So bless'd a life these thoughtless
realms display, ...255 Trav 13
Till, seeming bless'd, they grow to
what they seem. ....266 Trav 14
Too bless'd, indeed, were such
without alloy, ...337 Trav 16
How often have I bless'd the
coming day, ...15 DVil 23
She once, perhaps, in village
plenty bless'd, ...327 DVil 34
And bless'd the cot where every
pleasure rose ....380 DVil 35
Though very poor, may still be very
bless'd; ....426 DVil 37
Bless'd spirit thou, whose fame,
just born to bloom ....18 Thrn 74
And ah! bless'd spirit, wheresoe'er
thy flight, ...106 Thrn 77
BLESSING Hence every state to one
lov'd blessing prone, ...93 Trav 8
My blessing and repose. ....20 Ed&A 59
The wretch who wants each other
blessing, ...I:29 Capt 114
And he who wants each other
blessing, ...vI:29 Capt 250
Comes to heighten every
blessing, ...III:97 Capt 126
BLESSINGS Eternal blessings crown
my earliest friend, ...11 Trav 5
And estimate the blessings which
they share, ...76 Trav 7
To different nations makes their
blessings even. ....80 Trav 8
From Art more various are the
blessings sent; ....87 Trav 8
Thine, Freedom, thine the blessings
pictur'd here, ...335 Trav 16
These simple blessings of the
lowly train; ....252 DVil 31

Both similar blessings bestow; ..I:62 Capt 116
BLEST See also BLESSED
The sons of Italy were surely
blest. ....112 Trav 9
O blest retirement, friend to life's
decline, ...97 DVil 26
How blest is he who crowns in shades
like these, ...v99 DVil 183
In all my Enna's beauties blest, ...1 TrSA 51
Blest as the songsters of the
grove, ...v(163) Ed&A 211
In the hopes of being
blest. ....39, 47 Thrn 75
Is once again with Eden blest, ...118 Thrn 78
He forms a scene beyond Elysium
blest-- ....143 Thrn 79
The nightingale, with mutual
passion blest, ...11 Cati 94
A hopeful end indeed to such a
blest beginning. ....8 eSSC$_1$ 103
BLIND$_1$ O then how blind to all that
truth requires, ...377 Trav 17
That he should be, like Cupid,
blind, ...3 Byth 42
Now, now's our time! ye wretches
bold and blind, III:69 Capt 125
BLIND$_2$ Vida, 320
BLISS To see the hoard of human
bliss so small; ....58 Trav 7
To see the sum of human bliss so
small; ....v58 Trav 168
May gather bliss to see my
fellows bless'd. ....62 Trav 7
Or estimate their bliss on Reason's
plan, ...v76 Trav 168
Find that the bliss of all is
much the same, ...v(81) Trav 168
Still grants her bliss at
Labour's earnest call; ....82 Trav 8
But small the bliss that sense alone
bestows, ...123 Trav 9
And sensual bliss is all the nation
knows. ....124 Trav 9
Enhance the bliss his scanty fund
supplies. ....202 Trav 12
Till, buried in debauch, the bliss
expire. ....226 Trav 12
But while this softer art their
bliss supplies, ...267 Trav 14
That bliss which only centres in
the mind: ....424 Trav 19
Careful to see the mantling bliss
go round; ....248 DVil 31
Thou source of all my bliss, and
all my woe, ...413 DVil 37
She speaks! 'tis rapture all, and
nameless bliss, ...7 MrsX 49
The fifth was friendship mix'd
with bliss: ....32 DTrn 53
May every bliss be thine. ....105 Thrn 77
Hear the grove to bliss
beguiling; ....II:48 Capt 120
Awhile the bliss suspend; .....III:28 Capt 123
BLISSES 'Twas joy, and endless
blisses all around, ...11 MrsX 49
BLISSFUL Sweet Auburn! parent of
the blissful hour, ...75 DVil 25

May blissful endless peace be
thine above! ....111 Thrn 78
BLOATED A bloated mass of rank
unwieldy woe; ....392 DVil 36
BLOCK Vida, 139
BLOCKADE But when contending
chiefs blockade the throne, ...381 Trav 18
BLOCKS Are they but senseless
stones and blocks? ....64 NSim 58
To eat mutton cold, and cut blocks
with a razor. ....42 Rtal 88
BLOOD When wealth and rank and
noble blood, ...15 Thrn 74
Vida, 96, 263, 269, 335, 347, 374,
390
BLOODLESS Here may be seen, in
bloodless pomp array'd, ...149 Trav 10
BLOODS Regale the drabs and
bloods of Drury-lane; ....4 DABd 48
BLOODY Brutes never meet in bloody
fray, ...39 LogR 45
Vida, 110, 133, 163, 206, 249, 384,
408, 574, 636, 654
BLOOM$_1$ I'll strip all the spring
of its earliest bloom; ....248 Thrn 83
We'll rifle the spring of its
earliest bloom, ...256, 260 Thrn 83
Vida, 175
BLOOM$_2$ Those gentle hours that
plenty bade to bloom, ...69 DVil 25
Bless'd spirit thou, whose fame,
just born to bloom ....18 Thrn 74
BLOOMS$_1$ Whatever blooms in torrid
tracts appear, ...115 Trav 9
No vernal blooms their torpid rocks
array, ...171 Trav 11
Still may thy blooms the changeful
clime endure, ...369 Trav 17
And parting summer's lingering
blooms delay'd; ....4 DVil 23
BLOOMS$_2$ The country blooms--a
garden, and a grave. ....302 DVil 33
BLOOMY For all the bloomy flush
of life is fled. ....128 DVil 27
BLOSSOM$_1$ 'The blossom opening
to the day, ...121 Ed&A 63
'The dew, the blossom on the tree, 125 Ed&A 63
BLOSSOM$_2$ With vernal lives that
blossom but to die; ....118 Trav 9
BLOSSOMED With blossom'd furze
unprofitably gay, ...194 DVil 29
-BLOSSOMED The slow canal, the
yellow-blossom'd vale, ...293 Trav 15
And the new-blossomed thorn shall
whiten her tomb. ....250, 258 Thrn 83
BLOW To finish all their efforts
at a blow; ....57 Thrn 76
How shrinks my soul to meet the
threaten'd blow! ....II:26 Capt 119
In vain rebellion aims her
secret blow; ....III:4 Capt 122
Before they feel the blow! ....III:68 Capt 125
Vida, 88, 102, 155, 246, 310,
536, 593, 632
-BLOWN I'll give--but not the
full-blown rose, ...13 Gift 43
BLOWS Vida, 120

BLUNDER For making a blunder, or
picking a bone. ....30 HofV 96
Vida, 298
BLUNDERS Then, with chaos and
blunders encircling my head, ...21 Rtal 87
BLUNT Here Hickey reclines, a most
blunt, pleasant creature, ...125 Rtal 91
BLUNTED Fall blunted from each
indurated heart. ....232 Trav 13
BLUSH$_1$ But, while he spoke, a
rising blush ....83 Ed&A 62
BLUSH$_2$ When the ladies are calling,
to blush and hang back; ....60 eSSC$_1$ 106
BLUSHED Miss frown'd, and blush'd,
and then was--married. ....20 DTrn 52
BLUSHES Blushes when hir'd, and,
with unmeaning action, ...11 eSSC$_3$ 85
BLUSHING The modest matron, and
the blushing maid, ...408 Trav 18
BLUSTERING Vida, 366
BOARD Displays her cleanly platter
on the board: ....196 Trav 11
And five crack'd teacups dress'd
the chimney board; ....18 DABd 48
But when at home, at board or
bed, ...45 DTrn 53
Vida, 37, 673
-BOARD The paste-board triumph
and the cavalcade; ....150 Trav 10
BOAST$_1$ Such is the patriot's
boast, where'er we roam, ...73 Trav 7
BOAST$_2$ To boast one splendid
banquet once a year; ....278 Trav 14
Boast of a florid vigour not
their own; ....390 DVil 36
Our God alone is all we boast
below. ....I:6 Capt 113
Our God is all we boast below, ..I:7 Capt 113
Vida, 250, 444
BOASTED And that this boasted
lord of nature ....13 LogR 44
BOASTFUL While his lov'd partner,
boastful of her hoard, ...195 Trav 11
BOASTING And patriotic boasting
reason's shame! ....v(82) Trav 168
Vida, 572
-BOASTING Than reason-boasting
mortals' pride; ....16 LogR 44
BOASTS Boasts of his golden sands
and palmy wine, 70 Trav 7
While e'en the peasant boasts
these rights to scan, ...333 Trav 16
BODING Well had the boding
tremblers learn'd to trace ....199 DVil 29
BODY And lay my body where my
limbs were lost.' ....224 Thrn 82
A palled corse, and rest the body
there. ....III:18 Capt 123
BOISTEROUS Vida, 364
BOLD Rough, poor, content,
ungovernably bold; ....314 Trav 15
But a bold peasantry, their
country's pride, ...55 DVil 25
Yon broad, bold, angry spark, I
fix my eye on, ...27 eSis 71
In these bold times, when
Learning's sons explore ....1 pZob 72

'Twas a neck and a breast--that
might rival M--r--'s: ....24 HofV 95
'Twas a neck and a breast--that
might rival Monroe's: ....v24 HofV 238
We'll make his temple in our
breast, ...I:13 Capt 113
On God's supporting breast
reclin'd? ....I:98 Capt 117
Thou soft companion of the
breast! ....II:2 Capt 118
Tremble, thou vice-polluted
breast; ....II:73 Capt 121
BREASTS Breasts the keen air,
and carols as he goes; ....186 Trav 11
BREATH A breath can make them, as
a breath has made; ....54 DVil 25
His breath lent fragrance to the
gale, ...119 Ed&A 63
The transitory breath of fame
below: ....8 epTP 100
To the last moment of his
breath ....II:33 Capt 119
BREATHED Vida, 617
BRED But calm, and bred in
ignorance and toil, ...183 Trav 11
Heav'nly born, and bred on high, .114 Thrn 78
-BRED An under-bred, fine-
spoken fellow was he, ...37 HofV 96
BREECHES Then pull'd his breeches
tight, and thus began, ...v(22) DABd 200
-BREED No monster-breed to
mark the groves with shame; ....8 Cati 94
BREEZES There all around the
gentlest breezes stray, ...321 Trav 16
BREEZY The breezy covert of the
warbling grove, ...361 DVil 35
BRIBE If with a bribe his candour
you attack, ...39 eSis 71
BRIDAL Fears th' approaching
bridal night. ....4 Sonn 46
The raptures of the bridal night? .22 DTrn 52
BRIDE And the Jessamy Bride, ...14 Invt 128
Vida, 510, 558
BRIDLES Statesmen with bridles on;
and, close beside 'em, ...15 eSis 70
BRIGHT Bright as the summer, Italy
extends; ....106 Trav 8
Whose bright succession decks the
varied year; ....116 Trav 9
I turn; and France displays her
bright domain. ....240 Trav 13
Yet, why impair thy bright per-
fection? ....5 Sonn 46
For you, bright fair, the nine
address their lays, ...1 MrsX 49
As bright, as transient too. ......88 Ed&A 62
BRIGHTEN His children's looks,
that brighten at the blaze; ......194 Trav 11
But whence, when joy should
brighten o'er the land, ...I:77 Capt 116
BRIGHTENED Liv'd in each look,
and brighten'd all the green; .....72 DVil 25
BRIGHTENING Like flaring tapers
bright'ning as they waste; ....400 Trav 18
And, all his prospects bright'ning
to the last, ...111 DVil 27
BRIGHTER And brighter streams than
fam'd Hydaspes glide. ....320 Trav 15
Allur'd to brighter worlds, and
led the way. ....170 DVil 28
And quit for Venus, many a
brighter here; ....4 pZob 72
Emits a brighter ray. ....II:40 Capt 119
BRIGHTEST And, e'en while
fashion's brightest arts decoy, ..263 DVil 32
BRING Bring action for assault
and battery, ...21 LogR 44
Could any curtain-lectures
bring ....49 DTrn 53
To bring back lustre to her eyes. .84 DTrn 54
A guiltless feast I bring; ....26 Ed&A 60
Let each guest bring himself,
and he brings the best dish: ....4 Rtal 87
To deck it, bring with you
festoons of the vine, ...167 Rtal 93
Sure you mistake, Ma'am. The
Epilogue, I bring it. ....3 $eSSC_1$ 103
Vida, 70, 560
BRINGS With all those ills superfluous
treasure brings, ...302 Trav 15
'Alas! the joys that fortune brings 69 Ed&A 61
Let each guest bring himself, and he
brings the best dish: ....4 Rtal 87
And brings my long-lost country to
mine eyes. ....I:16 Capt 114
BRITAIN How much unlike the sons of
Britain now! ....316 Trav 15
And flies where Britain courts the
western spring; ....318 Trav 15
BRITAIN'S Have we not seen, round
Britain's peopled shore, ...397 Trav 18
For thine and Britain's wrongs they
feel, ...228 Thrn 82
BRITONS That independence Britons
prize too high, ...339 Trav 16
BROAD Where the broad ocean leans
against the land, ...284 Trav 14
Yon broad, bold, angry spark, I fix
my eye on, ...27 eSis 71
BROCADE Here, while the courtier glit-
ters in brocade, ...315 DVil 33
BROGUE With his long-winded speeches,
his smiles and his brogue; ....90 HofV 98
BROILS And on the gridiron broils
her lovers' hearts: ....20 $eSSC_3$ 85
BROKE Jack suck'd his pipe, and
often broke ....57 DTrn 54
Vida, 591
BROKEN The broken soldier, kindly
bade to stay, ...155 DVil 28
While broken tea-cups, wisely kept
for show, ...235 DVil 31
BROOD How hast thou fill'd the scene
with all thy brood, ...11 epLL 101
BROOK The never-failing brook, the
busy mill, ...11 DVil 23
No more thy glassy brook reflects
the day, ...41 DVil 24
To strip the brook with mantling
cresses spread, ...132 DVil 27
The cooling brook, the grassy-vested
green, ...360 DVil 35

BROOKS Where brooks refreshing
stray; ....III:40 Capt 124
BROOM He turns old woman, and
bestrides a broom. ....36 eSis 71
BROTHER Still to my brother turns
with ceaseless pain, ...9 Trav 5
Yes, brother, curse with me that
baleful hour, ...393 Trav 18
Your brother Doctor there, perhaps,
may try.' ....14 eGNM 68
BROUGHT The second brought its
transports too. ....30 DTrn 53
His goods, he hopes, are prime, and
brought from far, ...35 pZob 73
Each guest brought his dish, and the
feast was united; ....2 Rtal 87
What justice, when both to the Old
Bailey brought! ....41 LetB 133
Vida, 22, 283, 666
-BROUGHT While soul-brought tears
steal down each shining face. ....6 MrsX 49
BROW War in each breast, and freedom
on each brow; ....315 Trav 15
No more the smith his dusky brow
shall clear, ...245 DVil 31
How piercing is that eye! how sleek
that brow! ....35 epLL 102
BROWN And the brown Indian marks
with murd'rous aim; ....416 Trav 19
And the brown Indian takes a deadly
aim; ....v416 Trav 175
She left her wheel and robes of
country brown. ....336 DVil 34
-BROWN Low lies that house where
nut-brown draughts inspir'd, ...221 DVil 30
BROWS A nightcap deck'd his brows
instead of bay, ...19 DABd 48
BRUSH'D Thus snatching his hat, he
brush'd off like the wind, ...57 HofV 97
BRUTE$_1$ Who ever knew an honest brute 19 LogR 44
No single brute his fellow leads. ..38 LogR 45
Vida, 247
BRUTE$_2$ And that brute beasts are far
before 'em, ...17 LogR 44
BRUTES Brutes never meet in bloody
fray, ...39 LogR 45
BRUTORUM Deus est anima brutorum. ..18 LogR 44
-BUD Or rose-bud more in fashion; ..14 Gift 43
BUDGE But not a soul will budge to
give him place. ....30 eGNM 69
BUFFOON The old buffoon will fit my
name as well; ....18 pLab 41
BUILDS The shelter-seeking peasant
builds his shed, ...162 Trav 10
BULL Vida, 261, 522
BULWARK The firm-connected bulwark
seems to grow; ....288 Trav 14
Vida, 266
BULWARKS Vida, 71
BUMPER He cherish'd his friend, and
he relish'd a bumper; ....127 Rtal 91
BUNBURY 'What does Mrs. Bunbury?'
'I, Sir? I pass.' ....16 LetB 132
Mr. Bunbury frets, and I fret like
the devil, ...19 LetB 132
BUNCHES With bunches of fennel, and
nosegays before 'em; ....44 LetB 133
BURIED Till, buried in debauch, the
bliss expire. ....226 Trav 12
BURKE Our Burke shall be tongue,
with a garnish of brains; ....6 Rtal 87
We'll have Johnson, and Burke; all
the wits will be there; ....49 HofV 96
Yet Johnson, and Burke, and a good
venison pasty, ...62 HofV 97
With tidings that Johnson and Burke
would not come; ....70 HofV 97
BURN$_1$ Then what was his failing? come,
tell it, and, burn ye! ....135 Rtal 91
Vida, 262
BURN$_2$ See also BYRNE.
It's a truth--and your Lordship may
ask Mr. Burn. ....v18 HofV 238
BURNS Vida, 259, 352
-BURNT Vida, 80
BURST But I've eat of your tripe
till I'm ready to burst.' ....94 HofV 98
Vida, 373, 502, 516
BURSTING Vida, 587
BURTHEN Has frisk'd beneath the
burthen of threescore. ....254 Trav 13
BUSH The hawthorn bush, with seats
beneath the shade, ...13 DVil 23
BUSINESS And half the business of
destruction done; ....396 DVil 36
Hold, Ma'am, your pardon. What's
your business here? ....1 eSSC$_1$ 103
BUSTARDS Your bustards, your ducks,
and your widgeons; ....24 "LSm 84
BUSTLING Warm'd up each bustling
scene, and in her rage ....5 eSis 70
BUSY Ye lakes, whose vessels catch the
busy gale, ...47 Trav 6
Thus idly busy rolls their world
away: ....256 Trav 13
The never-failing brook, the busy
mill, ...11 DVil 23
Remembrance wakes with all her busy
train, ...81 DVil 26
No busy steps the grass-grown foot-
way tread, ...127 DVil 27
Full well the busy whisper, circling
round, ...203 DVil 30
And now, when busy crowds retire ...45 Ed&A 60
BUTT Where Calvert's butt, and Parsons'
black champagne, ...3 DABd 48
BUYS The needy sell it, and the rich
man buys; ....308 Trav 15
BUZZ When uncover'd, a buzz of
enquiry runs round,-- ....47 LetB 133
BY- (By-the-bye you may tell him, 19 Invt 128
-BYE (By-the-bye you may tell him, 19 Invt 128
BYRNE It's a truth--and your Lordship
may ask Mr. Byrne. ....18 HofV 95

C--Y There's H--d, and C--y, and
H--rth, and H--ff, ...27 HofV 96
CADUCEUS By classic authors term'd
caduceus, ...33 NSim 57
CAESAR Caesar persuades, submission
must be mine; ....12 pLab 41
CAESARS As in those domes, where
Caesars once bore sway, ...159 Trav 10
CAITIFF As puffing quacks some

caitiff wretch procure ....1 eGNM 68
CALL$_1$ Still grants her bliss at
Labour's earnest call; ....82 Trav 8
Have we not seen, at pleasure's lordly
call, ...405 Trav 18
But in his duty prompt at every call,165 DVil 28
Relentless tyrant, at thy call ......72 Thrn 76
CALL$_2$ To call it freedom when them-
selves are free; ....384 Trav 18
Call on their mistress--now no more--
and weep. ....162 Thrn 80
Macpherson write bombast, and call
it a style, ...87 Rtal 90
CALLED That call'd them from their
native walks away; ....364 DVil 35
An acquaintance, a friend as he
call'd himself, enter'd; ....36 HofV 96
'I wish I'd been called in a little
sooner:' ....54 eSSC$_1$ 106
May well be call'd picking of
pockets in law; ....38 LetB 133
Vida, 63, 172, 313, 418, 658, 660
CALLING When the ladies are calling,
to blush and hang back; ....60 eSSC$_1$ 106
CALLOUS Whose callous hand had
form'd the scene, ...168 Thrn 80
Till his relish grown callous,
almost to disease, ...111 Rtal 90
CALLS Quits the Ballet, and calls
for Nancy Dawson. ....22 eSSC$_2$ 108
The sun calls us out on this
festival day, ...I:59 Capt 115
CALM But calm, and bred in
ignorance and toil, ...183 Trav 11
Calm is my soul, nor apt to rise
in arms, ...379 Trav 17
Those calm desires that ask'd
but little room, ...70 DVil 25
And calm Religion shall repair .....134 Thrn 78
Vida, 36
CALMLY And calmly bent, to servi-
tude conform, ...311 Trav 15
CALVERT'S Where Calvert's butt,
and Parsons' black champagne, ...3 DABd 48
CAME The mingling notes came
soften'd from below; ....116 DVil 27
Comfort came down the trembling
wretch to raise, ...175 DVil 29
And fools, who came to scoff,
remain'd to pray. ....180 DVil 29
Unnumber'd suitors came; ....106 Ed&A 62
But soon a wonder came to light, ...29 MDog 66
First of the train the patient
rustic came, ...167 Thrn 80
Kindly came in beauty's aid; ....234 Thrn 82
'Twas death,--'twas the death of
my mistress that came. ....246 Thrn 83
Of praise a mere glutton, he
swallow'd what came, ...109 Rtal 90
They enter'd, and dinner was
serv'd as they came. ....80 HofV 97
That she came with some terrible
news from the baker: ....112 HofV 98
'Hoicks! hark forward!' came
thund'ring from behind, ...39 epLL 102
Vida, 48, 338, 342, 507, 528, 554

CAMP Vida, 98, 580
CAMPANIA'S Or where Campania's
plain forsaken lies, ...5 Trav 5
CAMPS From courts, to camps, to
cottages it strays, ...263 Trav 14
Vida, 82, 358
CAN Trav, 41, 64, 175, 242, 373,
430; DVil, 54, 56, 429; LogR, 4, 56;
DABd, 2, v(20); MrsX, 4; GRos, 5;
"wlw, 3, 4; eGNM, 33; Thrn, 174;
Rtal, 30, 93, 147, 169; HofV, 31;
eSSC$_2$, 38; Capt, I:84, 97, II:59,
62; Invt, 33; Vida, 89, 105, 125, 156,
202, 319, 386, 444, 482; Tr, 2
CANAL The slow canal, the yellow-
blossom'd vale, ...293 Trav 15
CANCEL And cancel at threescore
a life of fame; ....16 pLab 41
CANDID Blame where you must, be
candid where you can; ....33 eGNM 69
But let us be candid, and speak
out our mind, ...113 Rtal 91
CANDID- Ye candid-judging few,
hold up your hands. ....16 eSSC$_1$ 104
CANDOUR If with a bribe his candour
you attack, ...39 eSis 71
CANNIBALS Priests, cannibals, and
hoity-toity queens: ....8 pZob 72
CANNOT LogR, 10; MDog, 4; Thrn, 202;
Rtal, 173; Vida, 568
CAN'T eGNM, 9; Rtal, 27, 132; eSSC$_1$,
71
CANVAS The canvas glow'd beyond e'en
Nature warm, ...137 Trav 9
CAP A cap by night--a stocking
all the day! ....20 DABd 48
CAPON That Hickey's a capon, and
by the same rule, ...15 Rtal 87
CAPTAIN The 'squire and captain
took their stations, ...55 DTrn 53
And e'en the captain quit the
field. ....90 DTrn 55
Good Savages, our Captain craves
assistance; ....30 pZob 73
And the Captain in lace, ...18 Invt 128
CAPTIVE$_1$ To chain the strong, and
set the captive free. ....III:90 Capt 126
Vida, 148
CAPTIVE$_2$ Ye captive tribes, that
hourly work and weep ....I:1 Capt 113
This sullen gloom in Judah's
captive band? ....I:78 Capt 116
Begin, ye captive bands, and
strike the lyre, ...II:45 Capt 120
But hush! see, foremost of the
captive choir, ...II:63 Capt 120
See where dethron'd your captive
monarch lies, ...II:88 Capt 121
CAPTIVE'S Vida, 100
CAPTIVES Vida, 398, 421
CARCASE Vida, 410
CARDS She sits all night at cards,
and ogles at spadille. ....31 eSSC$_3$ 86
Round and round go the cards, while
I inwardly damn ....5 LetB 131
The whole pool as my own--'Come, give
me five cards.' ....24 LetB 132

CARE$_1$ My prime of life in wand'ring
spent and care, ...24 Trav 6
In all my wand'rings round this
world of care, ...83 DVil 26
Retreats from care, that never
must be mine, ...98 DVil 26
To sweet oblivion of his daily
care; ....242 DVil 31
Contented toil, and hospitable
care, ...403 DVil 36
And to perform takes equal
care. ....52 LogR 45
Such pleasures, unalloy'd with
care, ...7 DTrn 52
Requir'd a master's care; 42 Ed&A 60
With answ'ring care oppress'd; .....62 Ed&A 61
Forgive, and let thy pious
care ....v97 Ed&A 209
And ev'ry care resign; ....154 Ed&A 64
Thus 'tis with all--their chief
and constant care ....25 eSis 70
Fever and pain and pale con-
sumptive care, ...54 Thrn 76
A sleek and idle race is all
their care. ....176 Thrn 80
Augusta's care had well
supplied. ....186 Thrn 81
A flattering painter, who made
it his care ....63 Rtal 89
Vida, 196, 216, 242, 611
CARE$_2$ 'I don't care if I keep a
corner for't too.' ....102 HofV 98
CAREER And, plac'd on high above
the storm's career, ...33 Trav 6
Vida, 123, 608
CAREFUL Careful to see the mantling
bliss go round; ....248 DVil 31
Vida, 186
CARELESS There, as I pass'd with
careless steps and slow, ...115 DVil 27
Careless their merits, or their
faults to scan, ...161 DVil 28
Vida, 270
CARES Here for a while my proper
cares resign'd, ...101 Trav 8
By sports like these are all their
cares beguil'd, ...153 Trav 10
Their welfare pleas'd him, and
their cares distress'd; ....186 DVil 29
'Then, pilgrim, turn, thy cares
forgo; ....29 Ed&A 60
All earth-born cares are wrong: ....30 Ed&A 60
For earth-born cares are
wrong: ....v30 Ed&A 208
His rising cares the hermit
spied, ...61 Ed&A 61
When they have journeyed through
a world of cares, ...88 Thrn 77
CARINTHIAN Or onward, where the
rude Carinthian boor ....3 Trav 5
CARNAGE Vida, 636
CARO Pretends to taste, at Operas
cries caro, ...25 eSSC$_3$ 85
CAROL My voice shall be ready to
carol away ....44 eSSC$_1$ 105
CAROLLED He caroll'd lays of
love; ....118 Ed&A 63

CAROLS Breasts the keen air, and
carols as he goes; ....186 Trav 11
CARRIED Till, carried to excess
in each domain, ...97 Trav 8
So with decorum all things
carried; ....19 DTrn 52
CARRY That one small head could
carry all he knew. ....216 DVil 30
He, fond youth, that could
carry me, ...3 "Amw 94
Vida, 312
CASE Each case, however bad, he'll
new japan; ....6 GRos 51
'If that be the case, then,'
cried he, very gay, ...45 HofV 96
'My Lord,--your Lordship miscon-
ceives the case;' ....52 eSSC$_1$ 106
'But consider their case,--it
may be your own! ....63 LetB 134
CASES 'But where is your justice?
their cases are hard.' ....61 LetB 133
CAST Like yon neglected shrub
at random cast, ...103 Trav 8
On her grave shall the cowslip
and primrose be cast, ...249 Thrn 83
And there shall the cowslip and
primrose be cast, ...257, 261 Thrn 83
He cast off his friends, as
a huntsman his pack, ...107 Rtal 90
Vida, 253
CASTLES Vida, 70
CASTS Casts a long look where
England's glories shine, ...421 Trav 19
CATCH Ye lakes, whose vessels
catch the busy gale, ...47 Trav 6
Catch every nerve, and vibrate
through the frame. ....220 Trav 12
To catch the heart, or strike
for honest fame; ....410 DVil 36
Oh! for a Richard's voice to
catch the theme: ....23 epLL 101
CATERS Who whisks about the
house, at market caters, ...15 eSSC$_3$ 85
CAUGHT Where once the sign-post
caught the passing eye, ...220 DVil 30
Say, where has our poet this
malady caught? ....73 Rtal 89
Strephon caught thy ravish'd
eye; ....24 eSSC$_1$ 104
CAUSE$_1$ She long had wanted
cause of fear. ....8 Sonn 46
Assist my cause with hands and
voices hearty; ....55 eSSC$_1$ 106
Have we not cause for triumph
when we see ....I:33 Capt 114
And vindicate thy people's
cause; ....II:94 Capt 122
Vida, 163, 345, 654
CAUSE$_2$ That part which laws or
kings can cause or cure. ....430 Trav 19
CAUSED That caused his putrid
kennel to o'erflow, ...9 GRos 51
CAUTION 'Tis in vain that at
niggardly caution I scold, ...13 LetB 132
Vida, 142, 455
CAUTIOUS While novelty, with
cautious cunning, ...148 Thrn 79

I fret in my gizzard, yet, cautious
and sly, ...9 LetB 132
Vida, 274
CAVALCADE The paste-board triumph
and the cavalcade; ....150 Trav 10
CAVES Vida, 422
CAVILLED And cavill'd at his
image in the flood. ....30 epLL 102
CEASE O!--But let exclamation
cease, ...17 DTrn 52
And when in death my vows shall
cease, ...205 Thrn 81
If I cease Harlequin, I cease
from eating. ....26 epLL 101
CEASED Vida, 598
CEASELESS Still to my brother turns
with ceaseless pain, ...9 Trav 5
CEDARS Ye hills of Lebanon, with
cedars crown'd, ...I:19 Capt 114
CELESTIAL Celestial themes con-
fess'd his tuneful aid; ....5 epTP 100
Vida, 82
CELESTIAL- Celestial-like her
bounty fell, ...122 Thrn 78
CELL Whate'er my cell bestows; ......18 Ed&A 59
And follows to the cell. ....36 Ed&A 60
Vida, 396
CENSURE When Satire and Censure
encircl'd his throne, ...83 Rtal 89
CENTRE He eyes the centre, where
his friends sit snug; ....26 eGNM 68
And ogling the stake which is
fix'd in the centre. ....4 LetB 131
CENTRED While thus I debated, in
reverie centred, ...35 HofV 96
-CENTRED Thy towering mind self-
centred stood, ...26 Thrn 75
CENTRES That bliss which only
centres in the mind: ....424 Trav 19
CERTAIN 'Twas certain he could
write, and cypher too; ....208 DVil 30
Add too, what certain writers
tell, ...41 NSim 57
To make out the dinner, full
certain I am, ...13 Rtal 87
CHAFED Vida, 597
CHAIN$_1$ And drags at each remove a
lengthening chain. ....10 Trav 5
Depriv'd of sight and rankling in
his chain; ....II:89 Capt 121
CHAIN$_2$ To chain the strong, and
set the captive free. ....III:90 Capt 126
CHAINED Insulted, chain'd, and
all the world a foe, ...I:5 Capt 113
CHAINS Bow'd down with chains,
the scorn of all mankind, ...I:85 Capt 117
More ponderous chains, and
dungeons more confin'd. ......II:92 Capt 122
CHAIR And every stranger finds
a ready chair; ....16 Trav 5
Vida, 499
CHAIR- (A chair-lumber'd closet
just twelve feet by nine:) ....68 HofV 97
CHAMBERS I had thoughts, in my
chambers, to place it in view, ...7 HofV 95
CHAMPAGNE Where Calvert's butt,
and Parsons' black champagne, ...3 DABd 48
CHAMPION The reverend champion stood.
At his control, ...173 DVil 29
Vida, 198, 463
CHAMPIONESS Vida, 535
CHAMPIONS Vida, 441, 451
CHANCE$_1$ In passive ease they
leave the world to chance. .....v(156) Trav 170
Vida, 190, 287, 402, 505, 582
CHANCE$_2$ Or you may chance to
spoil a thriving trade. ....34 pZob 73
CHANGE$_1$ Trace every scene, and
wonder at the change, ...v(82) DVil 182
CHANGE$_2$ Nor e'er had chang'd,
nor wished to change his place; ....144 DVil 28
Both prone to change, no settled
limits fix, ...11 eSSC$_2$ 108
CHANGED Nor e'er had chang'd,
nor wished to change his place; ....144 DVil 28
CHANGEFUL Still may thy blooms the
changeful clime endure, ...369 Trav 17
CHANGES Vida, 159
CHAOS Then, with chaos and blunders
encircling my head, ...21 Rtal 87
CHAPTER A chapter out of Tooke's
Pantheon, ...6 NSim 56
CHARACTERS Or, wherefore his
characters thus without fault? ......74 Rtal 89
CHARGE$_1$ Vida, 199
CHARGE$_2$ Vida, 550
CHARGE$_3$ And picking of pockets, with
which I now charge ye, ...39 LetB 133
CHARGE$_4$ Vida, 89
CHARIOT The coachman was tipsy, the
chariot drove home; ....48 Rtal 88
Vida, 178
CHARIOTS The rattling chariots clash,
the torches glare. ....322 DVil 34
CHARITY His pity gave ere charity
began. ....162 DVil 28
To ask for charity? ....190 Thrn 81
CHARLES First Sir Charles advances
with phrases well strung, ...55 LetB 133
CHARM$_1$ Yet still, e'en here, content
can spread a charm, ...175 Trav 11
How often have I paus'd on every
charm, ...9 DVil 23
One native charm, than all the gloss
of art; ....254 DVil 31
Slights every borrow'd charm that
dress supplies, ...289 DVil 32
The heartfelt power of every charm
divine, ...3 MrsX 49
But nothing could a charm impart ....57 Ed&A 61
A charm that lulls to sleep; ....74 Ed&A 61
What charm can soothe her melancholy, 3 "wlw 67
CHARM$_2$ Through life's more cultur'd
walks, and charm the way, ...236 Trav 13
In vain, to charm thy ravish'd sight, 28 Thrn 75
CHARMED Far different there from all
that charm'd before, ...345 DVil 34
In sweet succession charmed the
senses, ...237 Thrn 82
CHARMER My charmer, turn to see ....150 Ed&A 64
CHARMING Dear charming nymph,
neglected and decried, ...411 DVil 37
I'll give thee--Ah! too charming
maid, ...19 Gift 43
CHARMS$_1$ When thus Creation's charms

around combine, ...37 Trav 6
Such are the charms to barren
states assign'd; ....209 Trav 12
At gold's superior charms all
freedom flies, ...307 Trav 15
Creation's mildest charms are
there combin'd, ...323 Trav 16
Thine are those charms that
dazzle and endear; ....336 Trav 16
Till time may come, when stripp'd
of all her charms, ...355 Trav 17
These were thy charms, sweet
village; sports like these, ...31 DVil 24
These were thy charms--But all
these charms are fled. ....34 DVil 24
Thy sports are fled, and all
thy charms withdrawn; ....36 DVil 24
But when those charms are pass'd,
for charms are frail, ...291 DVil 33
In nature's simplest charms at
first array'd; ....296 DVil 33
Silent went next, neglectful of
her charms, ...377 DVil 35
And felt her charms, without
disguise, within. ....14 MrsX 49
Let it suffice, that each had
charms; ....25 DTrn 52
Found half the charms that deck'd
her face ....35 DTrn 53
A maid in all her charms. ....92 Ed&A 62
Who prais'd me for imputed
charms, ...107 Ed&A 62
Their chief pretence my flatter'd
charms, ...v107 Ed&A 209
With charms inconstant shine; .....126 Ed&A 63
Their charms were his, but woe
to me! ....127 Ed&A 63
And lent him fancied charms! ....v128 Ed&A 210
Vida, 3, 410
CHARMS$_2$ Sings to its mate, and
nightly charms the nest; ....12 Cati 94
Vida, 488
CHASE Vida, 490
CHASED Vida, 625
CHASTE Chaste are their instincts,
faithful is their fire, ...1 Cati 94
But the chaste blackbird, to
its partner true, ...9 Cati 94
CHE And quits her <u>Nancy Dawson</u>,
for <u>Che faro</u>, ...26 eSSC$_3$ 85
CHEAPSIDE Swims round the room, the
Heinel of Cheapside; ....28 eSSC$_3$ 85
CHEAT$_1$ Vida, 416
CHEAT$_2$ And Scotchman meet Scotch-
man, and cheat in the dark. ....92 Rtal 90
Vida, 319
CHEATS Vida, 312
CHEEK 'The tripe,' quoth the Jew,
with his chocolate cheek. ....95 HofV 98
CHEEKS With modesty her cheeks
are dy'd, ...97 DTrn 55
CHEER$_1$ Here beggar pride defrauds
her daily cheer, ...277 Trav 14
CHEER$_2$ Unfit for raptures, or,
if raptures cheer ....223 Trav 12
Why, let them come, one good
remains to cheer; ....I:95 Capt 117
Those streams which cheer the sore
opprest, ...III:45 Capt 124
CHEERED Where health and plenty
cheer'd the labouring swain, ...2 DVil 23
And cheer'd his pensive guest: .....48 Ed&A 60
CHEERFUL Bless'd be that spot,
where cheerful guests retire ....13 Trav 5
Cheerful at morn he wakes from
short repose, ...185 Trav 11
Smiles by his cheerful fire, and
round surveys ....193 Trav 11
These round thy bowers their
cheerful influence shed, ...33 DVil 24
No cheerful murmurs fluctuate in
the gale, ...126 DVil 27
Vida, 380, 460, 646
CHEERFULLY Vida, 489
CHEERS To where yon taper cheers
the vale ....3 Ed&A 59
To yonder fire, that cheers the
vale ....v3 Ed&A 208
Adorns and cheers our way; .....II:38 Capt 119
Adorns and chears the way; ....vII:38 Capt 250
CHEQUERED Vida, 23, 388, 673
CHERISHED He cherish'd his friend,
and he relish'd a bumper; ....127 Rtal 91
CHERUBS May cherubs welcome their
expected guest; ....108 Thrn 77
CHEST The chest contriv'd a
double debt to pay, ...229 DVil 30
A bed by night, a chest of drawers
by day; ....230 DVil 30
CHID He chid their wand'rings,
but reliev'd their pain; ....150 DVil 28
CHIDE The wondering fair one turn'd
to chide,-- ....147 Ed&A 64
The astonish'd fair one turned to
chide, ...v147 Ed&A 211
CHIEF$_1$ Vida, 381, 436
CHIEF$_2$ Their chief pretence my
flatter'd charms, ...v107 Ed&A 209
Thus 'tis with all--their chief
and constant care ....25 eSis 70
CHIEF$_3$ But chief to Thee, our God,
defender, friend, ...III:103 Capt 127
CHIEFLY Vida, 526
CHIEFS But when contending
chiefs blockade the throne, ...381 Trav 18
CHIELS Where are the chiels?
Ah! Ah, I well discern ....39 eSSC$_1$ 105
CHILD The sports of children
satisfy the child; ....154 Trav 10
And as a child, when scaring
sounds molest, ...205 Trav 12
'Here to the houseless child of
want ....13 Ed&A 59
CHILDREN The sports of children
satisfy the child; ....154 Trav 10
Have led their children through
the mirthful maze, ...252 Trav 13
Far, far away, thy children leave
the land. ....50 DVil 24
The playful children just let loose
from school; ....120 DVil 27
Even children follow'd with en-
dearing wile, ...183 DVil 29
No more my titles shall my

children tell, ...17 pLab 41
Her weeping children round ....62 Thrn 76
My children shall the note
prolong. ....206 Thrn 81
See where he mourns his friends
and children slain. ....II:90 Capt 121
CHILDREN'S His children's looks,
that brighten at the blaze; ....194 Trav 11
CHILLED The hearth, except when
winter chill'd the day, ...233 DVil 31
CHILLING With smiling hopes and
chilling fears, ...14 Tr 267
CHILLS But winter ling'ring chills
the lap of May; ....172 Trav 11
CHIMNEY Rang'd o'er the chimney,
glisten'd in a row. ....236 DVil 31
And five crack'd teacups dress'd the
chimney board; ....18 DABd 48
CHINA From China borrows aid to deck
the scene-- ....150 Thrn 79
CHIRRUPS The cricket chirrups in the
hearth; ....55 Ed&A 61
CHOCOLATE 'The tripe,' quoth the
Jew, with his chocolate cheek, ...95 HofV 98
CHOICE Whither shall my choice
incline? ....I:73 Capt 116
CHOIR How often have I led thy
sportive choir, ...243 Trav 13
Dismiss your griefs, and join our
warbling choir, ...I:83 Capt 117
But hush! see, foremost of the
captive choir, ...II:63 Capt 120
CHOKE Vida, 223
CHOKED But chok'd with sedges,
works its weedy way. ....42 DVil 24
CHOOSE Vida, 86
CHOOSES Vida, 60
CHOOSING I'll waste no longer thought
in choosing; ....I:74 Capt 116
CHOP- The chop-house toast of ogling
connoisseurs. ....18 $eSSC_3$ 85
CHRISTIAN To every Christian eye; ..26 MDog 66
CHURCH The decent church that topp'd
the neighbouring hill, ...12 DVil 23
At church, with meek and unaffected
grace, ...177 DVil 29
At church, in silks and satins new, 13 MBlz 47
CHURCHILL'S You, I, he, wrote it
not--'twas Churchill's all. ....4 GCRL 51
CHURLISH And force a churlish soil for
scanty bread; ....168 Trav 10
CINNA Some think he writes Cinna--
he owns to Panurge. ....78 HofV 97
CIRCLE That, like the circle bounding
earth and skies, ...27 Trav 6
Vida, 322, 521
CIRCLED While many a pastime circled
in the shade, ...19 DVil 23
CIRCLING See, though by circling
deeps together held, ...v343 Trav 174
Full well the busy whisper,
circling round, ...203 DVil 30
He starts, he pants, he takes the
circling maze. ....42 epLL 102
Vida, 136, 168
CITIES Lakes, forests, cities, plains,
extending wide, ...35 Trav 6
CITIZENS See CITS
CITS On 'Squires and Cits she there
displays her arts, ...19 $eSSC_3$ 85
To this strange spot, Rakes,
Macaronies, Cits, ...15 $eSSC_2$ 108
CITY$_1$ If to the city sped--What waits
him there? ....309 DVil 33
CITY$_2$ Her country beaux and city
cousins, ...87 DTrn 55
Hither the affected city dame
advancing, ...19 $eSSC_2$ 108
CIVIL Not less sincere, than civil: 18 Gift 43
And, though her fops are wond'rous
civil, ...69 DTrn 54
To see them so cowardly, lucky, and
civil. ....20 LetB 132
CIVILLY To coxcombs averse, yet most
civilly steering, ...143 Rtal 92
CLAD 'In humble, simplest habit clad,113 Ed&A 63
The naked every day he clad, ...11 MDog 65
The modest matron, clad in homespun
gray, ...156 Thrn 79
CLAIM Where beasts with man divided
empire claim, ...415 Trav 19
When titles are the smallest claim-- 14 Thrn 74
CLAIMED Claim'd kindred there, and had
his claims allow'd; ....154 DVil 28
May peace that claimed while here thy
warmest love, ...110 Thrn 78
Vida, 20
CLAIMS All claims that bind and
sweeten life unknown; ....342 Trav 16
Claim'd kindred there, and had his
claims allow'd; ....154 DVil 28
CLAMOUR Amidst the clamour of exulting
joys, ...1 Queb 46
CLANG Vida, 225
CLARE My acquaintance is slight, or I'd
ask my Lord Clare. ....50 HofV 96
CLARION'S The clarion's note proclaims
the finish'd war! ....III:84 Capt 126
CLASH The rattling chariots clash,
the torches glare. ....322 DVil 34
Vida, 523
CLASHES Vida, 513
CLASP Vida, 147
CLASPED And clasp'd them close, in
sorrow doubly dear; ....382 DVil 36
He clasp'd a goddess in his arms; ...26 DTrn 52
And clasp'd her to his breast: .....146 Ed&A 64
Clasp'd in her hand a godly book was
borne, ...183 Thrn 81
CLASSIC By classic authors term'd
caduceus, ...33 NSim 57
CLAY Jack found his goddess made of
clay; ....34 DTrn 53
To bless the tomb that wraps thy
clay; ....133 Thrn 78
CLEAN A person ever neatly clean: 100 DTrn 55
In decent dress, and coarsely clean,181 Thrn 80
CLEANLY Displays her cleanly platter
on the board: ....196 Trav 11
CLEAR No more the smith his dusky
brow shall clear, ...245 DVil 31
CLEMENCY All whom her clemency
sustain'd; ....154 Thrn 79
CLERGY Is, by quinto Elizabeth,

Death without Clergy. ....40 LetB 133
CLEVER And let us be merry and
clever; ....20 "LSm 84
With two full as clever, and ten
times as hearty. ....74 HofV 97
Pity take on your swain so clever, 25 eSSC$_1$ 104
CLICKED The varnish'd clock that
click'd behind the door; ....228 DVil 30
CLIFF As some tall cliff, that lifts
its awful form, ...189 DVil 29
CLIFFS On Idra's cliffs as Arno's
shelvy side; ....84 Trav 8
On Torno's cliffs, or Pambamarca's
side, ...418 DVil 37
Vida, 9
CLIMATE The distant climate and the
savage shore; ....2 pZob 72
--what a sultry climate am I under! 17 pZob 72
CLIME Redress the clime, and all its
rage disarm, ...176 Trav 11
Still may thy blooms the changeful
clime endure, ...369 Trav 17
Redress the rigours of th' inclement
clime; ....422 DVil 37
CLIMES Whatever fruits in different
climes were found, ...113 Trav 9
Where rougher climes a nobler race
display, ...166 Trav 10
The wealth of climes, where savage
nations roam, ...387 Trav 18
To traverse climes beyond the
western main; ....410 Trav 18
Ah, no. To distant climes, a
dreary scene, ...341 DVil 34
CLING But silent bats in drowsy
clusters cling; ....350 DVil 34
CLINGS Clings close and closer to
the mother's breast, ...206 Trav 12
CLOCK The varnish'd clock that
click'd behind the door; ....228 DVil 30
CLOGGED Though clogg'd with a coxcomb, and Kitty his wife. ....64 HofV 97
CLOSE$_1$ To husband out life's taper
at the close, ...87 DVil 26
My anxious day to husband near the
close, ...v87 DVil 182
Sweet was the sound, when oft at
evening's close ....113 DVil 27
CLOSE$_2$ Clings close and closer to
the mother's breast, ...206 Trav 12
And clasp'd them close, in sorrow
doubly dear; ....382 DVil 36
Statesmen with bridles on; and, close
beside 'em, ...15 eSis 70
Vida, 253, 521, 588, 641
CLOSED Or draw the curtains clos'd
around? ....24 DTrn 52
Vida, 256
CLOSER But let us try these truths
with closer eyes, ...99 Trav 8
Clings close and closer to the
mother's breast, ...206 Trav 12
But view them closer, craft and
fraud appear, ...305 Trav 15
CLOSES Vida, 665
CLOSET (A chair-lumber'd closet just
twelve feet by nine:) ....68 HofV 97

CLOTHES When he put on his clothes. 12 MDog 65
CLOUD Yon ill foreboding cloud
seems big with thunder. ....18 pZob 72
CLOUDS Though round its breast the
rolling clouds are spread, ...191 DVil 29
Like clouds that deck the morning
skies, ...v87 Ed&A 209
Awful as clouds that nurse the
growing storm; ....II:68 Capt 121
CLOVER 'Young man,' cries one--a
bard laid up in clover-- ....11 eGNM 68
CLOY Unknown to them, when sensual
pleasures cloy, ...217 Trav 12
CLUE Vida, 10
CLUSTERS But silent bats in drowsy
clusters cling; ....350 DVil 34
COACH I drove to his door in my own
hackney coach. ....66 HofV 97
COACHMAN The coachman was tipsy, the
chariot drove home; ....48 Rtal 88
COARSELY But not their joys alone
thus coarsely flow: ....227 Trav 12
In decent dress, and coarsely clean,181 Thrn 80
COARSER He thinks her features
coarser grown; ....62 DTrn 54
COAST This seems a barren and a
dangerous coast. ....16 pZob 72
I'll seek that less inhospitable
coast, ...223 Thrn 82
Vida, 293
COAXING Who knows each art of
coaxing up the town, ...5 eGNM 68
COEVAL Coeval with man ....III:7 Capt 122
COLD$_1$ And, pinch'd with cold, and
shrinking from the shower, ...333 DVil 34
E'en now, perhaps, by cold and
hunger led, ...339 DVil 34
COLD$_2$ The morn was cold, he views
with keen desire ....15 DABd 48
While Botanists, all cold to smiles
and dimpling, ...5 pZob 72
To eat mutton cold, and cut blocks
with a razor. ....42 Rtal 88
While the matter was cold, ...8 Invt 128
COLEY There's COLEY, and WILLIAMS,
and HOWARD, and HIFF ....v27 HofV 238
COLLECT Come thronging to collect
their scatter'd wits. ....16 eSSC$_2$ 108
COLLEGE Jack Book-worm led a college
life; ....2 DTrn 52
COLOUR Vida, 60
COLOURED Vida, 131, 357, 390
-COLOURED Patriots, in party-
coloured suits, that ride 'em. ..16 eSis 70
Vida, 98
COLOURS Like colours o'er the morning
skies, ...87 Ed&A 62
Like an ill-judging beauty, his
colours he spread, ...99 Rtal 90
Vida, 32, 76
COLUMN$_1$ Again the long-fall'n column
sought the skies; ....136 Trav 9
COLUMN$_2$ Whose daily <u>bons</u> <u>mots</u> half
a column might fill; ....154 Rtal 93
COMBAT$_1$ Vida, 110, 325
COMBAT$_2$ Minds combat minds, repelling
and repell'd. ....344 Trav 16

And, since 'tis hard to combat,
learns to fly! ....102 DVil 26
But I will rally, and combat the
ruiner: ....5 "Amw 94
COMBATANTS Vida, 329, 407
COMBINE When thus Creation's charms
around combine, ...37 Trav 6
For me your tributary stores
combine; ....49 Trav 7
Vida, 71
COMBINED Creation's mildest charms
are there combin'd, ...323 Trav 16
To see ten thousand baneful arts
combin'd ....311 DVil 33
COME Till time may come, when
stripp'd of all her charms, ...355 Trav 17
O had the archer ne'er come down ...11 DTrn 52
There Faith shall come, a pil-
grim gray, ...132 Thrn 78
There promised a lover to come--
but, O me! ....245 Thrn 83
When Methodist preachers come
down ....10 "LSm 84
But when you come down with your
pence, ...14 "LSm 84
Then come, put the jorum about, ...19 "LSm 84
Come, all ye quack bards, and ye
quacking divines, ...81 Rtal 89
Come, and dance on the spot where
your tyrant reclines: ....82 Rtal 89
Then what was his failing? come,
tell it, and, burn ye! ....135 Rtal 91
Ye tame imitators, ye servile
herd, come, ...165 Rtal 93
When come to the place where we
all were to dine, ...67 HofV 97
With tidings that Johnson and
Burke would not come; ....70 HofV 97
'O--Oh!' quoth my friend, 'he'll
come on in a trice, ...99 HofV 98
I don't think he'll wish to come
back. ....4 epEP 100
Come, end the contest here, and
aid my party. ....56 eSSC$_1$ 106
Come thronging to collect their
scatter'd wits. ....16 eSSC$_2$ 108
Here come the sons of scandal and
of news, ...31 eSSC$_2$ 109
Come on, my companions, the
triumph display; ....I:57 Capt 115
Come, take the lyre, and pour the
strain along, ...I:81 Capt 116
Why, let them come, one good
remains to cheer ....I:95 Capt 117
Come on, and bid the warbling
rapture rise, ...II:43 Capt 119
Conspiring nations come; ....II:72 Capt 121
Come ponder his severer
fate, ...III:25 Capt 123
'Pray what does Miss Horneck?
take courage, come do,'-- ......17 LetB 132
The whole pool as my own-- 'Come,
give me five cards.' ....24 LetB 132
Ah! the Doctor is loo'd! Come,
Doctor, put down.' ....32 LetB 132
Whether crimes such as yours should
not come before Fielding? ......36 LetB 132
Then their friends all come round
me with cringing and leering, ..53 LetB 133
Vida, 517
COMEDY And comedy wonders at
being so fine; ....66 Rtal 89
COMEDY'S Little Comedy's face, ...17 Invt 128
COMES Comes nearest us in human
shape; ....42 LogR 45
Comes here at night, and goes a
prude away. ....18 eSSC$_2$ 108
Comes here to saunter, having
made his bets, ...25 eSSC$_2$ 108
He comes pursuant to divine
decree, ...III:89 Capt 126
Cyrus comes, our wrongs re-
dressing, ...III:93 Capt 126
Comes to give the world re-
pose. ....III:94 Capt 126
Cyrus comes, the world re-
dressing, ...III:95 Capt 126
Comes to heighten every
blessing, ...III:97 Capt 126
Comes to soften every pain. ...III:98 Capt 126
When he comes to enlist. ....22 Invt 128
Vida, 128, 618
COMFORT$_1$ Comfort came down the
trembling wretch to raise, ...175 DVil 29
They stood, while hope and com-
fort fail, ...69 Thrn 76
COMFORT$_2$ To comfort friends and
foes; ....10 MDog 65
COMFORTER Comforter of every woe, .113 Thrn 78
COMIC Besides, a singer in a
comic set!-- ....9 eSSC$_1$ 104
COMING And, sedulous to stop the
coming tide, ...285 Trav 14
How often have I bless'd the
coming day, ...15 DVil 23
COMMAND At her command the palace
learn'd to rise, ...135 Trav 9
But if, rebellious to his high
command, ...II:11 Capt 118
Vida, 198
-COMMANDING Who can withstand
their all-commanding shine? ....4 MrsX 49
COMMANDS$_1$ They, I am sure, will
answer my commands: ....15 eSSC$_1$ 104
The king's commands must fully
be obey'd; ....II:8 Capt 118
Vida, 56, 86
COMMANDS$_2$ Vida, 22, 168
COMMENCES His Heaven commences
ere the world be pass'd! ....112 DVil 27
COMMERCE Wealth, commerce, honour,
liberty, content. ....88 Trav 8
And honour sinks where commerce
long prevails. ....92 Trav 8
When commerce proudly flourish'd
through the state; ....134 Trav 9
Commerce on other shores display'd
her sail; ....140 Trav 10
Soon Commerce turn'd on other
shores her sail; ....v140 Trav 169
What a commerce was yours, while
you got and you gave! ....116 Rtal 91
COMMISSION Vida, 193
COMMISSIONED Vida, 180

COMMON$_1$ And e'en the bare-worn common
is denied. ....308 DVil 33
COMMON$_2$ Vida, 438, 612
COMMON- Even Common-Councilmen
forget to eat. ....22 eSSC$_3$ 85
COMMON'S If to some common's fence-
less limits stray'd, ...305 DVil 33
COMPANION The fond companion of
his helpless years, ...376 DVil 35
Companion of her way. ....100 Ed&A 62
Companion of the way. ....v100 Ed&A 209
Thou soft companion of the
breast! ....II:2 Capt 118
COMPANIONS His best companions,
innocence and health; ....61 DVil 25
Of old, when Scarron his com-
panions invited, ...1 Rtal 87
Till all my companions sink under
the table; ....20 Rtal 87
Come on, my companions, the
triumph display; ....I:57 Capt 115
Yes, my companions, Heaven's
decrees are past, ...III:1 Capt 122
Vida, 623
COMPANY The company set, and the
word to be, Loo; ....2 LetB 131
COMPARE And yet, perhaps, if
countries we compare, ...75 Trav 7
COMPARED Ye gods! what transport
e'er compared to this. ....8 MrsX 49
COMPARISON A just comparison,--
proceed. ....22 NSim 56
COMPENSATION An easy compensation
seem to find. ....148 Trav 10
COMPILE Our Townshend make speeches,
and I shall compile; ....88 Rtal 90
COMPLAIN Yet, why complain?
What, though by bonds confin'd, ..I:31 Capt 114
COMPLAINED Forlorn, a rural bard
complain'd, ...152 Thrn 79
COMPLAINING Weeping, murmuring,
complaining, ...1 Sonn 46
In innocence and youth complain-
ing, ...231 Thrn 79
COMPLAINT With fond complaint
addressed the listening Jove, ...10 MrsX 49
COMPLETE And as she smiles, her
triumphs to complete, ...21 eSSC$_3$ 85
COMPLETELY Vida, 571
COMPLIANCE Compliance with his will
your peace secures, ...II:9 Capt 118
I read your looks, and see
compliance there. ....II:42 Capt 119
COMPLYING His manners were gentle,
complying, and bland; ....140 Rtal 91
COMPOSED Our life is all a play,
compos'd to please, ...7 eSSC$_3$ 85
COMPOUND Rare compound of oddity,
frolic, and fun! ....149 Rtal 92
CONCEAL Vida, 278
CONDEMN To slaughter I condemn: .....22 Ed&A 59
Condemn the stubborn fool who
can't submit ....71 eSSC$_1$ 107
CONDEMNED Poor Madam, now con-
demn'd to hack ....91 DTrn 55
The Wretch condemn'd with life
to part, ...vII:33 Capt 250
Vida, 662
CONDESCEND Could so much beauty
condescend ....47 DTrn 53
-CONDITIONED Here ill-condition'd
oranges abound-- ....21 pZob 72
CONDUCE Alike too both conduce
to sleep. ....50 NSim 57
CONDUCT Aping the conduct of
superiors; ....50 LogR 45
His conduct still right, with his
argument wrong; ....46 Rtal 88
CONDUCTS For as the line of life
conducts me on ....95 Thrn 77
CONFESS Thy glades forlorn con-
fess the tyrant's power. ....76 DVil 25
CONFESSED Of beasts, it is con-
fess'd, the ape ....41 LogR 45
The lovely stranger stands
confess'd ....91 Ed&A 62
As an actor, confess'd without
rival to shine: ....95 Rtal 90
Yet happy if Woodfall confess'd
him a wit. ....162 Rtal 93
Celestial themes confess'd his
tuneful aid; .... 5 epTP 100
CONFIDED Perhaps he confided in
men as they go, ...133 Rtal 91
CONFINE$_1$ Vida, 118, 232
CONFINE$_2$ Vida, 643
CONFINED Their wants but few, their
wishes all confin'd ....210 Trav 12
Should so long be to news-paper
essays confin'd; ....158 Rtal 93
Yet, why complain? What, though
by bonds confin'd, ...I:31 Capt 114
More ponderous chains, and
dungeons more confin'd. ......II:92 Capt 122
Vida, 124, 397, 405
CONFIRMS Secure to please while
youth confirms her reign, ...288 DVil 32
CONFLICT Vida, 202, 363
CONFORM And calmly bent, to
servitude conform, ...311 Trav 15
Since then, unhelp'd, our bard
must now conform ....31 eGNM 69
CONFORMS Conforms and models life
to that alone. ....94 Trav 8
Dear is that shed to which his
soul conforms, ...203 Trav 12
CONFOUND 'The deuce confound,'
he cries, 'these drumstick shanks, .31 epLL 102
CONFOUNDEDLY Though secure of our
hearts, yet confoundedly sick .....105 Rtal 90
CONFOUNDS Vida, 540
CONFUSEDLY Vida, 358
CONFUSION These all in sweet con-
fusion sought the shade, ...123 DVil 27
Shall ever in confusion end; ....I:44 Capt 115
CONGENIAL To me more dear, con-
genial to my heart, ...253 DVil 31
-CONNECTED The firm-connected
bulwark seems to grow; ....288 Trav 14
CONNOISSEURS The chop-house
toast of ogling connoisseurs. .....18 eSSC$_3$ 85
CONNUBIAL And kind connubial
tenderness, are there; ....404 DVil 36
CONQUER Well, having stoop'd to

conquer with success, ...1 eSSC$_3$ 85
As I have conquer'd him, to
conquer you: ....4 eSSC$_3$ 85
Vida, 576
He sure must conquer, who himself
can tame! ....2 Tr 267
CONQUERED As I have conquer'd him,
to conquer you: ....4 eSSC$_3$ 85
CONQUEREST Yet they shall know thou
conquerest, though dead-- ....11 Queb 46
CONQUEROR Cyrus, the conqueror of the
world, prevails, ...III:60 Capt 125
CONQUEST Sighing we pay, and
think e'en conquest dear; ....6 Queb 46
CONSCIENCE Leave reason, faith, and
conscience, all our own. ....438 Trav 19
I'd speak a word or two, to ease
my conscience. ....2 epLL 101
CONSCIOUS But for himself, in
conscious virtue brave, ...373 DVil 35
Conscious of this, our bard has
gone about, ...7 eGNM 68
Unmov'd in conscious rectitude, ...25 Thrn 75
CONSIDER 'Consider, dear Doctor,
the girls are but young.' ....56 LetB 133
'But consider their case,--it may
yet be your own! ....63 LetB 134
CONSIGNED Some spot to real
happiness consign'd, ...60 Trav 7
Still to ourselves in every place
consign'd, ...431 Trav 19
To want, to toil, and every ill
consign'd, ...I:86 Capt 117
CONSORT'S Vida, 379
CONSORTS Vida, 46, 465
CONSPIRE Whilst his strong limbs
conspire to set him free, ...45 epLL 102
The time, the theme, the place,
and all conspire. ....II:46 Capt 120
CONSPIRING Conspiring nations
come; ....II:72 Capt 121
CONSTANCY Their constancy was
mine. ....128 Ed&A 63
CONSTANT A constant heart was all
he had, ...v115 Ed&A 209
The sigh that rends thy constant
heart ....159 Ed&A 64
Thus 'tis with all--their chief
and constant care ....25 eSis 70
Her constant pity fed the poor-- ...126 Thrn 78
Unseen, though constant, used to
flow; ....179 Thrn 80
While these a constant revel
keep, ...II:51 Capt 120
CONSULTED Had she consulted <u>me</u>,
she should have made ....3 eSis 70
-CONSUMING And own his all-
consuming power ....III:67 Capt 125
CONSUMPTIVE Fever and pain and
pale consumptive care, ...54 Thrn 76
CONTAINS And man contains it in
his breast. ....119 Thrn 78
CONTAMINATE All evils here contaminate the mind, ...131 Trav 9
CONTEMPT By proud contempt, or
favour's fostering sun, ...368 Trav 17
Vida, 591

CONTEND Though patriots flatter,
and though fools contend, ...v77 Trav 168
CONTENDING But when contending
chiefs blockade the throne, ...381 Trav 18
The young contending as the
old survey'd; ....20 DVil 23
CONTENT$_1$ Wealth, commerce, honour,
liberty, content. ....88 Trav 8
Yet still, e'en here, content can
spread a charm, ...175 Trav 11
CONTENT$_2$ Rough, poor, content,
ungovernably bold; ....314 Trav 15
Or Flavia been content to stop ......13 DTrn 52
Yet content 'if the table he set
on a roar'; ....160 Rtal 93
CONTENTED Contented toil, and
hospitable care, ...403 DVil 36
Contented with her own. ....198 Thrn 81
CONTENTION Vida, 261
CONTENTMENT Where wealth and free-
dom reign, contentment fails, ...91 Trav 8
CONTEST$_1$ Come, end the contest
here, and aid my party. ....56 eSSC$_1$ 106
CONTEST$_2$ Yet these each other's
power so strong contest, ...89 Trav 8
CONTESTS No, no; I've other con-
tests to maintain; ....17 eGNM 68
CONTIGUOUS Sees no contiguous
palace rear its head ....179 Trav 11
To 'scape the pressure of
contiguous pride? ....304 DVil 33
CONTINUE Yet still I sit snug,
and continue to sigh on, ...21 LetB 132
CONTRACT Their master's manners
still contract, ...55 LogR 45
CONTRACTING Each wish contract-
ing, fits him to the soil. ....184 Trav 11
Contracting regal power to
stretch their own; ....382 Trav 18
CONTRASTED Contrasted faults
through all his manners reign; ......127 Trav 9
CONTRIVED The chest contriv'd
a double debt to pay, ...229 DVil 30
CONTROL See also CONTROUL
Each nobler aim, repress'd by
long control, ...155 Trav 10
True to imagin'd right, above control,332 Trav 16
The reverend champion stood.
At his control, ...173 DVil 29
CONTROUL See also CONTROL
When struggling Virtue sinks by
long controul, ...v155 Trav 170
When noble aims have suffer'd
long controul, ...v155 Trav 171
CONVENIENCE Convenience, plenty,
elegance, and arts; ....304 Trav 15
CONVERSATION Suspend your con-
versation while I sing. ....6 eSSC$_1$ 103
CONVERTS While converts thank
their poet in the skies. ....10 epTP 100
CONVEX Where half the convex
world intrudes between, ...342 DVil 34
CONVEYED Convey'd the dismal
tidings when he frown'd; ....204 DVil 30
CONVINCING And thought of con-
vincing, while they thought of
dining; ....36 Rtal 88

COOL For a patriot, too cool; for a
drudge, disobedient; ....39 Rtal 88
I lay down my stake, apparently
cool, ...7 LetB 131
COOLING The cooling brook, the
grassy-vested green, ...360 DVil 35
COPIED Who copied his squibs,
and re-echoed his jokes; ....164 Rtal 93
COPIOUS And copious libations
bestow on his shrine: ....168 Rtal 93
COPPER And trims her robes of
frieze with copper lace; ....276 Trav 14
COPSE Near yonder copse, where
once the garden smil'd, ...137 DVil 27
COPY Still stoops among the low
to copy nature. ....40 $eSSC_2$ 109
COQUETS Talks loud, coquets the
guests, and scolds the waiters. ...16 $eSSC_3$ 85
COQUETTE The gay coquette, who
ogles all the day, ...17 $eSSC_2$ 108
COQUETTING By day, 'twas gadding
or coquetting. ....52 DTrn 53
CORNER He's keeping a corner for
something that's nice: ....100 HofV 98
'I don't care if I keep a
corner for't too.' ....102 HofV 98
'Though splitting, I'll still
keep a corner for thot.' ....104 HofV 98
'We'll all keep a corner,' the
lady cried out; ....105 HofV 98
'We'll all keep a corner,' was
echoed about. ....106 HofV 98
CORONET Without a star, a
coronet or garter, ...37 $eSSC_2$ 109
CORPSE Vida, 413
CORRECT Vida, 321
CORREGGIOS When they talk'd of
their Raphaels, Correggios and
stuff, ...145 Rtal 92
CORSE A palled corse, and rest
the body there. ....III:18 Capt 123
Behold his wretched corse with
sorrow worn, ...III:31 Capt 123
COSTLY No costly lord the
sumptuous banquet deal ....181 Trav 11
COT The shelter'd cot, the
cultivated farm, ...10 DVil 23
And bless'd the cot where every
pleasure rose ....380 DVil 35
COTTAGE Exults, and owns his
cottage with a smile. ....164 Trav 10
Where once the cottage stood, the
hawthorn grew, ...80 DVil 25
Indignant spurns the cottage from
the green; ....282 DVil 32
Her modest looks the cottage
might adorn, ...329 DVil 34
COTTAGES From courts, to camps,
to cottages it strays, ...263 Trav 14
COUCH My rushy couch, and
frugal fare, ...19 Ed&A 59
COUGH Doctors, who cough and
answer every misfortuner, ...53 $eSSC_1$ 106
COULD Trav, 111, 163; DVil, 6,
208, 209, 210, 212, 216, 237; pLab,
6; DRtH, 12; DTrn, 8, 9, 47, 49;
Ed&A, 57, v57, 123, v149;
eGNM, 10; $eSSC_3$, 3; Rtal, 26,
108, 136, 159; "Amw, 3; HofV,
5, 61, 96, v96, 111; Invt, 7, 43;
Vida, 309, 536, 543, 599, 601, 644,
656
-COUNCILMEN Even Common-Council-
men forget to eat. ....22 $eSSC_3$ 85
COUNSEL For thus retain'd, as
learned counsel can, ...5 GRos 51
If virtue fail her counsel
sage; ....82 Thrn 77
COUNT Yet count our gains. This
wealth is but a name ....273 DVil 32
COUNTERFEITED Full well they
laugh'd, with counterfeited glee, 201 DVil 30
COUNTRIES And yet, perhaps, if
countries we compare, ...75 Trav 7
COUNTRY$_1$ Boldly asserts that
country for his own, ...v66 Trav 168
His first, best country ever is,
at home. ....74 Trav 7
A man he was to all the country
dear, ...141 DVil 28
The country blooms--a garden,
and a grave. ....302 DVil 33
And the tears of her country
shall water her tomb. ....262 Thrn 83
And brings my long-lost country
to mine eyes. ....I:16 Capt 114
COUNTRY$_2$ She left her wheel and
robes of country brown. ....336 DVil 34
To ravage in a country town! ....12 DTrn 52
Her country beaux and city
cousins, ...87 DTrn 55
The First Act shows the simple
country maid, ...9 $eSSC_3$ 85
Th' unblushing Bar-maid of a
country inn, ...14 $eSSC_3$ 85
COUNTRYMAN No countryman living
their tricks to discover; ....90 Rtal 90
There's my countryman H--gg--ns--
Oh! let him alone, ...29 HofV 96
COUNTRY'S But a bold peasantry,
their country's pride, ...55 DVil 25
COUNTS Bends at his treasure,
counts, re-counts it o'er; ....52 Trav 7
-COUNTS Bends at his treasure,
counts, re-counts it o'er; ....52 Trav 7
COURAGE By a bounce now and then,
to get courage to fly. ....16 HofV 95
'Pray what does Miss Horneck?
take courage, come do,'-- ......17 LetB 132
Thus foil'd in my courage, on
all sides perplex'd, ...27 LetB 132
Vida, 189, 355, 392, 478, 611
COURSE With secret course, which
no loud storms annoy, ...433 Trav 19
He this way steers his course,
in hopes of trading-- ....12 pZob 72
Vida, 136, 531, 639
COURSER Vida, 314, 338
COURSERS The curling waves before
his coursers fly: ....5 Tr 267
COURT$_1$ Nor know who's in or out
at court; ....26 LogR 44
At court, the porters, lacqueys,

waiters, ...54 LogR 45
Thus at the court both great and
small ....57 LogR 45
To Death's great court, the
prospect seems more fair. ....96 Thrn 77
COURT$_2$ That proudly rise, or humbly
court the ground; ....114 Trav 9
I mean to flatter kings, or court
the great; ....362 Trav 17
While the dark owl to court its
partner flies, ...13 Cati 94
COURTEOUS Too courteous, perhaps,
or obligingly flat? ....131 Rtal 91
COURTIER Here, while the courtier
glitters in brocade, ...315 DVil 33
A courtier any ape surpasses. ......46 LogR 45
COURTS$_1$ From courts, to camps,
to cottages it strays, ...263 Trav 14
COURTS$_2$ And flies where Britain
courts the western spring; ....318 Trav 15
COUSINS Her country beaux and
city cousins, ...87 DTrn 55
COVENT Those things are not our
forte at Covent Garden.' ....20 eGNM 68
COVER The only art her guilt to
cover, ...5 "wlw 67
Both cover their faces with mobs
and all that; ....45 LetB 133
COVERED Vida, 263
COVERS See where an army covers
all the ground, ...III:49 Capt 124
COVERT The breezy covert of the
warbling grove, ...361 DVil 35
COWARD Till half a patriot, half
a coward grown, ...391 Trav 18
And should we mourn? should coward
virtue fly, ...I:39 Capt 115
COWARDLY To see them so cowardly,
lucky, and civil. ....20 LetB 132
COWARDS Brave but to God, and
cowards to mankind, ...III:70 Capt 125
COWERING May sit, like falcons
cow'ring on the nest; ....234 Trav 13
COWS Vida, 519
COWSLIP On her grave shall the
cowslip and primrose be cast, ...249 Thrn 83
And there shall the cowslip and
primrose be cast, ...257, 261 Thrn 83
COXCOMB Though clogg'd with a
coxcomb, and Kitty his wife. ....64 HofV 97
COXCOMBS Of powder'd coxcombs
at her levy; ....54 DTrn 53
And coxcombs, alike in their
failings alone, ...71 Rtal 89
To coxcombs averse, yet most
civilly steering, ...143 Rtal 92
COY Nor the coy maid, half will-
ing to be press'd, ...249 DVil 31
CRACK Ye brave Irish lads, hark
away to the crack, ...57 eSSC$_1$ 106
CRACKED And five crack'd teacups
dress'd the chimney board; ....18 DABd 48
He drank his glass and crack'd
his joke, ...5 DTrn 52
CRACKLING The crackling faggot
flies. ....56 Ed&A 61
CRAFT But view them closer, craft
and fraud appear, ...305 Trav 15
CRAVES Good Savages, our Captain
craves assistance; ....30 pZob 73
CREAMS In vain she tries her paste
and creams, ...85 DTrn 54
-CREATED Vida, 510
CREATION A new creation rescu'd
from his reign. ....296 Trav 15
CREATION'S When thus Creation's
charms around combine, ...37 Trav 6
Creation's heir, the world, the
world is mine! ....50 Trav 7
Creation's mildest charms are
there combin'd, ...323 Trav 16
CREATURE Is both a weak and erring
creature; ....14 LogR 44
Here Hickey reclines, a most
blunt, pleasant creature, ...125 Rtal 91
'Twas thus that Aesop's stag, a
creature blameless, ...27 epLL 102
No high-life scenes, no sentiment:--
the creature ....39 eSSC$_2$ 109
Yet still they sit snug, not a
creature will aim ....11 LetB 132
CREATURE'S Extorted from his
fellow creature's woe. ....314 DVil 33
CRECY'S Shall crowd from Crecy's
laurell'd field, ...226 Thrn 82
CREDIT But for my soul I cannot
credit 'em; ....10 LogR 44
CREEK Our ship's well stor'd;--in
yonder creek we've laid her; ....31 pZob 73
CRESSES To strip the brook with
mantling cresses spread, ...132 DVil 27
CRESTED Vida, 67
-CRESTED And though the rocky-
crested summits frown, ...85 Trav 8
CREW And shall I mix in this un-
hallow'd crew? ....17 epLL 101
With the rest of the crew, ...15 Invt 128
Your Devonshire crew, ...36 Invt 129
Vida, 227, 621
CRICKET The cricket chirrups in
the hearth; ....55 Ed&A 61
CRIED 'And whence, unhappy youth,'
he cried, ...63 Ed&A 61
A wretch forlorn,' she cried; ......94 Ed&A 62
'Forbid it, heaven!' the hermit
cried, ...145 Ed&A 64
'Thou shalt not thus,' the Hermit
cried, ...v145 Ed&A 211
'And where,' he cried, 'shall now
my babes have bread, ...171 Thrn 80
'Why, whose should it be?' cried
I with a flounce, ...41 HofV 96
'If that be the case, then,' cried
he, very gay, ...45 HofV 96
'For I knew it,' he cried, 'both
eternally fail, ...71 HofV 97
'We'll all keep a corner,' the
lady cried out; ....105 HofV 98
Vida, 294
The shouting army cry'd with joy
extreme, ...1 Tr 267
CRIES$_1$ And tires their echoes with
unvaried cries. ....46 DVil 24
Vida, 433, 605

CRIES$_2$ 'Forbear, my son,' the hermit
cries, ...9 Ed&A 59
'Young man,' cries one--a bard laid
up in clover-- ....11 eGNM 68
'And ah!' she cries, all woe-
begone, ...187 Thrn 81
Pretends to taste, at Operas
cries caro, ...25 eSSC$_3$ 85
'The deuce confound,' he cries,
'these drumstick shanks, ...31 epLL 102
'I advise,' cries the lady, 'to
try it, I own.-- ....31 LetB 132
Vida, 251
CRIMES Whether crimes such as
yours should not come before Field-
ing? ....36 LetB 132
'Pray what are their crimes?'--
'They've been pilfering found.' .48 LetB 133
CRIMSON Vida, 353
CRIMSONED Vida, 223
CRINGE Nor ever cringe to men
in place; ....30 LogR 45
CRINGES He nods, they nod; he
cringes, they grimace; ....29 eGNM 69
CRINGING Behold him humbly cring-
ing wait ....47 LogR 45
Then their friends all come round
me with cringing and leering, ..53 LetB 133
CRITIC And be each critic the
Good Natur'd Man. ....34 eGNM 69
Yon critic, too--but whither do
I run? ....41 eSis 71
CRITICS I've all the critics and
the wits for me. ....14 eSSC$_1$ 104
CROOK 'No more shall my crook or
my temples adorn, ...240 Thrn 83
No more will her crook or her
temples adorn; ....252 Thrn 83
CROSS$_1$ While winds and waves
their wishes cross-- ....68 Thrn 76
New Lauders and Bowers the Tweed
shall cross over, ...89 Rtal 90
CROSS-$_2$ Cross-readings, Ship-
news, and Mistakes of the Press. ..170 Rtal 93
CROUCHING Where crouching tigers
wait their hapless prey, ...355 DVil 35
CROWD$_1$ Each hour a mercenary
crowd ....109 Ed&A 63
Each hour the gay phantastic
crowd ....v109 Ed&A 209
His fools have their follies so
lost in a crowd ....69 Rtal 89
CROWD$_2$ Shall crowd from Crecy's
laurell'd field, ...226 Thrn 82
Vida, 206, 521
CROWDED The crowded mart, the
cultivated plain, ...295 Trav 15
CROWDS$_1$ My shame in crowds, my
solitary pride; ....412 DVil 37
And now, when busy crowds re-
tire ....45 Ed&A 60
And now, when worldly crowds
retire ....v45 Ed&A 208
CROWDS$_2$ Tumultuous grandeur
crowds the blazing square, ...321 DVil 34
CROWN$_1$ Luke's iron crown, and
Damiens' bed of steel, ...436 Trav 19
The snow-white vesture, and the
glittering crown, ...3 Cati 94
Vida, 488, 499
CROWN$_2$ I'll wager the rascals a
crown ....12 "LSm 84
CROWN$_3$ Eternal blessings crown
my earliest friend, ...11 Trav 5
I still had hopes my latest hours
to crown, ...85 DVil 26
To crown the favourites of the
sky-- ....115 Thrn 78
CROWNED Bless'd be those feasts
with simple plenty crown'd, ...17 Trav 5
Ye glitt'ring towns, with wealth
and splendour crown'd, ...45 Trav 6
Those pois'nous fields with rank
luxuriance crown'd, ...351 DVil 35
Ye hills of Lebanon, with cedars
crown'd, ...I:19 Capt 114
Exulting rocks have crown'd the
power of song! ....9 Tr 267
CROWNS How happy he who crowns in
shades like these, ...99 DVil 26
How blest is he who crowns in
shades like these, ...v99 DVil 183
CRUEL Say, cruel Iris, pretty
rake, ...1 Gift 43
Nor did the cruel ravagers
design ....56 Thrn 76
CRUSH And still our vengeance
crush the traitor's head. .....III:6 Capt 122
CRUSHED But crush'd, or trodden
to the ground, ...I:49 Capt 115
CRUST And my wife, little Kitty,
is famous for crust. ....54 HofV 97
CRUTCH Shoulder'd his crutch, and
show'd how fields were won. ......158 DVil 28
CRY Let some cry up woodcock or
hare, ...23 "LSm 84
'Well done!' cry the ladies; 'Ah,
Doctor, that's good! ....25 LetB 132
CRY'D See CRIED
CUE But how? ay, there's the
rub! --I've got my cue: ....11 eSis 70
CULPRITS Two handsomer culprits I
never set eyes on!' ....52 LetB 133
CULTIVATED The crowded mart, the
cultivated plain, ...295 Trav 15
The shelter'd cot, the cultivated
farm, ...10 DVil 23
CULTURED Through life's more
cultur'd walks, and charm the way, 236 Trav 13
CUMBERLAND Here Cumberland lies,
having acted his parts, ...61 Rtal 89
CUMBERLAND'S Our Cumberland's
sweet-bread its place shall obtain, .9 Rtal 87
CUMBROUS Unwieldy wealth, and
cumbrous pomp repose; ....66 DVil 25
CUNNING$_1$ While novelty, with
cautious cunning, ...148 Thrn 79
CUNNING$_2$ That sly-boots was
cursedly cunning to hide 'em. .....28 Rtal 88
CUP Shall kiss the cup to pass
it to the rest. ....250 DVil 31
To take us in when we have
drained the cup ....98 Thrn 77
CUPID That he should be, like

Cupid, blind, ...3 Byth 42
CUPID'S Could Cupid's shaft at
length transfix ....9 DTrn 52
CUPIDS To raise a flame in Cupids of
threescore. ....18 eSis 70
-CUPS While broken tea-cups, wisely
kept for show, ...235 DVil 31
CURB Vida, 141
CURE$_1$ To swear the pill, or drop,
has wrought a cure; ....2 eGNM 68
CURE$_2$ That part which laws or kings can
cause or cure. ....430 Trav 19
And tries to kill, ere she's got
power to cure. ....24 eSis 70
CURIOUSLY Vida, 674
CURLING The curling waves before
his coursers fly: ....5 Tr 267
CURRENT$_1$ Glides the smooth current
of domestic joy. ....434 Trav 19
CURRENT$_2$ Here passes current; paid
from hand to hand, ...261 Trav 14
CURS And curs of low degree. ....16 MDog 65
CURSE Yes, brother, curse with me
that baleful hour, ...393 Trav 18
CURSED O Luxury! thou curs'd by
Heaven's decree, ...385 DVil 36
Pray a slice of your liver, though
may I be curs'd, ...93 HofV 98
Vida, 534
CURSEDLY That sly-boots was
cursedly cunning to hide 'em. ......28 Rtal 88
CURTAIL And a long one to curtail.)--32 Invt 129
CURTAIN- Could any curtain-
lectures bring ....49 DTrn 53
CURTAINS Or draw the curtains
clos'd around? ....24 DTrn 52
Wak'd Priam in drawing his
curtains by night. ....110 HofV 98
CURVET Vida, 68
CUSTOM These rocks, by custom,
turn to beds of down. ....86 Trav 8
CUSTOM- A fine-spoken Custom-house
Officer he, ...v37 HofV 239
CUT Nor cut each others' throats,
for pay. ....40 LogR 45
To eat mutton cold, and cut blocks
with a razor. ....42 Rtal 88
So I cut it, and sent it to Reynolds
undress'd, ...21 HofV 95
CUTS Vida, 377
CYGNETS Vida, 669
CYPHER 'Twas certain he could write,
and cypher too; ....208 DVil 30
CYRUS Cyrus, the conqueror of the
world, prevails, ...III:60 Capt 125
Cyrus, our great restorer, is at
hand, ...III:85 Capt 126
Cyrus comes, our wrongs
redressing, ...III:93 Capt 126
Cyrus comes, the world
redressing, ...III:95 Capt 126

D-- Looking, as who should say,
D----! who's afraid? ....30 eSis 71
D--D But what vex'd me most was
that d--'d Scottish rogue, ...89 HofV 98
DABBLE Who dabble and write in the
Papers--like you; ....v76 HofV 241
DAILY Here beggar pride defrauds
her daily cheer, ...277 Trav 14
To sweet oblivion of his daily
care; ....242 DVil 31
By use and daily meditation
worn; ....184 Thrn 81
Whose daily bons mots half a
column might fill; ....154 Rtal 93
DAINTIES Such dainties to them,
their health it might hurt, ...33 HofV 96
Such dainties to them! It would
look like a flirt, ...v33 HofV 239
DALE 'Turn, gentle hermit of the
dale, ...1 Ed&A 59
Deign saint-like tenant of the
dale, ...v1 Ed&A 208
'And when beside me in the dale ....117 Ed&A 63
DAME Hither the affected city
dame advancing, ...19 eSSC$_2$ 108
Vida, 339, 585
DAMES Alike all ages. Dames of
ancient days ....251 Trav 13
DAMIENS' Luke's iron crown, and
Damiens' bed of steel, ...436 Trav 19
DAMME Looking, as who should say,
D----! who's afraid? ....30 eSis 71
As 'D-- --, Sir,' and 'Sir, I wear
a sword'; ....28 eSSC$_2$ 109
DAMN See also D-- and DAMME
Round and round go the cards,
while I inwardly damn ....5 LetB 131
DAMNABLE This tale of the bacon a
damnable bounce? ....14 HofV 95
He led such a damnable life in this
world,-- ....3 epEP 100
DAMN'D See also D--D
But what vex'd me most was that
d--'d Scottish rogue, ...89 HofV 98
DAMNS Instead of others, damns
himself. ....54 NSim 57
DANCE And dance, forgetful of the
noon-tide hour. ....250 Trav 13
Come, and dance on the spot where
your tyrant reclines: ....82 Rtal 89
DANCER'S But mock'd all tune, and
marr'd the dancer's skill; ....248 Trav 13
DANCING$_1$ Doats upon dancing, and
in all her pride, ...27 eSSC$_3$ 85
Who sighs for operas, and dotes on
dancing, ...20 eSSC$_2$ 108
DANCING- No judges, fiddlers,
dancing-masters, ...35 LogR 45
DANCING$_2$ The dancing pair that
simply sought renown, ...25 DVil 24
DANGER Except when fast-approaching
danger warms: ....380 Trav 17
But every danger felt before-- ....217 Thrn 82
Vida, 93, 214, 290, 342, 538
DANGEROUS Through tangled forests,
and through dangerous ways; ....414 Trav 19
Explore the mine, or tempt the
dangerous deep; ....104 DVil 26
'To tempt the dangerous gloom; .....10 Ed&A 59
This seems a barren and a danger-
ous coast. ....16 pZob 72

Vida, 241
DANGERS Vida, 132, 272, 275
DANGLE Still to gallant and dangle
with the ladies;-- ....20 eSSC$_1$ 104
DANGLING And from above the
dangling deities; ....16 epLL 101
DARE Nor dare I pretend to know
more than my betters; ....4 ClRp 100
Vida, 96, 141, 304, 614
DARES Grief dares to mingle her
soul-piercing voice, ...3 Queb 46
DARING With daring aims irregular-
ly great; ....326 Trav 16
Vida, 573
DARK$_1$ And Scotchman meet Scotchman,
and cheat in the dark. ....92 Rtal 90
DARK$_2$ Where the dark scorpion
gathers death around; ....352 DVil 35
While the dark owl to court its
partner flies, ...13 Cati 94
Vida, 422, 663
DARKEN Pass from the shore, and
darken all the strand. ....402 DVil 36
DARKER And still, as darker grows
the night, ...II:39 Capt 119
DART$_1$ And love's and friend-
ship's finely pointed dart ....231 Trav 13
When vice my dart and scythe
supply, ...76 Thrn 76
Vida, 125
DART$_2$ Those blazing suns that dart
a downward ray, ...347 DVil 34
DASHING Vida, 310
DATE For wealth was theirs, not
far remov'd the date, ...133 Trav 9
DAUGHTER His lovely daughter,
lovelier in her tears, ...375 DVil 35
Vida, 306
DAUGHTERS Begin, ye daughters of
immortal verse; ....8 Tr 267
DAVID Here lies David Garrick,
describe me, who can, ...93 Rtal 90
DAWSON And quits her Nancy Dawson,
for Che faro, ...26 eSSC$_3$ 85
Quits the Ballet, and calls for
Nancy Dawson. ....22 eSSC$_2$ 108
DAY And drags the struggling
savage into day. ....190 Trav 11
How often have I bless'd the
coming day, ...15 DVil 23
No more thy glassy brook reflects
the day, ...41 DVil 24
My anxious day to husband near
the close, ...v87 DVil 182
A bed by night, a chest of
drawers by day; ....230 DVil 30
The hearth, except when winter
chill'd the day, ...233 DVil 31
And fiercely shed intolerable
day; ....348 DVil 34
Good heaven! what sorrows gloom'd
that parting day, ...363 DVil 35
This day beyond its term my fate
extends, ...19 pLab 41
A cap by night--a stocking all
the day! ....20 DABd 48
By day, 'twas gadding or coquet-
ting. ....52 DTrn 53
Thus as her faults each day were
known, ...61 DTrn 54
She learns good-nature every day; .102 DTrn 55
Till reading, I forget what day
on, ...5 NSim 56
'The blossom opening to the day, .121 Ed&A 63
The naked every day he clad, ...11 MDog 65
Then only poor, indeed, the day
she died. ....127 Thrn 78
But ev'ry day her name I'll
bless, ...199 Thrn 81
Each day, each hour, her name
I'll bless-- ....203 Thrn 81
Than what I feel this fatal
day. ....220 Thrn 82
That we wish'd him full ten times
a day at Old Nick; ....58 Rtal 89
He turn'd and he varied full ten
times a day. ....104 Rtal 90
So next day, in due splendour to
make my approach, ...65 HofV 97
I'll sing to amuse you by night
and by day, ...41 eSSC$_1$ 105
The gay coquette, who ogles
all the day, ...17 eSSC$_2$ 108
Do not our tyrant lords this
day ordain ....I:37 Capt 114
The sun calls us out on this
festival day, ...I:59 Capt 115
The day demands it; sing us
Sion's song. ....I:82 Capt 116
Vida, 133, 181, 386, 660
-DAY She had not died to-
day. ....28 MBlz 47
He had not died to-day. ....4 DRtH 50
The pleasures that we lose to-
day; ....II:60 Capt 120
DAY'S The day's disasters in
his morning face; ....200 DVil 29
-DAY'S When both have been
spoil'd in to-day's Adver-
tiser? ....44 Invt 129
DAYS Alike all ages. Dames of
ancient days ....251 Trav 13
'Alas, young man, my writing days
are over; ....12 eGNM 68
Of life, or worn our days to
wretchedness. ....99 Thrn 77
'I could dine on this tripe seven
days in the week: ....96 HofV 98
I could eat of this Tripe seven
days in the week.' ....v96 HofV 242
That a few days ago, ...24 Invt 128
DAZZLE Thine are those charms
that dazzle and endear; ....336 Trav 16
DAZZL'D Jack soon was dazzl'd
to behold ....95 DTrn 55
DEAD$_1$ There in the ruin, heed-
less of the dead, ...161 Trav 10
Let me ponder, and tell what I
think of the dead ....22 Rtal 87
Vida, 405
DEAD$_2$ Yet they shall know thou
conquerest, though dead-- ....11 Queb 46
The doctors found, when she was

dead,-- ....23 MBlz 47
As ever dead man did. ....20 DRtH 50
They're perfectly disgraceful!
strike me dead! ....33 epLL 102
Vida, 223, 384, 410, 465
DEADLY And the brown Indian takes
a deadly aim; ....v416 Trav 175
DEAL No costly lord the sumptuous
banquet deal ....181 Trav 11
DEALT An equal portion dealt to
all mankind, ...78 Trav 7
DEAN Our Dean shall be venison,
just fresh from the plains; ....5 Rtal 87
Here lies the good Dean, re-united
to earth, ...23 Rtal 87
DEAR Dear is that shed to which
his soul conforms, ...203 Trav 12
And dear that hill which lifts him
to the storms; ....204 Trav 12
Dear lovely bowers of innocence
and ease, ...5 DVil 23
A man he was to all the country
dear, ...141 DVil 28
To me more dear, congenial to my
heart, ...253 DVil 31
And clasp'd them close, in sorrow
doubly dear; ....382 DVil 36
Dear charming nymph, neglected
and decried, ...411 DVil 37
With honest thrift I held my
honour dear: ....8 pLab 41
Dear mercenary beauty, ...2 Gift 43
Sighing we pay, and think e'en
conquest dear; ....6 Queb 46
'Turn, Angelina, ever dear, ...149 Ed&A 64
'What I? dear Sir,' the Doctor
interposes; ....15 eGNM 68
No stirring--I beg--my dear friend--
my dear friend! ....56 HofV 97
No words, my dear GOLDSMITH! my
very good Friend! ....v56 HofV 240
The Epilogue. The Epilogue?
Yes, the Epilogue, my dear. 2 $eSSC_1$ 103
'Consider, dear Doctor, the girls
are but young.' ....56 LetB 133
Vida, 489
DEAREST To treat as dearest friend,
a foe; ....28 LogR 45
DEARLY For praise too dearly lov'd,
or warmly sought, ...269 Trav 14
DEATH Where the dark scorpion
gathers death around; ....352 DVil 35
Death, with its formidable band, ...53 Thrn 76
Let us prize death as the best
gift of nature-- ....86 Thrn 77
Death, when unmasked, shows me a
friendly face, ...93 Thrn 77
And when in death my vows shall
cease, ...205 Thrn 81
'Twas death,--'twas the death of
my mistress that came. ....246 Thrn 83
And death is your only pre-
ventive: ....63 $eSSC_1$ 106
And e'en the pang preceding
death ....II:35 Capt 119
Is, by quinto Elizabeth, Death
without Clergy. ....40 LetB 133
Vida, 126, 511, 578, 591
DEATH'S Death's growing power, ...64 Thrn 76
To Death's great court, the pros-
pect seems more fair. ....96 Thrn 77
DEBARRED Vida, 299
DEBATE Yon politician, famous in
debate, ...33 eSis 71
DEBATED While thus I debated, in
reverie centred, ...35 HofV 96
DEBAUCH Till, buried in debauch,
the bliss expire. ....226 Trav 12
DEBT The chest contriv'd a double
debt to pay, ...229 DVil 30
This debt to thy mem'ry I can-
not refuse, ...173 Rtal 93
DEBTOR Seize the debtor as it
flies. ....II:58 Capt 120
DEBTS Finds his lost senses
out, and pay his debts. ....26 $eSSC_2$ 108
DECAY$_1$ Defac'd by time and
tottering in decay, ...160 Trav 10
Bends to the grave with unper-
ceiv'd decay, ...109 DVil 26
Sinks to the grave with unper-
ceiv'd decay, ...v109 DVil 183
That trade's proud empire hastes
to swift decay, ...427 DVil 37
The good old sire, unconscious
of decay, ...155 Thrn 79
DECAY$_2$ Nor this the worst. As
nature's ties decay, ...349 Trav 16
Nor this the worst. As social
bonds decay, ...v349 Trav 174
Where wealth accumulates, and
men decay: ....52 DVil 25
The rich man's joys increase, the
poor's decay, ...266 DVil 32
Are trifling, and decay; ....70 Ed&A 61
DECAYED Beheld the duteous son,
the sire decay'd, ...407 Trav 18
And as my strength decay'd, her
bounty grew.' ....180 Thrn 80
DECEIT Vida, 417
DECEITS Vida, 311
DECEIVE Offers to love, but means
to deceive me. ....4 "Amw 94
DECEIVER O Memory, thou fond
deceiver, ...I:23 Capt 114
DECENCY To decency so fine a
thing? ....50 DTrn 53
DECENT The decent church that
topp'd the neighbouring hill, ...12 DVil 23
In all the decent manliness of
grief. ....v384 DVil 190
In decent dress, and coarsely
clean, ...181 Thrn 80
That decent dress, this holy
guide, ...185 Thrn 81
DECIDES Vida, 93
DECISION Vida, 568
DECK Its uplands sloping deck the
mountain's side, ...107 Trav 8
Like clouds that deck the morning
skies, ...v87 Ed&A 209
From China borrows aid to deck
the scene-- ....150 Thrn 79
To deck it, bring with you festoons

of the vine, ...167 Rtal 93
DECKED Here, richly deck'd, admits
the gorgeous train; ....320 DVil 33
A nightcap deck'd his brows in-
stead of bay, ...19 DABd 48
Found half the charms that deck'd
her face ....35 DTrn 53
DECKS Whose bright succession decks
the varied year; ....116 Trav 9
And oh! for this! while sculpture
decks thy shrine, ...128 Thrn 78
DECLARED The village all declar'd
how much he knew; ....207 DVil 30
Yet some have declar'd, and it
can't be denied 'em, ...27 Rtal 88
DECLARES The growing sound their
swift approach declares;-- ......I:55 Capt 115
DECLINE O blest retirement,
friend to life's decline, ...97 DVil 26
But verging to decline, its
splendours rise, ...297 DVil 33
For ah! too partial to my life's
decline, ...11 pLab 41
DECLINED Vida, 585
DECORUM So with decorum all things
carried; ....19 DTrn 52
Both are plac'd at the bar, with
all proper decorum, ...43 LetB 133
DECOY And, e'en while fashion's
brightest arts decoy, ...263 DVil 32
DECREE O Luxury! thou curs'd by
Heaven's decree, ...385 DVil 36
He comes pursuant to divine
decree, ...III:89 Capt 126
DECREED Such as to modern bard's
decreed; ....21 NSim 56
Vida, 140
DECREES Yes, my companions,
Heaven's decrees are past, ...III:1 Capt 122
DECRIED Dear charming nymph,
neglected and decried, ...411 DVil 37
DEED And shame prevents the
deed, ...192 Thrn 81
DEEP$_1$ With patient angle trolls
the finny deep, ...187 Trav 11
Embosom'd in the deep where
Holland lies. ....282 Trav 14
Explore the mine, or tempt the
dangerous deep; ....104 DVil 26
And shudd'ring still to face the
distant deep, ...369 DVil 35
These sadly join beside the
murmuring deep, ...159 Thrn 80
The raging deep, the whirl-
wind's roar-- ....218 Thrn 82
Where flows Euphrates murmuring
to the deep, ...I:2 Capt 113
Vida, 35, 365
DEEP$_2$ Who, too deep for his hear-
ers, still went on refining, ...35 Rtal 88
Vida, 564
DEEPEST Vida, 480, 663
DEEPLY With Scythian stores, and
trinkets deeply laden, ...11 pZob 72
DEEPS See, though by circling
deeps together held, ...v343 Trav 174
DEFACED Defac'd by time and
tottering in decay, ...160 Trav 10
They robb'd the relic and
defac'd the shrine. ....59 Thrn 76
DEFECT 'Twas no defect of yours,
but pocket low, ...8 GRos 51
DEFENCELESS Vida, 623
DEFEND Vida, 427
DEFENDER But chief to Thee, our
God, defender, friend, ...III:103 Capt 127
DEFIANCE Pride in their port,
defiance in their eye, ...327 Trav 16
Vida, 191
DEFINED Logicians have but ill
defin'd ....1 LogR 44
DEFINITION With definition and
division, ...8 LogR 44
DEFRAUDS Here beggar pride defrauds
her daily cheer, ...277 Trav 14
DEFY While self-dependent power
can time defy, ...429 DVil 37
DEGENERATE Unfit in these degener-
ate times of shame, ...409 DVil 36
DEGREE My father liv'd, of high
degree, ...v101 Ed&A 209
And curs of low degree. ....16 MDog 65
DEIGN Deign saint-like tenant of
the dale, ...v1 Ed&A 208
DEIGNS Yet, when he deigns his
real shape t' assume, ...35 eSis 71
DEITIES And from above the
dangling deities; ....16 epLL 101
DEITY'S But ev'n this deity's
existence ....61 NSim 58
DEJECTED 'Till quite dejected with
my scorn, ...133 Ed&A 63
Till quite dejected by my
scorn, ...v133 Ed&A 210
DEJECTION Yet, why this killing
soft dejection? ....v5 Sonn 196
DELAY He tried each art, re-
prov'd each dull delay, ...169 DVil 28
Why this delay? at length for
joy prepare; ....II:41 Capt 119
And give repentance but an
hour's delay. ....III:64 Capt 125
Thy fall more dreadful from
delay! ....III:79 Capt 126
Vida, 542
DELAYED And parting summer's
lingering blooms delay'd: ....4 DVil 23
While thus we resolv'd, and the
pasty delay'd, ...107 HofV 98
No more! Too long has justice
been delay'd, ...II:7 Capt 118
DELIAN Vida, 251
DELICATE To spoil such a delicate
picture by eating; ....6 HofV 95
DELIGHT Lost to every gay de-
light; ....2 Sonn 46
Vida, 64
DELIGHTED And till delighted even
to pain, ...v123 Ed&A 210
DELIGHTS But me, not destin'd
such delights to share, ...23 Trav 6
While low delights, succeeding
fast behind, ...157 Trav 10
Or rather, Love's delights

despising. ....I:68 Capt 116
DELIVER Should I at once de-
liver, ...6 Gift 43
DEMANDS The day demands it; sing
us Sion's song. ....I:82 Capt 116
DEMONS Whilst from below the
trap-door Demons rise, ...15 epLL 101
DEN Or seeks the den where snow-
tracks mark the way, ...189 Trav 11
A land of tyrants, and a den of
slaves, ...309 Trav 15
DENIAL I'll take no denial--you
shall, and you must, ...v53 HofV 240
DENIED And e'en the bare-worn
common is denied. ....308 DVil 33
Yet some have declar'd, and it
can't be denied 'em, ...27 Rtal 88
DENIES Vida, 664
DENOTE Sure these denote one
universal joy! ....324 DVil 34
Why these denote a brain of
feather. ....18 NSim 56
Denote him of the reptile kind; ....46 NSim 57
Denote the rage with which he
writes, ...47 NSim 57
DENY Here Whitefoord reclines,
and deny it who can, ...147 Rtal 92
DEPARTED That opulence departed
leaves behind; ....132 Trav 9
DEPARTING These, far departing,
seek a kinder shore, ...73 DVil 25
DEPEND Thus on the stage, our play-
wrights still depend ....3 eGNM 68
-DEPENDENT The self-dependent
lordlings stand alone, ...341 Trav 16
While self-dependent power can
time defy, ...429 DVil 37
DEPLORE He left me to deplore; ..v134 Ed&A 210
Let all your echoes now de-
plore ....165 Thrn 80
Is taught his former folly to
deplore; ....44 epLL 102
DEPLORES With heavy heart deplores
that luckless hour, ...334 DVil 34
DEPOPULATION Lead stern depopu-
lation in her train, ...402 Trav 18
DEPRIVED Depriv'd of sight and
rankling in his chain; ....II:89 Capt 121
DERIDE Yes! let the rich deride,
the proud disdain, ...251 DVil 31
DESCENDING Whose beard descend-
ing swept his aged breast; ....152 DVil 28
DESCENDS Soft as the dew from
heav'n descends, ...33 Ed&A 60
DESCRIBE Here lies David Garrick,
describe me, who can, ...93 Rtal 90
DESCRIBED While thus he describ'd
them by trade, and by name, ...79 HofV 97
DESERT Amidst thy desert walks
the lapwing flies, ...45 DVil 24
Vida, 638
DESERTED Vida, 466
DESERTING Deserting fifty, fasten
on fifteen, ...20 eSis 70
DESIGN$_1$ Vida, 233, 328, 479
DESIGN$_2$ Nor did the cruel ravagers
design ....56 Thrn 76
DESIGNED Sure 'twas by Providence
design'd, ...1 Byth 42
Design'd, no doubt, their part to
bear, ...25 NSim 56
Vida, 526
DESIGNS Intent on high designs, a
thoughtful band, ...329 Trav 16
Vida, 582
DESIRE That first excites desire,
and then supplies; ....216 Trav 12
Unquench'd by want, unfann'd by
strong desire; ....222 Trav 12
Far from my bosom drive the
low desire; ....364 Trav 17
The morn was cold, he views with
keen desire ....15 DABd 48
No foreign beauty tempts to false
desire; ....2 Cati 94
DESIRED John Trott was desired by
two witty peers ....1 ClRp 100
DESIRES Those calm desires that
ask'd but little room, ...70 DVil 25
DESIST Desist, my sons, nor mix
the strain with theirs. ....I:56 Capt 115
DESOLATION And desolation sad-
dens all thy green: ....38 DVil 24
DESPAIR$_1$ Despair and anguish fled
the struggling soul; ....174 DVil 29
Who seeks for rest, but finds
despair ....99 Ed&A 62
That seeks repose, but finds
despair ....v99 Ed&A 209
Vida, 649
DESPAIR$_2$ Vida, 610
DESPAIRING 'And there forlorn,
despairing, hid, ...141 Ed&A 64
Despairing of relief, ...61 Thrn 76
Vida, 450, 474
DESPERATE Oft risks his fortune on
one desperate throw, ...24 eSSC$_2$ 108
DESPISING Or rather, Love's
delights despising, ...I:68 Capt 116
DESTINED But me, not destin'd
such delights to share, ...23 Trav 6
DESTROY Diffuse their pleasures
only to destroy! ....388 DVil 36
Vida, 94, 227, 507
DESTROYED When once destroy'd, can
never be supplied. ....56 DVil 25
DESTRUCTION Seen all her triumphs
but destruction haste, ...399 Trav 18
And half the business of de-
struction done; ....396 DVil 36
Saps the strong wall, and pours
destruction round; ....III:50 Capt 124
The ruin smokes, destruction
pours along; ....III:51 Capt 124
Vida, 134, 285
DESTRUCTIVE That either seems
destructive of the rest. ....90 Trav 8
Vida, 590
DETECTED Vida, 419
DETECTION Detection her taper shall
quench to a spark, ...91 Rtal 90
DETECTOR But now he is gone, and
we want a detector, ...85 Rtal 90
DETERMINED Determin'd took their

stand: ....55 Thrn 76
Vida, 194
DETHRONED See where dethron'd
your captive monarch lies, ...II:88 Capt 121
DEUCE 'The deuce confound,' he
cries, 'these drumstick shanks, ...31 epLL 102
DEUS Deus est anima brutorum. ......18 LogR 44
DEVASTATION E'en now the devas-
tation is begun, ...395 DVil 36
DEVIL I'll give thee--To the
devil. ....20 Gift 43
He thinks her ugly as the
devil. ....70 DTrn 54
In short, so provoking a devil
was Dick, ...57 Rtal 89
'What the de'il, mon, a pasty!'
re-echoed the Scot, ...103 HofV 98
'What the de'il, mon, a pasty!'
returned the Scot, ...v103 HofV 242
Mr. Bunbury frets, and I fret like
the devil, ...19 LetB 132
DEVONSHIRE Your Devonshire
crew, ...36 Invt 129
DEW Soft as the dew from heav'n
descends, ...33 Ed&A 60
'The dew, the blossom on the
tree, ...125 Ed&A 63
Her bounty, like the morning
dew, ...178 Thrn 80
DEWS The dews of heaven refin'd, ..122 Ed&A 63
DEXTEROUS Vida, 48
DICK And Dick with his pepper
shall heighten their savour: ....8 Rtal 87
In short, so provoking a devil
was Dick, ...57 Rtal 89
As often we wish'd to have Dick
back again ....60 Rtal 89
DID As ever dead man did. ....20 DRtH 50
'Twas so for me that Edwin did, ...143 Ed&A 64
'Twas thus for me my lover did, .v143 Ed&A 211
Nor did the cruel ravagers
design ....56 Thrn 76
How did Grub-street re-echo the
shouts that you rais'd, ...117 Rtal 91
Vida, 382, 610, 629
DIE With vernal lives that blossom
but to die; ....118 Trav 9
And scholars, soldiers, kings,
unhonour'd die. ....360 Trav 17
Here to return--and die at home
at last. ....96 DVil 26
I'll lay me down and die; ....142 Ed&A 64
I'll linger till I die; ....v142 Ed&A 211
They swore the man would die. ......28 MDog 66
And wring his bosom, is--to
die. ....8 "wlw 67
Who without your aid must die. ...26 eSSC$_1$ 104
Yes, I shall die, hu, hu, hu,
hu! ....27 eSSC$_1$ 105
Yes, I must die, ho, ho, ho,
ho! ....28 eSSC$_1$ 105
Vida, 215, 576
DIED She had not died to-day. ......28 MBlz 47
He had not died to-day. ....4 DRtH 50
In secret, where he died. ....136 Ed&A 63
The dog it was that died. ....32 MDog 66
Then only poor, indeed, the day
she died. ....127 Thrn 78
DIES She sinks, she groans, she
dies. ....II:78 Capt 121
DIFFERENCE This diff'rence
only, as the god ....51 NSim 57
DIFFERENT$_1$ As different good, by
Art or Nature given, ...79 Trav 8
To different nations makes their
blessings even. ....80 Trav 8
Whatever fruits in different
climes were found, ...113 Trav 9
Far different there from all that
charm'd before, ...345 DVil 34
Far different these from every
former scene, ...359 DVil 35
As each a different way pursues, ...72 DTrn 54
I'm for a different set.--Old men,
whose trade is ....19 eSSC$_1$ 104
Each to different joys exciting, .I:72 Capt 116
Vida, 25, 44, 76, 639
DIFFERENT$_2$ Vida, 131, 357, 390
DIFFUSE Diffuse their pleasures
only to destroy! ....388 DVil 36
Diffuse their balmy sweets
around. ....I:50 Capt 115
DIFFUSED Vida, 18
DIGNITY An equal dignity of
mind-- ....13 Thrn 74
DILIGENTLY Onward, methinks, and
diligently slow, ...287 Trav 14
DIM Or dim thy beauty with a
tear? ....6 Sonn 46
Why dim thy beauty with a tear? ...v6 Sonn 196
DIMLY That dimly show'd the state
in which he lay; ....8 DABd 48
DIMPLES The joy that dimples, and
the woe that weeps. ....10 epLL 101
DIMPLING While Botanists, all
cold to smiles and dimpling, ...5 pZob 72
DINE And giving each your bounty,
let him dine; ....4 GRos 51
When come to the place where we
all were to dine, ...67 HofV 97
'I could dine on this tripe seven
days in the week: ....96 HofV 98
DINING And thought of convincing,
while they thought of dining; ......36 Rtal 88
DINNER To make out the dinner,
full certain I am, ...13 Rtal 87
At a dinner so various, at such
a repast, ...17 Rtal 87
To-morrow you take a poor dinner
with me; ....47 HofV 96
We wanted this venison to make
out the dinner. ....52 HofV 96
They enter'd, and dinner was
serv'd as they came. ....80 HofV 97
A prettier dinner I never set
eyes on; ....92 HofV 98
DINNERS I like these here dinners
so pretty and small; ....97 HofV 98
DIRE That dire disease, whose
ruthless power ....75 DTrn 54
DIRECT$_1$ Vida, 129
DIRECT$_2$ Who can direct, when all
pretend to know? ....64 Trav 7
Vida, 144

DIRECTING Say, was it that vainly
directing his view ....75 Rtal 89
DIRECTION Had Myra followed my
direction, ...7 Sonn 46
DIRECTLY Vida, 54, 108, 287
DIRTY Nor undertake a dirty job, ...31 LogR 45
DISAPPEARED Vida, 562
DISARM Redress the clime, and all
its rage disarm ....176 Trav 11
DISASTERS The day's disasters in his
morning face; ....200 DVil 29
DISCERN Where are the chiels? Ah!
Ah, I well discern ....39 eSSC$_1$ 105
DISCERNED Vida, 416
DISCERNING Gives genus a better
discerning. ....4 "LSm 84
You've got an odd something--a
kind of discerning-- ....119 HofV 99
DISCLOSE There, where a few torn
shrubs the place disclose, ...139 DVil 27
Such short-liv'd offerings but
disclose ....15 Gift 43
Vida, 28
DISCLOSES ---, what a group the
motley scene discloses! ....13 eSis 70
Whose ins and outs no ray of sense
discloses, ...13 epLL 101
DISCOVER No countryman living their
tricks to discover; ....90 Rtal 90
Not a look, not a smile shall my
passion discover: ....6 "Amw 94
DISDAIN Say, should the philosophic
mind disdain ....39 Trav 6
Yes! let the rich deride, the proud
disdain, ...251 DVil 31
DISDAINS Vida, 128, 566
DISEASE That dire disease, whose
ruthless power ....75 DTrn 54
Till his relish grown callous,
almost to disease, ...111 Rtal 90
DISGRACE Vida, 461
DISGRACEFUL They're perfectly dis-
graceful! strike me dead! ....33 epLL 102
DISGUISE$_1$ And felt her charms,
without disguise, within. ....14 MrsX 49
Vida, 564
DISGUISE$_2$ Vida, 321
DISH Each guest brought his dish,
and the feast was united; ....2 Rtal 87
Let each guest bring himself, and
he brings the best dish: ....4 Rtal 87
DISHONOURABLE Here wretches seek
dishonourable graves, ...310 Trav 15
DISLIKED Were things that I never
dislik'd in my life, ...63 HofV 97
DISMAL Convey'd the dismal tidings
when he frown'd; ....204 DVil 30
Vida, 264
DISMAY$_1$ Less dreadful struck me
with dismay, ...219 Thrn 82
DISMAY$_2$ Vida, 132
DISMAYED And sorrow, guilt, and
pain, by turns dismay'd, ...172 DVil 29
The shatter'd veteran, now first
dismay'd; ....158 Thrn 79
DISMISS Dismiss your griefs, and
join our warbling choir, ...I:83 Capt 117

DISOBEDIENT For a patriot, too cool;
for a drudge, disobedient; ....39 Rtal 88
DISOBEYED Vida, 171
DISORDER Her last disorder mortal. 24 MBlz 47
DISOWNS Nature disowns, and
reason scorns thy mirth, ...8 epLL 101
DISPENSE Dispense thy balmy store.II:3 Capt 118
DISPENSES Every grace that grief
dispenses, ...235 Thrn 82
DISPERSED These far dispers'd,
on timorous pinions fly, ...237 Trav 13
DISPERSES But this vile hour
disperses all my store, ...9 pLab 41
DISPLACES Humility displaces pride; 98 DTrn 55
DISPLAY Where rougher climes a nobler
race display, ...166 Trav 10
So bless'd a life these thoughtless
realms display, ...255 Trav 13
Here, while the proud their long-
drawn pomps display, ...317 DVil 33
Each bard might well display; ......14 DRtH 50
Could nought of purity display, ...123 Ed&A 63
Come on, my companions, the triumph
display; ....I:57 Capt 115
DISPLAYED Commerce on other shores
display'd her sail; ....140 Trav 10
Are here displayed. Their much-
lov'd wealth imparts ....303 Trav 15
DISPLAYS Displays her cleanly
platter on the board: ....196 Trav 11
I turn; and France displays her
bright domain. ....240 Trav 13
Her Second Act displays a livelier
scene-- ....13 eSSC$_3$ 85
On 'Squires and Cits she there
displays her arts, ...19 eSSC$_3$ 85
DISPORTING These here disporting own
the kindred soil, ...119 Trav 9
DISPOSE Of the neck and the breast I
had next to dispose; ....23 HofV 95
DISPOSSESS Usurp the land and
dispossess the swain; ....64 DVil 25
DISPROPORTIONED Hence, should one
order disproportion'd grow, ...375 Trav 17
DISPUTE Vida, 569
DISSEMBLE Let school-taught pride
dissemble all it can, ...41 Trav 6
-DISSEMBLED And still with ill-
dissembled power ....v131 Ed&A 210
DISTANCE Our Author's friends, thus
plac'd at happy distance, ...21 eGNM 68
'Tis best, however, keeping at a
distance. ....29 pZob 73
And is a terror only at a distance; 94 Thrn 77
Vida, 274
DISTANT Ah, no. To distant climes,
a dreary scene, ...341 DVil 34
And shudd'ring still to face the
distant deep, ...369 DVil 35
The distant climate and the savage
shore; ....2 pZob 72
Vida, 69, 447, 645
DISTRACT May oft distract us with
their sad solemnity: ....91 Thrn 77
DISTRESS$_1$ But pitying his distress,
let virtue shine, ...3 GRos 51
A heart's distress allay; ....v98 Ed&A 209

DISTRESS$_2$ Vida, 459
DISTRESSED Their welfare pleas'd
him, and their cares distress'd; ..186 DVil 29
Has wept at tales of innocence
distress'd; ....328 DVil 34
Mute for a while, and sullenly
distress'd, ...211 Thrn 82
Vida, 615
DISTRESSFUL And all around dis-
tressful yells arise, ...418 Trav 19
DISTRESSING Hence, intruder, most
distressing, ...I:27 Capt 114
DISTREST Thus we, O Lord, alike
distrest, ...III:43 Capt 124
DISTRUSTING The heart distrusting
asks, if this be joy. ....264 DVil 32
DISTURB No politics disturb their
mind; ....24 LogR 44
DIVERSION Vida, 11
DIVERT Vida, 21
DIVIDE Those fenceless fields the
sons of wealth divide, ...307 DVil 33
DIVIDED Where beasts with man
divided empire claim, ...415 Trav 19
DIVINE The heartfelt power of every
charm divine, ...3 MrsX 49
His gallants are all faultless, his
women divine, ...65 Rtal 89
He comes pursuant to divine
decree, ...III:89 Capt 126
DIVINES Come, all ye quack bards,
and ye quacking divines, ...81 Rtal 89
DIVISION With definition and division,8 LogR 44
DIZENED Like a tragedy queen he has
dizen'd her out, ...67 Rtal 89
DO Do thine, sweet AUBURN, thine,
the loveliest train, ...337 DVil 34
Do thy fair tribes participate her
pain? ....338 DVil 34
How do thy potions, with insidious
joy ....387 DVil 36
Her love was sought, I do aver, ...17 MBlz 47
Yon critic, too-but whither do I run?41 eSis 71
Do you spare her, and I'll for once
spare you. ....44 eSis 71
How do the good, the virtuous fall! 73 Thrn 76
To do thy memory right; ....227 Thrn 82
Then strew all around it (you can do
no less) ....169 Rtal 93
May rosined lightning blast me, if
I do! ....18 epLL 101
Do not our tyrant lords this day
ordain ....I:37 Capt 114
'Pray what does Miss Horneck? take
courage, come do,'-- ....17 LetB 132
Vida, 569
DOATS See DOTES
DOCTOR Your brother Doctor there,
perhaps, may try.' ....14 eGNM 68
'What I? dear Sir,' the Doctor
interposes; ....15 eGNM 68
But your friend there, the Doctor,
eats nothing at all.' ....98 HofV 98
'Well done!' cry the ladies; 'Ah,
Doctor, that's good! ....25 LetB 132
The pool's very rich--ah! the Doctor
is loo'd!' ....26 LetB 132
Ah! the Doctor is loo'd! Come, Doctor,
put down.' ....32 LetB 132
'But, pray, whom have they pil-
fer'd?'--' A Doctor, I hear.' ..49 LetB 133
'Consider, dear Doctor, the girls
are but young.' ....56 LetB 133
DOCTORS The doctors found, when
she was dead,-- ....23 MBlz 47
Doctors, who cough and answer
every misfortuner, ...53 eSSC$_1$ 106
DOCTRINES By doctrines fashion'd
to the varying hour; ....146 DVil 28
DODDS Our Dodds shall be pious,
our Kenricks shall lecture; ....86 Rtal 90
DOES 'What does Mrs. Bunbury?'
'I, Sir? I pass.' ....16 LetB 132
'Pray what does Miss Horneck?
take courage, come do,'-- ......17 LetB 132
'The same.'--'What a pity! how
does it surprise one! ....51 LetB 133
Vida, 197
DOG And in that town a dog was
found, ...13 MDog 65
This dog and man at first were
friends; ....17 MDog 65
The dog, to gain some private
ends, ...19 MDog 65
The dog, to gain his private
ends, ...v19 MDog 212
And swore the dog had lost his
wits, ...23 MDog 65
And while they swore the dog was
mad, ...27 MDog 66
The dog it was that died. ....32 MDog 66
DOGS As many dogs there be, ...14 MDog 65
DOING And learn the luxury of
doing good. ....22 Trav 6
But aid the power of doing good-- ..16 Thrn 74
DOMAIN Till, carried to excess in
each domain, ...97 Trav 8
I turn; and France displays her
bright domain. ....240 Trav 13
One only master grasps the whole
domain, ...39 DVil 24
DOME The dome where Pleasure holds
her midnight reign ....319 DVil 33
DOMES As in those domes, where
Caesars once bore sway, ...159 Trav 10
DOMESTIC Glides the smooth current
of domestic joy. ....434 Trav 19
Secluded from domestic strife, ...1 DTrn 52
To be a dull domestic friend? ......48 DTrn 53
DONE Wept o'er his wounds, or tales
of sorrow done, ...157 DVil 28
And half the business of de-
struction done; ....396 DVil 36
That pretty Bar-maids have done
execution. ....6 eSSC$_3$ 85
'I hold the odds.--Done, done,
with you, with you;' ....50 eSSC$_1$ 106
'Tis fixed--it shall be done. ..II:82 Capt 121
And let thy will be done. .....III:58 Capt 124
'Well done!' cry the ladies;
'Ah, Doctor, that's good! ......25 LetB 132
Vida, 296, 323
DON'T But hold--let me pause--
Don't I hear you pronounce ....13 HofV 95

'I don't care if I keep a corner
for't too.' ....102 HofV 98
I don't think he'll wish to come
back. ....4 epEP 100
For sure I don't wrong you, you
seldom are slack, ...59 eSSC$_1$ 106
Don't you think the best way is
to venture for't twice?' ....30 LetB 132
DOOM To lure thee to thy doom. .....12 Ed&A 59
The king himself shall judge, and
fix their doom. ....II:84 Capt 121
DOOR Against the houseless
stranger shuts the door; ....4 Trav 5
The varnish'd clock that click'd
behind the door; ....228 DVil 30
Near her betrayer's door she lays
her head, ...332 DVil 34
The needy seldom pass'd her
door, ...5 MBlz 47
My door is open still; ....14 Ed&A 59
The door just opening with a
latch, ...v43 Ed&A 208
At the Pit door stands elbowing
a way, ...24 eGNM 68
Want pass'd for merit at her
door, ...124 Thrn 78
I drove to his door in my own
hackney coach. ....66 HofV 97
-DOOR Whilst from below the
trap-door Demons rise, ...15 epLL 101
DOORS At proud men's doors they
ask a little bread! ....340 DVil 34
DOST Reluctant dost thou rove; .....66 Ed&A 61
DOTAGE What in the name of dotage
drives me here? ....4 pLab 41
DOTES Doats upon dancing, and in
all her pride, ...27 eSSC$_3$ 85
Who sighs for operas, and dotes
on dancing, ...20 eSSC$_2$ 108
DOUBLE$_1$ Its double weight must
ruin all below. ....376 Trav 17
Gave wealth to sway the mind with
double force. ....396 Trav 18
Truth from his lips prevail'd
with double sway, ...179 DVil 29
The chest contriv'd a double debt
to pay, ...229 DVil 30
Vida, 130, 196, 262, 267, 356
DOUBLE- Vida, 75
DOUBLE$_2$ Vida, 111
DOUBLY And clasp'd them close, in
sorrow doubly dear; ....382 DVil 36
DOUBT Design'd, no doubt, their
part to bear, ...25 NSim 56
No doubt they're all barbarians.--
Yes, 'tis so, ...27 pZob 73
If he had any faults, he had left
us in doubt, ...25 Rtal 87
Vida, 562
DOUBTFUL Here, as with doubtful,
pensive steps I range, ...v(81) Dvil 182
DOUGLAS And Douglas is pudding,
substantial and plain: ....10 Rtal 87
Here Douglas retires, from his
toils to relax, ...79 Rtal 89
DOWN$_1$ These rocks, by custom, turn
to beds of down. ....86 Trav 8
The simple plumage, or the glossy
down ....4 Cati 94
DOWN$_2$ Trav, 32, 192; DVil, 26, 86,
175, 394, 399; MrsX, 6; DTrn, 11;
Ed&A, 142; eGNM, 6; eSis, 22; "LSm,
10, 14; eSSC$_2$, 10; Capt, I:85, II:77,
79, III:55; LetB, 7, 32; Vida, 554
DOWNWARD Look downward where a hundred
realms appear; ....34 Trav 6
Those blazing suns that dart a
downward ray, ...347 DVil 34
Downward they move, a melan-
choly band, ...401 DVil 36
DOZENS Lovers no more, flew off
by dozens: ....88 DTrn 55
DRABS Regale the drabs and bloods
of Drury-lane; ....4 DABd 48
DRAGS And drags at each remove a
lengthening chain. ....10 Trav 5
And drags the struggling savage in-
to day. ....190 Trav 11
DRAINED To take us in when we have
drained the cup. ....98 Thrn 77
DRANK He drank his glass and
crack'd his joke, ...5 DTrn 52
DRAUGHT At every draught more large
and large they grow, ...391 DVil 36
DRAUGHTS Low lies that house where
nut-brown draughts inspir'd, ...221 DVil 30
DRAW$_1$ Each wanton judge new penal
statutes draw, ...385 Trav 18
Around my fire an evening group
to draw, ...91 DVil 26
Nor draw the quill to write for
B--b. ....32 LogR 45
Or draw the curtains clos'd
around? ....24 DTrn 52
Vida, 302
DRAW$_2$ To draw men as they ought to
be, not as they are. ....64 Rtal 89
DRAWERS A bed by night, a chest
of drawers by day; ....230 DVil 30
DRAWING Wak'd Priam in drawing
his curtains by night. ....110 HofV 98
-DRAWN Here, while the proud their
long-drawn pomps display, ...317 DVil 33
DRAWS The mind still turns where
shifting fashion draws, ...279 Trav 14
Vida, 344, 653
DREADFUL Alive, the foe thy dread-
ful vigour fled, ...9 Queb 46
O there the natives are--a dread-
ful race! ....25 pZob 73
Less dreadful struck me with
dismay, ...219 Thrn 82
Less dreadful show ....II:22 Capt 119
Thy fall more dreadful from
delay! ....III:79 Capt 126
Vida, 393, 523
DREAM Where, splendid as the
youthful poet's dream, ...142 Thrn 79
'Give me another horse! bind up
my wounds!--soft--'twas but a
dream.' ....24 epLL 101
Aye, 'twas but a dream, for now
there's no retreating: ....25 epLL 101
DREARY Ah, no. To distant climes,

a dreary scene, ...341 DVil 34
Oswego's dreary shores shall be
my grave; ....222 Thrn 82
DRESS$_1$ Slights every borrow'd
charm that dress supplies, ...289 DVil 32
In all the glaring impotence of
dress. ....294 DVil 33
In decent dress, and coarsely
clean, ...181 Thrn 80
That decent dress, this holy
guide, ...185 Thrn 81
And gain'd a husband without aid
from dress, ...2 eSSC$_3$ 85
DRESS$_2$ Ye bending swains, that
dress the flow'ry vale, ...48 Trav 6
To dress, and look like awkward
Frenchmen here, ...34 eSSC$_1$ 105
DRESSED See also DREST
And five crack'd teacups dress'd
the chimney board; ....18 DABd 48
'Tis true she dress'd with modern
grace, ...43 DTrn 53
Ye fields of Sharon, dress'd in
flow'ry pride, ...I:17 Capt 114
DRESSING But dressing, patching,
repartee; ....40 DTrn 53
DREST And though no temple richly
drest, ...I:11 Capt 113
DREW$_1$ And the twelve rules the
royal martyr drew; ....12 DABd 48
Near, and more near, the hounds
and huntsmen drew. ....38 epLL 102
Vida, 246, 281, 347
DREW$_2$ He grew lazy at last, and
drew from himself? ....78 Rtal 89
DRINKING A-preaching that drink-
ing is sinful, ...11 "LSm 84
DRIVE Far from my bosom drive the
low desire; ....364 Trav 17
In vain, to drive thee from the
right, ...30 Thrn 75
Vida, 580
DRIVEN Where are we driven? our
reck'ning sure is lost! ....15 pZob 72
Vida, 178
DRIVES Or drives his vent'rous
plough-share to the steep; ....188 Trav 11
He drives his flock to pick the
scanty blade, ...306 DVil 33
What in the name of dotage drives
me here? ....4 pLab 41
With this he drives men's souls
to hell. ....42 NSim 57
DROP$_1$ To swear the pill, or drop,
has wrought a cure; ....2 eGNM 68
DROP$_2$ Even pitying hills would
drop a tear!-- ....11 DRtH 50
Sad Philomel thus--but let
similes drop-- ....115 HofV 99
DROPS Vida, 348
DROVE Drove souls to Tart'rus
with his rod, ...52 NSim 57
The coachman was tipsy, the
chariot drove home; ....48 Rtal 88
I drove to his door in my own
hackney coach. ....66 HofV 97
Vida, 334

DROWSY But silent bats in drowsy
clusters cling; ....350 DVil 34
DRUDGE For a patriot, too cool;
for a drudge, disobedient; ....39 Rtal 88
DRUMSTICK 'The deuce confound,'
he cries, 'these drumstick shanks, .31 epLL 102
DRURY- Regale the drabs and
bloods of Drury-lane; ....4 DABd 48
DRY The parting surface leaves his
brazen axle dry. ....6 Tr 267
DUCKS Your bustards, your ducks,
and your widgeons; ....24 "LSm 84
DUDS Or to put on my duds; ....10 Invt 128
DUE Yet let them only share the
praises due, ...211 Trav 12
So next day, in due splendour to
make my approach, ...65 HofV 97
Vida, 324
DUKES And footmen, lords and dukes
can act. ....56 LogR 45
DULL Dull as their lakes that
slumber in the storm. ....312 Trav 15
He tried each art, reprov'd each
dull delay, ...169 DVil 28
To be a dull domestic friend? ......48 DTrn 53
DULY Vida, 530
DUMB My friend bade me welcome,
but struck me quite dumb, ...69 HofV 97
Blasphemers, all be dumb. ......II:74 Capt 121
DUNCE And the puff of a dunce
he mistook it for fame; ....110 Rtal 90
DUNCES If dunces applauded, he
paid them in kind. ....114 Rtal 91
DUNGEON To yonder gloomy dungeon
turn your eyes; ....II:87 Capt 121
DUNGEONS More ponderous chains,
and dungeons more confin'd. ....II:92 Capt 122
DUPE The man had his failings,
a dupe to his art, ...98 Rtal 90
DUSKY No more the smith his dusky
brow shall clear, ...245 DVil 31
DUST Down with her, Lord, to lick
the dust, ...II:79 Capt 121
Down with them, Lord, to lick
the dust; ....III:55 Capt 124
DUTEOUS Beheld the duteous
son, the sire decay'd, ...407 Trav 18
DUTY As duty, love, and honour
fail to sway, ...350 Trav 16
But in his duty prompt at every
call, ...165 DVil 28
Expressive of my duty? ....4 Gift 43
Serenely gay, and strict in
duty, ...103 DTrn 55
DWELL Where modest want and
patient sorrow dwell; ....123 Thrn 78
To dwell a weeping hermit
there. ....135 Thrn 78
Vida, 662
DWELLING And round his dwelling
guardian saints attend: ....12 Trav 5
DWINDLES Man seems the only growth
that dwindles here. ....126 Trav 9
DYED With modesty her cheeks are
dy'd, ...97 DTrn 55
'It shows that their habits are
all dyed in grain.' ....58 LetB 133

DYES Vida, 25
DYING Loses ev'ry pain of dying 38,46 Thrn 75
Vida, 388, 555, 665

EACH Trav, 10, 40, 56, 61, v79, 89, 95, 97, 155, 184, 215, 232, 299, v299, 315, 325, 374, 385, 426; DVil, 8, 23, 26, 72, 124, 167, 169, 182, 283, v313, 353; LogR 40, 43; DABd, 2; MrsX, 6; DRtH, 14; GRos, 4, 6; DTrn, 25, 61, 72, 83; NSim, 60; Ed&A, 109, v109, 129; eGNM, 5, 8, 34; eSis, 5; Thrn, 63, 175, 203, 233; Rtal, 2, 4, 77; eSSC$_1$, 40; Capt, I:29, vI:29, 72, 89, II:66; Invt, 30, 35; Vida, 17, 24, 41, 59, 65, 69, 75, 124, 145, 163, 182, 203, 220, 396, 402, 422, 436, 467, 479, 561, 580, 581, 638
EAGER Ye gamesters, who, so eager in pursuit, ...47 eSSC$_1$ 105
Thus, playing, and playing, I still grow more eager, ...33 LetB 132
EAR Give ear unto my song; ....2 MDog 65
The sounds of barb'rous pleasure strike mine ear; ....I:52 Capt 115
EARLIEST Eternal blessings crown my earliest friend, ...11 Trav 5
Where smiling spring its earliest visit paid, ...3 DVil 23
I'll strip all the spring of its earliest bloom; ....248 Thrn 83
We'll rifle the spring of its earliest bloom, ...256,260 Thrn 83
EARLY For grief had seized his early age, ...v59 Ed&A 208
EARNEST Still grants her bliss at Labour's earnest call; ....82 Trav 8
EARS To tell them the reason why asses had ears? ....2 ClRp 100
EARTH That, like the circle bounding earth and skies, ...27 Trav 6
On earth unseen, or only found .....79 Ed&A 61
Here lies the good Dean, re-united to earth, ...23 Rtal 87
With no reason on earth to go out of his way, ...103 Rtal 90
Till earth, receding from our eyes, ...II:5 Capt 118
Vida, 165, 515, 555, 667
EARTH- All earth-born cares are wrong: ....30 Ed&A 60
For earth-born cares are wrong: ....v30 Ed&A 208
EASE$_1$ And his long nights of revelry and ease; ....68 Trav 7
In passive ease they leave the world to chance. ....v(156) Trav 170
Gay sprightly land of mirth and social ease, ...241 Trav 13
Dear lovely bowers of innocence and ease, ...5 DVil 23
A youth of labour with an age of ease; ....100 DVil 26
Vida, 535
EASE$_2$ I'd speak a word or two, to ease my conscience. ....2 epLL 101

EAST From north, from south, from east, from west, ...II:71 Capt 121
EASY An easy compensation seem to find. ....148 Trav 10
EAT They eat their meals, and take their sport, ...25 LogR 44
Even Common-Councilmen forget to eat. ....22 eSSC$_3$ 85
To eat mutton cold, and cut blocks with a razor. ....42 Rtal 88
To paint it, or eat it, just as he lik'd best. ....22 HofV 95
But hang it--to poets who seldom can eat, ...31 HofV 96
But I've eat of your tripe till I'm ready to burst.' ....94 HofV 98
I could eat of this Tripe seven days in the week.' ....v96 HofV 242
EATABLES And the porter and eatables follow'd behind. ....58 HofV 97
EATING To spoil such a delicate picture by eating; ....6 HofV 95
But for eating a rasher of what they take pride in, ...11 HofV 95
They'd as soon think of eating the pan it is fried in. ....12 HofV 95
'What have we got here?--Why, this is good eating! ....39 HofV 96
If I cease Harlequin, I cease from eating. ....26 epLL 101
EATS But your friend there, the Doctor, eats nothing at all,' ......98 HofV 98
EBBS Vida, 362
ECHO Vida, 264
-ECHO How did Grub-street re-echo the shouts that you rais'd, ...117 Rtal 91
Vida, 524
ECHOED 'We'll all keep a corner,' was echoed about. ....106 HofV 98
-ECHOED Who copied his squibs, and re-echoed his jokes; ....164 Rtal 93
'What the de'il, mon, a pasty!' re-echoed the Scot., ...103 HofV 98
ECHOES$_1$ And tires their echoes with unvaried cries. ....46 DVil 24
Let all your echoes now deplore ....165 Thrn 80
The echoes of Thames shall my sorrows proclaim, ...244 Thrn 83
ECHOES$_2$ Vida, 354
ECLIPSED My heels eclips'd the honours of my head; ....4 epLL 101
EDEN Is once again with Eden blest, ...118 Thrn 78
EDMUND Here lies our good Edmund, whose genius was such, ...29 Rtal 88
EDWARD'S Old Edward's sons, unknown to yield, ...225 Thrn 82
EDWIN Amongst the rest young Edwin bow'd, ...111 Ed&A 63
Among the rest young Edwin bow'd, ...v111 Ed&A 209
'Twas so for me that Edwin did, ...143 Ed&A 64
Thy own, thy long-lost Edwin here, ...151 Ed&A 64
EDWIN'S 'Twas Edwin's self that

prest. ....148 Ed&A 64
Shall break thy Edwin's too.' .....160 Ed&A 64
E'EN Trav, 31, 130, 137, 175, 201, 260, 306, 333, 338, 413; DVil, 32, 164, 210, 212, 263, 271, 308, 339, 395, 397; Queb, 6; DTrn, 90; Capt, II:35; Vida, 84
E'ER DVil, 144, 323; MrsX, 8; Vida, 543
EFFORTS To finish all their efforts at a blow; ....57 Thrn 76
EIGHT Vida, 24, 72
EITHER That either seems destructive of the rest. ....90 Trav 8
Wings upon either side--mark that. .16 NSim 56
Vida, 69, 169, 184, 576
ELAPSED And, many a year elaps'd, return to view ....79 DVil 25
ELATE Vida, 547
ELBOWING At the Pit door stands elbowing a way, ...24 eGNM 68
ELEGANCE Convenience, plenty, elegance, and arts; ....304 Trav 15
Where sculptur'd elegance and native grace ....144 Thrn 79
ELEPHANT Vida, 240, 336, 371, 506
ELEPHANTS Vida, 49, 70
ELF With his goosequill the scribbling elf, ...53 NSim 57
Quite sick of pursuing each troublesome elf, ...77 Rtal 89
ELIZABETH Is, by quinto Elizabeth, Death without Clergy. ....40 LetB 133
ELMS Where shading elms along the margin grew, ...245 Trav 13
ELYSIUM He forms a scene beyond Elysium blest-- ....143 Thrn 79
'EM Gift, 10, 12; LogR, 10, 17; eSis, 15, 16; pZob, 19, 20; Rtal, 26, 27, 28; HofV, v34; LetB, 44; Vida, 406, 515, 577, 614
EMBOSOMED Embosom'd in the deep where Holland lies. ....282 Trav 14
EMBOSSED Vida, 673
EMBRACE Vida, 671
EMITS Emits a brighter ray. ....II:40 Capt 119
EMPIRE Scoops out an empire, and usurps the shore; ....290 Trav 14
Where beasts with man divided empire claim, ...415 Trav 19
That trade's proud empire hastes to swift decay, ...427 DVil 37
And our fix'd empire shall for ever last; ....III:2 Capt 122
Our empire began, ...III:8 Capt 122
EMPLOY Let rapture the minutes employ; ....I:58 Capt 115
Vida, 95
EMPTIED Have emptied all the green-room on the stage. ....6 eSis 70
Left alone to reflect, having emptied my shelf, ...59 HofV 97
EMPTIER 'And love is still an emptier sound, ...77 Ed&A 61
EMULATE To emulate his mind. ......124 Ed&A 63
ENCAMPMENTS Vida, 52
ENCIRCLED When Satire and Censure encircl'd his throne, ...83 Rtal 89
-ENCIRCLED Filled with a snake-encircl'd wand; ....32 NSim 57
ENCIRCLING Then, with chaos and blunders encircling my head, ...21 Rtal 87
ENCOMPASS Vida, 151
END$_1$ But on he moves to meet his latter end, ...107 DVil 26
A thousand sorrows urg'd thy end: 31 Thrn 75
A hopeful end indeed to such a blest beginning. ....8 eSSC$_1$ 103
O Thou, without beginning, without end, ...III:105 Capt 127
-END Here, porter!--this venison with me to Mile-end; ...55 HofV 97
END$_2$ Come, end the contest here, and aid my party. ....56 eSSC$_1$ 106
We both agree, like friends, to end our jarring? ....66 eSSC$_1$ 106
Shall ever in confusion end; ...I:44 Capt 115
Like his, your lives shall end.III:30 Capt 123
Let us, and all, begin and end, in Thee! ....III:106 Capt 127
Vida, 544
ENDEAR Theirs are those arts that mind to mind endear, ...257 Trav 13
Thine are those charms that dazzle and endear; ....336 Trav 16
ENDEARED Where humble happiness endear'd each scene; ....8 DVil 23
ENDEARING Even children follow'd with endearing wile, ...183 DVil 29
ENDEARMENT And, as a bird each fond endearment tries ....167 DVil 28
ENDED For life is ended when our honour ends. ....20 pLab 41
Vida, 532, 654
ENDLESS 'Twas joy, and endless blisses all around, ...11 MrsX 49
May blissful endless peace be thine above! ....111 Thrn 78
ENDS$_1$ And spurns the plan that aims at other ends; ....96 Trav 8
The dog, to gain some private ends, 19 MDog 65
The dog, to gain his private ends,v19 MDog 212
ENDS$_2$ For life is ended when our honour ends. ....20 pLab 41
ENDUED To wit--most wond'rously endu'd, ...35 NSim 57
ENDURE Still may thy blooms the changeful clime endure, ...369 Trav 17
How small, of all that human hearts endure, ...429 Trav 19
ENFEEBLES Enfeebles all internal strength of thought; ....270 Trav 14
ENGAGE Truth, beauty, worth, and all that most engage, ...74 Thrn 76
If folly, fraud, your hearts engage,78 Thrn 76
Vida, 1, 165, 268, 390, 455
ENGAGED Vida, 369
ENGLAND The Terence of England, the mender of hearts; ....62 Rtal 89
ENGLAND'S Casts a long look where England's glories shine, ... 421 Trav 19
A time there was, ere England's griefs began, ...57 DVil 25
ENGLISH The English laws forbid to

punish lunatics. ....42 eSSC$_2$ 109
ENHANCE Enhance the bliss his
scanty fund supplies. ....202 Trav 12
ENJOY By the gods, I'll enjoy it;
though 'tis but in thought! ....42 LetB 133
ENLIST When he comes to enlist. ...22 Invt 128
ENLIVENED Vida, 407
ENLIVENS And our monarch enlivens
below. ....I:64 Capt 116
ENNA'S In all my Enna's beauties
blest, ...1 TrSA 51
ENOUGH Yet in a man 'twas well
enough. ....28 DTrn 53
ENQUIRY When uncover'd, a buzz of
enquiry runs round,-- ....47 LetB 133
ENSUES Vida, 389
ENTER That modern judges seldom
enter here. ....18 eSSC$_1$ 104
ENTERED An acquaintance, a friend
as he call'd himself, enter'd; .....36 HofV 96
They enter'd, and dinner was
serv'd as they came. ....80 HofV 97
With looks that quite petrified,
enter'd the maid; ....108 HofV 98
ENTERS Our bard into the general
spirit enters, ...9 pZob 72
ENTIRE In nought entire--except
his heart. ....210 Thrn 81
ENTRANCE Vida, 509
ENTRANCES 'We have our exits and
our entrances.' ....8 eSSC$_3$ 85
ENTRENCHED Vida, 219
ENVY Whenever rage or envy rise, ...65 DTrn 54
EPILOGUE 'An Epilogue--things can't
go on without it; ....9 eGNM 68
The Epilogue. The Epilogue? Yes,
the Epilogue, my dear. ....2 eSSC$_1$ 103
Sure you mistake, Ma'am. The
Epilogue, I bring it. ....3 eSSC$_1$ 103
Why, sure the girl's beside her-
self: an Epilogue of singing, 7 eSSC$_1$ 103
What if we leave the Epilogue
unspoken? ....68 eSSC$_1$ 106
-EPILOGUED Un-epilogued the Poet
waits his sentence. ....70 eSSC$_1$ 107
EPILOGUES For Epilogues and
Prologues on some friend, ...4 eGNM 68
EQUAL An equal portion dealt to
all mankind, ...78 Trav 7
He promises with equal air, ...51 LogR 45
And to perform takes equal care. ...52 LogR 45
An equal semblance still to keep, ..49 NSim 57
An equal dignity of mind-- ....13 Thrn 74
Though equal to all things, for all
things unfit, ...37 Rtal 88
Vida, 24, 41, 45, 175, 199, 381, 559, 561
EQUALLY Equally fit for gallantry
and war. ....36 pZob 73
Vida, 439
EQUINOCTIAL Whether where
equinoctial fervours glow, ...419 DVil 37
EQUIPAGE Space for his horses,
equipage, and hounds; ....278 DVil 32
ERE A time there was, ere England's
griefs began, ...57 DVil 25
His Heaven commences ere the world
be pass'd! ....112 DVil 27
His pity gave ere charity began. ...162 DVil 28
In these, ere triflers half their
wish obtain, ...261 DVil 32
And tries to kill, ere she's got
power to cure. ....24 eSis 70
Yet ere he lands he 'as ordered
me before, ...13 pZob 72
Ere I forget the land that gave me
birth, ...I:91 Capt 117
Ere yonder setting sun; ....II:80 Capt 121
Shall wrath vindictive threaten
ere it fall! ....III:38 Capt 124
ERRING Teach erring man to spurn
the rage of gain; ....424 DVil 37
Is both a weak and erring creature; 14 LogR 44
ERROR Where prostrate error hails
the rising sun? ....I:36 Capt 114
ESCAPE To 'scape the pressure of
contiguous pride? ....304 DVil 33
ESCAPED Vida, 454
ESPIED Vida, 668
ESSAY Vida, 483
ESSAYS Should so long be to news-
paper essays confin'd; ....158 Rtal 93
EST <u>Homo</u> <u>est</u> <u>ratione</u> <u>praeditum</u>,-- ....9 LogR 44
<u>Deus</u> <u>est</u> <u>anima</u> <u>brutorum</u>. ....18 LogR 44
ESTABLISHED Vida, 162
ESTEEM They please, are pleas'd,
they give to get esteem, ...265 Trav 14
ESTIMATE And estimate the blessings
which they share, ...76 Trav 7
Or estimate their bliss on Reason's
plan, ...v76 Trav 168
Teach us to estimate what all must
suffer; ....85 Thrn 77
ETERNAL Eternal blessings crown my
earliest friend, ...11 Trav 5
Eternal sunshine settles on its head.192 DVil 29
Ye prophets, skill'd in Heaven's
eternal truth, ...II:27 Capt 119
ETERNALLY 'For I knew it,' he
cried, 'both eternally fail, ...71 HofV 97
ETERNITY Let praise be given to all
eternity; ....III:104 Capt 127
ETHIOPIA'S Vida, 15
ETIQUETTE Excuse me, Ma'am, I
know the etiquette. ....10 eSSC$_1$ 104
EUPHRATES Where flows Euphrates
murmuring to the deep, ...I:2 Capt 113
EVEN$_1$ See also EV'N and E'EN
DVil, 183; MrsX, 13; DRtH, 11; Ed&A, v123; Thrn,
21; eSSC$_3$, 22
EVEN$_2$ To different nations makes
their blessings even. ....80 Trav 8
To these or those, but makes the
balance even: ....v80 Trav 168
EVENING To pause from toil, and trim
their ev'ning fire; ....14 Trav 5
Around my fire an evening group to
draw, ...91 DVil 26
To take their evening rest, ...46 Ed&A 60
My morning prayer, my evening song, 200 Thrn 81
My morning and my evening song; ....204 Thrn 81
EVENING'S Sweet was the sound, when
oft at evening's close ....113 DVil 27
EVENTFUL Such, through our lives,
the eventful history-- ....32 eSSC$_3$ 86

master's mind! ....324 Trav 16
EXULT Vida, 500
EXULTING Amidst the clamour of exulting joys, ...1 Queb 46
Vida, 604
Exulting rocks have crown'd the power of song! ....9 Tr 267
EXULTS Exults in all the good of all mankind. ....44 Trav 6
Exults, and owns his cottage with a smile. ....164 Trav 10
EYE Pride in their port, defiance in their eye, ...327 Trav 16
Where once the sign-post caught the passing eye, ...220 DVil 30
With sulky eye he smoak'd the patient man, ...v(21) DABd 200
To every Christian eye; ....26 MDog 66
To hide her shame from every eye, ...6 "wlw 67
Yon broad, bold, angry spark, I fix my eye on, ...27 eSis 71
Where wildly huddled to the eye, ..103 Thrn 77
How piercing is that eye! how sleek that brow! ....35 epLL 102
Strephon caught thy ravish'd eye; ....24 eSSC$_1$ 104
Vida, 253, 284, 326, 398, 420, 470, 508, 640
EYEBALLS Vida, 414
EYELESS Those eyeless orbs that shock with ghastly glare, ...III:33 Capt 123
EYES$_1$ But let us try these truths with closer eyes, ...99 Trav 8
Nor shares with art the triumph of her eyes: ....290 DVil 32
Are these thy serious thoughts?--Ah, turn thine eyes ....325 DVil 34
My heart, a victim to thine eyes, ...5 Gift 43
And saw thee fall with joy-pronouncing eyes: ....10 Queb 46
<u>But when she shut her eyes.</u> ....16 MBlz 47
O had her eyes forgot to blaze! ....15 DTrn 52
Or Jack had wanted eyes to gaze. ....16 DTrn 52
How wide her mouth, how wild her eyes! ....66 DTrn 54
To bring back lustre to her eyes. ..84 DTrn 54
His simp'ring friends, with pleasure in their eyes, ...27 eGNM 69
Have pleas'd our eyes, and sav'd the pain of thinking. ....8 eSis 70
Perhaps, to vulgar eyes, bestrides the state; ....34 eSis 71
Our vows are heard! Long, long to mortal eyes, ...120 Thrn 78
And owns its offspring in their yellow eyes. ....14 Cati 94
A prettier dinner I never set eyes on; ....92 HofV 98
To him we turn our eyes; ....I:8 Capt 113
And brings my long-lost country to mine eyes. ....I:16 Capt 114
Till earth, receding from our eyes, ...II:5 Capt 118
To yonder gloomy dungeon turn your eyes; ....II:87 Capt 121
Alas! too well mine eyes indignant trace ....III:19 Capt 123
Two handsomer culprits I never set eyes on!' ....52 LetB 133
Vida, 34, 241, 273, 289, 308, 320, 488, 665
EYES$_2$ He eyes the centre, where his friends sit snug; ....26 eGNM 68

FACE$_1$ The swain mistrustless of his smutted face, ...27 DVil 24
The day's disasters in his morning face; ....200 DVil 29
And brave prince William show'd his lamp-black face: ....14 DABd 48
And Prussia's monarch shew'd his lamp-black face ....v14 DABd 200
Not with that face, so servile and so gay, ...v(19) DABd 200
While soul-brought tears steal down each shining face. ....6 MrsX 49
Found half the charms that deck'd her face ....35 DTrn 53
That very face had robb'd her mind. ....38 DTrn 53
Her face is grown a knowing phiz; ....68 DTrn 54
Left but the remnant of a face. ....80 DTrn 54
Her present face surpass the old; ....96 DTrn 55
The men have tails, the women paint the face! ....26 pZob 73
Death, when unmasked, shows me a friendly face, ...93 Thrn 77
Little Comedy's face, ...17 Invt 128
Vida, 174
FACE$_2$ And shudd'ring still to face the distant deep, ...369 DVil 35
-FACED 'What, yon solemn-faced, odd-looking man that stands near!' ....50 LetB 133
FACES His pencil our faces, his manners our heart: ....142 Rtal 92
Both cover their faces with mobs and all that; ....45 LetB 133
FACTION Even now reproach and faction mourn, ...21 Thrn 74
FACTIONS Ferments arise, imprison'd factions roar, ...345 Trav 16
FACTIOUS When I behold a factious band agree ....383 Trav 18
FADE Princes and lords may flourish, or may fade; ....53 DVil 25
Vida, 26
FAGGOT To pick her wintry faggot from the thorn, ...133 DVil 27
The crackling faggot flies. ....56 Ed&A 61
FAIL Laugh at the jests or pranks that never fail, ...19 Trav 6
As duty, love, and honour fail to sway, ...350 Trav 16
But now the sounds of population fail, ...125 DVil 27
When time advances, and when lovers fail, ...292 DVil 33
And when this life of love shall

fail, ...v(167) Ed&A 211
It could not fail, would you
but set about it.' ....10 eGNM 68
They stood, while hope and com-
fort fail, ...69 Thrn 76
If virtue fail her counsel
sage, ...82 Thrn 77
Lovers are plenty; but fail to
relieve me: ....2 "Amw 94
'For I knew it,' he cried, 'both
eternally fail, ...71 HofV 97
Insulting slaves! if gentler
methods fail, ...I:93 Capt 117
And never shall fail ....III:9 Capt 122
FAILING Moreover, Merc'ry had
a failing: ....57 NSim 58
Then what was his failing? come,
tell it, and, burn ye! ....135 Rtal 91
-FAILING The never-failing brook,
the busy mill, ...11 DVil 23
FAILINGS And e'en his failings
lean'd to Virtue's side; ....164 DVil 28
And coxcombs, alike in their
failings alone, ...71 Rtal 89
The man had his failings, a dupe
to his art. ....98 Rtal 90
FAILS Where wealth and freedom
reign, contentment fails, ...91 Trav 8
All, all is lost. The Syrian army
fails, ...III:59 Capt 125
FAINT To stop too fearful, and
too faint to go, ...420 Trav 19
FAINTING Through torrid tracts
with fainting steps they go, ...343 DVil 34
With fainting steps and slow; ....6 Ed&A 59
FAIR$_1$ For you, bright fair, the nine
address their lays, ...1 MrsX 49
Levell'd its terrors at the fair; ..78 DTrn 54
Forsake the fair, and patiently--
go simpling; ....6 pZob 72
Still thus address the fair with voice
beguiling:-- ....22 eSSC$_1$ 104
FAIR$_2$ And thou, fair Freedom,
taught alike to feel ....365 Trav 17
As some fair female unadorn'd and
plain, ...287 DVil 32
Do thy fair tribes participate her
pain? ....338 DVil 34
Say, would the angry fair one prize 7 Gift 43
The modern fair one's jest: ....78 Ed&A 61
The haughty fair one's jest: .....v78 Ed&A 209
The wondering fair one turn'd to
chide, ...147 Ed&A 64
The astonish'd fair one turned to
chide,-- ....v147 Ed&A 211
To Death's great court, the
prospect seems more fair. ....96 Thrn 77
These hills how sweet! those plains
how wond'rous fair, ...I:21 Capt 114
Vida, 174, 626, 668
FAIREST Turn, my fairest, turn,
if ever ....23 eSSC$_1$ 104
Love presents the fairest treasure,I:66 Capt 116
FAIRLY Perceiving others fairly
flown, ...93 DTrn 55
FAIRY Ye nodding towers, ye fairy
scenes-- ....164 Thrn 80

FAITH Leave reason, faith, and
conscience, all our own. ....438 Trav 19
FAITH There Faith shall come, a
pilgrim gray, ...132 Thrn 78
FAITHFUL And steady loyalty, and
faithful love. ....406 DVil 36
Chaste are their instincts,
faithful is their fire, ...1 Cati 94
Vida, 151
FAITHLESS For yonder faithless
phantom flies ....11 Ed&A 59
FALCONS May sit, like falcons
cow'ring on the nest; ....234 Trav 13
FALL$_1$ Reprieve the tottering mansion
from its fall! ....238 DVil 31
In barren splendour feebly waits
the fall. ....286 DVil 32
See yonder tower just nodding to
the fall: ....III:48 Capt 124
Now press thy fall, ...III:76 Capt 125
Thy fall more dreadful from
delay! ....III:79 Capt 126
FALL$_2$ Yet oft a sigh prevails,
and sorrows fall, ...57 Trav 7
Fall blunted from each indurated
heart. ....232 Trav 13
The smiling long-frequented village
fall? ....406 Trav 18
And saw thee fall with joy-
pronouncing eyes: ....10 Queb 46
How do the good, the virtuous fall! 73 Thrn 76
Fall, round me fall, ye little
things, ...80 Thrn 77
Beheld our power in Zedekiah's
fall? ....II:86 Capt 121
Then shall Babylon fall. ......III:12 Capt 122
Shall wrath vindictive threaten
ere it fall! ....III:38 Capt 124
Vida, 224
FALLEN Heroes themselves had
fallen behind!-- ....7 DRtH 50
O Babylon, how art thou fallen! III:78 Capt 126
Vida, 533
-FALLEN Again the long-fall'n
column sought the skies; ....136 Trav 9
From these the feeble heart and long-
fall'n mind ....147 Trav 10
FALLS Our monarch falls, and now
our fears are o'er, ...III:21 Capt 123
FALSE False wits, false wives,
false virgins, and false spouses! ..14 eSis 70
She that gives all to the false
one pursuing her, ...7 "Amw 94
No foreign beauty tempts to false
desire; ....2 Cati 94
FALTERING And haply, though my
harsh touch falt'ring still, ...247 Trav 13
And his last falt'ring accents
whisper'd praise. ....176 DVil 29
FAME Where kings have toil'd, and
poets wrote for fame, ...358 Trav 17
And monarchs toil, and poets pant
for fame, ...v358 Trav 174
But past is all his fame. The
very spot ....217 DVil 30
To catch the heart, or strike
for honest fame; ....410 DVil 36

FATE This day beyond its term my
fate extends, ...19 pLab 41
To save him from Narcissus'
fate. ....4 Byth 42
Whilst thy sad fate extorts the
heart-wrung tear. ....8 Queb 46
Yet, ah! what terrors frowned up-
on her fate-- ....52 Thrn 76
In short, 'twas his fate, un-
employ'd, or in place, Sir, ...41 Rtal 88
Here lies honest Richard, whose
fate I must sigh at; ....51 Rtal 88
Come ponder his severer fate, .III:25 Capt 123
Such be her fate. But listen!
from afar ....III:83 Capt 126
Vida, 30, 74, 98, 143, 161, 236,
240, 257, 265, 374, 395, 456,
534, 548, 633
FATES Vida, 153
FATHER 'My father liv'd beside the
Tyne, ...101 Ed&A 62
My father liv'd, of high de-
gree, ...v101 Ed&A 209
And turn to God, your Father
and your Friend. ....I:4 Capt 113
Vida, 81
FATHER'S And left a lover's for
a father's arms. ....378 DVil 35
And left a lover's for her
father's arms. ....v378 DVil 190
FATTER Thanks, my Lord, for
your venison, for finer or fat-
ter ....1 HofV 95
FAULT The love he bore to learn-
ing was in fault; ....206 DVil 30
'But mine the sorrow, mine the
fault, ...137 Ed&A 64
Then since he perish'd by my
fault, ...v137 Ed&A 210
Or, wherefore his characters
thus without fault? ....74 Rtal 89
Yet one fault he had, and that
one was a thumper. ....128 Rtal 91
FAULTLESS His gallants are all
faultless, his women divine, ...65 Rtal 89
FAULTS Contrasted faults through
all his manners reign; ....127 Trav 9
Careless their merits, or their
faults to scan, ...161 DVil 28
Thus as her faults each day were
known, ...61 DTrn 54
If he had any faults, he has left
us in doubt, ...25 Rtal 87
What was good was spontaneous,
his faults were his own. ....50 Rtal 88
FAVOUR And view with favour, the
'Good-natur'd Man.' ....v34 eGNM 215
Has he not seen how you your
favour place, ...35 eSSC$_2$ 109
FAVOURED Vida, 122
FAVOURING Vida, 169
FAVOURITE$_1$ Vida, 613
FAVOURITE$_2$ Each to the favourite
happiness attends, ...95 Trav 8
This favourite good begets peculiar
pain. ....98 Trav 8
Thinks black alone is beauty's
favourite hue. ....10 Cati 94
FAVOURITES To crown the favourites
of the sky-- ....115 Thrn 78
Vida, 63
FAVOUR'S By proud contempt, or
favour's fostering sun, ...368 Trav 17
FAVOURS You spurn the favours
offer'd from his hand, ...II:12 Capt 118
FAWN Unpractis'd he to fawn,
or seek for power, ...145 DVil 28
Unskilful he to fawn, or seek
for power, ...v145 DVil 184
FEAR$_1$ Fear, pity, justice,
indignation start, ...389 Trav 18
Unaw'd by pow'r, and unappall'd
by fear, ...7 pLab 41
She long had wanted cause of
fear. ....8 Sonn 46
A stranger to flatt'ry, a stranger
to fear; ....152 Rtal 93
We fear the Lord, and know no
other fear. ....I:96 Capt 117
Vida, 145, 438, 577, 595
FEAR$_2$ The place is uninhabited,
I fear! ....23 pZob 73
What! no return? I find too
late, I fear, ...17 eSSC$_1$ 104
We fear the Lord, and know no
other fear. ....I:96 Capt 117
Vida, 157
FEARED I fear'd for your safety,
I fear'd for my own; ....84 Rtal 89
Vida, 561
FEARFUL To stop too fearful, and
too faint to go, ...420 Trav 19
FEARING Still aiming at honour,
yet fearing to roam, ...47 Rtal 88
Vida, 327
FEARS$_1$ Forgive my sex's fears,
forgive my youth! ....II:28 Capt 119
I wish for life, and yield me
to my fears. ....II:30 Capt 119
Our monarch falls, and now our
fears are o'er, ...III:21 Capt 123
Vida, 378, 600
With smiling hopes and chill-
ing fears, ...14 Tr 267
FEARS$_2$ Where at each step the
stranger fears to wake ....353 DVil 35
Fears th' approaching bridal
night. ....4 Sonn 46
FEAST$_1$ A guiltless feast I bring; ..26 Ed&A 60
Each guest brought his dish, and
the feast was united; ....2 Rtal 87
Vida, 20
FEAST$_2$ Vida, 34
FEASTS Bless'd be those feasts with
simple plenty crown'd, ...17 Trav 5
Bless'd be those feasts where mirth
and peace abound, ...v17 Trav 167
Though poor the peasant's hut,
his feasts though small, ...177 Trav 11
Are not this very morn those
feasts begun, ...I:35 Capt 114
FEATHER Why these denote a brain
of feather. ....18 NSim 56
A brain of feather! very right, ...19 NSim 56

wishes all confin'd. ....210 Trav 12
If few their wants, their pleasures
are but few; ....212 Trav 12
There, where a few torn shrubs
the place disclose, ...139 DVil 27
To find out men's virtues, and
finding them few, ...76 Rtal 89
Ye jockey tribe, whose stock of
words are few, ...49 $eSSC_1$ 106
That a few days ago, ...24 Invt 128
FICKLE 'For still I tried each
fickle art, ...129 Ed&A 63
FICTITIOUS Fictitious bonds, the
bonds of wealth and law, ...351 Trav 17
Vida, 413, 422
FIDDLERS No judges, fiddlers,
dancing-masters, ...35 LogR 45
FIELD And e'en the captain quit
the field. ....90 DTrn 55
Shall crowd from Crecy's laurell'd
field, ...226 Thrn 82
Vida, 30, 98, 119, 149, 200, 223,
289, 354, 360, 426, 494
FIELDING Whether crimes such as
yours should not come before Fielding? ....36 LetB 132
FIELDS Ye fields, where summer
spreads profusion round, ...46 Trav 6
In florid beauty groves and fields
appear, ...125 Trav 9
And over fields where scatter'd
hamlets rose, ...403 Trav 18
Shoulder'd his crutch, and show'd
how fields were won. ....158 DVil 28
Has robb'd the neighbouring fields
of half their growth, ...280 DVil 32
Those fenceless fields the sons
of wealth divide, ...307 DVil 33
Those pois'nous fields with rank
luxuriance crown'd, ...351 DVil 35
Through rolling worlds, or fields
of liquid light, ...107 Thrn 77
Ye fields of Sharon, dress'd in
flow'ry pride, ...I:17 Capt 114
FIERCE Fierce in their native
hardiness of soul, ...331 Trav 16
Fierce is the whirlwind howl-
ing ....II:15 Capt 118
And fierce the tempest roll-
ing ....II:17 Capt 118
Vida, 132, 454, 618
FIERCELY And fiercely shed in-
tolerable day; ....348 DVil 34
FIERY Vida, 127
FIFTEEN Deserting fifty, fasten
on fifteen, ...20 eSis 70
Miss, not yet full fifteen, with
fire uncommon, ...21 eSis 70
FIFTH The fifth was friendship
mix'd with bliss: ....32 DTrn 53
The Fifth and Last Act still re-
mains for me. ....33 $eSSC_3$ 86
FIFTY There Hebes, turn'd of
fifty, try once more ....17 eSis 70
Deserting fifty, fasten on
fifteen, ...20 eSis 70
FIGHT$_1$ Lopp'd of his limbs in
many a gallant fight, ...209 Thrn 81
And wish the avenging fight. ......230 Thrn 82
Vida, 32, 79, 85, 93, 116, 170,
209, 393, 452
FIGHT$_2$ Vida, 291
FIGURE Vida, 40
FILL Hoards after hoards his
rising raptures fill, ...53 Trav 7
To fill the languid pause with
finer joy; ....218 Trav 12
Whose daily <u>bons mots</u> half a
column might fill; ....154 Rtal 93
Whose talents to fill any station
were fit, ...161 Rtal 93
Vida, 23, 50
FILLED And fill'd each pause the
nightingale had made. ....124 DVil 27
Filled with a snake-encircl'd
wand; ....32 NSim 57
How hast thou fill'd the scene
with all thy brood, ...11 epLL 101
Vida, 293, 388, 433, 503, 605
FILLS See how prophetic rapture
fills his form, ...II:67 Capt 121
FIND And find no spot of all the
world my own. ....30 Trav 6
And oft I wish, amidst the scene,
to find ....59 Trav 7
But where to find that happiest
spot below, ...63 Trav 7
Though patriots flatter, still
shall wisdom find ....77 Trav 7
We still shall find uncertainty
suspend; ....v78 Trav 168
Find that each good, by Art or
Nature given, ...v79 Trav 168
Find that the bliss of all is
much the same, ...v(81) Trav 168
An easy compensation seem to
find. ....148 Trav 10
Vain, very vain, my weary search
to find ....423 Trav 19
Our own felicity we make or find: .432 Trav 19
Long had I sought in vain to
find ....1 NSim 56
I long had rack'd my brains to
find ....v1 NSim 205
You'll find him pictur'd at full
length ....11 NSim 56
And if you find it wond'rous
short, ...3 MDog 65
You'll find his lionship a very
lamb. ....32 eSis 71
At least, in six weeks, I could
not find 'em out; ....26 Rtal 87
To find out men's virtues, and
finding them few, ...76 Rtal 89
What! no return? I find too late,
I fear, ...17 $eSSC_1$ 104
And they, who lose their senses,
there may find them. ....4 $eSSC_2$ 108
That mortals visit both to find
their senses. ....14 $eSSC_2$ 108
But find no sense--for they had
none to lose. ....32 $eSSC_2$ 109
In thee must ever find a foe. vI:30 Capt 250
FINDING To find out men's virtues,

and finding them few, ...76 Rtal 89
At never once finding a visit
from Pam. ....6 LetB 131
FINDS And every stranger finds a
ready chair; ....16 Trav 5
He in his turn finds imitators; ....53 LogR 45
Jack finds his wife a perfect
beauty. ....104 DTrn 55
Who seeks for rest, but finds
despair ....99 Ed&A 62
That seeks repose, but finds
despair ....v99 Ed&A 209
And finds too late that men
betray, ...2 "wlw 67
Finds his lost senses out, and
pay his debts. ....26 eSSC$_2$ 108
FINE To decency so fine a
thing? ....50 DTrn 53
And comedy wonders at being so
fine, ...66 Rtal 89
FINE- An under-bred, fine-
spoken fellow was he, ...37 HofV 96
A fine-spoken Custom-house
Officer he, ...v37 HofV 239
FINELY And love's and friendship's
finely pointed dart ....231 Trav 13
FINER To fill the languid pause
with finer joy; ....218 Trav 12
Thanks, my Lord, for your venison,
for finer or fatter ....1 HofV 95
FINERY But now her wealth and
finery fled, ...21 MBlz 47
For tawdry finery is seen ....99 DTrn 55
FINESSING If they were not his own
by finessing and trick, ...106 Rtal 90
FINISH To finish all their efforts
at a blow; ....57 Thrn 76
FINISHED The clarion's note pro-
claims the finish'd war! ......III:84 Capt 126
FINNY With patient angle trolls
the finny deep, ...187 Trav 11
FIRE$_1$ To pause from toil, and trim
their ev'ning fire; ....14 Trav 5
Smiles by his cheerful fire, and
round surveys ....193 Trav 11
Their level life is but a
smould'ring fire, ...221 Trav 12
In wild excess the vulgar breast
takes fire, ...225 Trav 12
Around my fire an evening group
to draw, ...91 DVil 26
Sat by his fire, and talk'd the
night away; ....156 DVil 28
The rusty grate unconscious of a
fire; ....16 DABd 48
A rusty grate unconscious of a
fire. ....v16 DABd 200
To yonder fire, that cheers the
vale ....v3 Ed&A 208
The hermit trimm'd his little
fire, ... 47 Ed&A 60
Miss, not yet full fifteen, with
fire uncommon, ...21 eSis 70
Or how shall age support its feeble
fire? ....172 Thrn 80
Chaste are their instincts, faith-
ful is their fire, ...1 Cati 94
Vida, 661
FIRE$_2$ Its motions stop, or frenzy
fire the wheels. ....348 Trav 16
FIRED Fir'd at the sound, my
genius spreads her wing, ...317 Trav 15
At last the impetuous sorrow
fir'd his breast. ....212 Thrn 82
Vida, 267, 342, 355, 485
FIRM- The firm-connected bulwark
seems to grow; ....288 Trav 14
FIRST His first, best country
ever is, at home. ....74 Trav 7
That first excites desire, and
then supplies; ....216 Trav 12
When first ambition struck at
regal power; ....394 Trav 18
Pants to the place from whence
at first she flew, ...94 DVil 26
In nature's simplest charms at
first array'd; ....296 DVil 33
When idly first, ambitious of
the town, ...335 DVil 34
The good old sire, the first
prepar'd to go ....371 DVil 35
Still first to fly where sensual
joys invade; ....408 DVil 36
That found'st me poor at first,
and keep'st me so; ....414 DVil 37
Then first, at last even Jove
was taken in, ...13 MrsX 49
First please to turn to god
Mercurius; ....10 NSim 56
What first to hide he strove; ...v150 Ed&A 211
This dog and man at first were
friends; ....17 MDog 65
This is his first adventure; lend
him aid, ...33 pZob 73
The shatter'd veteran, now first
dismay'd; ....158 Thrn 79
First of the train the patient
rustic came, ...167 Thrn 80
The First Act shows the simple
country maid, ...9 eSSC$_3$ 85
As a wit, if not first, in the
very first line: ....96 Rtal 90
And first I hope, you'll readily
agree ....13 eSSC$_1$ 104
First let me suppose, what may
shortly be true, ...1 LetB 131
First Sir Charles advances with
phrases well strung, ...55 LetB 133
Vida, 12, 87, 109, 159, 188, 191,
193, 210, 242, 302, 382, 482,
486, 667
FIRST- The soul adopts, and owns
their first-born sway; ....256 DVil 31
FISH If our landlord supplies us
with beef, and with fish, ...3 Rtal 87
Of all the fish that graze beneath
the flood, ...11 Tr 267
FIT$_1$ Equally fit for gallantry and
war. ....36 pZob 73
Whose talents to fill any station
were fit, ...161 Rtal 93
FIT$_2$ The old buffoon will fit my
name as well; ....18 pLab 41
FITS$_1$ In short, by night, 'twas

product flies, ...283 DVil 32
While oft in whirls the mad
tornado flies, ...357 DVil 35
For yonder faithless phantom
flies ....11 Ed&A 59
For yonder phantom only flies ....v11 Ed&A 208
The crackling faggot flies. ....56 Ed&A 61
But peace to his spirit, wherever
it flies, ...119 Rtal 91
While the dark owl to court its
partner flies, ...13 Cati 94
Seize the debtor as it flies. ..II:58 Capt 120
As panting flies the hunted
hind, ...III:39 Capt 124
Vida, 490, 512, 563
FLIGHT And ah! bless'd spirit,
wheresoe'er thy flight, ...106 Thrn 77
Vida, 92, 244, 255, 292, 297
FLIGHTS For in a modern poet's
flights, ...28 NSim 57
FLIGHTY With wit that's flighty,
learning light; ....20 NSim 56
FLING Ye Gilead groves, that fling
perfumes around, ...I:20 Capt 114
FLINGS Flings down her sampler,
and takes up the woman: ....22 eSis 70
FLIRT Such dainties to them! It
would look like a flirt, ...v33 HofV 239
FLOATING Vida, 76, 384
FLOATS Triumphant music floats
along the vale; ....I:53 Capt 115
FLOCK$_1$ He drives his flock to
pick the scanty blade, ...306 DVil 33
FLOCK$_2$ And rich men flock from
all the world around. ....272 DVil 32
FLOCKS 'No flocks that range the
valley free ....21 Ed&A 59
FLOOD O Wolfe! to thee a stream-
ing flood of woe, ...5 Queb 46
And cavill'd at his image in the
flood. ....30 epLL 102
Of all the fish that graze be-
neath the flood, ...11 Tr 267
FLOOR The white-wash'd wall, the
nicely sanded floor, ...227 DVil 30
The sanded floor that grits be-
neath the tread; ....9 DABd 48
FLORID In florid beauty groves and
fields appear, ...125 Trav 9
Boast of a florid vigour not their
own; ....390 DVil 36
FLOUNCE 'Why, whose should it
be?' cried I with a flounce, ...41 HofV 96
FLOURISH Princes and lords may
flourish, or may fade; ....53 DVil 25
Shall spread and flourish from
the tomb, ...19 Thrn 74
FLOURISHED When commerce proudly
flourish'd through the state; ......134 Trav 9
FLOW But not their joys alone
thus coarsely flow: ....227 Trav 12
And tears began to flow. ....60 Ed&A 61
And tears would often flow. ......v60 Ed&A 208
Unseen, though constant, used
to flow; ....179 Thrn 80
FLOWED And rivers listen'd as
they flow'd along. ....10 Tr 267
FLOWER Thou transitory flower,
alike undone ....367 Trav 17
And still where many a garden
flower grows wild; ....138 DVil 27
Withers the beauty's transient
flower: ....76 DTrn 54
FLOWERS With aspen boughs, and
flowers, and fennel gay; ....234 DVil 31
FLOWERY Ye bending swains, that
dress the flow'ry vale, ...48 Trav 6
That leads to truth through
pleasure's flowery way! ....4 epTP 100
Ye fields of Sharon, dress'd in
flow'ry pride, ...I:17 Capt 114
FLOWN Perceiving others fairly
flown, ...93 DTrn 55
Vida, 603
FLOWS Where flows Euphrates
murmuring to the deep, ...I:2 Capt 113
Every moment, as it flows, ...II:55 Capt 120
Vida, 362
FLUCTUATE No cheerful murmurs
fluctuate in the gale, ...126 DVil 27
FLUENT Ye barristers, so fluent
with grimace, ...51 eSSC$_1$ 106
FLUSH$_1$ For all the bloomy flush
of life is fled. ....128 DVil 27
FLUSH$_2$ And flush with honest
love. ....v152 Ed&A 211
FLUTTER To sport and flutter in
a kinder sky. ....238 Trav 13
FLY These far dispers'd, on
timorous pinions fly, ...237 Trav 13
I fly from petty tyrants to the
throne. ....392 Trav 18
And, since 'tis hard to combat,
learns to fly! ....102 DVil 26
Still first to fly where sensual
joys invade; ....408 DVil 36
Oh, let me fly a land that spurns
the brave, ...221 Thrn 82
By a bounce now and then, to get
courage to fly. ....16 HofV 95
And should we mourn? should coward
virtue fly, ...I:39 Capt 115
But storms that fly, ...II:19 Capt 118
Vida, 204, 399, 575, 641
The curling waves before his
coursers fly: ....5 Tr 267
FOAMED Vida, 308
FOE To treat as dearest friend, a
foe; ....28 LogR 45
Alive, the foe thy dreadful
vigour fled, ...9 Queb 46
His very worst foe can't accuse
him of that: ....132 Rtal 91
Insulted, chain'd, and all the
world a foe, ...I:5 Capt 113
In thee must ever find a foe. ..vI:30 Capt 250
The foe prevails, the lofty walls
recline-- ....III:53 Capt 124
Alike of Heaven and man the foe;III:74 Capt 125
Vida, 41, 89, 103, 139, 154, 191, 211, 304,
331, 343, 361, 377, 459, 476, 479, 526, 539,
592, 630
FOES To comfort friends and foes; ..10 MDog 65
Vida, 482, 517, 580

FOILED Thus foil'd in my courage,
on all sides perplex'd, ...27 LetB 132
FOLKS To folks at Pater-Noster-Row; 34 LogR 45
For let folks only get a touch, ...37 NSim 57
Ye news-paper witlings! ye pert
scribbling folks ....163 Rtal 93
And sure the folks of both are
lunatics. ....12 eSSC$_2$ 108
FOLLIES It gives their follies
also room to rise, ...268 Trav 14
His fools have their follies so
lost in a crowd ....69 Rtal 89
FOLLOW Allures from far, yet, as I
follow, flies; ....28 Trav 6
Still follow your master, and visit
his tomb: ....166 Rtal 93
FOLLOWED Even children follow'd
with endearing wile, ...183 DVil 29
Had Myra followed my direction, ...7 Sonn 46
And never follow'd wicked ways,-- ..11 MBlz 47
The king himself has follow'd her,-- 19 MBlz 47
And the porter and eatables follow'd
behind. ....58 HofV 97
Vida, 641
FOLLOWS And follows to the cell. ...36 Ed&A 60
A shade that follows wealth or fame, 75 Ed&A 61
FOLLY And every pang that folly
pays to pride. ....68 DVil 25
And shouting Folly hails them from
her shore; ....270 DVil 32
When lovely woman stoops to folly, ..1 "wlw 67
If folly, fraud, your hearts engage, 78 Thrn 76
Of virtues and feelings, that folly
grows proud; ....70 Rtal 89
Is taught his former folly to
deplore; ....44 epLL 102
When impious folly rears her front
on high? ....I:40 Capt 115
FOND And, as a bird each fond
endearment tries ....167 DVil 28
The fond companion of his helpless
years, ...376 DVil 35
Whilst her fond husband strove to
lend relief ....383 DVil 36
With fond complaint addressed the
listening Jove, ...10 MrsX 49
Fond to be seen, she kept a bevy ...53 DTrn 53
'For shame, fond youth, thy sorrows
hush, ...81 Ed&A 62
And too fond of the right to pursue
the expedient. ....40 Rtal 88
He, fond youth, that could carry me, 3 "Amw 94
O Memory, thou fond deceiver, ...I:23 Capt 114
FONDLY My heart untravell'd fondly
turns to thee; ....8 Trav 5
No Zephyr fondly sues the mountain's
breast, ...173 Trav 11
Imagination fondly stoops to trace 225 DVil 30
Hung round their bowers, and fondly
look'd their last, ...366 DVil 35
FOOD Or press the bashful stranger
to his food, ...21 Trav 6
With food as well the peasant is
supplied ....83 Trav 8
He, only, ruminates his former food. 12 Tr 267
FOOL Magnanimous Goldsmith a
gooseberry fool. ....16 Rtal 87
Condemn the stubborn fool who
can't submit ....71 eSSC$_1$ 107
FOOLISHLY And so was too foolishly
honest? Ah no! ....134 Rtal 91
FOOLS Though patriots flatter, and
though fools contend, ...v77 Trav 168
Pants for the vulgar praise which
fools impart; ....274 Trav 14
And fools, who came to scoff,
remain'd to pray. ....180 DVil 29
His fools have their follies so
lost in a crowd ....69 Rtal 89
Of fools pursuing, and of fools
pursu'd! ....12 epLL 101
FOOT$_1$ Vida, 72, 104, 107, 210, 223, 231, 252,
256, 277, 291, 350, 351, 357, 385, 391, 442,
504, 552, 557
FOOT- Vida, 47, 404
FOOT$_2$ For the foot guards so stout 26 Invt 128
FOOT- No busy steps the grass-
grown foot-way tread, ...127 DVil 27
FOOTE'S Both shine at night, for,
but at Foote's alone, ...9 eSSC$_2$ 108
FOOTMEN And footmen, lords and
dukes can act. ....56 LogR 45
FOPS And, though her fops are
wond'rous civil, ...69 DTrn 54
FOR See FOR'T
FORBEAR 'Forbear, my son,' the
hermit cries, ...9 Ed&A 59
FORBID His obsequies forbid, ...18 DRtH 50
'Forbid it, heaven!' the hermit
cried, ...145 Ed&A 64
The English laws forbid to punish
lunatics. ....42 eSSC$_2$ 109
FORBIDS My pride forbids it ever
should be said, ...3 epLL 101
FORCE$_1$ Gave wealth to sway the mind
with double force. ....396 Trav 18
Nor force nor fraud could turn my
steps aside; ....6 pLab 41
Vida, 332
FORCE$_2$ And force a churlish soil for
scanty bread; ....168 Trav 10
Still gather strength, and force
unwilling awe. ....352 Trav 17
Vida, 8, 484, 581
FORCED Forc'd from their homes, a
melancholy train, ...409 Trav 18
She, wretched matron, forc'd, in
age, for bread, ...131 DVil 27
The pupil of impulse, it forc'd him
along, ...45 Rtal 88
FORCES Which triumph forces from
the patriot heart, ...2 Queb 46
FORCING Vida, 412
FOREBODING Yon ill foreboding cloud
seems big with thunder. ....18 pZob 72
FOREIGN At sports like these, while
foreign arms advance, ...v(155) Trav 170
No foreign beauty tempts to
false desire; ....2 Cati 94
FOREMOST But hush! see, foremost of
the captive choir, ...II:63 Capt 120
FOREST Never rang'd in a forest, or
smok'd in a platter; ....2 HofV 95
FORESTS Lakes, forests, cities,

plains, extending wide, ...35 Trav 6
Through tangled forests, and through
dangerous ways; ....414 Trav 19
FORGET Those matted woods where
birds **forget to sing,** ....**349** DVil 34
Till reading, I forget what day on, .5 NSim 56
Even Common-Councilmen forget
to eat. ....22 eSSC$_3$ 85
No, never! May this hand forget
each art ....I:89 Capt 117
Ere I forget the land that gave
me birth, ...I:91 Capt 117
FORGETFUL And dance, forgetful
of the noon-tide hour. ....250 Trav 13
FORGIVE 'And, ah! forgive a
stranger rude, ...93 Ed&A 62
Forgive, and let thy pious care ..v97 Ed&A 209
Forgive my sex's fears, forgive
my youth! ....II:28 Capt 119
FORGIVEN Request to be for-
given. ....23 Thrn 75
FORGO 'Then, pilgrim, turn, thy
cares forgo; ....29 Ed&A 60
FORGOT And quite forgot their
vices in the woe; ....160 DVil 28
Where many a time he triumph'd,
is forgot. ....218 DVil 30
And rocks forgot their hardness
at the sound. ....12 MrsX 49
O had her eyes forgot to blaze! ....15 DTrn 52
FORLORN Thy glades forlorn confess
the tyrant's power. ....76 DVil 25
'For here, forlorn and lost I
tread, ...5 Ed&A 59
A wretch forlorn,' she cried; ......94 Ed&A 62
And sought a solitude forlorn, ...135 Ed&A 63
'And there forlorn, despairing,
hid, ...141 Ed&A 64
Forlorn, a rural bard com-
plain'd, ...152 Thrn 79
Thy streets forlorn ....III:80 Capt 126
Vida, 649
FORM$_1$ The pregnant quarry teem'd
with human form; ....138 Trav 9
As some tall cliff, that lifts
its awful form, ...189 DVil 29
See how prophetic rapture fills
his form, ...II:67 Capt 121
Vida, 25
FORM$_2$ Ye beaux and belles, that
form this splendid ring, ...5 eSSC$_1$ 103
Vida, 52, 72, 518
FORMED Processions form'd for
piety and love, ...151 Trav 10
That she who form'd your beauties
is no more. ....166 Thrn 80
Whose callous hand had form'd
the scene, ...168 Thrn 80
FORMER Its former strength was
but plethoric ill. ....144 Trav 10
By arts, the splendid wrecks of
former pride; ....146 Trav 10
Some splendid arts, the wrecks of
former pride; ....vl46 Trav 170
Far different these from every
former scene, ...359 DVil 35
Each former art she vainly tries ...83 DTrn 54
Is taught his former folly to
deplore; ....44 epLL 102
To former joys recurring ever, ..I:25 Capt 114
Vida, 468, 471
He, <u>only</u>, ruminates his former
food. ....12 Tr 267
FORMIDABLE Death, with its formi-
dable band, ...53 Thrn 76
And this way leads his formidable
band. ....III:86 Capt 126
FORMS$_1$ By forms unfashion'd,
fresh from Nature's hand; ....330 Trav 16
FORMS$_2$ For honour forms the
social temper here: ....258 Trav 13
He forms a scene beyond Elysium
blest-- ....143 Thrn 79
FORSAKE Forsake the fair, and
patiently--go simpling; ....6 pZob 72
FORSAKEN Or where Campania's
plain forsaken lies, ...5 Trav 5
FOR'T 'I don't care if I keep a
corner for't too.' ....102 HofV 98
Don't you think the best way is
to venture for't twice?' ....30 LetB 132
FORTE Those things are not our
forte at Covent Garden.' ....20 eGNM 68
FORTH She then shines forth,
solicitous to bless, ...293 DVil 33
Vida, 209, 329, 433
FORTITUDE Truth, Fortitude, and
Friendship shall agree ....136 Thrn 78
That fortitude is victory. .....I:100 Capt 117
FORTUNE My fortune leads to
traverse realms alone, ...29 Trav 6
'Alas! the joys that fortune
brings ....69 Ed&A 61
A thousand gifts would fortune
send; ....29 Thrn 75
Make but of all your fortune one
<u>va toute</u>; ....48 eSSC$_1$ 105
Oft risks his fortune on one
desperate throw, ...24 eSSC$_2$ 108
And as our fortune sinks, our
wishes soar. ....I:42 Capt 115
Yet, though to fortune lost,
here still abide ....vl45 Trav 170
Vida, 149, 359
FORTUNE'S Ye wretches who, by
fortune's hate, ...III:23 Capt 123
FORTY And passing rich with
forty pounds a year; ....142 DVil 28
FORWARD 'Hoicks! hark forward!'
came thund'ring from behind, ...39 epLL 102
Vida, 117, 406, 573, 595
FOSTERED But foster'd e'en by
Freedom, ills annoy: ....338 Trav 16
FOSTERING By proud contempt, or
favour's fostering sun, ...368 Trav 17
FOUGHT Vida, 611
FOUL Vida, 409
FOUND Whatever fruits in different
climes were found, ...113 Trav 9
And late the nation found, with
fruitless skill, ...143 Trav 10
The host himself no longer shall
be found ....247 DVil 31
And always found her kind; ....6 MBlz 47

The doctors found, when she was
dead,-- ....23 MBlz 47
The Muse found Scroggen stretch'd
beneath a rug; ....6 DABd 48
The seasons, fram'd with listing,
found a place, ...13 DABd 48
Jack found his goddess made of
clay; ....34 DTrn 53
Found half the charms that deck'd
her face ....35 DTrn 53
On earth unseen, or only found .....79 Ed&A 61
And in that town a dog was found, ..13 MDog 65
But we quickly found out, for who
could mistake her? ....111 HofV 98
That I found humour in a piebald
vest, ...5 epLL 101
'Pray what are their crimes?'--
'They've been pilfering found.' .48 LetB 133
Vida, 453
-FOUND To new-found worlds, and
wept for others' woe; ....372 DVil 35
FOUNDEST That found'st me poor
at first, and keep'st me so; ......414 DVil 37
FOUNTAIN Once on the margin of
a fountain stood, ...29 epLL 102
-FOUR Vida, 23
FOURTH A third, a fourth, were
not amiss, ...31 DTrn 53
The Fourth Act shows her wedded
to the 'Squire, ...23 $eSSC_3$ 85
Vida, 53, 496, 531
-FOWL Our Will shall be wild-fowl
of excellent flavour, ...7 Rtal 87
FRAGRANCE To winnow fragrance
round the smiling land. ....122 Trav 9
His breath lent fragrance to the
gale, ...119 Ed&A 63
No spicy fragrance while they
grow; ....I:48 Capt 115
FRAIL But when those charms are
pass'd, for charms are frail, ...291 DVil 33
FRAME Catch every nerve, and
vibrate through the frame. ....220 Trav 12
FRAMED The seasons, fram'd with
listing, found a place, ...13 DABd 48
FRANCE I turn; and France dis-
plays her bright domain. ....240 Trav 13
FRAUD But view them closer, craft
and fraud appear, ...305 Trav 15
Nor force nor fraud could turn
my steps aside; ....6 pLab 41
If folly, fraud, your hearts
engage, ...78 Thrn 76
Vida, 316
FRAUGHT Fraught with invective
they ne'er go ....33 LogR 45
Though fraught with all learning,
yet straining his throat ....33 Rtal 88
FRAY Brutes never meet in bloody
fray, ...39 LogR 45
Vida, 83, 180, 585
FRAYS Say heavenly muse, their
youthful frays rehearse; ....7 Tr 267
FREAKS With all the freaks of
wanton wealth array'd, ...260 DVil 31
FREE To call it freedom when
themselves are free; ....384 Trav 18
And all the village train, from
labour free, ...17 DVil 23
'No flocks that range the valley
free ....21 Ed&A 59
Pain met thee like a friend that
set thee free; ....34 Thrn 75
A Scotchman, from pride and from
prejudice free; ....155 Rtal 93
Whilst his strong limbs conspire
to set him free, ...45 epLL 102
Seek the happy and the free: ....I:28 Capt 114
Ourselves alone from idol-
worship free? ....I:34 Capt 114
Wine shall bless the brave and
free. ....I:70 Capt 116
To chain the strong, and set the
captive free. ....III:90 Capt 126
Vida, 93, 232
FREED Here lies poor Ned
Purdon, from misery freed, ...1 epEP 100
FREEDOM Where wealth and freedom
reign, contentment fails, ...91 Trav 8
At gold's superior charms all
freedom flies, ...307 Trav 15
War in each breast, and freedom
on each brow; ....315 Trav 15
Thine, Freedom, thine the blessings
pictur'd here, ...335 Trav 16
But foster'd e'en by Freedom,
ills annoy: ....338 Trav 16
And thou, fair Freedom, taught
alike to feel ....365 Trav 17
Who think it freedom when a part
aspires! ....378 Trav 17
To call it freedom when themselves are free; ....384 Trav 18
FREEDOM'S Yet think not, thus
when Freedom's ills I state, ...361 Trav 17
And all that freedom's highest
aims can reach, ...373 Trav 17
FREELY She freely lent to all
the poor,-- ....7 MBlz 47
'Then turn to-night, and freely
share ....17 Ed&A 59
FREIGHTED Proud swells the tide
with loads of freighted ore, ...269 DVil 32
FRENCH Of French friseurs, and
nosegays, justly vain, ...32 $eSSC_1$ 105
FRENCHMEN To dress, and look like
awkward Frenchmen here, ...34 $eSSC_1$ 105
FRENZY Its motions stop, or frenzy
fire the wheels. ....348 Trav 16
FREQUENT Vida, 411, 565
-FREQUENTED The smiling long-
frequented village fall? ....406 Trav 18
FRESH By forms unfashion'd, fresh
from Nature's hand; ....330 Trav 16
Our Dean shall be venison, just
fresh from the plains; ....5 Rtal 87
Vida, 252
FRESHENED And freshen'd from the
wave the Zephyr flew; ....246 Trav 13
FRESHMEN And freshmen wonder'd
as he spoke. ....6 DTrn 52
FRET I fret in my gizzard, yet,
cautious and sly, ...9 LetB 132
Mr. Bunbury frets, and I fret

like the devil, ...19 LetB 132
FRETFUL Vida, 137, 450, 502
FRETS Mr. Bunbury frets, and I
fret like the devil, ...19 LetB 132
FRETTED Vida, 308
FRETTING In short, by night, 'twas
fits or fretting; ....51 DTrn 53
FRIED They'd as soon think of eat-
ing the pan it is fried in. ....12 HofV 95
At the top a fried liver and
bacon were seen, ...81 HofV 97
FRIEND Eternal blessings crown
my earliest friend, ...11 Trav 5
O blest retirement, friend to life's
decline, ...97 DVil 26
Angels around befriending Virtue's
friend; ....108 DVil 26
Or friend beguile with lies and
flattery? ....22 LogR 44
To treat as dearest friend, a
foe; ....28 LogR 45
To be a dull domestic friend? ......48 DTrn 53
How sigh for such a friend! .....v124 Ed&A 210
For Epilogues and Prologues on
some friend, ...4 eGNM 68
And teas'd each rhyming friend to
help him out. ....8 eGNM 68
Pain met thee like a friend that
set thee free; ....34 Thrn 75
But you, my good friend, are the
pigeon. ....17 "LSm 84
He cherish'd his friend, and he
relish'd a bumper; ....127 Rtal 91
I thought of a friend that was
trusty and staunch; ....20 HofV 95
An acquaintance, a friend as he
call'd himself, enter'd; ....36 HofV 96
No stirring--I beg--my dear friend--
my dear friend! ....56 HofV 97
No words, my dear GOLDSMITH! my
very good Friend! ....v56 HofV 240
My friend bade me welcome, but
struck me quite dumb, ...69 HofV 97
But your friend there, the Doctor,
eats nothing at all.' ....98 HofV 98
'O--Oh!' quoth my friend, 'he'll
come on in a trice, ...99 HofV 98
And turn to God, your Father and
your Friend. ....I:4 Capt 113
Ever wants a friend in thee. ....I:30 Capt 114
But chief to Thee, our God,
defender, friend, ...III:103 Capt 127
Vida, 139, 403
FRIENDLY Death, when unmasked,
shows me a friendly face, ...93 Thrn 77
FRIENDS Ye friends to truth, ye
statesmen, who survey ....265 DVil 32
Now lost to all; her friends, her
virtue fled, ...331 DVil 34
To comfort friends and foes; ....10 MDog 65
This dog and man at first were
friends; ....17 MDog 65
Our Author's friends, thus plac'd
at happy distance, ...21 eGNM 68
He eyes the centre, where his
friends sit snug; ....26 eGNM 68
His simp'ring friends, with pleasure
in their eyes; ....27 eGNM 69
As helpless friends who view
from shore ....66 Thrn 76
Groans, weeping friends, indeed,
and gloomy sables, ...90 Thrn 77
He cast off his friends, as a
huntsman his pack, ...107 Rtal 90
To be shown to my friends as a
piece of virtu; ....8 HofV 95
We both agree, like friends, to
end our jarring? ....66 eSSC$_1$ 106
See where he mourns his friends
and children slain. ....II:90 Capt 121
I wish all my friends may be
bolder than I: ....10 LetB 132
Then their friends all come round
me with cringing and leering, ..53 LetB 133
FRIENDSHIP The fifth was friend-
ship mix'd with bliss: ....32 DTrn 53
Or grieve for friendship un-
return'd, ...67 Ed&A 61
'And what is friendship but a
name, ...73 Ed&A 61
Truth, Fortitude, and Friendship
shall agree ....136 Thrn 78
And that our friendship may
remain unbroken, ...67 eSSC$_1$ 106
Vida, 400
FRIENDSHIP'S And love's and
friendship's finely pointed dart ..231 Trav 13
FRIEZE$_1$ And trims her robes of
frieze with copper lace; ....276 Trav 14
FRIEZE$_2$ With beer and milk arrears
the frieze was scor'd, ...17 DABd 48
An unpaid reck'ning on the frieze
was scor'd, ...v17 DABd 200
FRIGATE And fits his little
frigate for adventures: ....10 pZob 72
FRIGHT Reflected now a perfect
fright: ....82 DTrn 54
Vida, 290
FRIGID The shudd'ring tenant of
the frigid zone ....65 Trav 7
FRISEURS Of French friseurs, and
nosegays, justly vain, ...32 eSSC$_1$ 105
FRISKED Has frisk'd beneath the
burthen of threescore. ....254 Trav 13
FROLIC$_1$ Alas, that such frolic
should now be so quiet! ....52 Rtal 88
Rare compound of oddity, frolic,
and fun! ....149 Rtal 92
FROLIC$_2$ Lightly they frolic o'er
the vacant mind, ...257 DVil 31
To be frolick like him, ...42 Invt 129
FROLICKED And many a gambol
frolick'd o'er the ground, ...21 DVil 24
FRONT$_1$ When impious folly rears
her front on high? ....I:40 Capt 115
FRONT$_2$ Vida, 200, 427
FRONT$_3$ Vida, 211, 277, 577
FRONTS Vida, 101
FROTHY His frothy slaver, venom'd
bites; ....48 NSim 57
FROWN And though the rocky-crested
summits frown, ...85 Trav 8
And though rough rocks or gloomy
summits frown, ...v85 Trav 169

I'll not wear a garland until
she return; ....242 Thrn 83
For who'd wear a garland when she
is away, ...253 Thrn 83
On the grave of Augusta this
garland be plac'd, ...259 Thrn 83
GARLANDS With garlands of beauty
the queen of the May ....251 Thrn 83
On the grave of Augusta these
garlands be plac'd, ...255 Thrn 83
GARNISH Our Burke shall be tongue,
with a garnish of brains; ....6 Rtal 87
GARRICK Here lies David Garrick,
describe me, who can, ...93 Rtal 90
GARRICK'S Our Garrick's a salad;
for in him we see ....11 Rtal 87
GARTER Without a star, a coronet
or garter, ...37 $eSSC_2$ 109
GASPING Vida, 383
GATE To spurn imploring famine
from the gate; ....106 DVil 26
GATHER May gather bliss to see my
fellows bless'd. ....62 Trav 7
Still gather strength, and force
unwilling awe. ....352 Trav 17
Well! what is it from thence we
gather? ....17 NSim 56
GATHERS Where the dark scorpion
gathers death around; ....352 DVil 35
Near, nearer still, it gathers
on the gale; ....I:54 Capt 115
The tempest gathers all around, II:75 Capt 121
GAUGE And e'en the story ran that
he could gauge. ....210 DVil 30
GAULS Vida, 77
GAVE And thanks his gods for all
the good they gave. ....72 Trav 7
While nought remain'd of all that
riches gave, ...141 Trav 10
Gave wealth to sway the mind with
double force. ....396 Trav 18
Just gave what life requir'd, but
gave no more: ....60 DVil 25
His pity gave ere charity began. ..162 DVil 28
And to party gave up what was meant
for mankind. ....32 Rtal 88
What a commerce was yours, while
you got and you gave! ....116 Rtal 91
Ere I forget the land that gave
me birth, ...I:91 Capt 117
Vida, 190, 658, 673
GAY Woods over woods in gay
theatric pride; ....108 Trav 8
Gay sprightly land of mirth and
social ease, ...241 Trav 13
And the gay grandsire, skill'd in
gestic lore, ...253 Trav 13
With blossom'd furze unprofitably
gay, ...194 DVil 29
With aspen boughs, and flowers,
and fennel gay; ....234 DVil 31
Lost to every gay delight; ....2 Sonn 46
Not with that face, so servile and
so gay, ...v(19) DABd 200
Serenely gay, and strict in duty, 103 DTrn 55
Each hour the gay phantastic
crowd ....v109 Ed&A 209

'If that be the case, then,' cried
he, very gay, ...45 HofV 96
Give me the young, the gay, the
men of spirit. ....30 $eSSC_1$ 105
And be unco merry when you are
but gay; ....42 $eSSC_1$ 105
The gay coquette, who ogles all
the day, ...17 $eSSC_2$ 108
Vida, 67, 503
GAZE Or Jack had wanted eyes to
gaze. ....16 DTrn 52
GAZED And still they gaz'd, and still
the wonder grew, ...215 DVil 30
To go on with my tale--as I gaz'd
on the haunch, ...19 HofV 95
Who smil'd as he gaz'd on the Ven'son
and me. ....v38 HofV 239
GAZER And seems to every gazer all
in white, ...38 eSis 71
GAZING Amazed the gazing rustics
rang'd around, ...214 DVil 30
GEESE The noisy geese that gabbled
o'er the pool, ...119 DVil 27
GELID While sea-born gales their
gelid wings expand ....121 Trav 9
GEMS If gems, or gold, impart a joy, 11 Gift 43
GENERAL Till over-wrought, the
general system feels ....347 Trav 16
Our bard into the general spirit
enters, ...9 pZob 72
Vida, 90
GENERALS Vida, 357
GENEROUS Whose temper was generous,
open, sincere; ....151 Rtal 93
GENIUS See also GENUS
Fir'd at the sound, my genius
spreads her wing, ...317 Trav 15
Here lies our good Edmund, whose
genius was such, ...29 Rtal 88
And Heaven, that lent him genius,
was repaid. ....6 epTP 100
GENTLE There gentle music melts on
ev'ry spray; ....322 Trav 16
Those gentle hours that plenty
bade to bloom, ...69 DVil 25
'Turn, gentle hermit of the dale, ...1 Ed&A 59
His gentle accents fell: ....34 Ed&A 60
A kind and gentle heart he had, ...9 MDog 65
His manners were gentle, complying,
and bland; ....140 Rtal 91
This tomb, inscrib'd to gentle
Parnell's name, ...1 epTP 100
GENTLEMAN Though I could not help
thinking my gentleman hasty, ...61 HofV 97
GENTLER But all the gentler morals,
such as play ....235 Trav 13
To kinder skies, where gentler
manners reign, ...239 Trav 13
Insulting slaves! if gentler methods
fail, ...I:93 Capt 117
GENTLEST There all around the
gentlest breezes stray, ...321 Trav 16
GENTLY While Resignation gently
slopes the way; ....110 DVil 26
GENUS Gives <u>genus</u> a better discerning. ....4 "LSm 84
GESTIC And the gay grandsire,

skill'd in gestic lore, ...253 Trav 13
GET They please, are pleas'd,
they give to get esteem, ...265 Trav 14
I'll give them--when I get 'em. ....12 Gift 43
For let folks only get a
touch, ...37 NSim 57
By a bounce now and then, to
get courage to fly. ....16 HofV 95
'I get these things often;'--
but that was a bounce: ....42 HofV 96
GHASTLY Those eyeless orbs that
shock with ghastly glare, ...III:33 Capt 123
GIBBET There the black gibbet
glooms beside the way. ....318 DVil 33
GIDDY There, while above the
giddy tempest flies, ...417 Trav 19
GIFT The gift, who slights the
giver? ....8 Gift 43
Let us prize death as the best
gift of nature-- ....86 Thrn 77
GIFTS To spurn the venal gifts
as flattery. ....11 Thrn 74
A thousand gifts would fortune
send; ....29 Thrn 75
GILEAD Ye Gilead groves, that
fling perfumes around, ...I:20 Capt 114
GIRD Vida, 46
GIRL'S Why, sure the girl's
beside herself: an Epilogue
of singing, ...7 eSSC$_1$ 103
GIRLS 'Consider, dear Doctor,
the girls are but young.' ....56 LetB 133
GIVE They please, are pleas'd,
they give to get esteem, ...265 Trav 14
My rivals give--and let 'em; ....10 Gift 43
I'll give them--when I get 'em. ....12 Gift 43
I'll give--but not the full-
blown rose, ...13 Gift 43
I'll give thee something yet
unpaid, ...17 Gift 43
I'll give thee--Ah! too charm-
ing maid, ...19 Gift 43
I'll give thee--To the devil. ......20 Gift 43
I give it with good will. ....16 Ed&A 59
Give ear unto my song; ....2 MDog 65
To give repentance to her lover, ...7 "wlw 67
Give him good words indeed, but
no assistance. ....22 eGNM 68
But not a soul will budge to give
him place. ....30 eGNM 69
What if I give a masquerade?--I
will. ....10 eSis 70
'I hopes as how to give you
satisfaction.' ....12 eSSC$_3$ 85
'Give me another horse!.bind up
my wounds!--soft--'twas but
a dream,' ....24 epLL 101
Give me the young, the gay, the
men of spirit. ....30 eSSC$_1$ 105
Give me my bonny Scot, that
travels from the Tweed. ....38 eSSC$_1$ 105
And give repentance but an
hour's delay. ....III:64 Capt 125
Give, give your songs of Sion
to the wind, ...III:87 Capt 126
Comes to give the world re-
pose. ....III:94 Capt 126
The whole pool as my own--'Come,
give me five cards.' ....24 LetB 132
'Pray, Ma'am, be so good as
to give your advice; ....29 LetB 132
Vida, 457, 489
GIVEN As different good, by Art
or Nature given, ...79 Trav 8
Find that each good, by Art or
Nature given, ...v79 Trav 168
In all my griefs--and GOD has
given my share-- ....84 DVil 26
To them his heart, his love, his
griefs were given, ...187 DVil 29
Our pity shall be given, ...v(166) Ed&A 211
The incense given to kings, ...7 Thrn 74
'An't please you,' quoth John,
'I'm not given to letters, ...3 ClRp 100
Let praise be given to all
eternity; ....III:104 Capt 127
GIVER The gift, who slights
the giver? ....8 Gift 43
GIVES It gives their follies also
room to rise; ....268 Trav 14
For though she gives me up her
breast, ...3 TrSA 51
Gives genus a better discerning. ....4 "LSm 84
She that gives all to the false
one pursuing her, ...7 "Amw 94
Vida, 498, 664
GIVING And giving each your
bounty, let him dine; ....4 GRos 51
Or rather like tragedy giving
a rout. ....68 Rtal 89
For giving advice that is not
worth a straw, ...37 LetB 133
GIZZARD I fret in my gizzard,
yet, cautious and sly, ...9 LetB 132
GLAD 'I'm glad I have taken
this house in my way. ....46 HofV 96
GLADE Far shelter'd in a glade
obscure ....v37 Ed&A 208
GLADES Along thy glades, a
solitary guest, ...43 DVil 24
Thy glades forlorn confess the
tyrant's power. ....76 DVil 25
GLADLY Vida, 345
GLANCE The matron's glance that
would those looks reprove: ....30 DVil 24
Every glance that warms the
soul, ...236 Thrn 82
GLANCING Vida, 123
GLARE$_1$ Basks in the glare, or
stems the tepid wave, ...71 Trav 7
Lo! the small-pox, whose horrid
glare ....77 DTrn 54
Those eyeless orbs that shock
with ghastly glare, ...III:33 Capt 123
Vida, 414
GLARE$_2$ But meteors glare, and
stormy glooms invest. ....174 Trav 11
The rattling chariots clash,
the torches glare. ....322 DVil 34
GLARING In all the glaring im-
potence of dress. ....294 DVil 33
GLASS$_1$ He drank his glass and
crack'd his joke, ...5 DTrn 52
GLASS$_2$ The glass, grown hateful

reclin'd? ....I:98 Capt 117
GODS And thanks his gods for all
the good they gave. ....72 Trav 7
Ye gods! what transport e'er compared
to this. ....8 MrsX 49
Let them brag of their heathenish
gods, ...5 "LSm 84
Praise but our gods, and every good
is yours. ....II:10 Capt 118
By the gods, I'll enjoy it; though
'tis but in thought! ....42 LetB 133
Vida, 29, 165, 169, 185, 317, 655
GODSHIP And waft his godship
through the air; ....26 NSim 56
GOES Breasts the keen air, and carols
as he goes; 186 Trav.11
We scarce exhibit till the sun goes
down. ....10 eSSC$_2$ 108
Comes here at night, and goes a
prude away. ....18 eSSC$_2$ 108
Goes out, affronts his man, and
takes a beating. ....30 eSSC$_2$ 109
Vida, 627
GOLD If gems, or gold, impart a
joy, ...11 Gift 43
Vida, 674
GOLDEN Boasts of his golden sands
and palmy wine, ...70 Trav 7
Vida, 67, 179
GOLD'S At gold's superior charms
all freedom flies, ...307 Trav 15
GOLDSMITH Magnanimous Goldsmith a
gooseberry fool. ....16 Rtal 87
No words, my dear GOLDSMITH! my
very good Friend! ....v56 HofV 240
GONE Conscious of this, our bard
has gone about, ...7 eGNM 68
But now he is gone, and we want
a detector, ...85 Rtal 90
Yes, he's far gone:--and yet some
pity fix, ...41 eSSC$_2$ 109
GOOD$_1$ And learn the luxury of doing
good. ....22 Trav 6
Some fleeting good, that mocks me
with the view; ....26 Trav 6
That good, which makes each humbler
bosom vain? ....40 Trav 6
Exults in all the good of all mankind.44 Trav 6
Pleas'd with each good that heaven
to man supplies: ....56 Trav 7
And thanks his gods for all the good
they gave. ....72 Trav 7
As different good, by Art or Nature
given, ...79 Trav 8
Find that each good, by Art or Nature
given, ...v79 Trav 168
This favourite good begets peculiar
pain. ....98 Trav 8
Thus every good his native wilds
impart, ...199 Trav 11
Hence all the good from opulence
that springs, ...301 Trav 15
To seek a good each government
bestows? ....426 Trav 19
The base bestow them: but the
good agree ....10 Thrn 74
But aid the power of doing good-- ..16 Thrn 74
Some increasing good bestows, ...41,49 Thrn 75
How do the good, the virtuous fall! 73 Thrn 76
While the owner ne'er knew half the
good that was in't; ....44 Rtal 88
Why, let them come, one good remains
to cheer; ....I:95 Capt 117
Praise but our gods, and every
good is yours. ....II:10 Capt 118
GOOD$_2$ Pleas'd with his guests,
the good man learn'd to glow, ...159 DVil 28
And pluck'd his gown, to share the
good man's smile. ....184 DVil 29
The twelve good rules, the royal
game of goose; ....232 DVil 31
Good heaven! what sorrows gloom'd
that parting day, ...363 DVil 35
The good old sire, the first
prepar'd to go ....371 DVil 35
Good people all, with one accord, ...1 MBlz 47
Who never wanted a good word-- ......3 MBlz 47
No poppy water half so good; ....36 NSim 57
I give it with good will. ....16 Ed&A 59
Good people all, of every sort, ...1 MDog 65
To bite so good a man. ....24 MDog 65
Give him good words indeed, but
no assistance. ....22 eGNM 68
And be each critic the Good Natur'd
Man. ....34 eGNM 69
Good Savages, our Captain craves
assistance; ....30 pZob 73
The good old sire, unconscious of
decay, ...155 Thrn 79
Good liquor, I stoutly maintain, ...3 "LSm 84
But you, my good friend, are the
pigeon. ....17 "LSm 84
Here lies the good Dean, re-united
to earth, ...23 Rtal 87
Here lies our good Edmund, whose
genius was such, ...29 Rtal 88
What was good was spontaneous, his
faults were his own. ....50 Rtal 88
And slander itself must allow him
good nature: ....126 Rtal 91
Your very good mutton's a very good
treat; ....32 HofV 96
'What have we got here?--Why, this
is good eating! ....39 HofV 96
No words, my dear GOLDSMITH! my very
good Friend! ....v56 HofV 240
Yet Johnson, and Burke, and a good
venison pasty, ...62 HofV 97
To be plain, my good Lord, it's but
labour misplac'd ....117 HofV 99
To send such good verses to one of
your taste; ....118 HofV 99
The good man suffers but to gain, I:45 Capt 115
But, whence that shout? Good
heavens! amazement all! ....III:47 Capt 124
But, alas! your good worships,
how could they be wiser, ...43 Invt 129
'Well done!' cry the ladies; 'Ah,
Doctor, that's good! ....25 LetB 132
'Pray, Ma'am, be so good as to give
your advice; ....29 LetB 132
GOOD- She learns good-nature
every day; ....102 DTrn 55
And view with favour, the 'Good-

natur'd Man.' ....v34 eGNM 215
GOODS His goods, he hopes, are
prime, and brought from far, ...35 pZob 73
GOOSE The twelve good rules, the
royal game of goose; ....232 DVil 31
The royal game of goose was there
in view, ...11 DABd 48
The game of goose was there
expos'd to view ....v11 DABd 200
GOOSEBERRY Magnanimous Goldsmith
a gooseberry fool. ....16 Rtal 87
GOOSEQUILL With his goosequill the
scribbling elf, ...53 NSim 57
GORE Vida, 64
GORGEOUS Here, richly deck'd,
admits the gorgeous train; ....320 DVil 33
GOT But how? ay, there's the
rub!--I've got my cue: ....11 eSis 70
And tries to kill, ere she's got
power to cure. ....24 eSis 70
What a commerce was yours, while
you got and you gave! ....116 Rtal 91
'What have we got here?--Why,
this is good eating! ....39 HofV 96
You've got an odd something--a
kind of discerning-- ....119 HofV 99
Your mandate I got, ...1 Invt 128
Now I've got him a scale ....29 Invt 129
GOVERN That those who think must
govern those that toil; ....372 Trav 17
GOVERNMENT To seek a good each
government bestows? ....426 Trav 19
In every government, though
terrors reign, ...427 Trav 19
GOWN And pluck'd his gown, to
share the good man's smile. ....184 DVil 29
GRACE$_1$ At church, with meek and
unaffected grace, ...177 DVil 29
See how she moves along with
every grace, ...5 MrsX 49
'Tis true she dress'd with modern
grace, ...43 DTrn 53
And, rifling ev'ry youthful
grace, ...79 DTrn 54
Where sculptur'd elegance and
native grace ....144 Thrn 79
Every grace that grief dis-
penses, ...235 Thrn 82
Vida, 175
GRACE$_2$ They never importune his
grace, ...29 LogR 45
GRACE$_3$ Vida, 16
GRACED Those healthful sports
that grac'd the peaceful scene, ...71 DVil 25
GRACEFUL Vida, 40
GRACES Howe'er, from this time
I shall ne'er see your graces, ...5 ClRp 100
GRAIN 'It shows that their habits
are all dyed in grain.' ....58 LetB 133
GRAMMAR With grammar, and non-
sense, and learning; ....2 "LSm 84
GRAND His pencil was striking,
resistless, and grand; ....139 Rtal 91
GRANDEUR With venerable grandeur
mark the scene. ....110 Trav 9
Seen opulence, her grandeur to
maintain, ...401 Trav 18
Tumultuous grandeur crowds the
blazing square, ...321 DVil 34
GRANDSIRE And the gay grandsire,
skill'd in gestic lore, ...253 Trav 13
GRANT Yet grant a word by way
of postscript. ....56 NSim 57
GRANTS Still grants her bliss
at Labour's earnest call; ....82 Trav 8
GRASP Grasp the red bolt, and
lay the guilty low? ....III:36 Capt 123
GRASPS One only master grasps
the whole domain, ...39 DVil 24
The master-prophet grasps his
full-ton'd lyre. ....II:64 Capt 120
GRASS And the long grass o'er-
tops the mould'ring wall; ....48 DVil 24
GRASS- No busy steps the
grass-grown foot-way tread, ...127 DVil 27
GRASSY 'But from the mountain's
grassy side ....25 Ed&A 60
GRASSY- The cooling brook, the
grassy-vested green, ...360 DVil 35
GRATE The rusty grate unconscious
of a fire; ....16 DABd 48
A rusty grate unconscious of a
fire. ....v16 DABd 200
GRATEFUL The grateful stranger
lowly bends. ....v35 Ed&A 208
GRATITUDE May speak our gratitude,
but not his fame. ....2 epTP 100
They never have my gratitude
nor thanks; ....32 epLL 102
GRAVE$_1$ Bends to the grave with
unperceiv'd decay, ...109 DVil 26
Sinks to the grave with un-
perceiv'd decay, ...v109 DVil 183
The country blooms--a garden,
and a grave. ....302 DVil 33
He only wish'd for worlds beyond
the grave. ....374 DVil 35
Oswego's dreary shores shall be
my grave; ....222 Thrn 82
On her grave shall the cowslip
and primrose be cast, ...249 Thrn 83
On the grave of Augusta these
garlands be plac'd, ...255 Thrn 83
On the grave of Augusta this
garland be plac'd, ...259 Thrn 83
GRAVE$_2$ Though grave, yet trifling;
zealous, yet untrue; ....129 Trav 9
Ye Kenricks, ye Kellys, and
Woodfalls so grave, ...115 Rtal 91
Though he merrily liv'd, he is
now a grave man; ....148 Rtal 92
GRAVES Here wretches seek dis-
honourable graves, ...310 Trav 15
GRAY See also GREY-
There Faith shall come, a pilgrim
gray, ...132 Thrn 78
The modest matron, clad in home-
spun gray, ...156 Thrn 79
GRAZE Of all the fish that graze
beneath the flood, ...11 Tr 267
GREASY Five greasy nightcaps wrapp'd
her head. ....46 DTrn 53
GREAT$_1$ I mean to flatter kings, or
court the great; ....362 Trav 17

Thus at the court both great and small ....57 LogR 45
Where all the humble, all the great, ...101 Thrn 77
How low the great, how feeble are the strong! ....III:52 Capt 124
$GREAT_2$ These little things are great to little man; ....42 Trav 6
With daring aims irregularly great; ....326 Trav 16
Have strove to prove with great precision, ...7 LogR 44
This, I believe, between us great or small, ...3 GCRL 51
Being each as great a thief as he: .60 NSim 58
Nor wanted man's opinion to be great. ....27 Thrn 75
How great a king of terrors I! .....77 Thrn 76
To Death's great court, the prospect seems more fair. ....96 Thrn 77
Like the sun, our great monarch all rapture supplies, ...I:61 Capt 116
Cyrus, our great restorer, is at hand, ...III:85 Capt 126
Vida, 86, 114, 233, 247, 267, 309, 319, 375, 382, 412, 604
GREATER Vida, 142, 184, 455
GREATNESS Kingdoms, by thee, to sickly greatness grown, ...389 DVil 36
GREECE Vida, 63
GREEN How often have I loiter'd o'er thy green, ...7 DVil 23
And desolation saddens all thy green: ....38 DVil 24
Liv'd in each look, and brighten'd all the green; ....72 DVil 25
Indignant spurns the cottage from the green; ....282 DVil 32
The cooling brook, the grassy-vested green, ...360 DVil 35
The wavy lawn, the sloping green-- 147 Thrn 79
GREEN- Have emptied all the green-room on the stage. ....6 eSis 70
GREENS Ye shady walks, ye waving greens, ...163 Thrn 80
GREW Where shading elms along the margin grew, ...245 Trav 13
Where once the cottage stood, the hawthorn grew, ...80 DVil 25
And still they gaz'd, and still the wonder grew, ...215 DVil 30
And as my strength decay'd, her bounty grew.' ....180 Thrn 80
He grew lazy at last, and drew from himself? ....78 Rtal 89
GREY- Where grey-beard mirth and smiling toil retir'd, ...222 DVil 30
GRIDIRON And on the gridiron broils her lovers' hearts: ....20 $eSSC_3$ 85
GRIEF In all the silent manliness of grief. ....384 DVil 36
In all the decent manliness of grief. ....v384 DVil 190
Grief dares to mingle her soul-piercing voice, ...3 Queb 46
For grief was heavy at his heart, ..59 Ed&A 61
For grief had seized his early age, ...v59 Ed&A 208
With unavailing grief, ...60 Thrn 76
Every grace that grief dispenses, .235 Thrn 82
Vida, 259, 418, 437
GRIEFS A time there was, ere England's griefs began, ...57 DVil 25
In all my griefs--and GOD has given my share-- ....84 DVil 26
To them his heart, his love, his griefs were given, ...187 DVil 29
Dismiss your griefs, and join our warbling choir, ...I:83 Capt 117
GRIEVE Or grieve for friendship unreturn'd, ...67 Ed&A 61
GRIEVED Vida, 239, 451
GRIEVES 'But then they're so handsome, one's bosom it grieves.' 59 LetB 133
$GRIMACE_1$ Here vanity assumes her pert grimace, ...275 Trav 14
Ye barristers, so fluent with grimace, ...51 $eSSC_1$ 106
$GRIMACE_2$ He nods, they nod; he cringes, they grimace; ....29 eGNM 69
GRIMACES But both in malice and grimaces ....45 LogR 45
GRIMLY Who mump their passion, and who, grimly smiling, ...21 $eSSC_1$ 104
GRIND Laws grind the poor, and rich men rule the law; ....386 Trav 18
GRITS The sanded floor that grits beneath the tread; ....9 DABd 48
GROAN In want and sorrow groan; III:24 Capt 123
GROANS Groans, weeping friends, indeed, and gloomy sables, ...90 Thrn 77
She sinks, she groans, she dies. ....II:78 Capt 121
GROUND That proudly rise, or humbly court the ground; ....114 Trav 9
And many a gambol frolick'd o'er the ground, ...21 DVil 24
When every rood of ground main-tain'd its man; ....58 DVil 25
Need we intrude on hallow'd ground, ...23 DTrn 52
And apples, bitter apples strew the ground. ....22 pZob 73
But crush'd, or trodden to the ground, ...I:49 Capt 115
Down with her! down--**down to the** ground; ....II:77 Capt 121
See where an army covers all the ground, ...III:49 Capt 124
Vida, 55, 131, 218, 348, 353
GROUNDS Amidst thy tangling walks, and ruin'd grounds, ...78 DVil 25
GROUP Around my fire an evening group to draw, ...91 DVil 26
---,what a group the motley scene discloses! ....13 eSis 70
GROVE A mistress or a saint in every grove. ....152 Trav 10
The breezy covert of the warbling grove, ...361 DVil 35
And music to the grove. ....120 Ed&A 63
Blest as the songsters of the grove, ...v(163) Ed&A 211
Hear the grove to bliss be-

guiling; ....II:48 Capt 120
GROVES In florid beauty groves
and fields appear, ...125 Trav 9
As when in Paphian groves the
Queen of Love ....9 MrsX 49
How sad the groves and plains
appear, ...9 DRtH 50
No monster-breed to mark the groves
with shame; ....8 Cati 94
Ye Gilead groves, that fling
perfumes around, ...I:20 Capt 114
Vida, 524
GROW Till, seeming bless'd, they
grow to what they seem. ....266 Trav 14
The firm-connected bulwark seems
to grow; ....288 Trav 14
Hence, should one order dis-
proportion'd grow, ...375 Trav 17
At every draught more large and
large they grow, ...391 DVil 36
Wings grow again from both his
shoes; ....24 NSim 56
Our Author's the least likely to
grow wiser; ....34 eSSC$_2$ 109
No spicy fragrance while they
grow; ....I:48 Capt 115
Ah, me! what angry terrors
round us grow; ....II:25 Capt 119
Thus, playing, and playing, I
still grow more eager, ...33 LetB 132
GROWING Death's growing power, ...64 Thrn 76
The growing sound their swift
approach declares;-- ....I:55 Capt 115
Awful as clouds that nurse the
growing storm; ....II:68 Capt 121
Still shall our fame and grow-
ing power be spread, ...III:5 Capt 122
GROWN Till half a patriot, half
a coward grown, ...391 Trav 18
Kingdoms, by thee, to sickly
greatness grown, ...389 DVil 36
He thinks her features coarser
grown; ....62 DTrn 54
Her face is grown a knowing phiz; ..68 DTrn 54
The glass, grown hateful to her
sight, ...81 DTrn 54
Till his relish grown callous,
almost to disease, ...111 Rtal 90
-GROWN No busy steps the grass-
grown foot-way tread, ...127 DVil 27
GROWS And still where many a
garden flower grows wild; ....138 DVil 27
Of virtues and feelings, that folly
grows proud; ....70 Rtal 89
And still, as darker grows the
night, ...II:39 Capt 119
Vida, 363
GROWTH Man seems the only growth
that dwindles here. ....126 Trav 9
Has robb'd the neighbouring fields
of half their growth, ...280 DVil 32
GRUB- How did Grub-street re-
echo the shouts that you rais'd, ..117 Rtal 91
GRUDGING Each grudging master keeps
the labourer bare-- ....175 Thrn 80
GRUMBLING Now wrangling and
grumbling to keep up the ball, ...55 Rtal 89

GUARD$_1$ Vida, 587
GUARD$_2$ Vida, 155, 195, 300, 437, 644
GUARDED Vida, 237
GUARDIAN And round his dwelling
guardian saints attend: ....12 Trav 5
GUARDS$_1$ For the foot guards so
stout ....26 Invt 128
GUARDS$_2$ The hollow-sounding
bittern guards its nest; ....44 DVil 24
Vida, 58, 88
GUEST Along thy glades, a solitary
guest, ...43 DVil 24
The long-remember'd beggar was
his guest, ...151 DVil 28
And cheer'd his pensive guest: ....48 Ed&A 60
His love-lorn guest betray'd. .....84 Ed&A 62
The bashful guest betray'd. .....v84 Ed&A 209
May cherubs welcome their ex-
pected guest; ....108 Thrn 77
Each guest brought his dish, and
the feast was united; ....2 Rtal 87
Let each guest bring himself,
and he brings the best dish: ....4 Rtal 87
O peace of mind, angelic
guest! ....II:1 Capt 118
GUESTS Bless'd be that spot,
where cheerful guests retire ....13 Trav 5
Pleas'd with his guests, the good
man learn'd to glow, ...159 DVil 28
Talks loud, coquets the guests,
and scolds the waiters. ....16 eSSC$_3$ 85
GUIDE$_1$ Thou guide by which the
nobler arts excel, ...415 DVil 37
A time there was, when glory
was my guide, ...5 pLab 41
That instinct is a surer guide ....15 LogR 44
That decent dress, this holy
guide, ...185 Thrn 81
Nature, a better guide than
you. ....**II:54 Capt 120**
GUIDE$_2$ And guide my lonely
way, ...2 Ed&A 59
To guide my nightly way, ...v2 Ed&A 208
You vain, whom youth and
pleasure guide, ...III:27 Capt 123
Vida, 10, 112
GUILT And sorrow, guilt, and
pain, by turns dismay'd, ...172 DVil 29
What art can wash her guilt
away? ....4 "wlw 67
The only art her guilt to cover, ...5 "wlw 67
GUILTLESS A guiltless feast I
bring; ....26 Ed&A 60
GUILTY$_1$ Grasp the red bolt, and
lay the guilty low? ....III:36 Capt 123
Vida, 662
GUILTY$_2$ No surly porter stands
in guilty state ....105 DVil 26

H--D There's H--d, and C--y, and
H--rth, and H--ff, ...27 HofV 96
H--FF There's H--d, and C--y, and
H--rth, and H--ff, ...27 HofV 96
H--GG--NS There's my countryman
H--gg--ns--Oh! let him alone, ...29 HofV 96
H--RTH There's H--d, and C--y, and
H--rth, and H--ff, ...27 HofV 96

cheer'd the labouring swain, ...2 DVil 23
His best companions, innocence
and health; ....61 DVil 25
Such dainties to them, their
health it might hurt, ...33 HofV 96
HEALTH$_2$ Here's a health to the
Three Jolly Pigeons. ....26 "LSm 84
HEALTHFUL Those healthful sports
that grac'd the peaceful scene, ...71 DVil 25
HEAPS Vida, 223
HEAR Relax his pond'rous strength,
and lean to hear; ....246 DVil 31
And hark! I hear the tuneful
throng ....17 DRtH 50
The labouring ship, and hear the
tempest roar, ...67 Thrn 76
But hold--let me pause--Don't I
hear you pronounce ....13 HofV 95
Hear the grove to bliss be-
guiling; ....II:48 Capt 120
'But, pray, whom have they
pilfer'd?'--'A Doctor, I hear.' 49 LetB 133
HEARD And ne'er was heard of
more. ....v136 Ed&A 210
I heard a hissing--there are
serpents here! ....24 pZob 73
Our vows are heard! Long, long
to mortal eyes, ...120 Thrn 78
HEARERS Who, too deep for his
hearers, still went on refining, ...35 Rtal 88
HEARING When they judg'd without
skill he was still hard of hearing: ....144 Rtal 92
HEART My heart untravell'd
fondly turns to thee; ....8 Trav 5
From these the feeble heart and
long-fall'n mind ....147 Trav 10
Imprints the patriot passion on
his heart, ...200 Trav 11
Fall blunted from each indurated
heart. ....232 Trav 13
Tear off reserve, and bare my
swelling heart; ....390 Trav 18
Far other aims his heart had
learned to prize, ...147 DVil 28
To them his heart, his love, his
griefs were given, ...187 DVil 29
An hour's importance to the
poor man's heart; ....240 DVil 31
To me more dear, congenial to
my heart, ...253 DVil 31
The heart distrusting asks, if
this be joy. ....264 DVil 32
With heavy heart deplores that
luckless hour, ...334 DVil 34
To catch the heart, or strike
for honest fame; ....410 DVil 36
My heart, a victim to thine
eyes, ...5 Gift 43
Which triumph forces from the
patriot heart, ...2 Queb 46
For grief was heavy at his
heart, ...59 Ed&A 61
A constant heart was all he
had, ...v115 Ed&A 209
How would my heart attend! ......v122 Ed&A 210
And while his passion touch'd
my heart, ...131 Ed&A 63
'Thus let me hold thee to my
heart, ...153 Ed&A 64
The sigh that rends thy constant
heart ....159 Ed&A 64
And the last sigh that rends thy
heart, ...v159 Ed&A 211
A kind and gentle heart he
had, ...9 MDog 65
In nought entire--except his
heart. ....210 Thrn 81
Here lies honest William, whose
heart was a mint, ...43 Rtal 88
Yet, with talents like these, and
an excellent heart, ...97 Rtal 90
His pencil our faces, his manners
our heart: ....142 Rtal 92
What heart but feels his sweetly-
moral lay, ...3 epTP 100
That speeds the power of music
to the heart, ...I:90 Capt 117
And ev'ry pang that rends the
heart, ...vII:35 Capt 250
Feels for each tone, and speeds
it to the heart; ....II:66 Capt 120
Only binds the willing
heart. ....III:102 Capt 127
And see how they kneel! Is
your heart made of stone?' .....64 LetB 134
Vida, 537
Thus, when soft love subdues
the heart ....13 Tr 267
HEART- Whilst thy sad fate ex-
torts the heart-wrung tear. ......8 Queb 46
HEARTFELT The heartfelt power of
every charm divine, ...3 MrsX 49
HEARTH The hearth, except when
winter chill'd the day, ...233 DVil 31
The cricket chirrups in the
hearth; ....55 Ed&A 61
HEART'S A heart's distress
allay; ....v98 Ed&A 209
HEARTS How small, of all that
human hearts endure, ...429 Trav 19
If folly, fraud, your hearts
engage, ...78 Thrn 76
Our hearts and our liquors are
stout; ....21 "LSm 84
And on the gridiron broils her
lovers' hearts: ....20 eSSC$_3$ 85
The Terence of England, the mender
of hearts; ....62 Rtal 89
Though secure of our hearts, yet
confoundedly sick ....105 Rtal 90
HEARTY With two full as clever,
and ten times as hearty. ....74 HofV 97
Assist my cause with hands and
voices hearty; ....55 eSSC$_1$ 106
HEATED Vida, 355
HEATHENISH Let them brag of their
heathenish gods, ...5 "LSm 84
HEAVEN To spurn the splendid things
by heaven supply'd. ....v40 Trav 168
Pleas'd with each good that
heaven to man supplies: ....56 Trav 7
His Heaven commences ere the world
be pass'd! ....112 DVil 27

But all his serious thoughts had
rest in Heaven. ....188 DVil 29
Good heaven! what sorrows gloom'd
that parting day, ...363 DVil 35
Him I obey, whom heaven itself
obeys, ...13 pLab 41
Soft as the dew from heav'n
descends, ...33 Ed&A 60
Where heaven and you reside. ....96 Ed&A 62
The dews of heaven refin'd, ...122 Ed&A 63
'Forbid it, heaven!' the hermit
cried, ...145 Ed&A 64
We'll love again in heaven. ...v(168) Ed&A 211
How hast thou left mankind for
heaven! ....20 Thrn 74
And Heaven, that lent him genius,
was repaid. ....6 epTP 100
But sweeter still, when Heaven
was with us there! ....I:22 Capt 114
Or mix in rites that Heaven
regards with pain? ....I:88 Capt 117
And shall not Heaven for this
its terrors show, ...III:35 Capt 123
To Heaven their praise be-
stow, ...III:66 Capt 125
Alike of Heaven and man the
foe; ....III:74 Capt 125
Heaven, men, and all, ...III:75 Capt 125
HEAVENLY Heav'nly born, and
bred on high, ...114 Thrn 78
Vida, 296, 666
Say heavenly muse, their youthful
frays rehearse; ....7 Tr 267
HEAVEN'S O Luxury! thou curs'd
by Heaven's decree, ...385 DVil 36
Ye prophets, skill'd in Heaven's
eternal truth, ...II:27 Capt 119
Yes, my companions, Heaven's
decrees are past, ...III:1 Capt 122
HEAVENS Heavens! how unlike
their Belgic sires of old! ....313 Trav 15
But, whence that shout? Good
heavens! amazement all! ...III:47 Capt 124
HEAVY With heavy heart deplores
that luckless hour, ...334 DVil 34
For grief was heavy at his heart, ..59 Ed&A 61
HEBES There Hebes, turn'd of
fifty, try once more ....17 eSis 70
HECATE Vida, 412
HE'D Vida, 345
HEEDLESS There in the ruin, heedless
of the dead, ...161 Trav 10
HEELS My heels eclips'd the honours
of my head; ....4 epLL 101
HEIGHTEN And Dick with his pepper
shall heighten their savour: ....8 Rtal 87
Comes to heighten every bless-
ing, ...III:97 Capt 126
HEINEL Swims round the room,
the Heinel of Cheapside; ....28 $eSSC_3$ 85
Their hands are only lent to the
Heinel. ....36 $eSSC_1$ 105
HEIR Creation's heir, the world,
the world is mine! ....50 Trav 7
HELD Here by the bonds of nature
feebly held, ...343 Trav 16
See, though by circling deeps
together held, ...v343 Trav 174
With honest thrift I held
my honour dear: ....8 pLab 41
HE'LL Each case, however bad, he'll
new japan; ....6 GRos 51
'O--Oh!' quoth my friend, 'he'll
come on in a trice, ...99 HofV 98
I don't think he'll wish to come
back. ....4 epEP 100
HELL With this he drives men's
souls to hell. ....42 NSim 57
Vida, 412, 663
HELP And teas'd each rhyming friend
to help him out. ....8 eGNM 68
He was, could he help it?--a
special attorney. ....136 Rtal 91
Though my stomach was sharp, I
could scarce help regretting .....5 HofV 95
Though I could not help thinking
my gentleman hasty, ...61 HofV 97
HELPLESS The fond companion of
his helpless years, ...376 DVil 35
As helpless friends who view from
shore ....66 Thrn 76
Vida, 649
HENCE Hence every state to one
lov'd blessing prone, ...93 Trav 8
Hence ostentation here, with
tawdry art, ...273 Trav 14
Hence all the good from opulence
that springs, ...301 Trav 15
Hence all obedience bows to these
alone, ...353 Trav 17
Hence, should one order dis-
proportion'd grow, ...375 Trav 17
Hence through their tribes no
mix'd polluted flame, ...7 Cati 94
Here lesson'd for a while, and
hence retreating, ...29 $eSSC_2$ 109
Hence, intruder, most dis-
tressing, ...I:27 Capt 114
Hence, intruder! we'll
pursue ....II:53 Capt 120
Vida, 470
HENCEFORWARD Vida, 300
HERBS A scrip with herbs and
fruits supplied, ...27 Ed&A 60
HERD The sober herd that low'd to
meet their young, ...118 DVil 27
Ye tame imitators, ye servile
herd, come, ...165 Rtal 93
HERE Trav, 101, 102, 119, 126, 131,
145, v145, 149, 169, 175, 258, 261,
273, 275, 277, 303, 306, 310, 335,
343; DVil, 77, v(81), 96, 315, 317,
320, 397; pLab, 4, 15; NSim, 27, 55;
Ed&A, 5, 13, 31, 151, v(161); pZob,
4, 20, 21, 24; Thrn, 110, 117; Rtal,
19, 23, 29, 43, 51, 61, 79, 93, 125,
137, 147; HofV, 39, 55, 97; epEP, 1;
$eSSC_1$, 1, 18, 34, 56; $eSSC_2$, 18, 25,
29, 31, 33; Capt, I:12; Vida, 31, 47,
81, 164, 165, 255, 337, 463, 529,
594, 620
HERE'S Here's the Three Jolly
Pigeons for ever. ....22 "LSm 84
Here's a health to the Three Jolly

HITHER Hither the affected city
dame advancing, ...19 eSSC$_2$ 108
HO Yes, I must die, ho, ho, ho,
ho! ....28 eSSC$_1$ 105
HOARD To see the hoard of human
bliss so small; ....58 Trav 7
While his lov'd partner, boastful
of her hoard, ...195 Trav 11
And all my hoard of honour is no
more. ....10 pLab 41
HOARDS Hoards after hoards his
rising raptures fill, ...53 Trav 7
Yet still he sighs, for hoards are
wanting still: ....54 Trav 7
Hoards, e'en beyond the miser's
wish abound, ...271 DVil 32
HOARY Vida, 35
HOICKS 'Hoicks! hark forward!'
came thund'ring from behind, ...39 epLL 102
HOITY- Priests, cannibals, and
hoity-toity queens: ....8 pZob 72
HOLD Promis'd to hold them on
for life, ...74 DTrn 54
'Thus let me hold thee to my
heart, ...153 Ed&A 64
It cannot hold you long. ....4 MDog 65
And Madam now begins to hold it
higher; ....24 eSSC$_3$ 85
But hold--let me pause--Don't I
hear you pronounce ....13 HofV 95
Hold! Prompter, hold! a word
before your nonsense; ....1 epLL 101
Hold, Ma'am, your pardon. What's
your business here? ....1 eSSC$_1$ 103
Ye candid-judging few, hold up
your hands. ....16 eSSC$_1$ 104
'I hold the odds.--Done, done,
with you, with you;' ....50 eSSC$_1$ 106
HOLDING By holding out to tire
each other down; ....26 DVil 24
HOLDS Stern o'er each bosom reason
holds her state, ...325 Trav 16
The dome where Pleasure holds her
midnight reign ....319 DVil 33
HOLLAND Embosom'd in the deep where
Holland lies. ....282 Trav 14
HOLLOW- The hollow-sounding bittern
guards its nest; ....44 DVil 24
HOLY That decent dress, this holy
guide, ...185 Thrn 81
HOMAGE Let all the old pay
homage to your merit; ....29 eSSC$_1$ 105
Shall make our homage rise. .....I:10 Capt 113
HOME His first, best country
ever is, at home. ....74 Trav 7
Pillag'd from slaves to purchase
slaves at home; ....388 Trav 18
Here to return--and die at home
at last. ....96 DVil 26
But when at home, at board or
bed, ...45 DTrn 53
The coachman was tipsy, the
chariot drove home; ....48 Rtal 88
HOMES Forc'd from their homes,
a melancholy train, ...409 Trav 18
HOMESPUN The modest matron, clad
in homespun gray, ...156 Thrn 79
HOMO <u>Homo est ratione praeditum</u>,-- ..9 LogR 44
HONEST With steady zeal, each
honest rustic ran; ....182 DVil 29
To catch the heart, or strike
for honest fame; ....410 DVil 36
With honest thrift I held my
honour dear: ....8 pLab 41
Who ever knew an honest brute ......19 LogR 44
Are known to honest quadrupeds; ....37 LogR 45
And flush with honest love. .....v152 Ed&A 211
Here lies honest William, whose
heart was a mint, ...43 Rtal 88
Here lies honest Richard, whose
fate I must sigh at; ....51 Rtal 88
And so was too foolishly honest?
Ah no! ....134 Rtal 91
HONEY- The honey-moon like
lightning flew, ...29 DTrn 53
HONOUR Wealth, commerce, honour,
liberty, content. ....88 Trav 8
And honour sinks where commerce
long prevails. ....92 Trav 8
For honour forms the social temper
here: ....258 Trav 13
Honour, that praise which real
merit gains, ...259 Trav 13
As duty, love, and honour fail
to sway, ...350 Trav 16
And thus polluting honour in its
source, ...395 Trav 18
With honest thrift I held my
honour dear: ....8 pLab 41
And all my hoard of honour is no
more. ....10 pLab 41
For life is ended when our honour
ends. ....20 pLab 41
His honour is no mercenary trader; .32 pZob 73
Still aiming at honour, yet fear-
ing to roam, ...47 Rtal 88
HONOURED Vida, 676
HONOURS My heels eclips'd the
honours of my head; ....4 epLL 101
HOOFS Vida, 225
HOOP With hoop of monstrous size, ..14 MBlz 47
HOPE$_1$ Where my worn soul, each
wand'ring hope at rest, ...61 Trav 7
They stood, while hope and comfort
fail, ...69 Thrn 76
On hope the wretch relies; .....II:34 Capt 119
Still, still on Hope relies; ..vII:34 Capt 250
Hope, like the gleaming taper's
light, ...II:37 Capt 119
Hope, like the glim'ring taper's
light, ...vII:37 Capt 250
Vida, 145, 603, 628
HOPE$_2$ As I hope to be saved!
without thinking on asses.' ....6 ClRp 100
And first I hope, you'll readily
agree ....13 eSSC$_1$ 104
How can the piece expect or hope
for quarter? ....38 eSSC$_2$ 109
As I hope to be saved, ...5 Invt 128
Vida, 481
HOPED Vida, 561, 631
HOPEFUL A hopeful end indeed to
such a blest beginning. ....8 eSSC$_1$ 103
HOPELESS Hopeless of pleasing, yet

inclin'd to please. ....14 pLab 41
HOPES$_1$ I still had hopes my latest
hours to crown, ...85 DVil 26
I still had hopes, for pride
attends us still, ...89 DVil 26
I still had hopes, my long vex-
ations pass'd, ...95 DVil 26
He this way steers his course, in
hopes of trading-- ....12 pZob 72
In the hopes of being blest. ...39, 47 Thrn 75
Vida, 492
With smiling hopes and chilling
fears, ...14 Tr 267
HOPES$_2$ His goods, he hopes, are
prime, and brought from far, ...35 pZob 73
'I hopes as how to give you
satisfaction.' ....12 eSSC$_3$ 85
HOPING Vida, 335
HORN Vida, 262
HORNECK So tell Horneck and
Nesbitt, ...11 Invt 128
'Pray what does Miss Horneck?
take courage, come do,'-- ......17 LetB 132
HORNS$_1$ And, as a hare, whom hounds
and horns pursue, ...93 DVil 26
HORNS$_2$ My horns! I'm told horns
are the fashion now.' ....36 epLL 102
Vida, 523
HORRID The various terrors of that
horrid shore; ....346 DVil 34
Lo! the small-pox, whose horrid
glare ....77 DTrn 54
HORSE$_1$ So there I sat stuck, like
a horse in a pound, ...87 HofV 98
'Give me another horse! bind up
my wounds!--soft--'twas but a
dream,' ....24 epLL 101
HORSE$_2$ Vida, 137, 232, 333, 391,
448, 596
HORSES Space for his horses,
equipage, and hounds; ....278 DVil 32
HOSPITABLE Contented toil, and
hospitable care, ...403 DVil 36
With hospitable ray. ....4 Ed&A 59
HOST$_1$ The host himself no longer
shall be found ....247 DVil 31
HOST$_2$ Vida, 101, 259, 265
HOSTILE Vida, 581
HOSTS O God of hosts, the victory
is thine! ....III:54 Capt 124
Vida, 51, 75, 432
HOT At the sides there was
spinach and pudding made hot; ......83 HofV 98
HOUND Both mongrel, puppy, whelp,
and hound, ...15 MDog 65
HOUNDS And, as a hare, whom
hounds and horns pursue, ...93 DVil 26
Space for his horses, equipage,
and hounds; ....278 DVil 32
Near, and more near, the hounds
and huntsmen drew. ....38 epLL 102
HOUR I sit me down a pensive hour
to spend; ....32 Trav 6
And dance, forgetful of the noon-
tide hour. ....250 Trav 13
Yes, brother, curse with me that
baleful hour, ...393 Trav 18
Sweet Auburn! parent of the bliss-
ful hour, ...75 DVil 25
By doctrines fashion'd to the
varying hour; ....146 DVil 28
With heavy heart deplores that
luckless hour, ...334 DVil 34
But this vile hour disperses all
my store, ...9 pLab 41
Each hour a mercenary crowd ....109 Ed&A 63
Each hour the gay phantastic
crowd ....v109 Ed&A 209
Yet still (and woe betide the
hour!) ....v129 Ed&A 210
'No, never from this hour to
part, ...157 Ed&A 64
Are but the trappings of an
hour-- ....8 Thrn 74
Beheld each hour ....63 Thrn 76
Each day, each hour, her name
I'll bless-- ....203 Thrn 81
Let us one hour, one little hour
obey; ....II:31 Capt 119
Thrice happy, who in happy
hour ....III:65 Capt 125
Vida, 616
HOURLY Ye captive tribes, that
hourly work and weep ....I:1 Capt 113
HOUR'S An hour's importance to
the poor man's heart; ....240 DVil 31
And give repentance but an
hour's delay. ....III:64 Capt 125
HOURS Those gentle hours that
plenty bade to bloom, ...69 DVil 25
I still had hopes my latest hours
to crown, ...85 DVil 26
While all their hours were pass'd
between ....59 DTrn 54
The lingering hours beguil'd. ......52 Ed&A 60
Vida, 173
HOUSE$_1$ His house was known to all
the vagrant train, ...149 DVil 28
Low lies that house where nut-
brown draughts inspir'd, ...221 DVil 30
Who whisks about the house, at
market caters, ...15 eSSC$_3$ 85
'I'm glad I have taken this house
in my way. ....46 HofV 96
-HOUSE The chop-house toast of
ogling connoisseurs. ....18 eSSC$_3$ 85
A fine-spoken Custom-house
Officer he, ...v37 HofV 239
HOUSE$_2$ The one at the House, and
the other with THRALE. ....v72 HofV 241
HOUSE$_3$ What if we leave it to
the House? The House!--Agreed.
Agreed. ....11 eSSC$_1$ 104
HOUSELESS Against the houseless
stranger shuts the door; ....4 Trav 5
Where the poor houseless shiv'ring
female lies. ....326 DVil 34
'Here to the houseless child of
want ....13 Ed&A 59
HOUSES As in some Irish houses,
where things are so so, ...9 HofV 95
HOW Trav, 243, 313, 316, 377, 429;
DVil, 7, 9, 15, 99, v99, 158, 207,
267, 386, 387; MrsX, 5; DRtH, 9;

DTrn, 66, 67; Ed&A, v122, v124, v127;
eSis, 11; Thrn, 20, 22, 73, 77, 172;
eSSC$_3$, 12; Rtal, 117; HofV, 26; epLL,
11, 35; eSSC$_2$, 35, 38; Capt, I:21,
II:26, 67, III:37, 52, 62, 78; Invt,
33, 43; LetB, 51, 64; Vida, 3, 163,
383, 387, 402, 543, 551, 675

HOWARD There's COLEY, and WILLIAMS,
and HOWARD, and HIFF, ...v27 HofV 238

HOWE'ER Howe'er, from this time
I shall ne'er see your graces, ...5 ClRp 100
Vida, 94, 295, 475

HOWEVER See also HOWE'ER
Each case, however bad, he'll new
japan; ....6 GRos 51
'Tis best, however, keeping at a
distance. ....29 pZob 73
Vida, 156, 242, 316, 440, 610

HOWLING And wild the tempest howling ....215 Thrn 82
Fierce is the whirlwind howling II:15 Capt 118

HU Yes, I shall die, hu, hu,
hu, hu! ....27 eSSC$_1$ 105

HUDDLED Where wildly huddled to
the eye, ...103 Thrn 77

HUE Thinks black alone is beauty's
favourite hue. ....10 Cati 94

HUES His well acquainted tints, and
kindred hues. ....6 Cati 94

HUMAN To see the hoard of human
bliss so small; ....58 Trav 7
To see the sum of human bliss so
small; ....v58 Trav 168
The pregnant quarry teem'd with
human form; ....138 Trav 9
I see the lords of human kind
pass by, ...328 Trav 16
How small, of all that human
hearts endure, ...429 Trav 19
As rational, the human kind; ....2 LogR 44
Comes nearest us in human shape; ....42 LogR 45
Lost human wits have places there
assign'd them, ...3 eSSC$_2$ 108
Vida, 40

HUMBLE$_1$ Where all the humble, all
the great, ...101 Thrn 77

HUMBLE$_2$ To shame the meanness of
his humble shed; ....180 Trav 11
Where humble happiness endear'd
each scene; ....8 DVil 23
Amidst these humble bowers to lay
me down; ....86 DVil 26
The mournful peasant leads his
humble band; ....300 DVil 33
No stores beneath its humble
thatch ....41 Ed&A 60
'In humble, simplest habit clad, ...113 Ed&A 63

HUMBLER The pomp of kings, the
shepherd's humbler pride. ....36 Trav 6
That good, which makes each humbler
bosom vain? ....40 Trav 6

HUMBLY That proudly rise, or
humbly court the ground; ....114 Trav 9
Behold him humbly cringing wait .....47 LogR 45

HUMID The humid wall with paltry
pictures spread: ....10 DABd 48

HUMILITY Humility displaces pride; ..98 DTrn 55

HUMOUR And, just as humour rose
or fell, ...41 DTrn 53
Who scatter'd around wit and
humour at will; ....153 Rtal 93
That a Scot may have humour, I
had almost said wit: ....172 Rtal 93
That I found humour in a piebald
vest, ...5 epLL 101

HUMOURED 'Thou best humour'd man
with the worst humour'd muse.' ....174 Rtal 93

HUNDRED Look downward where a
hundred realms appear; ....34 Trav 6

HUNG Hung round their bowers, and
fondly look'd their last, ...366 DVil 35
Or why those harps on yonder
willows hung? ....I:80 Capt 116

HUNGER E'en now, perhaps, by cold
and hunger led, ...339 DVil 34
Vida, 19

HUNGRY Let not the hungry Bavius'
angry stroke ....1 GRos 51

HUNTED As panting flies the
hunted hind, ...III:39 Capt 124

HUNTER'S That stop the hunt-
er's way: ....III:42 Capt 124

HUNTSMAN He cast off his friends,
as a huntsman his pack, ...107 Rtal 90

HUNTSMEN Near, and more near, the
hounds and huntsmen drew. ....38 epLL 102

HURRIES Vida, 268

HURRY Vida, 486

HURRYING Vida, 32

HURT Such dainties to them, their
health it might hurt, ...33 HofV 96
Can whips or tortures hurt the
mind ....I:97 Capt 117

HUSBAND$_1$ Whilst her fond husband
strove to lend relief ....383 DVil 36
And gain'd a husband without aid
from dress, ...2 eSSC$_3$ 85

HUSBAND$_2$ To husband out life's
taper at the close, ...87 DVil 26
My anxious day to husband near
the close, ...v87 DVil 182

HUSH 'For shame, fond youth,
thy sorrows hush, ...81 Ed&A 62
But hush, my sons, our tyrant
lords are near; ....I:51 Capt 115
But hush! see, foremost of the
captive choir, ...II:63 Capt 120

HUSHED Ev'ry passion hush'd to
rest, ...37,45 Thrn 75

HUT Though poor the peasant's hut,
his feasts though small, ...177 Trav 11

HYDASPES And brighter streams
than fam'd Hydaspes glide. ....320 Trav 15

I See also I'D, I'LL, I'M, I'VE
Trav, 7, 28, 32, 59, 240, 243, 328,
361, 362, 370, 383, 392, 425; DVil,
7, 9, 15, 77, v(81), 85, 89, 92,
95, 115, 198, 397, 398; pLab, 8,
13, 15; Gift, 3, 6, 12; LogR, 10;
MBlz, 17; DRtH, 17; GCRL, 1, 3, 4;
TrSA, 2; NSim, 1, v1, 5, 7, 13;
Ed&A, 5, 8, 16, 22, 24, 26, v125,

v127, 129, v130, 132, v138, v142, 144; eGNM, 13, 15, 18; eSis, 10, 27, 31, 41, 42; pZob, 17, 23, 24; Thrn, 77, 194, 195, 220, 243; "LSm, 3; eSSC$_3$, 3, 4, 12; Rtal, 13, 22, 26, 51, 84, 88, 130, 171, 172, 173; "Amw, 1, 5; HofV, 5, 7, 13, 17, 19, 20, 21, 23, 25, 28, 35, 40, 41, 42, 44, 46, 48, 51, 56, 61, 63, 66, 71, 86, 87, 92, 93, v95, 96, v96, 97, 102, 116; ClRp, 4, 5, 6; epEP, 4; epLL, 5, 17, 18, 19, 26, 34; eSSC$_1$, 3, 6, 10, 13, 15, 17, 27, 28, 39, 50, 54, 58, 59; eSSC$_2$, 6, 7, 28; Capt, I:91, II:30, 42; Invt, 1, 5, 6, 7, 20, 21, 33; LetB, 5, 7, 9, 10, 13, 14, 16, 18, 19, 21, 23, 28, 31, 33, 35, 39, 49, 52, 57, 62, 65; Vida, 3, 7, 9, 572

I'D pZob, 38; HofV, 50; epLL, 2; eSSC$_1$, 54

IDLE A sleek and idle race is all their care. ....176 Thrn 80

IDLY Thus idly busy rolls their world away: ....256 Trav 13
When idly first, ambitious of the town, ...335 DVil 34
That idly waiting flaps with ev'ry gale, ...400 DVil 36
Vida, 161

IDOL- Ourselves alone from idol-worship free? ....I:34 Capt 114

IDRA'S On Idra's cliffs as Arno's shelvy side; ....84 Trav 8

IGNORANCE But calm, and bred in ignorance and toil, ...183 Trav 11
And his best riches, ignorance of wealth. ....62 DVil 25

I'LL Gift, 12, 13, 17, 19, 20; Ed&A, 139, 142, v142; eSis, 44; pZob, 28; Thrn, 199, 201, 203, 223, 241, 242, 248; "LSm, 12, 16; HofV, v53, 73, 104; epLL, 19; eSSC$_1$, 41; Capt, I:74, 76; LetB, 42; Vida, 570

ILL$_1$ Its former strength was but plethoric ill. ....144 Trav 10
To want, to toil, and every ill consign'd, ...I:86 Capt 117
Every ill presaging, ...II:21 Capt 119

ILL$_2$ Ill fares the land, to hast'ning ills a prey, ...51 DVil 25
How ill exchang'd are things like these for thee! ....386 DVil 36
Logicians have but ill defin'd ......1 LogR 44
Yon ill foreboding cloud seems big with thunder. ....18 pZob 72

ILL- And still with ill-dissembled power ....v131 Ed&A 210
Here ill-condition'd oranges abound-- ....21 pZob 72
Like an ill-judging beauty, his colours he spread, ...99 Rtal 90
Those ill-becoming rags--that matted hair! ....III:34 Capt 123

ILLS And e'en those ills, that round his mansion rise, ...201 Trav 12
With all those ills superfluous treasure brings, ...302 Trav 15
But foster'd e'en by Freedom, ills annoy: ....338 Trav 16
Yet think not, thus when Freedom's ills I state, ...361 Trav 17
Ill fares the land, to hast'ning ills a prey, ...51 DVil 25

ILLUMINES The sun with his splendour illumines the skies, ...I:63 Capt 116

I'M NSim, 29; Rtal, 19; HofV, 46, 94; ClRp, 3; epLL, 36; eSSC$_1$, 19; LetB, 34

IMAGE But ever, for ever, her image shall last, ...247 Thrn 83
And cavill'd at his image in the flood. ....30 epLL 102

IMAGINARY Or e'en imaginary worth obtains, ...260 Trav 13

IMAGINATION Imagination fondly stoops to trace ....225 DVil 30

IMAGINED True to imagin'd right, above control, ...332 Trav 16

IMITATES Like man he imitates each fashion, ...43 LogR 45

IMITATORS He in his turn finds imitators; ....53 LogR 45
Ye tame imitators, ye servile herd, come, ...165 Rtal 93

IMMATURELY Vida, 260

IMMEASURABLY Where wilds immeasurably spread, ...7 Ed&A 59

IMMEDIATE Vida, 633

IMMENSE Vida, 71

IMMORTAL Begin, ye daughters of immortal verse; ....8 Tr 267

IMPAIR Yet, why impair thy bright perfection? ....5 Sonn 46
Could any accident impair? ....8 DTrn 52

IMPART Thus every good his native wilds impart, ...199 Trav 11
Pants for the vulgar praise which fools impart; ....274 Trav 14
Obscure it sinks, nor shall it more impart ....239 DVil 31
If gems, or gold, impart a joy, ...11 Gift 43
But nothing could a charm impart ...57 Ed&A 61

IMPARTS Are here displayed. Their much-lov'd wealth imparts ....303 Trav 15

IMPATIENCE Vida, 582

IMPATIENT Vida, 118

IMPELLED Impell'd, with steps unceasing, to pursue ....25 Trav 6

IMPELS Impels the native to repeated toil, ...298 Trav 15

IMPENDING Vida, 593

IMPERIAL Vida, 95, 478

IMPERIOUS Vida, 395

IMPETUOUS At last the impetuous sorrow fir'd his breast. ....212 Thrn 82
Vida, 516

IMPIOUS When impious folly rears her front on high? ....I:40 Capt 115

IMPLORED Since none implor'd relief in vain!-- ....15 DRtH 50

IMPLORING To spurn imploring famine from the gate; ....106 DVil 26

INSTINCT That instinct is a surer
guide ....15 LogR 44
INSTINCTS Chaste are their instincts,
faithful is their fire, ...1 Cati 94
INSULT Vida, 501
INSULTED Insulted, chain'd, and all
the world a foe, ...I:5 Capt 113
INSULTING Insulting repartee or
spleen. ....60 DTrn 54
Insulting slaves! if gentler
methods fail, ...I:93 Capt 117
INSULTS Vida, 656
IN'T While the owner ne'er knew
half the good that was in't; ....44 Rtal 88
INTENT$_1$ Vida, 584
INTENT$_2$ Intent on high designs, a
thoughtful band, ...329 Trav 16
Vida, 161, 493
INTERNAL Enfeebles all internal
strength of thought; ....270 Trav 14
INTERPOSES 'What I? dear Sir,'
the Doctor interposes; ....15 eGNM 68
INTERRUPT Vida, 186
INTERWEAVE Vida, 311
INTO And drags the struggling savage
into day. ....190 Trav 11
The toiling pleasure sickens into
pain; ....262 DVil 32
Our bard into the general spirit
enters, ...9 pZob 72
Vida, 502, 531, 564, 596
INTOLERABLE And fiercely shed in-
tolerable day; ....348 DVil 34
INTRUDE Need we intrude on hallow'd
ground, ...23 DTrn 52
'Whose feet unhallow'd thus in-
trude ....95 Ed&A 62
INTRUDER Hence, intruder, most
distressing, ...I:27 Capt 114
Hence, intruder! we'll pursue .II:53 Capt 120
INTRUDES Where half the convex
world intrudes between, ...342 DVil 34
INVADE Still first to fly where
sensual joys invade; ....408 DVil 36
INVECTIVE$_1$ Fraught with invective
they ne'er go ....33 LogR 45
INVECTIVE$_2$ Vida, 566
INVENTIVE Still to amuse us in-
ventive, ...62 eSSC$_1$ 106
INVEST But meteors glare, and
stormy glooms invest. ....174 Trav 11
INVITED Of old,when Scarron his
companions invited, ...1 Rtal 87
INVITES Invites each passing stranger
that can pay; ....2 DABd 48
INVITING Wine and beauty thus in-
viting, ...I:71 Capt 116
INWARDLY Round and round go the
cards, while I inwardly damn ....5 LetB 131
IONIAN Vida, 365
IRIS Say, cruel Iris, pretty rake, ..1 Gift 43
IRISH As in some Irish houses,
where things are so so, ...9 HofV 95
Ye brave Irish lads, hark away to
the crack, ...57 eSSC$_1$ 106
IRON Luke's iron crown, and
Damiens' bed of steel, ...436 Trav 19
Vida, 225
IRREGULARLY With daring aims ir-
regularly great; ....326 Trav 16
ISLINGTON In Islington there was
a man, ...5 MDog 65
ISSUED Vida, 349
ITALIANS Vida, 667
ITALY Bright as the summer, Italy
extends; ....106 Trav 8
The sons of Italy were surely
blest. ....112 Trav 9
Vida, 12
IT'S But, my Lord, it's no bounce:
I protest in my turn, ...17 HofV 95
It's a truth--and your Lordship may
ask Mr. Byrne. ....18 HofV 95
It's a truth--and your Lordship **may**
ask Mr. Burn. ....v18 HofV 238
It's like sending them ruffles,
when wanting a shirt. ....34 HofV 96
Now, my Lord, as for tripe, it's
my utter aversion, ...85 HofV 98
To be plain, my good Lord, it's
but labour misplac'd ....117 HofV 99
At least, it's your temper, as
very well known, ...121 HofV 99
At least, it's your temper, 'tis
very well known, ...v121 HofV 242
ITSELF And the weak soul, within
itself unblest, ...271 Trav 14
E'en liberty itself is barter'd
here. ....306 Trav 15
Him I obey, whom heaven itself
obeys, ...13 pLab 41
This world itself, if thou art
here, ...117 Thrn 78
And slander itself must allow him
good **nature**: ....126 Rtal 91
I'VE eGNM, 17; eSis, 11; pZob, 19;
HofV, 94; eSSC$_1$, 14; Invt, 29
IVORY Vida, 613

JACK Jack Book-worm led a college
life; ....2 DTrn 52
Or Jack had wanted eyes to gaze. ...16 DTrn 52
Jack found his goddess made of
clay; ....34 DTrn 53
Jack suck'd his pipe, and often
broke ....57 DTrn 54
The rest of life with anxious
Jack, ...92 DTrn 55
Jack soon was dazzl'd to behold ....95 DTrn 55
Jack finds his wife a perfect
beauty. ....104 DTrn 55
JAPAN Each case, however bad, he'll
new japan; ....6 GRos 51
JARRING We both agree, like friends,
to end our jarring? ....66 eSSC$_1$ 106
JARVIE With Sawney, and Jarvie,
and Jockey. ....46 eSSC$_1$ 105
JAV'LIN Vida, 211
JEALOUS Vida, 326, 398
JESSAMY And the Jessamy Bride, ...14 Invt 128
JEST The modern fair one's jest: ...78 Ed&A 61
The haughty fair one's jest: ....v78 Ed&A 209
Now breaking a jest, and now
breaking a limb; ....54 Rtal 88

Or ever thought that jumping was
a jest. ....6 epLL 101
JESTS Laugh at the jests or pranks
that never fail, ...19 Trav 6
JET Vida, 42
JEW The one is a Scotchman, the
other a Jew, ...75 HofV 97
'The tripe,' quoth the Jew, with
his chocolate cheek, ...95 HofV 98
'Your Tripe!' quoth the Jew, 'if
the truth I may speak, ...v95 HofV 242
There's a pasty'--'A pasty!' re-
peated the Jew, ...101 HofV 98
JEWEL A bill, a jewel, watch, or
toy, ...9 Gift 43
JOB Nor undertake a dirty job, ...31 LogR 45
JOCKEY With Sandy, and Sawney,
and Jockey, ...45 eSSC$_1$ 105
With Sawney, and Jarvie, and
Jockey. ....46 eSSC$_1$ 105
Ye jockey tribe, whose stock of
words are few, ...49 eSSC$_1$ 106
JOHN John Trott was desired by
two witty peers ....1 ClRp 100
'An't please you,' quoth John, 'I'm
not given to letters, ...3 ClRp 100
JOHNSON We'll have Johnson, and
Burke; all the wits will be
there; ....49 HofV 96
Yet Johnson, and Burke, and a good
venison pasty, ...62 HofV 97
With tidings that Johnson and Burke
would not come; ....70 HofV 97
JOIN These sadly join beside the
murmuring deep, ...159 Thrn 80
Dismiss your griefs, and join our
warbling choir, ...I:83 Capt 117
Or join with sounds profane its
sacred mirth! ....I:92 Capt 117
Vida, 116, 329
JOINED But when to pomp and
power are join'd ....12 Thrn 74
Vida, 400
JOKE At all his jokes, for many a
joke had he; ....202 DVil 30
He drank his glass and crack'd
his joke, ...5 DTrn 52
Who relish'd a joke, and rejoic'd
in a pun; ....150 Rtal 92
JOKES At all his jokes, for many
a joke had he; ....202 DVil 30
Who copied his squibs, and re-
echoed his jokes; ....164 Rtal 93
JOLLY Here's the Three Jolly
Pigeons for ever. ....22 "LSm 84
Here's a health to the Three Jolly
Pigeons. ....26 "LSm 84
JORDAN Ye plains where Jordan rolls
its glassy tide, ...I:18 Capt 114
JORUM Then come, put the jorum
about, ...19 "LSm 84
JOURNEYED When they have journeyed
through a world of cares, ...88 Thrn 77
JOVE With fond complaint addressed
the listening Jove, ...10 MrsX 49
Then first, at last even Jove was
taken in, ...13 MrsX 49
Vida, 15, 168, 180, 306, 420, 658
JOY To fill the languid pause with
finer joy; ....218 Trav 12
Glides the smooth current of
domestic joy. ....434 Trav 19
The heart distrusting asks, if
this be joy. ....264 DVil 32
To see each joy the sons of
pleasure know ....v313 DVil 189
Sure these denote one universal
joy! ....324 DVil 34
How do thy potions, with insidious
joy ....387 DVil 36
If gems, or gold, impart a joy, ...11 Gift 43
'Twas joy, and endless blisses
all around, ...11 MrsX 49
The joy that dimples, and the woe
that weeps. ....10 epLL 101
And our monarch partakes in the
joy. ....I:60 Capt 115
But whence, when joy should
brighten o'er the land, ...I:77 Capt 116
Why this delay? at length for
joy prepare; ....II:41 Capt 119
Vida, 17, 547, 564, 605
The shouting army cry'd with joy
extreme, ...1 Tr 267
JOY- And saw thee fall with joy-
pronouncing eyes: ....10 Queb 46
JOYFUL Vida, 485
JOYS But not their joys alone thus
coarsely flow: ....227 Trav 12
Spontaneous joys, where Nature has
its play, ...255 DVil 31
The rich man's joys increase, the
poor's decay, ...266 DVil 32
To see those joys the sons of
pleasure know ....313 DVil 33
Still first to fly where sensual
joys invade; ....408 DVil 36
Amidst the clamour of exulting
joys, ...1 Queb 46
'Alas! the joys that fortune
brings ....69 Ed&A 61
To former joys recurring ever, ..I:25 Capt 114
Leave all other joys for me. ....I:67 Capt 116
Each to different joys excit-
ing, ...I:72 Capt 116
JUDAH Ye sons of Judah, why the
lute unstrung? ....I:79 Capt 116
JUDAH'S This sullen gloom in
Judah's captive band? ....I:78 Capt 116
The last remains of Judah's
royal race: ....III:20 Capt 123
JUDGE$_1$ Each wanton judge new
penal statutes draw, ...385 Trav 18
But the judge bids them, angrily,
take off their hat. ....46 LetB 133
JUDGE$_2$ 'Tis yours to judge, how
wide the limits stand ....267 DVil 32
The king himself shall judge,
and fix their doom. ....II:84 Capt 121
JUDGED When they judg'd without
skill he was still hard of
hearing: ....144 Rtal 92
JUDGES No judges, fiddlers,
dancing-masters, ...35 LogR 45

That modern judges seldom enter
here. ....18 eSSC$_1$ 104
-JUDGING Like an ill-judging beauty,
his colours he spread, ...99 Rtal 90
Ye candid-judging few, hold up your
hands. ....16 eSSC$_1$ 104
JUMPING Or ever thought that jumping
was a jest. ....6 epLL 101
JUST$_1$ Serve her as she hath served
the just! ....II:81 Capt 121
Serve them as they have serv'd the
just, ...III:57 Capt 124
JUST$_2$ For just experience tells, in
every soil, ...371 Trav 17
A just comparison,--proceed. ....22 NSim 56
JUST$_3$ Just gave what life requir'd,
but gave no more: ....60 DVil 25
The playful children just let loose
from school; ....120 DVil 27
And, just as humour rose or fell, ...41 DTrn 53
The door just opening with a latch, v43 Ed&A 208
Bless'd spirit thou, whose fame,
just born to bloom ....18 Thrn 74
Our Dean shall be venison, just fresh
from the plains; ....5 Rtal 87
To paint it, or eat it, just as he
lik'd best. ....22 HofV 95
(A chair-lumber'd closet just twelve
feet by nine:) ....68 HofV 97
See yonder tower just nodding to the
fall: ....III:48 Capt 124
Vida, 280, 362, 444
JUSTICE Fear, pity, justice,
indignation start, ...389 Trav 18
No more! Too long has justice been
delay'd, ...II:7 Capt 118
What justice, when both to the Old
Bailey brought! ....41 LetB 133
'But where is your justice? their
cases are hard.' ....61 LetB 133
'What signifies justice? I want
the reward. ....62 LetB 133
JUSTLY I'm sure it may be justly
said, ...29 NSim 57
Of French friseurs, and nosegays,
justly vain, ...32 eSSC$_1$ 105

KAUFFMANN And Kauffmann beside, ...13 Invt 128
KEEN Breasts the keen air, and carols
as he goes; ....186 Trav 11
The morn was cold, he views with
keen desire ....15 DABd 48
These in their turn, with appetites
as keen, ...19 eSis 70
Vida, 246, 653
KEEP And keep the flame from wasting
by repose. ....88 DVil 26
And keep life's flame from wasting
by repose. ....v88 DVil 182
An equal semblance still to keep, ...49 NSim 57
Now wrangling and grumbling to keep
up the ball, ...55 Rtal 89
'I don't care if I keep a corner
for't too.' ....102 HofV 98
'Though splitting, I'll still keep a
corner for thot.' ....104 HofV 98
'We'll all keep a corner,' the lady
cried out; ....105 HofV 98
'We'll all keep a corner,' was
echoed about. ....106 HofV 98
While these a constant revel keep,II:51 Capt 120
Vida, 601, 656
KEEPEST That found'st me poor at
first, and keep'st me so; ....414 DVil 37
KEEPING 'Tis best, however, keeping
at a distance. ....29 pZob 73
He's keeping a corner for something
that's nice: ....100 HofV 98
KEEPS Keeps man from man, and breaks
the social tie; ....340 Trav 16
Each grudging master keeps the
labourer bare-- ....175 Thrn 80
Vida, 508
KELLYS Ye Kenricks, ye Kellys, and
Woodfalls so grave, ...115 Rtal 91
And Beaumonts and Bens be his Kellys
above. ....124 Rtal 91
KENNEL That caused his putrid kennel
to o'erflow. ....9 GRos 51
KENRICKS Our Dodds shall be pious,
our Kenricks shall lecture; ....86 Rtal 90
Ye Kenricks, ye Kellys, and Woodfalls
so grave, ...115 Rtal 91
KENT- For Kent-street well may say, 26 MBlz 47
KEPT While broken tea-cups, wisely
kept for show, ...235 DVil 31
Fond to be seen, she kept a bevy ....53 DTrn 53
My life on't, this had kept her play
from sinking; ....7 eSis 70
KEW The towers of Kew, ...161 Thrn 80
KICK Let boys play tricks, and kick
the straw; not I: ....13 eGNM 68
KILL And tries to kill, ere she's
got power to cure. ....24 eSis 70
'Till having lost in age the power
to kill, ...30 eSSC$_3$ 86
KILLING Yet, why this killing soft
dejection? ....v5 Sonn 196
KIND$_1$ I see the lords of human kind
pass by, ...328 Trav 16
As rational, the human kind; ....2 LogR 44
A likeness for the scribbling kind; ..2 NSim 56
The modern scribbling kind, who write 3 NSim 56
Denote him of the reptile kind; .....46 NSim 57
If dunces applauded, he paid them in
kind. ....114 Rtal 91
You've got an odd something--a kind
of discerning-- ....119 HofV 99
KIND$_2$ Nature, a mother kind alike
to all, ...81 Trav 8
Yet he was kind; or if severe in
aught, ...205 DVil 30
And kind connubial tenderness, are
there; ....404 DVil 36
And always found her kind; ....6 MBlz 47
A kind and gentle heart he had, ...9 MDog 65
'Tis Nature's kind retreat, that's
always open ....97 Thrn 77
Are pleas'd to be kind--but I hate
ostentation.' ....44 HofV 96
KINDER To sport and flutter in a kinder
sky. ....238 Trav 13
To kinder skies, where gentler
manners reign, ...239 Trav 13

These, far departing, seek a
kinder shore, ...73 DVil 25
KINDLY The broken soldier, kindly
bade to stay, ...155 DVil 28
Kindly came in beauty's aid; ......234 Thrn 82
KINDRED$_1$ Claim'd kindred there, and
had his claims allow'd; ....154 DVil 28
KINDRED$_2$ These here disporting own
the kindred soil, ...119 Trav 9
Her soul was fitting to its kindred
skies: ....121 Thrn 78
His well acquainted tints, and
kindred hues. ....6 Cati 94
KING The king himself has follow'd
her,-- ....19 MBlz 47
How great a king of terrors I! .....77 Thrn 76
The king himself shall judge, and
fix their doom. ....II:84 Capt 121
Vida, 56, 73, 91, 216, 234, 236, 243, 339, 378,
492, 498, 517, 527, 533, 536, 586, 588, 593,
600, 615, 622, 640, 648, 652
KINGDOM Your wealth, your pride,
your kingdom, are no more. ....III:72 Capt 125
KINGDOMS Kingdoms, by thee, to
sickly greatness grown, ...389 DVil 36
KING'S$_1$ The king's commands must
fully be obey'd; ....II:8 Capt 118
KING'S$_2$ Vida, 146
KINGS The pomp of kings, the
shepherd's humbler pride. ....36 Trav 6
Where kings have toil'd, and poets
wrote for fame, ...358 Trav 17
And scholars, soldiers, kings,
unhonour'd die. ....360 Trav 17
I mean to flatter kings, or court
the great; ....362 Trav 17
Though tyrant kings, or tyrant laws
restrain, ...428 Trav 19
That part which laws or kings can
cause or cure. ....430 Trav 19
The incense given to kings, ...7 Thrn 74
Ye statesmen, warriors, poets, kings;81 Thrn 77
Vida, 45, 85, 465
KISS Shall kiss the cup to pass it
to the rest. ....250 DVil 31
KISSED And kiss'd her thoughtless
babes with many a tear, ...381 DVil 36
KITTEN Its tricks the kitten tries; 54 Ed&A 61
KITTY And my wife, little Kitty,
is famous for crust. ....54 HofV 97
Though clogg'd with a coxcomb, and
Kitty his wife. ....64 HofV 97
KNEEL And see how they kneel! Is
your heart made of stone?' ....64 LetB 134
KNEW I knew him well, and every truant
knew; ....198 DVil 29
The village all declar'd how much
he knew; ....207 DVil 30
That one small head could carry all
he knew. ....216 DVil 30
Who ever knew an honest brute ......19 LogR 44
While the owner ne'er knew half
the good that was in't; ....44 Rtal 88
For he knew when he pleas'd he could
whistle them back. ....108 Rtal 90
'For I knew it,' he cried, 'both
eternally fail, ...71 HofV 97
Vida, 650

They knew and own'd the monarch
of the main: ....3 Tr 267
KNIGHT Vida, 227, 245, 404, 549, 609
KNIGHTS Vida, 48, 67, 221, 353, 385
KNOW Who can direct, when all pretend
to know? ....64 Trav 7
To see those joys the sons of
pleasure know ....313 DVil 33
To see each joy the sons of pleasure
know ....v313 DVil 189
Nor know who's in or out at court; ..26 LogR 44
Yet they shall know thou conquerest,
though dead-- ....11 Queb 46
'Twas one, both, three of them,
they know not whether; ....2 GCRL 51
I think they love venison--I know
they love beef; ....28 HofV 96
Nor dare I pretend to know more
than my betters; ....4 ClRp 100
Excuse me, Ma'am, I know the
etiquette. ....10 eSSC$_1$ 104
We fear the Lord, and know no other
fear. ....I:96 Capt 117
Yet know, ye slaves, that still
remain behind ....II:91 Capt 122
Your worships must know ....23 Invt 128
Vida, 11
KNOWING Her face is grown a knowing
phiz; ....68 DTrn 54
KNOWN To men remote from power but
rarely known, ...437 Trav 19
His house was known to all the
vagrant train, ...149 DVil 28
Are known to honest quadrupeds; .....37 LogR 45
Thus as her faults each day were
known, ...61 DTrn 54
Were to my Mistress known; ....196 Thrn 81
At least, it's your temper, as very
well known, ...121 HofV 99
At least, it's your temper, 'tis
very well known, ...v121 HofV 242
Vida, 59, 179
KNOWS And sensual bliss is all
the nation knows. ....124 Trav 9
He knows not how, but so it is, ...67 DTrn 54
Who knows each art of coaxing up
the town, ...5 eGNM 68

LABOUR At night returning, every
labour sped, ...191 Trav 11
And all the village train, from
labour free, ...17 DVil 23
For him light labour spread her
wholesome store, ...59 DVil 25
A youth of labour with an age of
ease; ....100 DVil 26
To be plain, my good Lord, it's
but labour misplac'd ....117 HofV 99
Vida, 635
LABOURED As ocean sweeps the
labour'd mole away; ....428 DVil 37
LABOURER Each grudging master keeps
the labourer bare-- ....175 Thrn 80
LABOURING Where health and plenty
cheer'd the labouring swain, ...2 DVil 23
The labouring ship, and hear the
tempest roar, ...67 Thrn 76

LABOUR'S Still grants her bliss
at Labour's earnest call; ....82 Trav 8
LACE And trims her robes of frieze
with copper lace; ....276 Trav 14
Arose from powder, shreds, or lace; 36 DTrn 53
On sentimental Queens and Lords
in lace? ....36 $eSSC_2$ 109
And the Captain in lace, ...18 Invt 128
LACQUEYS At court the porters,
lacqueys, waiters, ...54 LogR 45
LADEN With Scythian stores, and
trinkets deeply laden, ...11 pZob 72
LADIES Still to gallant and dangle
with the ladies;-- ....20 $eSSC_1$ 104
When the ladies are calling, to
blush and hang back; ....60 $eSSC_1$ 106
'Well done!' cry the ladies; 'Ah,
Doctor, that's good! ....25 LetB 132
Now, ladies, I ask, if law-matters
you're skill'd in, ...35 LetB 132
LADS Ye brave Irish lads, hark away
to the crack, ...57 $eSSC_1$ 106
LADY 'We'll all keep a corner,'
the lady cried out; ....105 HofV 98
I ask for advice from the lady that's
next: ....28 LetB 132
'I advise,' cries the lady, 'to
try it, I own.-- ....31 LetB 132
LAID Beside the bed where parting
life was laid, ...171 DVil 29
'Young man,' cries one--a bard laid
up in clover-- ....11 eGNM 68
Our ship's well stor'd;--in yonder
creek we've laid her; ....31 pZob 73
Here Reynolds is laid, and, to tell
you my mind, ...137 Rtal 91
LAKE Space for his lake, his park's
extended bounds, ...277 DVil 32
LAKES Lakes, forests, cities,
plains, extending wide, ...35 Trav 6
Ye lakes, whose vessels catch the
busy gale, ...47 Trav 6
Dull as their lakes that slumber
in the storm. ....312 Trav 15
LAMB You'll find his lionship a
very lamb. ....32 eSis 71
That Ridge is anchovy, and Reynolds
is lamb; ....14 Rtal 87
LAMENT Lament for Madam Blaize, ...2 MBlz 47
Let us lament in sorrow sore, ...25 MBlz 47
LAMP- And brave prince William
show'd his lamp-black face: ....14 DABd 48
And Prussia's monarch shew'd his
lamp-black face ....v14 DABd 200
LANCE Vida, 221
LAND To winnow fragrance round the
smiling land. ....122 Trav 9
Gay sprightly land of mirth and
social ease, ...241 Trav 13
It shifts in splendid traffic round
the land: ....262 Trav 14
Where the broad ocean leans against
the land, ...284 Trav 14
A land of tyrants, and a den of
slaves, ...309 Trav 15
The land of scholars, and the nurse
of arms, ...356 Trav 17
Far, far away, thy children leave
the land. ....50 DVil 24
Ill fares the land, to hast'ning
ills a prey, ...51 DVil 25
Usurp the land and dispossess the
swain; ....64 DVil 25
Between a splendid and a happy land.268 DVil 32
While thus the land adorn'd for
pleasure, all ....285 DVil 32
Thus fares the land, by luxury
betray'd, ...295 DVil 33
While scourg'd by famine from the
smiling land, ...299 DVil 33
I see the rural virtues leave the
land: ....398 DVil 36
Oh, let me fly a land that spurns
the brave, ...221 Thrn 82
But whence, when joy should brighten
o'er the land, ...I:77 Capt 116
Ere I forget the land that gave me
birth, ...I:91 Capt 117
Till every tongue in every land II:95 Capt 122
Vida, 519
LANDLORD If our landlord supplies
us with beef, and with fish, ...3 Rtal 87
$LANDS_1$ Whence from such lands each
pleasing science flies, ...215 Trav 12
Lands he could measure, terms and
tides presage, ...209 DVil 30
$LANDS_2$ Yet ere he lands he 'as
ordered me before, ...13 pZob 72
LANDSCAPE Mingling the ravag'd
landscape with the skies. ....358 DVil 35
LANE To-night I head our troops at
Warwick Lane: ....18 eGNM 68
-LANE Regale the drabs and bloods
of Drury-lane; ....4 DABd 48
LANGUID To fill the languid pause
with finer joy; ....218 Trav 12
LAP But winter ling'ring chills the
lap of May; ....172 Trav 11
LAPWING Amidst thy desert walks the
lapwing flies, ...45 DVil 24
LARGE At every draught more large and
large they grow, ...391 DVil 36
LARGER And, wond'ring man could
want the larger pile, ...163 Trav 10
There Mangroves spread, and larger
than I've seen 'em-- ....19 pZob 72
LARGEST And she, whose party's
largest, shall proceed. ....12 $eSSC_1$ 104
LASH Vida, 367
$LAST_1$ Now sinks at last, or feebly
mans the soul; ....156 Trav 10
She leaves at last, or feebly mans
the soul; ....v156 Trav 170
They sink at last, or feebly man the
soul; ....v156 Trav 171
Here to return--and die at home
at last. ....96 DVil 26
And, all his prospects bright'ning
to the last, ...111 DVil 27
Hung round their bowers, and fondly
look'd their last, ...366 DVil 35
Then first, at last even Jove was
taken in, ...13 MrsX 49
At last the impetuous sorrow fir'd

his breast. ....212 Thrn 82
Who'd not be a glutton, and stick
to the last? ....18 Rtal 87
He grew lazy at last, and drew from
himself? ....78 Rtal 89
And so bold, and so bold, I'm at
last a bold beggar. ....34 LetB 132
This moves:--so at last I agree to
relent, ...65 LetB 134
Vida, 71, 382, 665
LAST$_2$ And his last falt'ring accents
whisper'd praise. ....176 DVil 29
Her last disorder mortal. ....24 MBlz 47
The Fifth and Last Act still remains
for me. ....33 eSSC$_3$ 86
And the last sigh that rends thy
heart, ...v159 Ed&A 211
To the last moment of his breath II:33 Capt 119
The last remains of Judah's
royal race: ....III:20 Capt 123
Vida, 558, 621
LAST$_3$ Then all their trophies
last; and flattery turns to fame. ..17 Thrn 74
I'll praise her while my life shall
last, ...201 Thrn 81
A life that cannot last me long. 202 Thrn 81
But ever, for ever, her image shall
last, ...247 Thrn 83
And our fix'd empire shall for
ever last; ....III:2 Capt 122
LASTING Lovely, lasting Peace
below, ...112 Thrn 78
Lovely, lasting Peace, appear; ....116 Thrn 78
More lasting rapture from his works
shall rise, ...9 epTP 100
LASTLY Lastly, vouchsafe t' observe
his hand, ...31 NSim 57
LATCH The wicket, opening with a
latch, ...43 Ed&A 60
The door just opening with a latch,v43 Ed&A 208
LATE$_1$ And late the nation found,
with fruitless skill, ...143 Trav 10
And finds too late that men betray, 2 "wlw 67
Too late in life for me to ask, ...191 Thrn 81
What! no return? I find too late,
I fear, ...17 eSSC$_1$ 104
Save us, O Lord! to thee, though
late, we pray, ...III:63 Capt 125
Too late you seek that power
unsought before, ...III:71 Capt 125
For sending so late ....37 Invt 129
LATE$_2$ Agreed. Agreed. And now
with late repentance, ...69 eSSC$_1$ 107
LATELY Vida, 445
LATEST I still had hopes my latest
hours to crown, ...85 DVil 26
Vida, 627
LATTER But on he moves to meet his
latter end, ...107 DVil 26
LAUDERS New Lauders and Bowers the
Tweed shall cross over, ...89 Rtal 90
LAUGH$_1$ And the loud laugh that spoke
the vacant mind; ....122 DVil 27
LAUGH$_2$ Laugh at the jests or pranks
that never fail, ...19 Trav 6
LAUGHED Full well they laugh'd, with
counterfeited glee, ...201 DVil 30

Vida, 322, 657
LAUGHING Now teasing and vexing,
yet laughing at all! ....56 Rtal 89
LAUGHTER While secret laughter
titter'd round the place; ....28 DVil 24
LAUREL Vida, 637
LAURELLED Shall crowd from Crecy's
laurell'd field, ...226 Thrn 82
LAW Fictitious bonds, the bonds of
wealth and law, ...351 Trav 17
Laws grind the poor, and rich men
rule the law; ....386 Trav 18
At law his neighbour prosecute, ...20 LogR 44
May well be call'd picking of
pockets in law; ....38 LetB 133
Vida, 301, 330
LAW- Now, ladies, I ask, if law-
matters you're skill'd in, ...35 LetB 132
LAWN Sweet smiling village, loveliest
of the lawn, ...35 DVil 24
Along the lawn, where scatter'd
hamlets rose, ...65 DVil 25
From lawn to woodland stray; ..v(162) Ed&A 211
The wavy lawn, the sloping
green-- ....147 Thrn 79
LAWNS Where lawns extend that
scorn Arcadian pride, ...319 Trav 15
LAWS Laws grind the poor, and
rich men rule the law; ....386 Trav 18
Though tyrant kings, or tyrant
laws restrain, ...428 Trav 19
That part which laws or kings
can cause or cure. ....430 Trav 19
The English laws forbid to punish
lunatics. ....42 eSSC$_2$ 109
Vida, 84, 104, 162
LAY$_1$ What heart but feels his
sweetly-moral lay, ...3 epTP 100
LAY$_2$ Is but to lay proportion'd
loads on each. ....374 Trav 17
Amidst these humble bowers to lay
me down; ....86 DVil 26
The stress of all my proofs on him
I lay, ...13 NSim 56
I'll lay me down and die; ....142 Ed&A 64
And lay my body where my limbs
were lost.' ....224 Thrn 82
Grasp the red bolt, and lay the
guilty low? ....III:36 Capt 123
I lay down my stake, apparently
cool, ...7 LetB 131
LAY$_3$ That dimly show'd the state in
which he lay; ....8 DABd 48
That feebly shew'd the state in
which he lay. ....v8 DABd 200
The lonely mansion lay; ....38 Ed&A 60
The modest mansion lay; ....v38 Ed&A 208
And stretch me where he lay. ......140 Ed&A 64
Vida, 383
LAYS$_1$ For you, bright fair, the
nine address their lays, ...1 MrsX 49
He caroll'd lays of love; ....118 Ed&A 63
LAYS$_2$ Near her betrayer's door she
lays her head, ...332 DVil 34
LAZY Or by the lazy Scheldt, or
wandering Po; ....2 Trav 5
He grew lazy at last, and drew from

himself? ....78 Rtal 89
LEAD Lead stern depopulation in her
train, ...402 Trav 18
Vida, 85, 189
LEADERS Vida, 387
LEADS My fortune leads to traverse
realms alone, ...29 Trav 6
The mournful peasant leads his
humble band; ....300 DVil 33
No single brute his fellow leads. ..38 LogR 45
That leads to truth through
pleasure's flowery way! ....4 epTP 100
And this way leads his formidable
band. ....III:86 Capt 126
Vida, 269, 376
LEAN₁ Relax his pond'rous strength,
and lean to hear; ....246 DVil 31
LEAN₂ The fat was so white, and the
lean was so ruddy. ....4 HofV 95
LEANED And e'en his failings lean'd
to Virtue's side; ....164 DVil 28
LEANS Leans for all pleasure on
another's breast. ....272 Trav 14
Where the broad ocean leans against
the land, ...284 Trav 14
LEAPED Vida, 547, 592
LEAPS Vida, 130
LEARN And learn the luxury of doing
good. ....22 Trav 6
If hills could learn to weep. ......12 DRtH 50
I learn to pity them. ....24 Ed&A 59
And learn to bless your own. ..III:26 Capt 123
Vida, 83, 568
LEARNED At her command the palace
learn'd to rise, ...135 Trav 9
Far other aims his heart had
learned to prize, ...147 DVil 28
Pleas'd with his guests, the good
man learn'd to glow, ...159 DVil 28
Well had the boding tremblers
learn'd to trace ....199 DVil 29
While words of learned length
and thund'ring sound ....213 DVil 30
For thus retain'd, as learned
counsel can, ...5 GRos 51
-LEARNED Amidst the swains to
show my book-learn'd skill, ...90 DVil 26
LEARNING The love he bore to learning was in fault; ....206 DVil 30
With wit that's flighty, learning
light; ....20 NSim 56
With grammar, and nonsense, and
learning; ....2 "LSm 84
Though fraught with all learning,
yet straining his throat ....33 Rtal 88
A relish--a taste--sicken'd over
by learning; ....120 HofV 99
LEARNING'S In these bold times,
when Learning's sons explore ....1 pZob 72
LEARNS And learns to venerate him-
self as man. ....334 Trav 16
And, since 'tis hard to combat,
learns to fly! ....102 DVil 26
She learns good-nature every day; .102 DTrn 55
LEAST₁ At least, in six weeks, I
could not find 'em out; ....26 Rtal 87
At least, it's your temper, as
very well known, ...121 HofV 99
At least, it's your temper, 'tis
very well known, ...v121 HofV 242
At least in many things, I think,
I see ....7 eSSC₂ 108
Twelve inches at least: 28 Invt 129
LEAST₂ Our Author's the least
likely to grow wiser; ....34 eSSC₂ 109
LEAVE In passive ease they leave
the world to chance. ....v(156) Trav 170
Leave reason, faith, and
conscience, all our own. ....438 Trav 19
Far, far away, thy children leave
the land. ....50 DVil 24
I see the rural virtues leave the
land: ....398 DVil 36
I'll leave it to all men of
sense, ...16 "LSm 84
What if we leave it to the House?
The House!--Agreed. Agreed. ..11 eSSC₁ 104
What if we leave the Epilogue
unspoken? ....68 eSSC₁ 106
Leave all other joys for me. ....I:67 Capt 116
Vida, 239, 457
LEAVES That opulence departed
leaves behind; ....132 Trav 9
She leaves at last, or feebly
mans the soul; ....v156 Trav 170
Swells from the vale, and mid-
way leaves the storm, ...190 DVil 29
That leaves our useful products
still the same. ....274 DVil 32
But leaves the wretch to weep? .....76 Ed&A 61
The parting surface leaves his
brazen axle dry. ....6 Tr 267
LEBANON Ye hills of Lebanon, with
cedars crown'd, ...I:19 Capt 114
LECTURE Our Dodds shall be pious,
our Kenricks shall lecture; ....86 Rtal 90
-LECTURES Could any curtain-lectures
bring ....49 DTrn 53
LED And haply too some pilgrim,
thither led, ...197 Trav 11
How often have I led thy sportive
choir, ...243 Trav 13
Have led their children through the
mirthful maze, ...252 Trav 13
Led up their sports beneath the
spreading tree; ....18 DVil 23
Allur'd to brighter worlds, and
led the way. ....170 DVil 28
E'en now, perhaps, by cold and
hunger led, ...339 DVil 34
Jack Book-worm led a college
life; ....2 DTrn 52
And strangers led astray. ....40 Ed&A 60
He led such a damnable life in this
world,-- ....3 epEP 100
Vida, 425, 495, 549, 573, 595
LEERING Then their friends all come
round me with cringing and leering, 53 LetB 133
LEERS Ogles and leers with
artificial skill, ...29 eSSC₃ 86
LEFT₁ She only left of all the
harmless train, ...135 DVil 27
She left her wheel and robes of
country brown. ....336 DVil 34

And left a lover's for a father's
arms. ....378 DVil 35
And left a lover's for her father's
arms. ....v378 DVil 190
What! no way left to shun th'
inglorious stage, ...1 pLab 41
Who left a pledge behind. ....8 MBlz 47
Left but the remnant of a face. .....80 DTrn 54
He left me to my pride; ....134 Ed&A 63
He left me to deplore; ....v134 Ed&A 210
How hast thou left mankind for heaven!20 Thrn 74
If he had any faults, he has left
us in doubt, ...25 Rtal 87
He has not left a better or wiser
behind: ....138 Rtal 91
Left alone to reflect, having emptied
my shelf, ...59 HofV 97
Vida, 464, 628, 632, 641, 652
LEFT$_2$ Vida, 58, 117, 135, 232, 283, 372, 496
LEFTWARD Vida, 212
LEGENDARY And, skill'd in legendary
lore, ...51 Ed&A 60
LEND Whilst her fond husband strove
to lend relief ....383 DVil 36
Shall lend my simile assistance. ...62 NSim 58
This is his first adventure; lend
him aid, ...33 pZob 73
To persuade Tommy Townshend to lend
him a vote; ....34 Rtal 88
Lend me your hands.--Oh! fatal
news to tell: ....35 eSSC$_1$ 105
LENGTH While words of learned
length and thund'ring sound ....213 DVil 30
Could Cupid's shaft at length
transfix ....9 DTrn 52
You'll find him pictur'd at full
length ....11 NSim 56
At length his silly head, so priz'd
before, ...43 epLL 102
Why this delay? at length for joy
prepare; ....II:41 Capt 119
Vida, 234, 257, 378, 653
LENGTHEN To lengthen a short tail, 31 Invt 129
LENGTHENING And drags at each remove
a lengthening chain. ....10 Trav 5
Seem length'ning as I go.' ....8 Ed&A 59
LENT When toil remitting lent its
turn to play, ...16 DVil 23
She freely lent to all the poor,-- ...7 MBlz 47
A window, patch'd with paper, lent
a ray, ...7 DABd 48
The window, patch'd with paper,
lent a ray, ...v7 DABd 200
His breath lent fragrance to the
gale, ...119 Ed&A 63
And lent him fancied charms! .....v128 Ed&A 210
And Heaven, that lent him genius,
was repaid. ....6 epTP 100
Their hands are only lent to the
Heinel. ....36 eSSC$_1$ 105
Vida, 491
LESS$_1$ Not less sincere, than civil: 18 Gift 43
Less dreadful struck me with dismay, 219 Thrn 82
I'll seek that less inhospitable
coast, ...223 Thrn 82
Then strew all around it (you can
do no less) ....169 Rtal 93
Less dreadful show ....II:22 Capt 119
LESS$_2$ Vida, 185
LESSEN Vida, 461
LESSONED Here lesson'd for a while,
and hence retreating, ...29 eSSC$_2$ 109
LEST Vida, 399, 539
LET Let school-taught pride dis-
semble all it can, ...41 Trav 6
But let us try these truths with
closer eyes, ...99 Trav 8
Here let me sit in sorrow for
mankind, ...102 Trav 8
Yet let them only share the praises
due, ...211 Trav 12
The playful children just let loose
from school; ....120 DVil 27
Yes! let the rich deride, the proud
disdain, ...251 DVil 31
Still let thy voice, prevailing over
time, ...421 DVil 37
My rivals give--and let 'em; ....10 Gift 43
But let them prove it if they can. ..4 LogR 44
Let us lament in sorrow sore, ...25 MBlz 47
Let not the hungry Bavius' angry
stroke ....1 GRos 51
But pitying his distress, let
virtue shine, ...3 GRos 51
And giving each your bounty, let
him dine; ....4 GRos 51
O!--But let exclamation cease, ...17 DTrn 52
Let it suffice, that each had charms;25 DTrn 52
But let us not proceed too furious, 9 NSim 56
For let folks only get a touch, ...37 NSim 57
'But let a maid thy pity share, ...97 Ed&A 62
Forgive, and let thy pious care ..v97 Ed&A 209
'Thus let me hold thee to my heart, 153 Ed&A 64
Let boys play tricks, and kick the
straw; not I: ....13 eGNM 68
Yet let that wisdom, urged by her
example, ...84 Thrn 77
Let us prize death as the best gift
of nature-- ....86 Thrn 77
Let us, let all the world agree, ..138 Thrn 79
Let all your echoes now deplore ...165 Thrn 80
Oh, let me fly a land that spurns
the brave, ...221 Thrn 82
Let school-masters puzzle their
brain, ...1 "LSm 84
Let them brag of their heathenish
gods, ...5 "LSm 84
And let us be merry and clever; ....20 "LSm 84
Let some cry up woodcock or
hare, ...23 "LSm 84
And let me say, for all your
resolution, ...5 eSSC$_3$ 85
Let each guest bring himself, and
he brings the best dish: ....4 Rtal 87
Here, waiter! more wine, let me sit
while I'm able, ...19 Rtal 87
Let me ponder, and tell what I think
of the dead. ....22 Rtal 87
But let us be candid, and speak
out our mind, ...113 Rtal 91
But hold--let me pause--Don't I
hear you pronounce ....13 HofV 95
There's my countryman H--gg--ns--
Oh! let him alone, ...29 HofV 96

world,-- ....3 epEP 100
I wish for life, and yield me to
    my fears. ....II:30 Capt 119
Like yours, his life began in
    pride, ...III:29 Capt 123
Vida, 345, 349, 395, 415, 472
The Wretch condemn'd with life
    to part, ...vII:33 Capt 250
-LIFE   No high-life scenes, no
    sentiment:--the creature ......39 eSSC₂ 109
LIFE'S   Through life's more cultur'd
    walks, and charm the way, ...236 Trav 13
To husband out life's taper at the
    close, ...87 DVil 26
And keep life's flame from wasting
    by repose. ....v88 DVil 182
O blest retirement, friend to
    life's decline, ...97 DVil 26
For ah! too partial to my life's
    decline, ...11 pLab 41
Vida, 175
LIFT   Lift the tall rampire's
    artificial pride. ....286 Trav 14
LIFTED   The lifted axe, the agonising
    wheel, ...435 Trav 19
LIFTS   And dear that hill which lifts
    him to the storms; ....204 Trav 12
As some tall cliff, that lifts its
    awful form, ...189 DVil 29
Near yonder thorn, that lifts its
    head on high, ...219 DVil 30
LIGHT₁   But soon a wonder came to
    light, ...29 MDog 66
Through rolling worlds, or fields
    of liquid light, ...107 Thrn 77
Hope, like the gleaming taper's
    light, ...II:37 Capt 119
Hope, like the glim'ring taper's
    light, ...vII:37 Capt 250
Vida, 626
LIGHT₂   For him light labour
    spread her wholesome store, ...59 DVil 25
With wit that's flighty, learning
    light; ....20 NSim 56
LIGHTLY   Lightly they frolic o'er
    the vacant mind, ...257 DVil 31
LIGHTNING   The honey-moon like
    lightning flew, ...29 DTrn 53
May rosined lightning blast me,
    if I do! ....18 epLL 101
Vida, 512
LIKE   That, like the circle bound-
    ing earth and skies, ...27 Trav 6
Like yon neglected shrub at random
    cast, ...103 Trav 8
By sports like these are all their
    cares beguil'd, ...153 Trav 10
At sports like these, while
    foreign arms advance, ...v(155) Trav 170
Their morals, like their
    pleasures, are but low; ....228 Trav 12
May sit, like falcons cow'ring on
    the nest; ....234 Trav 13
Like flaring tapers bright'ning
    as they waste; ....400 Trav 18
These were thy charms, sweet
    village; sports like these, ...31 DVil 24

How happy he who crowns in shades
    like these, ...99 DVil 26
How blest is he who crowns in
    shades like these, ...v99 DVil 183
Sure scenes like these no troubles
    e'er annoy! ....323 DVil 34
For seats like these beyond the
    western main; ....368 DVil 35
How ill exchang'd are things like
    these for thee! ....386 DVil 36
That he should be, like Cupid,
    blind, ...3 Byth 42
Like man he imitates each fashion, .43 LogR 45
The honey-moon like lightning
    flew, ...29 DTrn 53
Like colours o'er the morning
    skies, ...87 Ed&A 62
Like clouds that deck the morning
    skies, ...v87 Ed&A 209
Like some well-fashion'd arch thy
    patience stood, ...32 Thrn 75
Pain met thee like a friend that
    set thee free; ....34 Thrn 75
Her bounty, like the morning
    dew, ...178 Thrn 80
Like a tragedy queen he has dizen'd
    her out, ...67 Rtal 89
Or rather like tragedy giving a
    rout. ....68 Rtal 89
Yet, with talents like these, and
    an excellent heart, ...97 Rtal 90
Like an ill-judging beauty, his
    colours he spread, ...99 Rtal 90
Such dainties to them! It would
    look like a flirt, ...v33 HofV 239
It's like sending them ruffles,
    when wanting a shirt. ....34 HofV 96
Like sending 'em Ruffles when want-
    ing a Shirt. ....v34 HofV 239
Thus snatching his hat, he brush'd
    off like the wind, ...57 HofV 97
They('re) both of them merry and
    authors like you; ....76 HofV 97
Who dabble and write in the Papers--
    like you; ....v76 HofV 241
And your bacon I hate like a Turk
    or a Persian; ....86 HofV 98
So there I sat stuck, like a horse
    in a pound, ...87 HofV 98
Yet something vain, like one that
    shall be nameless, ...28 epLL 102
And at one bound he saves himself,--
    like me. ....46 epLL 102
To dress, and look like awkward
    Frenchmen here, ...34 eSSC₁ 105
We both agree, like friends, to
    end our jarring? ....66 eSSC₁ 106
Thou, like the world, th' opprest
    oppressing, ...vI:27 Capt 250
Like the sun, our great monarch
    all rapture supplies, ...I:61 Capt 116
For who like you can wake the
    sleeping lyre? ....I:84 Capt 117
Hope, like the gleaming taper's
    light, ...II:37 Capt 119
Hope, like the glim'ring taper's
    light, ...vII:37 Capt 250

merrily round. ....88 HofV 98
Pray a slice of your liver, though
may I be curs'd, ...93 HofV 98
LIVES With vernal lives that blossom
but to die; ....118 Trav 9
Such, through our lives, the event-
ful history-- ....32 eSSC$_3$ 86
Like his, your lives shall end. III:30 Capt 123
Vida, 387
LIVING No countryman living their
tricks to discover; ....90 Rtal 90
LO Lo! the small-pox, whose horrid
glare ....77 DTrn 54
Vida, 428
LOAD And purchas'd strength from
its increasing load. ....33 Thrn 75
LOADS Is but to lay proportion'd
loads on each. ....374 Trav 17
Proud swells the tide with loads of
freighted ore, ...269 DVil 32
LOATHE To make him loathe his
vegetable meal; ....182 Trav 11
Vida, 466
LOFTY The foe prevails, the lofty
walls recline-- ....III:53 Capt 124
LOGICIANS Logicians have but ill
defin'd ....1 LogR 44
LOIRE With tuneless pipe, beside the
murmuring Loire! ....244 Trav 13
LOITERED How often have I loiter'd
o'er thy green, ...7 DVil 23
LONE As some lone miser visiting his
store, ...51 Trav 7
LONELY There in a lonely room, from
bailiffs snug, ...5 DABd 48
And guide my lonely way, ...2 Ed&A 59
The lonely mansion lay; ....38 Ed&A 60
LONG$_1$ And his long nights of revelry
and ease; ....68 Trav 7
Each nobler aim, repress'd by long
control, ...155 Trav 10
When struggling Virtue sinks by
long controul, ...vl55 Trav 170
When noble aims have suffer'd long
controul, ...vl55 Trav 171
Spreads its long arms amidst the
wat'ry roar, ...289 Trav 14
Casts a long look where England's
glories shine, ...421 Trav 19
And the long grass o'ertops the
mould'ring wall; ....48 DVil 24
I still had hopes, my long vexations
pass'd, ...95 DVil 26
But the long pomp, the midnight
masquerade, ...259 DVil 31
And took a long farewell, and wish'd
in vain ....367 DVil 35
What! five long acts--and all to
make us wiser! ....1 eSis 70
And a long one to curtail.)-- .....32 Invt 129
Vida, 532
-LONG The bashful virgin's side-
long looks of love, ...29 DVil 24
LONG$_2$ And honour sinks where commerce
long prevails. ....92 Trav 8
She long had wanted cause of fear. ..8 Sonn 46
He still shall live, shall live
as long!-- ....19 DRtH 50
Long had I sought in vain to find ...1 NSim 56
I long had rack'd my brains to
find ....vl NSim 205
Nor wants that little long.' ....32 Ed&A 60
It cannot hold you long. ....4 MDog 65
Our vows are heard! Long, long to
mortal eyes, ...120 Thrn 78
A life that cannot last me long.' 202 Thrn 81
Should so long be to news-paper
essays confin'd; ....158 Rtal 93
Who long was a bookseller's hack; ..2 epEP 100
No more! Too long has justice been
delay'd, ...II:7 Capt 118
How long, how long, Almighty God
of all, ...III:37 Capt 124
LONG- Again the long-fall'n
column sought the skies; ....136 Trav 9
From these the feeble heart and
long-fall'n mind ....147 Trav 10
The smiling long-frequented village
fall? ....406 Trav 18
The long-remember'd beggar was his
guest, ...151 DVil 28
Here, while the proud their long-
drawn pomps display, ...317 DVil 33
Thy own, thy long-lost Edwin here, 151 Ed&A 64
With his long-winded speeches, his
smiles and his brogue; ....90 HofV 98
And brings my long-lost country to
mine eyes. ....I:16 Capt 114
Vida, 599
LONG$_3$ For streams of mercy long;III:44 Capt 124
LONGED Vida, 228
LONGER The ruin'd spendthrift,
now no longer proud, ...153 DVil 28
The host himself no longer shall be
found ....247 DVil 31
For now no longer could he hide, vl49 Ed&A 211
I'll waste no longer thought in
choosing; ....I:74 Capt 116
LOO The company set, and the word
to be, Loo; ....2 LetB 131
LOO'D The pool's very rich--ah! the
Doctor is loo'd!' ....26 LetB 132
Ah! the Doctor is loo'd! Come,
Doctor, put down.' ....32 LetB 132
LOOK$_1$ Casts a long look where
England's glories shine, ...421 Trav 19
Liv'd in each look, and brighten'd
all the green; ....72 DVil 25
The bashful look, the rising breast, 89 Ed&A 62
Not a look, not a smile shall my
passion discover: ....6 "Amw 94
LOOK$_2$ Look downward where a hundred
realms appear; ....34 Trav 6
Such dainties to them! It would look
like a flirt, ...v33 HofV 239
To dress, and look like awkward
Frenchmen here, ...34 eSSC$_1$ 105
LOOKED Hung round their bowers, and
fondly look'd their last, ...366 DVil 35
And he smil'd as he look'd at the
venison and me. ....38 HofV 96
Vida, 265
LOOKING Looking, as who should say,
D-- --! who's afraid? ....30 eSis 71

-LOOKING 'What, yon solemn-faced, odd-looking man that stands near!'50 LetB 133

LOOKS His children's looks, that brighten at the blaze; ....194 Trav 11

The bashful virgin's side-long looks of love, ...29 DVil 24

The matron's glance that would those looks reprove: ....30 DVil 24

His looks adorn'd the venerable place; ....178 DVil 29

Where village statesmen talk'd with looks profound, ...223 DVil 30

Her modest looks the cottage might adorn, ...329 DVil 34

Her looks, her lips, her panting breast, ...v89 Ed&A 209

His looks resume their youthful pride, ...v151 Ed&A 211

With looks that quite petrified, enter'd the maid; ....108 HofV 98

The smiling looks of each bewitching bairn. ....40 $eSSC_1$ 105

I read your looks, and see compliance there. ....II:42 Capt 119

LOOSE The playful children just let loose from school; ....120 DVil 27

LOPPED Lopp'd of his limbs in many a gallant fight, ...209 Thrn 81

LOQUACIOUS While sullen or loquacious strife, ...73 DTrn 54

LORD$_1$ We fear the Lord, and know no other fear. ....I:96 Capt 117

Down with her, Lord, to lick the dust, ...II:79 Capt 121

Thus we, O Lord, alike distrest,III:43 Capt 124

Down with them, Lord, to lick the dust; ....III:55 Capt 124

Save us, O Lord! to thee, though late, we pray, ...III:63 Capt 125

LORD$_2$ No costly lord the sumptuous banquet deal ....181 Trav 11

And that this boasted lord of nature 13 LogR 44

A wealthy lord was he; ....102 Ed&A 62

No lord will take me now, my vigour fled, ...173 Thrn 80

Thanks, my Lord, for your venison, for finer or fatter ....1 HofV 95

But, my Lord, it's no bounce: I protest in my turn, ...17 HofV 95

My acquaintance is slight, or I'd ask my Lord Clare. ....50 HofV 96

Now, my Lord, as for tripe, it's my utter aversion, ...85 HofV 98

To be plain, my good Lord, it's but labour misplac'd ....117 HofV 99

'My Lord,--your Lordship misconceives the case; ....52 $eSSC_1$ 106

LORD$_3$ Vida, 360

LORDLINGS The self-dependent lord-lings stand alone, ...341 Trav 16

LORDLY Have we not seen, at pleasure's lordly call, ...405 Trav 18

Vida, 522

LORDS But towns unmann'd, and lords without a slave; ....142 Trav 10

I see the lords of human kind pass by, ...328 Trav 16

Princes and lords may flourish, or may fade; ....53 DVil 25

And footmen, lords and dukes can act.56 LogR 45

'Some lords, my acquaintance, that settle the nation, ...43 HofV 96

On sentimental Queens and Lords in lace? ....36 $eSSC_2$ 109

Do not our tyrant lords this day ordain ....I:37 Capt 114

But hush, my sons, our tyrant lords are near; ....I:51 Capt 115

LORDSHIP It's a truth--and your Lordship may ask Mr. Byrne. ....18 HofV 95

It's a truth--and your Lordship may ask Mr. Burn. ....v18 HofV 238

'My Lord,--your Lordship misconceives the case;' ....52 $eSSC_1$ 106

LORE And the gay grandsire, skill'd in gestic lore, ...253 Trav 13

And, skill'd in legendary lore, ...51 Ed&A 60

-LORN His love-lorn guest betray'd. 84 Ed&A 62

LOSE And they, who lose their senses, there may find them. ......4 $eSSC_2$ 108

But find no sense--for they had none to lose. ....32 $eSSC_2$ 109

The pleasures that we lose to-day;II:60 Capt 120

Vida, 345

LOSES Loses ev'ry pain of dying ..38,46 Thrn 75

Makes but a penitent, loses a lover. 8 "Amw 94

Vida, 270

LOSING By losing their money to venture at fame. ....12 LetB 132

LOSS Yet still the loss of wealth is here supplied ....145 Trav 10

Not so the loss. The man of wealth and pride ....275 DVil 32

The inevitable loss. ....71 Thrn 76

Vida, 248

LOSSES Till made by my losses as bold as a lion, ...22 LetB 132

LOST Yet, though to fortune lost, here still abide ....v145 Trav 170

Now lost to all; her friends, her virtue fled, ...331 DVil 34

Lost to every gay delight; ....2 Sonn 46

'For here, forlorn and lost I tread, 5 Ed&A 59

And swore the dog had lost his wits, 23 MDog 65

Where are we driven? our reck'ning sure is lost! ....15 pZob 72

And lay my body where my limbs were lost.' ....224 Thrn 82

'Till having lost in age the power to kill, ...30 $eSSC_3$ 86

His fools have their follies so lost in a crowd ....69 Rtal 89

A treasury for lost and missing things; ....2 $eSSC_2$ 108

Lost human wits have places there assign'd them, ...3 $eSSC_2$ 108

Finds his lost senses out, and pay his debts. ....26 $eSSC_2$ 108

All, all is lost. The Syrian army fails, ...III:59 Capt 125

Vida, 260, 262, 294, 546, 672

-LOST Thy own, thy long-lost Edwin here, ...151 Ed&A 64

And brings my long-lost country to

mine eyes. ....I:16 Capt 114
LOT He sees his little lot the
lot of all; ....178 Trav 11
LOUD$_1$ So the loud torrent, and the
whirlwind's roar, ...207 Trav 12
With secret course, which no loud
storms annoy, ...433 Trav 19
And the loud laugh that spoke the
vacant mind; ....122 DVil 27
LOUD$_2$ Talks loud, coquets the
guests, and scolds the waiters. ...16 eSSC$_3$ 85
LOUDER With louder plaints the
mother spoke her woes, ...379 DVil 35
LOVE$_1$ Processions form'd for piety
and love, ...151 Trav 10
And industry begets a love of gain. 300 Trav 15
As duty, love, and honour fail to
sway, ...350 Trav 16
The bashful virgin's side-long looks
of love, ...29 DVil 24
To them his heart, his love, his
griefs were given, ...187 DVil 29
The love he bore to learning was
in fault; ....206 DVil 30
That only shelter'd thefts of harm-
less love. ....362 DVil 35
And steady loyalty, and faithful
love, ...406 DVil 36
Her love was sought, I do aver, ...17 MBlz 47
As when in Paphian groves the Queen
of Love ....9 MrsX 49
Or unregarded love? ....68 Ed&A 61
'And love is still an emptier sound, 77 Ed&A 61
Whom love has taught to stray; .....98 Ed&A 62
But never talk'd of love. ....112 Ed&A 63
Who offer'd only love. ....v112 Ed&A 209
He caroll'd lays of love; ....118 Ed&A 63
Repaid his love with pride. .....v132 Ed&A 210
Restor'd to love and thee. ....152 Ed&A 64
And flush with honest love. .....v152 Ed&A 211
Our love shall still be new; ....v158 Ed&A 211
And when this life of love shall
fail, ...v(167) Ed&A 211
May peace that claimed while
here thy warmest love, ...110 Thrn 78
Old Shakespeare, receive him, with
praise and with love, ...123 Rtal 91
Love presents the fairest
treasure, ...I:66 Capt 116
Love and pleasure in his
train; ....III:96 Capt 126
Vida, 468
Thus, when soft love subdues
the heart ....13 Tr 267
LOVE- His love-lorn guest be-
tray'd. ....84 Ed&A 62
Vida, 470
LOVE$_2$ We'll live and love so true; 158 Ed&A 64
We'll love again in heaven. ...v(168) Ed&A 211
Offers to love, but means to
deceive me. ....4 "Amw 94
I think they love venison--I know
they love beef; ....28 HofV 96
Vida, 166
LOVED Hence every state to one
lov'd blessing prone, ...93 Trav 8
While his lov'd partner, boastful
of her hoard, ...195 Trav 11
For praise too dearly lov'd, or
warmly sought, ...269 Trav 14
-LOVED Are here displayed.
Their much-lov'd wealth im-
parts ....303 Trav 15
LOVELIER His lovely daughter,
lovelier in her tears, ...375 DVil 35
LOVELIEST Sweet Auburn! loveliest
village of the plain, ...1 DVil 23
Sweet smiling village, loveliest of
the lawn, ...35 DVil 24
Do thine, sweet AUBURN, thine, the
loveliest train, ...337 DVil 34
And thou, sweet Poetry, thou
loveliest maid, ...407 DVil 36
Vida, 627, 670
LOVELY Dear lovely bowers of in-
nocence and ease, ...5 DVil 23
His lovely daughter, lovelier in
her tears, ...375 DVil 35
The lovely stranger stands
confess'd ....91 Ed&A 62
When lovely woman stoops to folly, ..1 "wlw 67
Lovely, lasting Peace below, ...112 Thrn 78
Lovely, lasting Peace, appear; ....116 Thrn 78
Next appear'd a lovely maid, ...232 Thrn 82
LOVER 'Twas thus for me my lover
did, ...v143 Ed&A 211
To give repentance to her lover, ...7 "wlw 67
There promised a lover to come--
but, O me! ....245 Thrn 83
Makes but a penitent, loses a
lover. ....8 "Amw 94
LOVER'S And left a lover's for a
father's arms. ....378 DVil 35
And left a lover's for her
father's arms. ....v378 DVil 190
LOVERS For talking age and
whisp'ring lovers made; ....14 DVil 23
When time advances, and when
lovers fail, ...292 DVil 33
Lovers no more, flew off by
dozens: ....88 DTrn 55
Lovers are plenty; but fail to
relieve me: ....2 "Amw 94
LOVERS' And on the gridiron broils
her lovers' hearts: ....20 eSSC$_3$ 85
LOVE'S And love's and friendship's
finely pointed dart ....231 Trav 13
Or rather, Love's delights
despising, ...I:68 Capt 116
LOVES Prompt not their loves:--
the patriot bird pursues ....5 Cati 94
LOW$_1$ Still stoops among the low to
copy nature. ....40 eSSC$_2$ 109
And sink thee lowest of the
low. ....III:77 Capt 125
LOW$_2$ While low delights,
succeeding fast behind, ...157 Trav 10
Their morals, like their pleasures,
are but low; ....228 Trav 12
Far from my bosom drive the low
desire; ....364 Trav 17
Low lies that house where nut-
brown draughts inspir'd, ...221 DVil 30
'Twas no defect of yours, but

heart made of stone?' ....64 LetB 134
Vida, 439, 553, 607, 614
MAGNANIMOUS Magnanimous Goldsmith
a gooseberry fool. ....16 Rtal 87
MAIA Vida, 174
MAIA'S Vida, 293, 322
MAID The modest matron, and the
blushing maid, ...408 Trav 18
Nor the coy maid, half willing to
be press'd, ...249 DVil 31
And thou, sweet Poetry, thou
loveliest maid, ...407 DVil 36
I'll give thee--Ah! too charming
maid, ...19 Gift 43
A maid in all her charms. ....92 Ed&A 62
'But let a maid thy pity share, ...97 Ed&A 62
The military boy, the orphan'd
maid, ...157 Thrn 79
Next appear'd a lovely maid, ...232 Thrn 82
The First Act shows the simple
country maid, ...9 $eSSC_3$ 85
With looks that quite petrified,
enter'd the maid; ....108 HofV 98
-MAID The swain responsive as the
milk-maid sung, ...117 DVil 27
Still, as a Bar-maid, I could wish
it too, ...3 $eSSC_3$ 85
Th' unblushing Bar-maid of a
country inn, ...14 $eSSC_3$ 85
The Bar-maid now for your protection
prays, ...34 $eSSC_3$ 86
-MAIDS That pretty Bar-maids have
done execution. ....6 $eSSC_3$ 85
MAIMED Scarr'd, mangled, maim'd in
every part, ...208 Thrn 81
MAIN To traverse climes beyond the
western main; ....410 Trav 18
For seats like these beyond the
western main; ....368 DVil 35
Along the billow'd main: ....216 Thrn 82
Along the furrow'd main: ....II:18 Capt 118
They knew and own'd the monarch
of the main: ....3 Tr 267
MAINTAIN Seen opulence, her grandeur
to maintain, ...401 Trav 18
And must in spite of them main-
tain, ...11 LogR 44
No, no; I've other contests to
maintain; ....17 eGNM 68
Good liquor, I stoutly maintain, ...3 "LSm 84
Vida, 295, 441
MAINTAINED When every rood of ground
maintain'd its man; ....58 DVil 25
MAINTAINS Vida, 163, 182
MAJESTIC Vida, 142
MAKE To make him loathe his
vegetable meal; ....182 Trav 11
Our own felicity we make or find: ..432 Trav 19
A breath can make them, as a breath
has made; ....54 DVil 25
What annual offering shall I make, ...3 Gift 43
And make full many a bitter pill go
down. ....6 eGNM 68
What! five long acts--and all to
make us wiser! ....1 eSis 70
To make an observation on the shore. 14 pZob 72
I'll try to make palaver with them
though; ....28 pZob 73
To make out the dinner, full
certain I am, ...13 Rtal 87
Our Townshend make speeches, and
I shall compile; ....88 Rtal 90
We wanted this venison to make out
the dinner. ....52 HofV 96
So next day, in due splendour to
make my approach, ...65 HofV 97
But no matter, I'll warrant we'll
make up the party ....73 HofV 97
You may make a mistake, and think
slightly of this. ....124 HofV 99
Make but of all your fortune one
<u>va toute</u>; ....48 $eSSC_1$ 105
Shall make our homage rise. .....I:10 Capt 113
We'll make his temple in our
breast, ...I:13 Capt 113
I'll make them both together
mine. ....I:76 Capt 116
For I could not make bold, ...7 Invt 128
Vida, 148, 301, 572
MAKES That good, which makes each
humbler bosom vain? ....40 Trav 6
To different nations makes their
blessings even. ....80 Trav 8
To these or those, but makes the
balance even: ....v80 Trav 168
Makes but a penitent, loses a
lover. ....8 "Amw 94
MAKING For making a blunder, or
picking a bone. ....30 HofV 96
Vida, 552
MALADY Say, where has our poet this
malady caught? ....73 Rtal 89
MALICE And malice is his ruling
passion; ....44 LogR 45
But both in malice and grimaces ....45 LogR 45
Ev'ry shock that malice offers .42, 50 Thrn 75
MALIGNANT Vida, 505
MAN$_1$ See also MON.
These little things are great
to little man; ....42 Trav 6
Pleas'd with each good that heaven
to man supplies: ....56 Trav 7
Man seems the only growth that
dwindles here. ....126 Trav 9
And, wond'ring man could want the
larger pile, ...163 Trav 10
But man and steel, the soldier and
his sword; ....170 Trav 10
The needy sell it, and the rich
man buys; ....308 Trav 15
And learns to venerate himself as
man. ....334 Trav 16
Keeps man from man, and breaks the
social tie; ....340 Trav 16
Where beasts with man divided
empire claim, ...415 Trav 19
When every rood of ground maintain'd its man; ....58 DVil 25
A man he was to all the country
dear, ...141 DVil 28
Pleas'd with his guests, the good
man learn'd to glow, ...159 DVil 28
The service pass'd, around the
pious man, ...181 DVil 29

A man severe he was, and stern to
view; ....197 DVil 29
Not so the loss. The man of wealth
and pride ....275 DVil 32
Teach erring man to spurn the rage
of gain; ....424 DVil 37
Reason, they say, belongs to man, ...3 LogR 44
That man and all his ways are vain; 12 LogR 44
Like man he imitates each fashion, .43 LogR 45
With sulky eye he smoak'd the
patient man, ...v(21) DABd 200
As ever dead man did. ....20 DRtH 50
Made him the happiest man alive; ....4 DTrn 52
Yet in a man 'twas well enough. ....28 DTrn 53
Man wants but little here below, ...31 Ed&A 60
In Islington there was a man, ...5 MDog 65
This dog and man at first were
friends; ....17 MDog 65
Went mad and bit the man. ....20 MDog 65
To bite so good a man. ....24 MDog 65
They swore the man would die. ......28 MDog 66
The man recover'd of the bite, ...31 MDog 66
'Young man,' cries one--a bard laid
up in clover-- ....11 eGNM 68
'Alas, young man, my writing days are
over; ....12 eGNM 68
And be each critic the Good Natur'd
Man. ....34 eGNM 69
And view with favour, the 'Good-
natur'd Man.' ....v34 eGNM 215
And man contains it in his breast. 119 Thrn 78
An abridgment of all that was
pleasant in man; ....94 Rtal 90
The man had his failings, a dupe to
his art. ....98 Rtal 90
Perhaps you may ask if the man was
a miser? ....129 Rtal 91
Though he merrily liv'd, he is now
a grave man; ....148 Rtal 92
'Thou best humour'd man with the
worst humour'd muse.' ....174 Rtal 93
Goes out, affronts his man, and
takes a beating. ....30 eSSC$_2$ 109
The good man suffers but to
gain, ...I:45 Capt 115
Coeval with man ....III:7 Capt 122
Alike of Heaven and man the
foe; ....III:74 Capt 125
'What, yon solemn-faced, odd-
looking man that stands near!' .50 LetB 133
Vida, 579

MAN$_2$ They sink at last, or feebly
man the soul; ....v156 Trav 171

MANAGER Go, ask your manager.'
'Who, me? Your pardon; ....19 eGNM 68

MANDATE Your mandate I got, ...1 Invt 128

MANGLED Scarr'd, mangled, maim'd
in every part, ...208 Thrn 81

MANGROVES There Mangroves spread,
and larger than I've seen 'em-- ....19 pZob 72

MANKIND Exults in all the good of
all mankind. ....44 Trav 6
An equal portion dealt to all mankind, ...78 Trav 7
Here let me sit in sorrow for mankind, ...102 Trav 8
To pamper luxury, and thin man-
kind; ....312 DVil 33
O! were he born to bless man-
kind, ...5 DRtH 50
How hast thou left mankind for
heaven! ....20 Thrn 74
And to party gave up what was
meant for mankind. ....32 Rtal 88
Bow'd down with chains, the scorn
of all mankind, ...I:85 Capt 117
Brave but to God, and cowards
to mankind, ...III:70 Capt 125
And hail the benefactor of
mankind: ....III:88 Capt 126

MANLINESS In all the silent
manliness of grief. ....384 DVil 36
In all the decent manliness of
grief. ....v384 DVil 190

MANNER Vida, 121

MANNERS Contrasted faults through
all his manners reign; ....127 Trav 9
Unalter'd, unimprov'd the manners
run; ....230 Trav 12
To kinder skies, where gentler
manners reign, ...239 Trav 13
And rural mirth and manners are
no more. ....74 DVil 25
Their master's manners still
contract, ...55 LogR 45
With manners wond'rous winning, ...10 MBlz 47
His manners were gentle, complying,
and bland; ....140 Rtal 91
His pencil our faces, his manners
our heart: ....142 Rtal 92

MAN'S$_1$ And pluck'd his gown, to
share the good man's smile. ....184 DVil 29
An hour's importance to the poor
man's heart; ....240 DVil 31
The rich man's joys increase, the
poor's decay, ...266 DVil 32
Nor wanted man's opinion to be
great. ....27 Thrn 75

-MAN'S No more the wood-man's
ballad shall prevail; ....244 DVil 31

MAN'S$_2$ He bows, turns round, and
whip--the man's a black! ....40 eSis 71

MANS Now sinks at last, or feebly
mans the soul; ....156 Trav 10
She leaves at last, or feebly
mans the soul; ....v156 Trav 170

MANSION And e'en those ills, that
round his mansion rise, ...201 Trav 12
The village preacher's modest
mansion rose. ....140 DVil 27
There, in his noisy mansion,
skill'd to rule, ...195 DVil 29
Reprieve the tottering mansion
from its fall! ....238 DVil 31
The lonely mansion lay; ....38 Ed&A 60
The modest mansion lay; ....v38 Ed&A 208

MANSIONS Where the bleak Swiss
their stormy mansions tread, ...167 Trav 10
Vida, 663

MANTLING To strip the brook with
mantling cresses spread, ...132 DVil 27
Careful to see the mantling bliss
go round; ....248 DVil 31
Swift mantling to the view; ....86 Ed&A 62

MANY With many a tale repays the
nightly bed. ....198 Trav 11
While many a pastime circled in
the shade, ...19 DVil 23
And many a gambol frolick'd o'er
the ground, ...21 DVil 24
And, many a year elaps'd, return
to view ....79 DVil 25
And still where many a garden flower
grows wild; ....138 DVil 27
At all his jokes, for many a joke
had he; ....202 DVil 30
Where many a time he triumph'd,
is forgot. ....218 DVil 30
Takes up a space that many poor
supplied; ....276 DVil 32
And kiss'd her thoughtless babes
with many a tear, ...381 DVil 36
Scarce half alive, oppress'd with
many a year, ...3 pLab 41
As many dogs there be, ...14 MDog 65
And make full many a bitter pill go
down. ....6 eGNM 68
While oft, with many a smile, and
many a shrug, ...25 eGNM 68
And quit for Venus, many a brighter
here; ....4 pZob 72
With many a tear and many a sigh
between; ....170 Thrn 80
Lopp'd of his limbs in many a gallant
fight, ...209 Thrn 81
At least in many things, I think,
I see ....7 $eSSC_2$ 108
Vida, 383, 387, 451, 464
MARCHED Vida, 274, 497
MARGIN Where shading elms along the
margin grew, ...245 Trav 13
Once on the margin of a fountain
stood, ...29 epLL 102
MARK With venerable grandeur mark
the scene. ....110 Trav 9
Or seeks the den where snow-tracks
mark the way, ...189 Trav 11
Wings upon either side--mark that. ..16 NSim 56
No monster-breed to mark the groves
with shame; ....8 Cati 94
Mark where he sits, with executing
art, ...II:65 Capt 120
MARKED And all his wealth was
mark'd as mine, ...103 Ed&A 62
MARKET Who whisks about the house,
at market caters, ...15 $eSSC_3$ 85
MARKS And the brown Indian marks
with murd'rous aim; ....416 Trav 19
MARRED But mock'd all tune, and
marr'd the dancer's skill; ....248 Trav 13
MARRIED Miss frown'd, and blush'd,
and then was--married. ....20 DTrn 52
MARRY Ah, me! when shall I marry
me? ....1 "Amw 94
MARS Vida, 122, 208, 400, 419, 421
MARS'S Vida, 63, 613
MART The crowded mart, the culti-
vated plain, ...295 Trav 15
MARTIAL Vida, 240, 336, 354, 473,
549, 650
MARTYR And the twelve rules the
royal martyr drew; ....12 DABd 48
MASKERS The world's a masquerade!
the maskers, you, you, you. ....12 eSis 70
MASQUERADE But the long pomp, the
midnight masquerade, ...259 DVil 31
Her moral play a speaking masquer-
ade; ....4 eSis 70
What if I give a masquerade?--I
will. ....10 eSis 70
The world's a masquerade! the
maskers, you, you, you. ....12 eSis 70
MASS A bloated mass of rank un-
wieldy woe; ....392 DVil 36
MASTER One only master grasps the
whole domain, ...39 DVil 24
The village master taught his little
school; ....196 DVil 29
Each grudging master keeps the
labourer bare-- ....175 Thrn 80
Still follow your master, and visit
his tomb: ....166 Rtal 93
MASTER- The master-prophet
grasps his full-ton'd lyre. .II:64 Capt 120
MASTER'S Extremes are only in the
master's mind! ....324 Trav 16
Their master's manners still
contract, ...55 LogR 45
Requir'd a master's care; ....42 Ed&A 60
-MASTERS No judges, fiddlers,
dancing-masters, ...35 LogR 45
Let school-masters puzzle their
brain, ...1 "LSm 84
MATE Sings to its mate, and nightly
charms the nest; ....12 Cati 94
MATRON The modest matron, and the
blushing maid, ...408 Trav 18
She, wretched matron, forc'd, in
age, for bread, ...131 DVil 27
The modest matron, clad in home-
spun gray, ...156 Thrn 79
The pious matron next was seen-- ..182 Thrn 80
MATRON'S The matron's glance that
would those looks reprove: ....30 DVil 24
MATTED Those matted woods where
birds forget to sing, ...349 DVil 34
Those ill-becoming rags--that
matted hair! ....III:34 Capt 123
MATTER But no matter, I'll
warrant we'll make up the party ....73 HofV 97
While the matter was cold, ...8 Invt 128
-MATTERS Now, ladies, I ask, if
law-matters you're skill'd in, ...35 LetB 132
MAY_1 But winter ling'ring chills
the lap of May; ....172 Trav 11
With garlands of beauty the queen
of the May ....251 Thrn 83
MAY_2 Trav, 62, 149, 234, 355, 369;
DVil, 53, 426; MBlz, 26; NSim, 29;
eGNM, 14; pZob, 34; Thrn, 89, 91,
105, 108, 109, 110, 111; Rtal, 129,
172; HofV, 15, 18, v18, 91, 93,
v95, 116, 124; epTP, 2; epLL, 18;
$eSSC_1$, 67; $eSSC_2$, 4; Capt, I:89,
II:32; Invt, 2, 19; LetB, 1, 10,
38, 63; Vida, 103, 109, 136, 138
MAZE Have led their children through
the mirthful maze, ...252 Trav 13

MERITS Careless their merits, or
their faults to scan, ...161 DVil 28
Would you ask for his merits? alas!
he had none; ....49 Rtal 88
Vida, 477
MERRILY Though he merrily liv'd,
he is now a grave man; ....148 Rtal 92
While the bacon and liver went
merrily round. ....88 HofV 98
MERRY And let us be merry and clever; 20 "LSm 84
Merry Whitefoord, farewell! for thy
sake I admit ....171 Rtal 93
They('re) both of them merry and
authors like you; ....76 HofV 97
And be unco merry when you are but
gay; ....42 eSSC$_1$ 105
MET I think I met with something
there, ...7 NSim 56
Pain met thee like a friend that set
thee free; ....34 Thrn 75
Vida, 4, 381, 594
METEORS But meteors glare, and
stormy glooms invest. ....174 Trav 11
METHINKS Methinks her patient sons
before me stand, ...283 Trav 14
Onward, methinks, and diligently
slow, ...287 Trav 14
E'en now, methinks, as pond'ring
here I stand, ...397 DVil 36
And now, methinks, to yonder bank
they bear ....III:17 Capt 123
METHODIST When Methodist preachers
come down ....10 "LSm 84
METHODS Insulting slaves! if gentler
methods fail, ...I:93 Capt 117
METTLED Vida, 448
MID Vida, 584, 608
MIDDLE$_1$ In the middle a place
where the pasty--was not. ....84 HofV 98
In the middle a place where the
Ven'son--was not. ....v84 HofV 241
MIDDLE$_2$ Vida, 217
MIDNIGHT But the long pomp, the
midnight masquerade, ...259 DVil 31
The dome where Pleasure holds her
midnight reign ....319 DVil 33
MIDST$_1$ Vida, 200, 368, 518, 622
MIDST$_2$ Vida, 231
MIDWAY Swells from the vale, and
midway leaves the storm, ...190 DVil 29
MIEN Vida, 357, 646
MIGHT$_1$ Vida, 57, 392
MIGHT$_2$ DVil, 329; DRtH, 14; MDog, 6; Rtal, 154;
HofV, 24, v24, 33; Vida, 45, 535
MIGHTY Vida, 4, 70, 297
MILDEST Creation's mildest charms
are there combin'd, ...323 Trav 16
MILE- Here, porter!--this venison
with me to Mile-end; ....55 HofV 97
MILITARY The military boy, the
orphan'd maid, ...157 Thrn 79
Vida, 181, 379
MILK With beer and milk arrears the
frieze was scor'd, ...17 DABd 48
MILK- The swain responsive as the
milk-maid sung, ...117 DVil 27
MILL The never-failing brook, the
busy mill, ...11 DVil 23
MIMIC$_1$ His lunar, and our mimic
world agree. ....8 eSSC$_2$ 108
Vida, 37, 297
MIMIC$_2$ Vida, 2
MIND Say, should the philosophic
mind disdain ....39 Trav 6
And wiser he, whose sympathetic
mind ....43 Trav 6
All evils here contaminate the
mind, ...131 Trav 9
From these the feeble heart and
long-fall'n mind ....147 Trav 10
In happier meanness occupy the
mind: ....158 Trav 10
Theirs are those arts that mind
to mind endear, ...257 Trav 13
The mind still turns where shift-
ing fashion draws, ...279 Trav 14
Extremes are only in the master's
mind! ....324 Trav 16
Gave wealth to sway the mind with
double force. ....396 Trav 18
That bliss which only centres in
the mind: ....424 Trav 19
And the loud laugh that spoke the
vacant mind; ....122 DVil 27
Lightly they frolic o'er the vacant
mind, ...257 DVil 31
No politics disturb their mind; ....24 LogR 44
That very face had robb'd her
mind. ....38 DTrn 53
To emulate his mind. ....124 Ed&A 63
An equal dignity of mind-- ....13 Thrn 74
Thy towering mind self-centred
stood, ...26 Thrn 75
Who, born for the Universe,
narrow'd his mind, ...31 Rtal 88
But let us be candid, and speak
out our mind, ...113 Rtal 91
Here Reynolds is laid, and, to tell
you my mind, ...137 Rtal 91
What pity, alas! that so lib'ral
a mind ....157 Rtal 93
Should bonds repress the vigour of
the mind? ....I:32 Capt 114
Can whips or tortures hurt the
mind ....I:97 Capt 117
O peace of mind, angelic
guest! ....II:1 Capt 118
Reflect, nor tempt to rage the
royal mind. ....II:14 Capt 118
MINDS To men of other minds my
fancy flies, ...281 Trav 14
Minds combat minds, repelling and
repell'd. ....344 Trav 16
MINE$_1$ Explore the mine, or tempt
the dangerous deep; ....104 DVil 26
MINE$_2$ Creation's heir, the world,
the world is mine! ....50 Trav 7
And bids his bosom sympathise with
mine. ....422 Trav 19
Retreats from care, that never must
be mine, ...98 DVil 26
Caesar persuades, submission must
be mine; ....12 pLab 41
Its panting tenant is not mine. .....4 TrSA 51

Such as to modern bard's decreed: ...21 NSim 56
For in a modern poet's flights, ...28 NSim 57
His wand's a modern author's pen; ...44 NSim 57
In which all modern bards agree, ...59 NSim 58
Our modern bards! why what a pox ...63 NSim 58
The modern fair one's jest: ....78 Ed&A 61
That modern judges seldom enter here. ....18 $eSSC_1$ 104
MODEST The modest matron, and the blushing maid, ...408 Trav 18
The village preacher's modest mansion rose. ....140 DVil 27
Her modest looks the cottage might adorn, ...329 DVil 34
The modest stranger lowly bends .....35 Ed&A 60
The modest mansion lay; ....v38 Ed&A 208
Where modest want and patient sorrow dwell; ....123 Thrn 78
Unseen the modest were supplied, ...125 Thrn 78
The modest matron, clad in home-spun gray, ...156 Thrn 79
MODESTY With modesty her cheeks are dy'd, ...97 DTrn 55
MOHAWK The Mohawk too--**with angry** phrases stored, ...27 $eSSC_2$ 109
MOLE As ocean sweeps the labour'd mole away; ....428 DVil 37
MOLEST And as a child, when scaring sounds molest, ...205 Trav 12
MOMENT To the last moment of his breath ....II:33 Capt 119
Every moment, as it flows, ...II:55 Capt 120
Vida, 650
MOMENTS And speaks in moments more than years. ....16 Tr 267
MON 'What the de'il, mon, a pasty!' re-echoed the Scot, ...103 HofV 98
'What the de'il, mon, a pasty!' returned the Scot, ...v103 HofV 242
MONARCH He sits him down the monarch of a shed; ....192 Trav 11
And Prussia's monarch shew'd his lamp-black face ....v14 DABd 200
The madd'ning monarch revels in my veins. ....22 epLL 101
And our monarch partakes in the joy. ....I:60 Capt 115
Like the sun, our great monarch all rapture supplies, ...I:61 Capt 116
And our monarch enlivens below. ..I:64 Capt 116
See where dethron'd your captive monarch lies, ...II:88 Capt 121
Our monarch falls, and now our fears are o'er, ...III:21 Capt 123
Vida, 65, 197, 239, 396, 467, 548, 556, 592, 619, 646
They knew and own'd the monarch of the main: ....3 Tr 267
MONARCH'S Than angry monarch's raging. ....II:24 Capt 119
Our monarch's fame the noblest theme supplies. ....II:44 Capt 119
Prepares our monarch's victories to sing. ....II:70 Capt 121
Vida, 609
MONARCHS And monarchs toil, and poets pant for fame, ...v358 Trav 174
Vida, 4, 54, 143, 424, 427, 481
MONEY By losing their money to venture at fame. ....12 LetB 132
MONGREL Both mongrel, puppy, whelp, and hound, ...15 MDog 65
MONROE'S 'Twas a neck and a breast--that might rival Monroe's: ....v24 HofV 238
MONSTER Vida, 554
MONSTER- No monster-breed to mark the groves with shame; ....8 Cati 94
MONSTROUS With hoop of monstrous size, ...14 MBlz 47
-MONTH That had she liv'd a twelve-month more,-- ....27 MBlz 47
MOON The Moon, says he:--but I affirm the Stage: ....6 $eSSC_2$ 108
-MOON The honey-moon like lightning flew, ...29 DTrn 53
MOORS Vida, 80
MORAL Her moral play a speaking masquerade; ....4 eSis 70
-MORAL What heart but feels his sweetly-moral lay, ...3 epTP 100
MORALS Their morals, like their pleasures, are but low; ....228 Trav 12
But all the gentler morals, such as play ....235 Trav 13
MORE Trav, 87, 139, 208, 236; DVil, 41, 60, 74; Trav, v139; DVil, 148, v148, 239, 241, 243, 244, 245, 253, 356, 391; pLab, 10, **17**; Gift, 14; MBlz, 18, 27; DTrn, 88, 101; Ed&A, 72, v136; eSis, 17; Thrn, 96, 162, 166, 240, 252; Rtal, 19; ClRp, 4; epTP, 9; epLL, 38; Capt, I:15, 41, II:7, 83, 92, III:22, 72, 79; LetB, 33; Vida, 19, 229, 320, 321, 363, 460, 584; Tr, 16
MOREOVER Moreover, Merc'ry had a failing: ....57 NSim 58
MORN Cheerful at morn he wakes from short repose, ...185 Trav 11
To seek her nightly shed, and weep till morn; ....134 DVil 27
The morn was cold, he views with keen desire ....15 DABd 48
Are not this very morn those feasts begun, ...I:35 Capt 114
O Lucifer, thou son of morn, ..III:73 Capt 125
Vida, 624
$MORNING_1$ See the ruddy morning smiling, ...II:47 Capt 120
$MORNING_2$ Like clouds that deck the morning skies, ...v87 Ed&A 209
The day's disasters in his morning face; ....200 DVil 29
Like colours o'er the morning skies, ...87 Ed&A 62
Her bounty, like the morning dew, .178 Thrn 80
My morning prayer, my evening song, ...200 Thrn 81
My morning and my evening song; ...204 Thrn 81
-MORROW To-morrow you take a poor dinner with me; ....47 HofV 96
Think not to-morrow can repay ..II:59 Capt 120
-MORROW'S To-morrow's tears may wash our stains away. ....II:32 Capt 119

To-morrow's most unbounded
store ....II:61 Capt 120
MORTAL$_1$ Her last disorder
mortal. ....24 MBlz 47
MORTAL$_2$ Our vows are heard! Long,
long to mortal eyes, ...120 Thrn 78
MORTALS Tremble, ye mortals, at
my rage! ....79,83 Thrn 76,77
That mortals visit both to find
their senses. ....14 eSSC$_2$ 108
MORTALS' Than reason-boasting
mortals' pride; ....16 LogR 44
MOST To wit--most wond'rously
endu'd, ...35 NSim 57
Truth, beauty, worth, and all that
most engage, ...74 Thrn 76
Here Hickey reclines, a most blunt,
pleasant creature, ...125 Rtal 91
To coxcombs averse, yet most
civilly steering, ...143 Rtal 92
But what vex'd me most was that
d--'d Scottish rogue, ...89 HofV 98
Hence, intruder, most distress-
ing, ...I:27 Capt 114
To-morrow's most unbounded
store ....II:61 Capt 120
Vida, 122, 160, 166
MOTHER Nature, a mother kind
alike to all, ...81 Trav 8
With louder plaints the mother
spoke her woes, ...379 DVil 35
MOTHER'S Clings close and closer
to the mother's breast, ...206 Trav 12
MOTION Vida, 324
MOTIONS Its motions stop, or frenzy
fire the wheels. ....348 Trav 16
Vida, 144, 402, 643
MOTLEY ---, what a group the
motley scene discloses! ....13 eSis 70
MOTS Whose daily bons mots half
a column might fill; ....154 Rtal 93
MOULDERING While oft some temple's
mould'ring tops between ....109 Trav 9
And the long grass o'ertops the
mould'ring wall; ....48 DVil 24
MOUNTAIN'S Its uplands sloping
deck the mountain's side, ...107 Trav 8
No Zephyr fondly sues the mountain's
breast, ...173 Trav 11
Some sterner virtues o'er the
mountain's breast ....233 Trav 13
'But from the mountain's grassy
side ....25 Ed&A 60
MOUNTAINS But bind him to his
native mountains more. ....208 Trav 12
MOURN Even now reproach and
faction mourn, ...21 Thrn 74
And should we mourn? should
coward virtue fly, ...I:39 Capt 115
MOURNFUL Or sigh with pity at
some mournful tale, ...20 Trav 6
The mournful peasant leads his
humble band; ....300 DVil 33
MOURNING Vida, 436
MOURNS See where he mourns his
friends and children slain. ....II:90 Capt 121
MOUTH How wide her mouth, how
wild her eyes! ....66 DTrn 54
MOVE$_1$ Vida, 634
MOVE$_2$ Downward they move, a
melancholy band, ...401 DVil 36
Vida, 107, 541
MOVED Vida, 75, 421, 558
MOVES$_1$ Vida, 275, 639
MOVES$_2$ But on he moves to meet his
latter end, ...107 DVil 26
See how she moves along with every
grace, ...5 MrsX 49
This moves:--so at last I agree to
relent, ...65 LetB 134
Vida, 150, 160, 415
MR. It's a truth--and your Lordship
may ask Mr. Byrne. ....18 HofV 95
It's a truth--and your Lordship
may ask Mr. Burn. ....v18 HofV 238
Mr. Bunbury frets, and I fret
like the devil, ...19 LetB 132
MRS. 'What does Mrs. Bunbury?'
'I, Sir? I pass.' ....16 LetB 132
MUCH Find that the bliss of all
is much the same, ...v(81) Trav 168
How much unlike the sons of
Britain now! ....316 Trav 15
The village all declar'd how much
he knew; ....207 DVil 30
And news much older than their ale
went round. ....224 DVil 30
Could so much beauty condescend ....47 DTrn 53
Though ne'er so much awake before, .39 NSim 57
We scarcely can praise it, or
blame it too much; ....30 Rtal 88
MUCH- Are here displayed. Their
much-lov'd wealth imparts ......303 Trav 15
MUMP Who mump their passion, and
who, grimly smiling, ...21 eSSC$_1$ 104
MURDER Vida, 536
MURDEROUS And the brown Indian
marks with murd'rous aim; ....416 Trav 19
And savage men more murd'rous
still than they; ....356 DVil 35
MURMUR Up yonder hill the village
murmur rose; ....114 DVil 27
MURMURING With tuneless pipe, be-
side the murmuring Loire! ....244 Trav 13
Weeping, murmuring, complaining, ...1 Sonn 46
These sadly join beside the
murmuring deep, ...159 Thrn 80
Where flows Euphrates murmuring
to the deep, ...I:2 Capt 113
Vida, 349
MURMURS$_1$ No cheerful murmurs
fluctuate in the gale, ...126 DVil 27
MURMURS$_2$ Where wild Altama mur-
murs to their woe. ....344 DVil 34
MUSE The Muse found Scroggen
stretch'd beneath a rug; ....6 DABd 48
'Thou best humour'd man with the
worst humour'd muse.' ....174 Rtal 93
Say heavenly muse, their youth-
ful frays rehearse; ....7 Tr 267
MUSES Ye Muses, pour the pitying
tear ....1 DRtH 50
MUSIC There gentle music melts on
ev'ry spray; ....322 Trav 16

Conspiring nations come; ....II:72 Capt 121
NATIVE$_1$ Impels the native to
repeated toil, ...298 Trav 15
NATIVE$_2$ Thus every good his native
wilds impart, ...199 Trav 11
But bind him to his native
mountains more. ....208 Trav 12
Fierce in their native hardiness
of soul, ...331 Trav 16
One native charm, than all the
gloss of art; ....254 DVil 31
That call'd them from their native
walks away; ....364 DVil 35
Teach him, that states of native
strength possess'd, ...425 DVil 37
Where sculptur'd elegance and
native grace ....144 Thrn 79
NATIVES O there the natives are--
a dreadful race! ....25 pZob 73
NATURAL And beplaster'd with rouge
his own natural red. ....100 Rtal 90
On the stage he was natural,
simple, affecting; ....101 Rtal 90
NATURE$_1$ As different good, by
Art or Nature given, ...79 Trav 8
Find that each good, by Art or
Nature given, ...v79 Trav 168
Nature, a mother kind alike to
all, ...81 Trav 8
The canvas glow'd beyond e'en
Nature warm, ...137 Trav 9
Here by the bonds of nature
feebly held, ...343 Trav 16
Spontaneous joys, where Nature
has its play, ...255 DVil 31
And that this boasted lord of
nature ....13 LogR 44
Let us prize death as the best
gift of nature-- ....86 Thrn 77
And slander itself must allow him
good nature: ....126 Rtal 91
Nature disowns, and reason scorns
thy mirth, ...8 epLL 101
Still stoops among the low to
copy nature. ....40 eSSC$_2$ 109
Nature, a better guide than
you. ....II:54 Capt 120
-NATURE$_2$ She learns good-nature
every day; ....102 DTrn 55
NATURED And be each critic the
Good Natur'd Man. ....34 eGNM 69
-NATURED And view with favour,
the 'Good-natur'd Man.' ....v34 eGNM 215
NATURE'S Could Nature's bounty
satisfy the breast, ...111 Trav 9
By forms unfashion'd, fresh from
Nature's hand; ....330 Trav 16
Nor this the worst. As nature's
ties decay, ...349 Trav 16
In nature's simplest charms at
first array'd; ....296 DVil 33
In wit, and sense, and nature's
spite: ....4 NSim 56
'Tis Nature's kind retreat, that's
always open ....97 Thrn 77
NEAR$_1$ And twenty other near
relations; ....56 DTrn 53

NEAR$_2$ My anxious day to husband
near the close, ...v87 DVil 182
Near yonder copse, where once the
garden smil'd, ...137 DVil 27
Near yonder thorn, that lifts its
head on high, ...219 DVil 30
Near her betrayer's door she lays
her head, ...332 DVil 34
Near, and more near, the hounds
and huntsmen drew. ....38 epLL 102
But hush, my sons, our tyrant
lords are near; ....I:51 Capt 115
Near, nearer still, it gathers
on the gale; ....I:54 Capt 115
'What, yon solemn-faced, odd-
looking man that stands near!' .50 LetB 133
Vida, 401, 658
NEARER Near, nearer still, it
gathers on the gale; ....I:54 Capt 115
NEAREST Comes nearest us in
human shape; ....42 LogR 45
Vida, 57
NEATLY A person ever neatly clean: 100 DTrn 55
Vida, 39
NECK Of the neck and the breast
I had next to dispose; ....23 HofV 95
'Twas a neck and a breast--that
might rival M--r--'s: ....24 HofV 95
'Twas a neck and a breast--that
might rival Monroe's: ....v24 HofV 238
NED Here lies poor Ned Purdon,
from misery freed, ...1 epEP 100
NEED Need we expose to vulgar sight 21 DTrn 52
Need we intrude on hallow'd
ground, ...23 DTrn 52
To succour, should I need. ....194 Thrn 81
Vida, 155
NEEDFUL Around the world each need-
ful product flies, ...283 DVil 32
NEEDLESS Needless to him the
tribute we bestow-- ....7 epTP 100
NEEDY The needy sell it, and the
rich man buys; ....308 Trav 15
The needy seldom pass'd her door, ...5 MBlz 47
NE'ER See also NEVER.
LogR, 33; DTrn, 11; NSim, 39; Ed&A,
v136; Rtal, 44; ClRp, 5; Vida,
6, 105, 120, 132, 250
NEGLECTED Like yon neglected
shrub at random cast, ...103 Trav 8
Dear charming nymph, neglected
and decried, ...411 DVil 37
NEGLECTFUL Silent went next,
neglectful of her charms, ...377 DVil 35
NEGLIGENT And so it fell out, for
that negligent sloven ....113 HofV 99
NEGRO The naked negro, panting
at the line, ...69 Trav 7
NEIGH Vida, 68
NEIGHBOR At law his neighbour
prosecute, ...20 LogR 44
NEIGHBOURHOOD She strove the
neighbourhood to please, ...9 MBlz 47
NEIGHBOURING The decent church that
topp'd the neighbouring hill, ...12 DVil 23
Has robb'd the neighbouring fields
of half their growth, ...280 DVil 32

A refuge to the neighbouring
poor ....39 Ed&A 60
Around from all the neighbouring
streets ....21 MDog 65
Vida, 243, 396
NEIGHBOURS The wond'ring neigh-
bours ran, ...22 MDog 65
Vida, 35
NEITHER But, neither this nor
that refusing, ...I:75 Capt 116
Vida, 106, 139, 202, 637
NEREIDS Vida, 34
NERVE Catch every nerve, and
vibrate through the frame. ....220 Trav 12
NESBITT So tell Horneck and
Nesbitt, ...11 Invt 128
NEST May sit, like falcons
cow'ring on the nest; ....234 Trav 13
The hollow-sounding bittern
guards its nest; ....44 DVil 24
To warm the turtle's nest. ....80 Ed&A 61
Sings to its mate, and nightly
charms the nest; ....12 Cati 94
NETTLED Vida, 545
NEVER See also NE'ER.
Trav, 19; DVil, 56, 98; LogR, 27,
29, 39; MBlz, 3, 11, 15; Ed&A,
112, 155, 157; Thrn, 24, 243,
254; HofV, 2, 63, 92; epLL, 32;
Capt, I:89, III:9; LetB, 6, 52;
Vida, 136, 176, 178
NEVER- The never-failing brook,
the busy mill, ...11 DVil 23
NEW A new creation rescu'd from
his reign. ....296 Trav 15
Each wanton judge new penal
statutes draw, ...385 Trav 18
At church, in silks and satins new, 13 MBlz 47
Each case, however bad, he'll new
japan; ....6 GRos 51
Surpris'd, he sees new beauties rise,85 Ed&A 62
Our love shall still be new; ....v158 Ed&A 211
As some unhappy wight, at some
new play, ...23 eGNM 68
Reflects new glories on his breast, 141 Thrn 79
New Lauders and Bowers the Tweed
shall cross over, ...89 Rtal 90
Off! off! vile trappings! a new
passion reigns! ....21 epLL 101
Vida, 413
NEW- To tempt its new-fledg'd
offspring to the skies, ...168 DVil 28
To new-found worlds, and wept for
others' woe; ....372 DVil 35
And the new-blossomed thorn shall
whiten her tomb.' ....250,258 Thrn 83
Vida, 510
NEWS And news much older than
their ale went round. ....224 DVil 30
No more the farmer's news, the
barber's tale, ...243 DVil 31
That she came with some terrible
news from the baker: ....112 HofV 98
Lend me your hands.--Oh! fatal
news to tell: ....35 eSSC$_1$ 105
Here come the sons of scandal and
of news, ...31 eSSC$_2$ 109
NEWS- Should so long be to news-paper
essays confin'd; ....158 Rtal 93
Ye news-paper witlings! ye pert
scribbling folks ....163 Rtal 93
-NEWS <u>Cross-readings</u>, <u>Ship-news</u>,
and <u>Mistakes of the Press</u>. .....170 Rtal 93
NEWSPAPER See NEWS-
NEXT$_1$ In the next place, his feet
peruse, ...23 NSim 56
So next day, in due splendour to
make my approach, ...65 HofV 97
I ask for advice from the lady
that's next: ....28 LetB 132
Vida, 634
NEXT$_2$ Silent went next, neglectful
of her charms, ...377 DVil 35
The pious matron next was seen-- ..182 Thrn 80
Next appear'd lovely maid, ...232 Thrn 82
Next the scene shifts to town,
and there she soars, ...17 eSSC$_3$ 85
Of the neck and the breast I had
next to dispose; ....23 HofV 95
Vida, 66, 275
NIAGARA And Niagara stuns with
thund'ring sound? ....412 Trav 19
NICE Too nice for a statesman,
too proud for a wit: ....38 Rtal 88
He's keeping a corner for something
that's nice: ....100 HofV 98
NICELY The white-wash'd wall, the
nicely sanded floor, ...227 DVil 30
NICK That we wish'd him full ten
times a day at Old Nick; ....58 Rtal 89
NIGGARDLY 'Tis in vain that at
niggardly caution I scold, ...13 LetB 132
NIGH Vida, 254, 285, 327
NIGHT At night returning, every
labour sped, ...191 Trav 11
Sat by his fire, and talk'd the
night away; ....156 DVil 28
A bed by night, a chest of drawers
by day; ....230 DVil 30
Fears th' approaching bridal night. 4 Sonn 46
A cap by night--a stocking all the
day! ....20 DABd 48
The raptures of the bridal night? ..22 DTrn 52
In short, by night, 'twas fits or
fretting; ....51 DTrn 53
She sits all night at cards, and
ogles at spadille. ....31 eSSC$_3$ 86
Wak'd Priam in drawing his curtains
by night. ....110 HofV 98
I'll sing to amuse you by night
and by day, ...41 eSSC$_1$ 105
Both shine at night, for, but at
Foote's alone, ...9 eSSC$_2$ 108
Comes here at night, and goes a
prude away. ....18 eSSC$_2$ 108
And still, as darker grows the
night, ...II:39 Capt 119
You'd have sent before night; ......4 Invt 128
Vida, 62, 544
-NIGHT 'Then turn to-night, and
freely share ....17 Ed&A 59
To-night I head our troops at
Warwick Lane: ....18 eGNM 68
NIGHTCAP A nightcap deck'd his

brows instead of bay, ...19 DABd 48
NIGHTCAPS Five greasy nightcaps
wrapp'd her head. ....46 DTrn 53
NIGHTINGALE And fill'd each pause
the nightingale had made. ....124 DVil 27
The nightingale, with mutual passion
blest, ...11 Cati 94
NIGHTLY With many a tale repays the
nightly bed. ....198 Trav 11
To seek her nightly shed, and weep
till morn; ....134 DVil 27
To guide my nightly way, ...v2 Ed&A 208
Sings to its mate, and nightly charms
the nest; ....12 Cati 94
NIGHTS And his long nights of
revelry and ease; ....68 Trav 7
NINE For you, bright fair, the nine
address their lays, ...1 MrsX 49
(A chair-lumber'd closet just twelve
feet by nine:) ....68 HofV 97
NOBLE When noble aims have suffer'd
long controul, ...v155 Trav 171
Where noble stems transmit the
patriot flame, ...357 Trav 17
When wealth and rank and noble
blood, ...15 Thrn 74
My noble mistress thought not so: ..177 Thrn 80
Vida, 229
NOBLER Each nobler aim, repress'd
by long control, ...155 Trav 10
Where rougher climes a nobler race
display, ...166 Trav 10
Thou guide by which the nobler arts
excel, ...415 DVil 37
Vida, 392, 546
NOBLEST Our monarch's fame the
noblest theme supplies. ....II:44 Capt 119
NOBLY Vida, 375
NOBODY 'And nobody with me at sea
but myself'; ....60 HofV 97
NOD He nods, they nod; he cringes,
they grimace; ....29 eGNM 69
NODDING Ye nodding towers, ye
fairy scenes-- ....164 Thrn 80
See yonder tower just nodding to
the fall: ....III:48 Capt 124
NODS He nods, they nod; he cringes,
they grimace; ....29 eGNM 69
NOISY The noisy geese that gabbled
o'er the pool, ...119 DVil 27
There, in his noisy mansion, skill'd
to rule, ...195 DVil 29
NONE Since none implor'd relief
in vain!-- ....15 DRtH 50
Would you ask for his merits? alas!
he had none; ....49 Rtal 88
But find no sense--for they had
none to lose. ....32 eSSC$_2$ 109
Vida, 156, 248, 481, 536, 633
NONSENSE With grammar, and nonsense,
and learning; ....2 "LSm 84
Hold! Prompter, hold! a word before
your nonsense; ....1 epLL 101
NOON- And dance, forgetful of the
noon-tide hour. ....250 Trav 13
NOOSE Now, to perplex the ravell'd
noose, ...71 DTrn 54

NOR Trav, 120, 280, 349, v349, 379; DVil, 144,
239, 249, 290; pLab, 6; LogR, 26, 30, 31, 32,
40; Ed&A, 32, 114; Thrn, 27, 56, 174, 197;
ClRp, 4; epLL, 32; Capt, I:12, 56, 75; II:
14; Vida, 44, 139, 492, 598, 620, 652
NORTH From north, from south, from
east, from west, ...II:71 Capt 121
NORTHERN Whatever sweets salute the
northern sky ....117 Trav 9
NOSE Or thins her lip, or points
her nose: ....64 DTrn 54
NOSEGAYS Of French friseurs, and
nosegays, justly vain, ...32 eSSC$_1$ 105
With bunches of fennel, and nosegays
before 'em; ....44 LetB 133
NOSES Whose only plot it is to
break our noses; ....14 epLL 101
-NOSTER- To folks at Pater-Noster-
Row; ....34 LogR 45
NOTE And waken every note of woe; ....2 Thrn 74
My children shall the note prolong. 206 Thrn 81
The clarion's note proclaims the
finish'd war! ....III:84 Capt 126
NOTES The mingling notes came
soften'd from below; ....116 DVil 27
-NOTES Vida, 679
NOTHING But nothing could a charm
impart ....57 Ed&A 61
But nothing mirthful could assuage v57 Ed&A 208
But your friend there, the Doctor,
eats nothing at all.' ....98 HofV 98
NOUGHT While nought remain'd of all
that riches gave, ...141 Trav 10
Could nought of purity display, ...123 Ed&A 63
In nought entire--except his heart. 210 Thrn 81
NOVELTY While novelty, with cautious
cunning, ...148 Thrn 79
NOW E'en now, where Alpine
solitudes ascend, ...31 Trav 6
Now sinks at last, or feebly mans the
soul; ....156 Trav 10
How much unlike the sons of Britain
now! ....316 Trav 15
E'en now, perhaps, as there some
pilgrim strays ....413 Trav 19
But now the sounds of population
fail, ...125 DVil 27
The ruin'd spendthrift, now no
longer proud, ...153 DVil 28
Now lost to all; her friends, her
virtue fled, ...331 DVil 34
E'en now, perhaps, by cold and
hunger led, ...339 DVil 34
E'en now the devastation is begun, 395 DVil 36
E'en now, methinks, as pond'ring
here I stand, ...397 DVil 36
But now her wealth and finery fled, 21 MBlz 47
Now, to perplex the ravell'd noose, 71 DTrn 54
Reflected now a perfect fright: .....82 DTrn 54
Poor Madam, now condemn'd to hack ...91 DTrn 55
And now proceed we to our simile. ...14 NSim 56
Now to apply, begin we then; ....43 NSim 57
And now, when busy crowds retire ....45 Ed&A 60
And now, when worldly crowds retire v45 Ed&A 208
For now no longer could he hide, ..v149 Ed&A 211
Since then, unhelp'd, our bard must
now conform ....31 eGNM 69

Even now reproach and faction
mourn, ...21 Thrn 74
The shatter'd veteran, now first
dismay'd; ....158 Thrn 79
Call on their mistress--now no
more--and weep. ....162 Thrn 80
Let all your echoes now deplore ...165 Thrn 80
'And where,' he cried, 'shall now
my babes have bread, ...171 Thrn 80
No lord will take me now, my
vigour fled, ...173 Thrn 80
'What now remains for me? ....188 Thrn 81
And Madam now begins to hold it
higher; ....24 eSSC$_3$ 85
The Bar-maid now for your pro-
tection prays, ...34 eSSC$_3$ 86
Alas, that such frolic should
now be so quiet! ....52 Rtal 88
Now breaking a jest, and now
breaking a limb; ....54 Rtal 88
Now wrangling and grumbling to
keep up the ball, ...55 Rtal 89
Now teasing and vexing, yet laugh-
ing at all! ....56 Rtal 89
But now he is gone, and we want
a detector, ...85 Rtal 90
Though he merrily liv'd, he is now
a grave man; ....148 Rtal 92
By a bounce now and then, to get
courage to fly. ....16 HofV 95
And now that I think on't, as I
am a sinner! ....51 HofV 96
Now, my Lord, as for tripe, it's
my utter aversion, ...85 HofV 98
And now that I think on't, the
story may stop. ....116 HofV 99
Aye, 'twas but a dream, for now
there's no retreating: ....25 epLL 101
My horns! I'm told horns are the
fashion now.' ....36 epLL 102
Agreed. Agreed. And now with
late repentance, ...69 eSSC$_1$ 107
And now his voice, accordant to
the string, ...II:69 Capt 121
And now, methinks, to yonder
bank they bear ....III:17 Capt 123
Our monarch falls, and now our
fears are o'er, ...III:21 Capt 123
Now, now's our time! ye
wretches bold and blind, ...III:69 Capt 125
Now press thy fall, ...III:76 Capt 125
Now I've got him a scale ....29 Invt 129
Now, ladies, I ask, if law-matters
you're skill'd in, ...35 LetB 132
And picking of pockets, with which
I now charge ye, ...39 LetB 133
Vida, 51, 83, 163, 210, 332, 360, 361, 424,
436, 496, 529, 559, 569, 595, 602, 645, 676
NOW'S Now, now's our time! ye
wretches bold and blind, ...III:69 Capt 125
NUMBER Vida. 41, 444
NUPTIAL Vida. 469, 490
NUPTIALS Vida, 16
NURSE$_1$ The land of scholars, and
the nurse of arms, ...356 Trav 17
Thou nurse of every virtue, fare
thee well! ....416 DVil 37
NURSE$_2$ Awful as clouds that nurse
the growing storm; ....II:68 Capt 121
NUT- Low lies that house where
nut-brown draughts inspir'd, ...221 DVil 30
NYMPH Dear charming nymph, neglected
and decried, ...411 DVil 37
NYMPHS Vida, 6, 10, 34

O_1 O then how blind to all that
truth requires, ...377 Trav 17
O! had he liv'd another year!-- .....3 DRtH 50
O! were he born to bless mankind, ...5 DRtH 50
O had the archer ne'er come down ...11 DTrn 52
O had her eyes forgot to blaze! ....15 DTrn 52
O!--But let exclamation cease, ...17 DTrn 52
O there the natives are--a dreadful
race! ....25 pZob 73
There promised a lover to come--
but, O me! ....245 Thrn 83
'O--Oh!' quoth my friend, 'he'll
come on in a trice, ...99 HofV 98
Vida, 248
O_2 O blest retirement, friend to
life's decline, ...97 DVil 26
O Luxury! thou curs'd by Heaven's
decree, ...385 DVil 36
O Wolfe! to thee a streaming flood
of woe, ...5 Queb 46
O thou--my all that's mine? .....v156 Ed&A 211
O Memory, thou fond deceiver, ...I:23 Capt 114
O peace of mind, angelic guest! II:1 Capt 118
Thus we, O Lord, alike distrest,III:43 Capt 124
O God of hosts, the victory is
thine! ....III:54 Capt 124
Save us, O Lord! to thee, though
late, we pray, ...III:63 Capt 125
O Lucifer, thou son of morn, ..III:73 Capt 125
O Babylon, how art thou fallen! III:78 Capt 126
O Thou, without beginning, without
end, ...III:105 Capt 127
OBEDIENCE Hence all obedience bows
to these alone, ...353 Trav 17
OBEDIENT Vida, 66
OBEY Him I obey, whom heaven itself
obeys, ...13 pLab 41
Let us one hour, one little hour
obey; ....II:31 Capt 119
Vida, 84
OBEYED The king's commands must
fully be obey'd; ....II:8 Capt 118
OBEYS Him I obey, whom heaven
itself obeys, ...13 pLab 41
OBLIGINGLY Too courteous, perhaps, or
obligingly flat? ....131 Rtal 91
OBLIQUE Vida, 113, 531
OBLIQUELY Vida, 120
OBLIVION To sweet oblivion of his
daily care; ....242 DVil 31
OBSCURE Obscure it sinks, nor shall
it more impart ....239 DVil 31
Far in a wilderness obscure ....37 Ed&A 60
Far shelter'd in a glade obscure v37 Ed&A 208
OBSEQUIES His obsequies forbid, ...18 DRtH 50
OBSERVANT Vida, 273, 640
OBSERVATION To make an observation
on the shore. ....14 pZob 72
OBSERVE Imprimis, pray observe his

hat, ...15 NSim 56
Lastly, vouchsafe t' observe his
hand, ...31 NSim 57
OBSERVED Vida, 402
OBTAIN Industrious habits in each
breast obtain, ...v299 Trav 173
In these, ere triflers half their
wish obtain, ...261 DVil 32
Our Cumberland's sweet-bread its
place shall obtain, ...9 Rtal 87
OBTAINS Or e'en imaginary worth
obtains, ...260 Trav 13
OCCUPY In happier meanness occupy
the mind: ....158 Trav 10
OCEAN Where the broad ocean leans
against the land, ...284 Trav 14
While the pent ocean rising o'er
the pile, ...291 Trav 15
As ocean sweeps the labour'd mole
away; ....428 DVil 37
Vida, 16, 21, 81
ODD You've got an odd something--
a kind of discerning-- ....119 HofV 99
ODD- 'What, yon solemn-faced,
odd-looking man that stands
near!' ....50 LetB 133
ODDITY Rare compound of oddity,
frolic, and fun! ....149 Rtal 92
ODDS 'I hold the odds.--Done, done,
with you, with you?' ....50 eSSC$_1$ 106
O'ER Trav, 52, 233, 291, 325; DVil, 7, 21, 119,
157, 236, 257; LogR, 23; DABd, 1; Ed&A, 87;
Thrn, 214, 233; Capt, I:77; II:16; III:21;
Vida, 9, 20, 78, 130, 193, 233, 263, 360,
410, 426, 489, 501, 519, 648
O'ERCOME Vida, 99
O'ERFLOW That caused his putrid
kennel to o'erflow. ....9 GRos 51
O'ERLEAP Vida, 140
O'ERTOPS And the long grass o'ertops
the mould'ring wall; ....48 DVil 24
O'ERTHROWN Vida, 271, 451
O'ERTURN'D Vida, 266
O'ERWHELM'D Vida, 600
OFF Trav, 390; DTrn, 88; eSis, 31; Thrn, 89;
Rtal, 102, 107; HofV, 57; epLL, 21; Invt, 6;
LetB, 46; Vida, 310, 591
OFFER And offer up a tear. ......I:14 Capt 113
Shall offer up unfeign'd
applause. ....II:96 Capt 122
OFFERED Who offer'd only love. ..v112 Ed&A 209
You spurn the favours offer'd
from his hand, ...II:12 Capt 118
OFFERING What annual offering shall
I make, ...3 Gift 43
OFFERINGS Such short-liv'd offerings
but disclose ....15 Gift 43
OFFERS Ev'ry shock that malice
offers ....42,50 Thrn 75
Offers to love, but means to
deceive me. ....4 "Amw 94
Vida, 472
OFFICER A fine-spoken Custom-house
Officer he, ...v37 HofV 239
OFFSPRING To tempt its new-fledg'd
offspring to the skies, ...168 DVil 28
And owns its offspring in their
yellow eyes. ....14 Cati 94
OFT Trav, 57, 59, 109; DVil, 113, 357; eGNM,
25; Thrn, 91; eSSC$_2$, 24; Vida, 33, 152, 167,
328
OFTEN Trav, 243; DVil, 7, 9, 15; DTrn, 57;
Ed&A, v60; Rtal, 60; HofV, 42; Vida, 276
OGLES Ogles and leers with
artificial skill, ...29 eSSC$_3$ 86
She sits all night at cards, and
ogles at spadille. ....31 eSSC$_3$ 86
The gay coquette, who ogles all
the day, ...17 eSSC$_2$ 108
OGLING The chop-house toast of
ogling connoisseurs. ....18 eSSC$_3$ 85
And ogling the stake which is fix'd
in the centre. ....4 LetB 131
OH See also O$_1$
Farewell, and Oh! where'er thy
voice be tried, ...417 DVil 37
And oh! for this! while sculpture
decks thy shrine, ...128 Thrn 78
Oh! where shall weeping want repair,189 Thrn 81
Oh, let me fly a land that spurns
the brave, ...221 Thrn 82
There's my countryman H--gg--ns--Oh!
let him alone, ...29 HofV 96
'O--Oh!' quoth my friend, 'he'll
come on in a trice, ...99 HofV 98
Oh! for a Richard's voice to catch
the theme: ....23 epLL 101
Lend me your hands.--Oh! fatal news
to tell: ....35 eSSC$_1$ 105
Vida, 505
OIL Oil, vinegar, sugar, and saltness
agree: ....12 Rtal 87
OLD$_1$ Heavens! how unlike their
Belgic sires of old! ....313 Trav 15
Of old, when Scarron his companions
invited, ...1 Rtal 87
OLD$_2$ The young contending as the
old survey'd; ....20 DVil 23
Let all the old pay homage to
your merit; ....29 eSSC$_1$ 105
OLD$_3$ The good old sire, the first
prepar'd to go ....371 DVil 35
The old buffoon will fit my name
as well; ....18 pLab 41
Her present face surpass the old; ..96 DTrn 55
He turns old woman, and bestrides
a broom. ....36 eSis 71
The good old sire, unconscious of
decay, ...155 Thrn 79
Old Edward's sons, unknown to yield,225 Thrn 82
That we wish'd him full ten times
a day at Old Nick; ....58 Rtal 89
Old Shakespeare, receive him, with
praise and with love, ...123 Rtal 91
I'm for a different set.--Old men,
whose trade is ....19 eSSC$_1$ 104
What justice, when both to the Old
Bailey brought! ....41 LetB 133
Vida, 16
OLDER And news much older than their
ale went round. ....224 DVil 30
-ON Her hangers-on out short all; ..22 MBlz 47
ONCE Trav, 159, 224, 278; DVil, 56, 80, 137,
220, 327; pLab, 15; Gift, 6; eSis, 17, 44;

Thrn, 118, 169; epLL, 29; eSSC$_1$, 33;
Capt, I:15; LetB, 6; Vida, 89, 236,
329, 339, 369, 435

ONE$_1$ Say, would the angry fair
one prize ....7 Gift 43
'Twas one, both, three of them,
they know not whether; ....2 GCRL 51
The wondering fair one turn'd to
chide, ...147 Ed&A 64
The astonish'd fair one turned to
chide,-- ....v147 Ed&A 211
'Young man,' cries one--a bard
laid up in clover-- ....11 eGNM 68
Yet one fault he had, and that one
was a thumper. ....128 Rtal 91
She that gives all to the false
one pursuing her, ...7 "Amw 94
The one with his speeches, and
t'other with Thrale; ....72 HofV 97
The one at the House, and the other
with THRALE. ....v72 HofV 241
The one is a Scotchman, the other
a Jew, ...75 HofV 97
The one writes the <u>Snarler</u>, the
other the <u>Scourge</u>; ....77 HofV 97
To send such good verses to one
of your taste; ....118 HofV 99
Yet something vain, like one that
shall be nameless, ...28 epLL 102
And a long one to curtail.)-- .....32 Invt 129
To one of my state. ....38 Invt 129
'The same.'--'What a pity! how
does it surprise one! ....51 LetB 133
Vida, 58, 88, 89, 260, 438, 472

ONE$_2$ Hence every state to one
lov'd blessing prone, ...93 Trav 8
To boast one splendid banquet once
a year; ....278 Trav 14
One sink of level avarice shall
lie, ...359 Trav 17
Hence, should one order dis-
proportion'd grow, ...375 Trav 17
One only master grasps the whole
domain, ...39 DVil 24
That one small head could carry
all he knew. ....216 DVil 30
One native charm, than all the
gloss of art; ....254 DVil 31
And while he sinks, without one
arm to save, ...301 DVil 33
Sure these denote one universal
joy! ....324 DVil 34
Good people all, with one accord, ...1 MBlz 47
Yet one fault he had, and that one
was a thumper. ....128 Rtal 91
One gammon of bacon hangs up for
a show: ....10 HofV 95
And at one bound he saves himself,--
like me. ....46 epLL 102
Make but of all your fortune one
<u>va toute</u>; ....48 eSSC$_1$ 105
Oft risks his fortune on one
desperate throw, ...24 eSSC$_2$ 108
Why, let them come, one good
remains to cheer; ....I:95 Capt 117
Let us one hour, one little
hour obey; ....II:31 Capt 119
Vida, 90, 102, 160, 203, 359, 505,
647

ONE'S The modern fair one's jest: ..78 Ed&A 61
The haughty fair one's jest: .....v78 Ed&A 209
'But they're so handsome, one's
bosom it grieves.' ....59 LetB 133

ONLY$_1$ Man seems the only growth
that dwindles here. ....126 Trav 9
One only master grasps the whole
domain, ...39 DVil 24
She only left of all the harmless
train, ...135 DVil 27
This diff'rence only, as the god ...51 NSim 57
And as he had but only me, ...v103 Ed&A 209
He had but only me. ....104 Ed&A 62
Who offer'd only love. ....v112 Ed&A 209
The only art her guilt to cover, ...5 "wlw 67
Whose only plot it is to break
our noses; ....14 epLL 101
And death is your only pre-
ventive: ....63 eSSC$_1$ 106
Vida, 89, 121
He, <u>only</u>, ruminates his former
food. ....12 Tr 267

ONLY$_2$ Yet let them only share the
praises due, ...211 Trav 12
Extremes are only in the master's
mind! ....324 Trav 16
I only would repress them to
secure: ....370 Trav 17
That bliss which only centres in
the mind: ....424 Trav 19
That only shelter'd thefts of
harmless love. ....362 DVil 35
He only wish'd for worlds beyond
the grave. ....374 DVil 35
Diffuse their pleasures only to
destroy! ....388 DVil 36
For let folks only get a touch, ...37 NSim 57
For yonder phantom only flies ....v11 Ed&A 208
On earth unseen, or only found .....79 Ed&A 61
Only rocks her to repose. ......43, 51 Thrn 75
And is a terror only at a
distance; ....94 Thrn 77
Then only poor, indeed, the day
she died. ....127 Thrn 78
'Twas only that when he was off he
was acting. ....102 Rtal 90
He shifted his trumpet, and only
took snuff. ....146 Rtal 92
Their hands are only lent to the
Heinel. ....36 eSSC$_1$ 105
Shall Reason only teach to
weep? ....II:52 Capt 120
Only binds the willing heart. III:102 Capt 127
Vida, 141, 155, 504

ON'T My life on't, this had
kept her play from sinking; ....7 eSis 70
No words--I insist on't--precisely
at three: ....48 HofV 96
And now that I think on't, as I
am a sinner! ....51 HofV 96
And now that I think on't, the
story may stop. ....116 HofV 99

ONWARD Or onward, where the rude
Carinthian boor ....3 Trav 5
Onward, methinks, and diligently

slow, ...287 Trav 14
Vida, 597
OPEN$_1$ My door is open still; ....14 Ed&A 59
'Tis Nature's kind retreat, that's always open ....97 Thrn 77
Whose temper was generous, open, sincere; ....151 Rtal 93
Vida, 585, 596
OPEN$_2$ Vida, 74
OPENING The wicket, opening with a latch, ...43 Ed&A 60
The door just opening with a latch, ...v43 Ed&A 208
'The blossom opening to the day, ..121 Ed&A 63
Vida, 515
OPERAS Pretends to taste, at Operas cries caro, ...25 eSSC$_3$ 85
Who sighs for operas, and dotes on dancing, ...20 eSSC$_2$ 108
OPINION Nor wanted man's opinion to be great. ....27 Thrn 75
Vida, 305
OPPORTUNITY Affliction still is virtue's opportunity! ....35 Thrn 75
OPPOSE Vida, 97, 550, 579
OPPOSED Vida, 255
OPPOSITE Vida, 54, 287
OPPRESSED See also OPPREST.
Scarce half alive, oppress'd with many a year, ...3 pLab 41
With answ'ring care oppress'd; .....62 Ed&A 61
OPPRESSING Thou, like the world, th' opprest oppressing, ...vI:27 Capt 250
OPPREST See also OPPRESSED.
Thou, like the world, th' opprest oppressing, ...vI:27 Capt 250
Those streams which cheer the sore opprest, ...III:45 Capt 124
OPULENCE That opulence departed leaves behind; ....132 Trav 9
Hence all the good from opulence that springs, ...301 Trav 15
Seen opulence, her grandeur to maintain, ...401 Trav 18
And every want to opulence allied, .67 DVil 25
ORANGES Here ill-condition'd oranges abound-- ....21 pZob 72
ORBS Those eyeless orbs that shock with ghastly glare, ...III:33 Capt 123
ORDAIN Do not our tyrant lords this day ordain ....I:37 Capt 114
Vida, 104
ORDER$_1$ An order went out, ...25 Invt 128
ORDER$_2$ Vida, 185
ORDER$_3$ Hence, should one order disproportion'd grow, ...375 Trav 17
ORDER$_4$ I'd best step back--and order up a sample. ....38 pZob 73
ORDERED Yet ere he lands he 'as ordered me before, ...13 pZob 72
Vida, 421
ORDERS$_1$ Vida, 498
ORDERS$_2$ Vida, 83
ORE Her useful sons exchang'd for useless ore? ....398 Trav 18
Proud swells the tide with loads of freighted ore, ...269 DVil 32
ORNAMENT The pictures plac'd for ornament and use, ...231 DVil 31
ORPHANED The military boy, the orphan'd maid, ...157 Thrn 79
OSTENTATION Hence ostentation here, with tawdry art, ...273 Trav 14
Are pleas'd to be kind--but I hate ostentation.' ....44 HofV 96
OSWEGO Where wild Oswego spreads her swamps around, ...411 Trav 19
OSWEGO'S Oswego's dreary shores shall be my grave; ....222 Thrn 82
OTHER$_1$ By holding out to tire each other down; ....26 DVil 24
The one with his speeches, and t'other with Thrale; ....72 HofV 97
The one at the House, and the other with THRALE. ....v72 HofV 241
The one is a Scotchman, the other a Jew, ...75 HofV 97
The one writes the Snarler, the other the Scourge; ....77 HofV 97
Tell each other to rue ....35 Invt 129
Vida, 58, 203
OTHER$_2$ And spurns the plan that aims at other ends; ....96 Trav 8
Commerce on other shores display'd her sail; ....140 Trav 10
Soon Commerce turn'd on other shores her sail; ....v140 Trav 169
To men of other minds my fancy flies, ...281 Trav 14
Far other aims his heart had learned to prize, ...147 DVil 28
Skill'd in no other arts was she ...39 DTrn 53
And twenty other near relations; ...56 DTrn 53
No, no; I've other contests to maintain; ....17 eGNM 68
The wretch who wants each other blessing, ...I:29 Capt 114
And he who wants each other blessing, ...vI:29 Capt 250
Leave all other joys for me. ....I:67 Capt 116
We fear the Lord, and know no other fear. ....I:96 Capt 117
OTHER'S Yet these each other's power so strong contest, ...89 Trav 8
OTHERS Perceiving others fairly flown, ...93 DTrn 55
Instead of others, damns himself. ....54 NSim 57
OTHERS' To new-found worlds, and wept for others' woe; ....372 DVil 35
Now cut each others' throats, for pay. ....40 LogR 45
OUGHT To draw men as they ought to be, not as they are. ....64 Rtal 89
OURSELVES Still to ourselves in every place consign'd, ...431 Trav 19
Ourselves alone from idol-worship free? ....I:34 Capt 114
OUTS Whose ins and outs no ray of sense discloses, ...13 epLL 101
OUTSTRIPS He bounds aloft, outstrips the fleeting wind: ....40 epLL 102
OVEN Had shut out the pasty on shutting his oven ....114 HofV 99

boastful of her hoard, ...195 Trav 11
But the chaste blackbird, to its
partner true, ...9 Cati 94
While the dark owl to court its
partner flies, ...13 Cati 94
PARTS Here Cumberland lies, having
acted his parts, ...61 Rtal 89
PARTY And to party gave up what was
meant for mankind. ....33 Rtal 88
But no matter, I'll warrant we'll
make up the party ....73 HofV 97
Come, end the contest here, and aid
my party. ....56 eSSC$_1$ 106
Vida, 182
PARTY- Patriots, in party-coloured
suits, that ride 'em. ....16 eSis 70
PARTY'S And she, whose party's
largest, shall proceed. ....12 eSSC$_1$ 104
PASS I see the lords of human
kind pass by, ...328 Trav 16
Shall kiss the cup to pass it to
the rest. ....250 DVil 31
Pass from the shore, and darken all
the strand. ....402 DVil 36
'What does Mrs. Bunbury?' 'I, Sir?
I pass.' ....16 LetB 132
'Who, I? let me see, Sir, why I
must pass too.' ....18 LetB 132
PASSAGE Vida, 256
PASSED See also $PAST_2$
I still had hopes, my long vexations
pass'd, ...95 DVil 26
His Heaven commences ere the world
be pass'd! ....112 DVil 27
There, as I pass'd with careless
steps and slow, ...115 DVil 27
The service pass'd, around the
pious man, ...181 DVil 29
But when those charms are pass'd,
for charms are frail, ...291 DVil 33
When the poor exiles, every pleasure
pass'd, ...365 DVil 35
The needy seldom pass'd her door, ...5 MBlz 47
But, when a twelvemonth pass'd away, 33 DTrn 53
While all their hours were pass'd
between ....59 DTrn 54
Want pass'd for merit at her door, 124 Thrn 78
Vida, 230, 434, 439
PASSES Here passes current; paid
from hand to hand, ...261 Trav 14
PASSING And passing rich with forty
pounds a year; ....142 DVil 28
Where once the sign-post caught
the passing eye, ...220 DVil 30
Invites each passing stranger that
can pay; ....2 DABd 48
PASSION Imprints the patriot passion
on his heart, ...200 Trav 11
A transitory passion. ....16 Gift 43
And malice is his ruling passion; ..44 LogR 45
And while his passion touch'd my
heart, ...131 Ed&A 63
Ev'ry passion hush'd to rest, ...37,45 Thrn 75
Not a look, not a smile shall my
passion discover: ....6 "Amw 94
The nightingale, with mutual passion
blest, ...11 Cati 94
In thy black aspect every passion
sleeps, ...9 epLL 101
Off! off! vile trappings! a new
passion reigns! ....21 epLL 101
Who mump their passion, and who,
grimly smiling, ...21 eSSC$_1$ 104
PASSIONS Thus to my breast alternate
passions rise, ...55 Trav 7
PASSIVE In passive ease they leave
the world to chance. ....v(156) Trav 170
$PAST_1$ Swells at my breast, and turns
the past to pain. ....82 DVil 26
And turning all the past to pain; I:26 Capt 114
$PAST_2$ See also PASSED
But past is all his fame. The very
spot ....217 DVil 30
Yes, my companions, Heaven's decrees
are past, ...III:1 Capt 122
Rise to transports past express-
ing, ...III:91 Capt 126
Vida, 635
PASTE In vain she tries her paste
and creams, ...85 DTrn 54
PASTE- The paste-board triumph and
the cavalcade; ....150 Trav 10
PASTIME While many a pastime circled
in the shade, ...19 DVil 23
Vida, 21
PASTURE Vida, 519
PASTY What say you--a pasty? it
shall, and it must, ...53 HofV 97
Yet Johnson, and Burke, and a good
venison pasty, ...62 HofV 97
In the middle a place where the
pasty--was not. ....84 HofV 98
There's a pasty'--'A pasty!' repeated
the Jew, ...101 HofV 98
'What the de'il, mon, a pasty!'
re-echoed the Scot, ...103 HofV 98
'What the de'il, mon, a pasty!'
returned the Scot, ...v103 HofV 242
While thus we resolv'd, and the
pasty delay'd, ...107 HofV 98
Had shut out the pasty on shutting
his oven ....114 HofV 99
PATCHED A window, patch'd with paper,
lent a ray, ...7 DABd 48
The window, patch'd with paper,
lent a ray, ...v7 DABd 200
PATCHING But dressing, patching,
repartee; ....40 DTrn 53
PATER- To folks at Pater-Noster-Row; 34 LogR 45
PATH Vida, 7, 129, 203
PATIENCE Like some well-fashion'd
arch thy patience stood, ...32 Thrn 75
PATIENT With patient angle trolls the
finny deep, ...187 Trav 11
Methinks her patient sons before me
stand, ...283 Trav 14
With sulky eye he smoak'd the
patient man, ...v(21) DABd 200
Where modest want and patient
sorrow dwell; ....123 Thrn 78
First of the train the patient rustic
came, ...167 Thrn 80
PATIENTLY Forsake the fair, and
patiently--go simpling; ....6 pZob 72

PATRIOT$_1$ Till half a patriot,
half a coward grown, ...391 Trav 18
Yon patriot, too, who presses on
your sight, ...37 eSis 71
For a patriot, too cool; for a
drudge, disobedient; ....39 Rtal 88
PATRIOT$_2$ Imprints the patriot passion
on his heart, ...200 Trav 11
Where noble stems transmit the
patriot flame, ...357 Trav 17
Which triumph forces from the
patriot heart, ...2 Queb 46
Prompt not their loves:--the patriot
bird pursues ....5 Cati 94
PATRIOTIC And patriotic boasting
reason's shame! ....v(82) Trav 168
PATRIOT'S Such is the patriot's
boast, where'er we roam, ...73 Trav 7
PATRIOTS Though patriots flatter,
still shall wisdom find ....77 Trav 7
Though patriots flatter, and though
fools contend, ...v77 Trav 168
Patriots, in party-coloured suits,
that ride 'em. ....16 eSis 70
PAUSE$_1$ To fill the languid pause
with finer joy; ....218 Trav 12
And fill'd each pause the night-
ingale had made. ....124 DVil 27
PAUSE$_2$ To pause from toil, and
trim their ev'ning fire; ....14 Trav 5
But hold--let me pause--Don't I
hear you pronounce ....13 HofV 95
Taught by our art her ridicule to
pause on, ...21 eSSC$_2$ 108
PAUSED How often have I paus'd on
every charm, ...9 DVil 23
Vida, 164
PAUSING Vida, 543
PAVILION Vida, 528
PAWED Vida, 597
PAWN Vida, 344, 496, 546
PAY$_1$ Nor cut each others' throats,
for pay. ....40 LogR 45
PAY$_2$ The chest contriv'd a double
debt to pay, ...229 DVil 30
Sighing we pay, and think e'en
conquest dear; ....6 Queb 46
Invites each passing stranger that
can pay; ....2 DABd 48
That welcomes every stranger that
can pay, ...v(20) DABd 200
And well my life shall pay; ....138 Ed&A 64
This pilgrimage I pay, ...v138 Ed&A 210
Let all the old pay homage to
your merit; ....29 eSSC$_1$ 105
Finds his lost senses out, and
pay his debts. ....26 eSSC$_2$ 108
Can but pay its proper score. ...II:62 Capt 120
PAYS And every pang that folly
pays to pride. ....68 DVil 25
PEACE Bless'd be those feasts where
mirth and peace abound, ...v17 Trav 167
Her presence banish'd all his peace. 18 DTrn 52
May peace that claimed while here
thy warmest love, ...110 Thrn 78
May blissful endless peace be thine
above! ....111 Thrn 78
Lovely, lasting Peace below, ...112 Thrn 78
Lovely, lasting Peace, appear; ....116 Thrn 78
But peace to his spirit, wherever
it flies, ...119 Rtal 91
O peace of mind, angelic guest! .II:1 Capt 118
Compliance with his will your
peace secures, ...II:9 Capt 118
Vida, 446
PEACEFUL Those healthful sports
that grac'd the peaceful scene, ...71 DVil 25
Skilled in every peaceful art; III:100 Capt 127
PEASANT With food as well the peasant
is supplied ....83 Trav 8
The shelter-seeking peasant builds
his shed, ...162 Trav 10
While e'en the peasant boasts
these rights to scan, ...333 Trav 16
Thither no more the peasant shall
repair ....241 DVil 31
The mournful peasant leads his
humble band; ....300 DVil 33
PEASANTRY But a bold peasantry, their
country's pride, ...55 DVil 25
PEASANT'S Though poor the peasant's
hut, his feasts though small, ...177 Trav 11
PECULIAR This favourite good begets
peculiar pain. ....98 Trav 8
Some peculiar pleasure owes; ...II:56 Capt 120
PEDANT A scholar, yet surely no
pedant was he. ....156 Rtal 93
PEEPS Sweet as the primrose peeps
beneath the thorn; ....330 DVil 34
PEERS John Trott was desired by
two witty peers ....1 ClRp 100
PELTING 'To 'bide the pelting of
this pitiless storm'-- ....32 eGNM 69
PEN His wand's a modern author's
pen; ....44 NSim 57
PENAL Each wanton judge new penal
statutes draw, ...385 Trav 18
Vida, 661
PENANCE And e'en in penance planning
sins anew. ....130 Trav 9
PENCE But when you come down with
your pence, ...14 "LSm 84
PENCIL His pencil was striking,
resistless, and grand; ....139 Rtal 91
His pencil our faces, his manners
our heart: ....142 Rtal 92
PENITENT Makes but a penitent, loses
a lover. ....8 "Amw 94
PENSIVE I sit me down a pensive
hour to spend; ....32 Trav 6
The pensive exile, bending with his
woe, ...419 Trav 19
Here, as with doubtful, pensive
steps I range, ...v(81) DVil 182
The sad historian of the pensive
plain. ....136 DVil 27
And cheer'd his pensive guest: .....48 Ed&A 60
The pensive stranger's woe; ......v58 Ed&A 208
PENT While the pent ocean rising
o'er the pile, ...291 Trav 15
PEOPLE Good people all, with one
accord, ...1 MBlz 47
Good people all, of every sort, ...1 MDog 65
'What signifies handsome, when people

are thieves?' ....60 LetB 133
PEOPLED Have we not seen, round
Britain's peopled shore, ...397 Trav 18
PEOPLE'S And vindicate thy people's
cause; ....II:94 Capt 122
PEPPER And Dick with his pepper
shall heighten their savour. ....8 Rtal 87
PEPPERED Who pepper'd the highest was
surest to please. ....112 Rtal 90
PERCEIVE Vida, 520
PERCEIVED Vida, 290, 538
PERCEIVING Perceiving others fairly
flown, ...93 DTrn 55
PERFECT Reflected now a perfect
fright: ....82 DTrn 54
Jack finds his wife a perfect
beauty. ....104 DTrn 55
Vida, 318
PERFECTION Yet, why impair thy bright
perfection? ....5 Sonn 46
PERFECTLY They're perfectly dis-
graceful! strike me dead! ....33 epLL 102
PERFORM And to perform takes equal
care. ....52 LogR 45
Nor can my strength perform what they
require; ....174 Thrn 80
PERFUMES Ye Gilead groves, that
fling perfumes around, ...I:20 Capt 114
PERHAPS And yet, perhaps, if countries
we compare, ...75 Trav 7
And yet, perhaps, if states with
states we scan, ...v75 Trav 168
E'en now, perhaps, as there some
pilgrim strays ....413 Trav 19
She once, perhaps, in village plenty
bless'd, ...327 DVil 34
E'en now, perhaps, by cold and
hunger led, ...339 DVil 34
My wealth perhaps their aim. .....v108 Ed&A 209
Your brother Doctor there, perhaps,
may try.' ....14 eGNM 68
Perhaps, to vulgar eyes, bestrides
the state; ....34 eSis 71
Perhaps you may ask if the man was
a miser? ....129 Rtal 91
Too courteous, perhaps, or obligingly
flat? ....131 Rtal 91
Perhaps he confided in men as they
go, ...133 Rtal 91
Who perhaps to the summit of science
could soar, ...159 Rtal 93
So, perhaps, in your habits of
thinking amiss, ...123 HofV 99
PERISHED Then since he perish'd by
my fault, ...v137 Ed&A 210
PERPETUALLY Vida, 578
PERPLEX Now, to perplex the ravell'd
noose, ...71 DTrn 54
PERPLEXED Thus foil'd in my courage,
on all sides perplex'd, ...27 LetB 132
PERSIAN And your bacon I hate like
a Turk or a Persian; ....86 HofV 98
PERSON A person ever neatly clean: 100 DTrn 55
Vida, 437
PERSUADE To persuade Tommy Townshend
to lend him a vote; ....34 Rtal 88
PERSUADES Caesar persuades, submission
must be mine; ....12 pLab 41
PERSUASIVE Aid slighted truth; with
thy persuasive strain ....423 DVil 37
PERT Here vanity assumes her pert
grimace, ...275 Trav 14
Ye news-paper witlings! ye pert
scribbling folks ....163 Rtal 93
PERUSE In the next place, his feet
peruse, ...23 NSim 56
PERVERSE Vida, 542
PETRIFIED With looks that quite
petrified, enter'd the maid; ....108 HofV 98
PETTY I fly from petty tyrants to
the throne. ....392 Trav 18
PEW She never slumber'd in her pew,-- 15 MBlz 47
PHALANX Vida, 256
PHANTASTIC Each hour the gay phantastic
crowd ....v109 Ed&A 209
PHANTOM For yonder faithless
phantom flies ....11 Ed&A 59
For yonder phantom only flies ....v11 Ed&A 208
PHILOMEL Sad Philomel thus--but
let similes drop-- ....115 HofV 99
PHILOSOPHIC Say, should the
philosophic mind disdain ....39 Trav 6
PHIZ Her face is grown a knowing phiz;68 DTrn 54
PHOEBUS Vida, 172, 226, 282, 286, 295, 316,
326, 401, 418, 419, 443, 460, 545, 555, 567,
594, 610
PHRASES The Mohawk too--with angry
phrases stored, ...27 $eSSC_2$ 109
First Sir Charles advances with
phrases well strung, ...55 LetB 133
PICK To pick her wintry faggot from
the thorn, ...133 DVil 27
He drives his flock to pick the
scanty blade, ...306 DVil 33
PICK- No pick-pockets, or
poetasters, ...36 LogR 45
PICKING For making a blunder, or
picking a bone. ....30 HofV 96
May well be call'd picking of pockets
in law; ....38 LetB 133
And picking of pockets, with which I
now charge ye, ...39 LetB 133
PICTURE The haunch was a picture for
painters to study, ...3 HofV 95
To spoil such a delicate picture by
eating; ....6 HofV 95
PICTURED Thine, Freedom, thine the
blessings pictur'd here, ...335 Trav 16
You'll find him pictur'd at full
length ....11 NSim 56
PICTURES The pictures plac'd for
ornament and use, ...231 DVil 31
The humid wall with paltry pictures
spread: ....10 DABd 48
PIEBALD That I found humour in a
piebald vest, ...5 epLL 101
PIECE To be shown to my friends as
a piece of virtu; ....8 HofV 95
How can the piece expect or hope for
quarter? ....38 $eSSC_2$ 109
PIERCE Vida, 113, 126, 480
PIERCED Vida, 350, 447
PIERCES Vida, 375, 526
PIERCING How piercing is that eye!

how sleek that brow! ....35 epLL 102
-PIERCING Grief dares to mingle
her soul-piercing voice, ...3 Queb 46
PIETY Processions form'd for piety
and love, ...151 Trav 10
And piety, with wishes plac'd
above, ...405 DVil 36
PIGEON But you, my good friend,
are the pigeon. ....17 "LSm 84
PIGEONS They're all but a parcel
of Pigeons. ....8 "LSm 84
Here's the Three Jolly Pigeons
for ever. ....22 "LSm 84
Here's a health to the Three Jolly
Pigeons. ....26 "LSm 84
PILE And, wond'ring man could want
the larger pile, ...163 Trav 10
While the pent ocean rising o'er
the pile, ...291 Trav 15
PILFERED 'But, pray, whom have
they pilfer'd?'--'A Doctor, I
hear.' ....49 LetB 133
PILFERING 'Pray what are their
crimes?'--'They've been pilfering
found.' ....48 LetB 133
PILGRIM And haply too some pilgrim,
thither led, ...197 Trav 11
E'en now, perhaps, as there some
pilgrim strays ....413 Trav 19
'Then, pilgrim, turn, thy cares
forgo; ....29 Ed&A 60
There Faith shall come, a pilgrim
gray, ...132 Thrn 78
PILGRIMAGE This pilgrimage I
pay, ...v138 Ed&A 210
PILL To swear the pill, or drop,
has wrought a cure; ....2 eGNM 68
And make full many a bitter pill
go down. ....6 eGNM 68
PILLAGED Pillag'd from slaves to
purchase slaves at home; ....388 Trav 18
PINCHED And, pinch'd with cold,
and shrinking from the shower, ...333 DVil 34
PINE Amidst profusion still I
pine; ....2 TrSA 51
PINIONS These far dispers'd, on
timorous pinions fly, ...237 Trav 13
PIOUS The service pass'd, around
the pious man, ...181 DVil 29
Forgive, and let thy pious care ..v97 Ed&A 209
The pious matron next was seen-- ..182 Thrn 80
Our Dodds shall be pious, our
Kenricks shall lecture; ....86 Rtal 90
PIPE$_1$ With tuneless pipe, beside
the murmuring Loire! ....244 Trav 13
PIPE$_2$ Jack suck'd his pipe, and
often broke ....57 DTrn 54
PIQUE But when a pique began, ...18 MDog 65
PIT At the Pit door stands elbow-
ing a way, ...24 eGNM 68
PITIES Taught by that power that
pities me, ...23 Ed&A 59
PITILESS 'To 'bide the pelting of
this pitiless storm'-- ....32 eGNM 69
PITY$_1$ Or sigh with pity at some
mournful tale, ...20 Trav 6
Fear, pity, justice, indignation
start, ...389 Trav 18
His pity gave ere charity began. ..162 DVil 28
Rather in pity, than in hate, ...2 Byth 42
'But let a maid thy pity share, ...97 Ed&A 62
Our pity shall be given, ...v(166) Ed&A 211
Her constant pity fed the
poor-- ....126 Thrn 78
While pity harmonized the whole. ..238 Thrn 82
What pity, alas! that so lib'ral
a mind ....157 Rtal 93
Pity take on your swain so
clever, ...25 eSSC$_1$ 104
Yes, he's far gone:--and yet some
pity fix, ...41 eSSC$_2$ 109
'The same.'--'What a pity! how
does it surprise one! ....51 LetB 133
To melt me to pity, and soften
my swearing. ....54 LetB 133
PITY$_2$ I learn to pity them. ....24 Ed&A 59
PITYING Ye Muses, pour the pitying
tear ....1 DRtH 50
Even pitying hills would drop a
tear!-- ....11 DRtH 50
But pitying his distress, let
virtue shine, ...3 GRos 51
Vida, 241, 284
PLACE Still to ourselves in every
place consign'd, ...431 Trav 19
While secret laughter titter'd
round the place; ....28 DVil 24
Pants to the place from whence at
first she flew, ...94 DVil 26
There, where a few torn shrubs the
place disclose, ...139 DVil 27
Nor e'er had chang'd, nor wished to
change his place; ....144 DVil 28
His looks adorn'd the venerable
place; ....178 DVil 29
The parlour splendours of that
festive place; ....226 DVil 30
Nor ever cringe to men in place; ...30 LogR 45
The seasons, fram'd with listing,
found a place, ...13 DABd 48
In the next place, his feet peruse, 23 NSim 56
But not a soul will budge to give
him place. ....30 eGNM 69
The place is uninhabited, I fear! ..23 pZob 73
Unite to stamp the beauties of the
place, ...145 Thrn 79
Our Cumberland's sweet-bread its
place shall obtain, ...9 Rtal 87
In short, 'twas his fate, unemploy'd,
or in place, Sir, ...41 Rtal 88
When come to the place where we all
were to dine, ...67 HofV 97
In the middle a place where the
pasty--was not. ....84 HofV 98
In the middle a place where the
Ven'son--was not. ....v84 HofV 241
There is a place, so Ariosto
sings, ...1 eSSC$_2$ 108
But where's this place, this
storehouse of the age? ....5 eSSC$_2$ 108
The time, the theme, the place,
and all conspire. ....II:46 Capt 120
Vida, 92, 213, 539, 652, 670
PLACE$_2$ I had thoughts, in my

chambers, to place it in view, ...7 HofV 95
Has he not seen how you your favour
place, ...35 $eSSC_2$ 109
PLACED And, plac'd on high above
the storm's career, ...33 Trav 6
The pictures plac'd for ornament
and use, ...231 DVil 31
And piety, with wishes plac'd
above, ...405 DVil 36
Our Author's friends, thus plac'd
at happy distance, ...21 eGNM 68
On the grave of Augusta these
garlands be plac'd, ...255 Thrn 83
On the grave of Augusta this
garland be plac'd, ...259 Thrn 83
Both are plac'd at the bar, with
all proper decorum, ...43 LetB 133
PLACES Lost human wits have places
there assign'd them, ...3 $eSSC_2$ 108
PLAIN$_1$ Or where Campania's plain
forsaken lies, ...5 Trav 5
The crowded mart, the cultivated
plain, ...295 Trav 15
Sweet Auburn! loveliest village
of the plain, ...1 DVil 23
And half a tillage stints thy
smiling plain: ....40 DVil 24
The sad historian of the pensive
plain. ....136 DVil 27
O'er Afric's sandy plain, ...214 Thrn 82
O'er Afric's sandy plain, ...II:16 Capt 118
That this way slowly bend along
the plain? ....III:16 Capt 123
Vida, 50, 115, 193, 207, 233,
254, 310, 350, 370, 388,
406, 560, 596, 622, 636, 629
The sea subsiding spreads a level
plain: ....4 Tr 267
PLAIN$_2$ As some fair female unadorn'd
and plain, ...287 DVil 32
And Douglas is pudding, substantial
and plain: ....10 Rtal 87
To be plain, my good Lord, it's
but labour misplac'd ....117 HofV 99
PLAINLY And by a quick transition,
plainly show ....7 GRos 51
PLAINS Lakes, forests, cities,
plains, extending wide, ...35 Trav 6
O'er plains they ramble unconfin'd, 23 LogR 44
How sad the groves and plains
appear, ...9 DRtH 50
Our Dean shall be venison, just
fresh from the plains; ....5 Rtal 87
Ye plains where Jordan rolls its
glassy tide, ...I:18 Capt 114
These hills how sweet! those
plains how wond'rous fair, ...I:21 Capt 114
PLAINTIVE But ha! what means
yon sadly plaintive train, ...III:15 Capt 123
PLAINTS With louder plaints
the mother spoke her woes, ...379 DVil 35
PLAN Or estimate their bliss on
Reason's plan, ...v76 Trav 168
And spurns the plan that aims at
other ends; ....96 Trav 8
PLANNING And e'en in penance
planning sins anew. ....130 Trav 9

PLANT 'What, plant my thistle,
Sir, among his roses! ....16 eGNM 68
PLANTER'S Nor ask luxuriance from
the planter's toil; ....120 Trav 9
PLANTS As aromatic plants be-
stow ....I:47 Capt 115
PLASHY That feebly bends beside
the plashy spring; ....130 DVil 27
PLATTER Displays her cleanly platter
on the board: ....196 Trav 11
Never rang'd in a forest, or
smok'd in a platter; ....2 HofV 95
PLAY$_1$ When toil remitting lent its
turn to play, ...16 DVil 23
Spontaneous joys, where Nature has
its play, ...255 DVil 31
Vida, 186
PLAY$_2$ As some unhappy wight, at
some new play, ...23 eGNM 68
Her moral play a speaking masquer-
ade; ....4 eSis 70
My life on't, this had kept her
play from sinking; ....7 eSis 70
Our life is all a play, compos'd
to please, ...7 $eSSC_3$ 85
PLAY- Thus on the stage, our
play-wrights still depend ....3 eGNM 68
PLAY$_3$ But all the gentler morals,
such as play ....235 Trav 13
Let boys play tricks, and kick
the straw; not I: ....13 eGNM 68
When you with your bagpipes are
ready to play, ...43 $eSSC_1$ 105
All play their own way, and they
think me an ass,-- ....15 LetB 132
PLAYED Vida, 675
PLAYFUL The playful children just
let loose from school; ....120 DVil 27
PLAYING Zephyrs through the wood-
land playing, ...II:49 Capt 120
Thus, playing, and playing, I
still grow more eager, ...33 LetB 132
PLAYS Vida, 208
PLAY-WRIGHT See PLAY-.
PLEADS Turns Female Barrister,
and pleads for Bayes. ....35 $eSSC_3$ 86
PLEASANT An abridgment of all
that was pleasant in man; ....94 Rtal 90
Here Hickey reclines, a most blunt,
pleasant creature, ...125 Rtal 91
All smirking, and pleasant, and
big with adventure, ...3 LetB 131
PLEASE Pleas'd with thyself, whom
all the world can please, ...242 Trav 13
They please, are pleas'd, they
give to get esteem, ...265 Trav 14
Seats of my youth, when every
sport could please, ...6 DVil 23
With sweet succession, taught e'en
toil to please; ....32 DVil 24
Secure to please while youth con-
firms her reign, ...288 DVil 32
Hopeless of pleasing, yet inclin'd
to please. ....14 pLab 41
She strove the neighbourhood to
please, ...9 MBlz 47
First please to turn to god

Mercurius; ....10 NSim 56
Our life is all a play, compos'd
to please, ...7 eSSC$_3$ 85
Who pepper'd the highest was surest
to please. ....112 Rtal 90
'An't please you,' quoth John,
'I'm not given to letters, ...3 ClRp 100
Vida, 31, 86, 321

PLEASED Pleas'd with each good
that heaven to man supplies: ....56 Trav 7
Pleas'd with thyself, whom all the
world can please, ...242 Trav 13
They please, are pleas'd, they
give to get esteem, ...265 Trav 14
Pleas'd with his guests, the good
man learn'd to glow, ...159 DVil 28
Their welfare pleas'd him, and
their cares distress'd; ....186 DVil 29
Have pleas'd our eyes, and sav'd
the pain of thinking. ....8 eSis 70
Adopting his portraits, are pleas'd
with their own. ....72 Rtal 89
For he knew when he pleas'd he
could whistle them back. ....108 Rtal 90
Are pleas'd to be kind--but I
hate ostentation.' ....44 HofV 96
Vida, 3, 12, 226, 305, 341, 498,
511, 550

PLEASING Whence from such lands
each pleasing science flies, ...215 Trav 12
Hopeless of pleasing, yet inclin'd
to please. ....14 pLab 41
Attempted pleasing him alone. ......94 DTrn 55
Vida, 14

PLEASURE Becomes a source of
pleasure when redrest. ....214 Trav 12
Leans for all pleasure on another's
breast. ....272 Trav 14
Why have I stray'd from pleasure
and repose, ...425 Trav 19
And still as each repeated pleasure
tir'd, ...23 DVil 24
The toiling pleasure sickens into
pain; ....262 DVil 32
While thus the land adorn'd for
pleasure, all ....285 DVil 32
To see those joys the sons of
pleasure know ....313 DVil 33
To see each joy the sons of
pleasure know ....v313 DVil 189
The dome where Pleasure holds
her midnight reign ....319 DVil 33
When the poor exiles, every
pleasure pass'd, ...365 DVil 35
And bless'd the cot where every
pleasure rose ....380 DVil 35
His simp'ring friends, with
pleasure in their eyes, ...27 eGNM 69
Who mix'd reason with pleasure,
and wisdom with mirth: ....24 Rtal 87
The sounds of barb'rous pleasure
strike mine ear; ....I:52 Capt 115
Haste, ye sprightly sons of
pleasure; ....I:65 Capt 116
Some peculiar pleasure owes; ...II:56 Capt 120
You vain, whom youth and
pleasure guide, ...III:27 Capt 123
Love and pleasure in his
train; ....III:96 Capt 126
Vida, 103, 138

PLEASURE'S Have we not seen, at
pleasure's lordly call, ...405 Trav 18
That leads to truth through
pleasure's flowery way! ....4 epTP 100

PLEASURES If few their wants,
their pleasures are but few; ......212 Trav 12
Unknown to them, when sensual
pleasures cloy, ...217 Trav 12
Their morals, like their pleasures,
are but low; ....228 Trav 12
Diffuse their pleasures only tc
destroy! ....388 DVil 36
And quells the raptures which from
pleasures start. ....4 Queb 46
Such pleasures, unalloy'd with
care, ...7 DTrn 52
The pleasures that we lose
to-day; ....II:60 Capt 120

PLEDGE Who left a pledge be-
hind. ....8 MBlz 47

PLENTY Bless'd be those feasts with
simple plenty crown'd, ...17 Trav 5
Convenience, plenty, elegance,
and arts; ....304 Trav 15
Where health and plenty cheer'd
the labouring swain, ...2 DVil 23
Those gentle hours that plenty
bade to bloom, ...69 DVil 25
She once, perhaps, in village
plenty bless'd, ...327 DVil 34
Lovers are plenty; but fail to
relieve me: ....2 "Amw 94

PLETHORIC Its former strength was
but plethoric ill. ....144 Trav 10

PLIES There the pale artist plies
the sickly trade; ....316 DVil 33

PLOT Whose only plot it is to
break our noses; ....14 epLL 101

PLOUGH Vida, 365

PLOUGH- Or drives his vent'rous
plough-share to the steep; ....188 Trav 11

PLUCKED And pluck'd his gown, to
share the good man's smile. ....184 DVil 29

PLUMAGE The simple plumage, or the
glossy down ....4 Cati 94

PO Or by the lazy Scheldt, or
wandering Po; ....2 Trav 5

POCKET$_1$ 'Twas no defect of yours,
but pocket low, ...8 GRos 51

POCKET$_2$ While the harpies about me
all pocket the pool. ....8 LetB 131

POCKETS May well be call'd picking
of pockets in law; ....38 LetB 133
And picking of pockets, with which
I now charge ye, ...39 LetB 133

-POCKETS No pick-pockets, or
poetasters, ...36 LogR 45

POET Say, where has our poet this
malady caught? ....73 Rtal 89
Well, suppose it a bounce--sure a
poet may try, ...15 HofV 95
While converts thank their poet in
the skies. ....10 epTP 100
Unepilogued the Poet waits his

sentence. ....70 eSSC$_1$ 107
POETASTERS No pick-pockets, or
poetasters, ...36 LogR 45
POETRY And thou, sweet Poetry,
thou loveliest maid, ...407 DVil 36
POET'S For in a modern poet's
flights, ...28 NSim 57
Where, splendid as the youthful
poet's dream, ...142 Thrn 79
POETS Where kings have toil'd, and
poets wrote for fame, ...358 Trav 17
And monarchs toil, and poets pant
for fame, ...v358 Trav 174
Ye statesmen, warriors, poets,
kings; ....81 Thrn 77
Those poets, who owe their best
fame to his skill, ...121 Rtal 91
But hang it--to poets who seldom
can eat, ...31 HofV 96
POINTED And love's and friendship's
finely pointed dart ....231 Trav 13
POINTS Or thins her lip, or points
her nose: ....64 DTrn 54
Vida, 479
POISE Vida, 221
POISON And, 'Madam,' quoth he,
'may this bit be my poison, ...91 HofV 98
POISONOUS Those pois'nous fields
with rank luxuriance crown'd, ...351 DVil 35
POLAR Or winter wraps the polar
world in snow, ...420 DVil 37
POLITE For you're always polite
and attentive, ...61 eSSC$_1$ 106
POLITICIAN Yon politician, famous
in debate, ...33 eSis 71
POLITICS No politics disturb their
mind; ....24 LogR 44
POLLIO For Pollio snatch'd away; ....2 DRtH 50
POLLUTED Hence through their
tribes no mix'd polluted flame, ...7 Cati 94
-POLLUTED Tremble, thou vice-
polluted breast; ....II:73 Capt 121
POLLUTING And thus polluting
honour in its source, ...395 Trav 18
POMP The pomp of kings, the
shepherd's humbler pride. ....36 Trav 6
Here may be seen, in bloodless
pomp array'd, ...149 Trav 10
In barren solitary pomp repose? ...404 Trav 18
Unwieldy wealth, and cumbrous
pomp repose; ....66 DVil 25
But the long pomp, the midnight
masquerade, ...259 DVil 31
The praise attending pomp and
power, ...6 Thrn 74
But when to pomp and power are
join'd ....12 Thrn 74
Vida, 511
POMPS Here, while the proud their
long-drawn pomps display, ...317 DVil 33
PONDER Let me ponder, and tell
what I think of the dead. ....22 Rtal 87
Come ponder his severer fate, .III:25 Capt 123
PONDERED Vida, 192
PONDERING E'en now, methinks,
as pond'ring here I stand, ...397 DVil 36
Vida, 551

PONDEROUS Relax his pond'rous
strength, and lean to hear; ....246 DVil 31
More ponderous chains, and
dungeons more confin'd. .....II:92 Capt 122
His squalid limbs with pond'rous
fetters torn; ....III:32 Capt 123
Vida, 211
POOL$_1$ The noisy geese that
gabbled o'er the pool, ...119 DVil 27
POOL$_2$ While the harpies about me
all pocket the pool. ....8 LetB 131
The whole pool as my own--'Come,
give me five cards.' ....24 LetB 132
POOL'S The pool's very rich--
ah! the Doctor is loo'd!' ....26 LetB 132
POOR$_1$ Laws grind the poor, and
rich men rule the law; ....386 Trav 18
Takes up a space that many poor
supplied; ....276 DVil 32
She freely lent to all the
poor,-- ....7 MBlz 47
A refuge to the neighbouring
poor ....39 Ed&A 60
Her constant pity fed the poor-- ..126 Thrn 78
POOR$_2$ Though poor, luxurious;
though submissive, vain; ....128 Trav 9
Though poor the peasant's hut,
his feasts though small, ...177 Trav 11
Rough, poor, content, ungovernably
bold; ....314 Trav 15
An hour's importance to the poor
man's heart; ....240 DVil 31
Where the poor houseless
shiv'ring female lies. ....326 DVil 34
When the poor exiles, every
pleasure pass'd, ...365 DVil 35
That found'st me poor at first,
and keep'st me so; ....414 DVil 37
Though very poor, may still be
very bless'd; ....426 DVil 37
Poor Madam, now condemn'd to
hack ....91 DTrn 55
Then only poor, indeed, the day
she died. ....127 Thrn 78
To-morrow you take a poor dinner
with me; ....47 HofV 96
Here lies poor Ned Purdon, from
misery freed, ...1 epEP 100
Vida, 519, 612
POOR'S The rich man's joys in-
crease, the poor's decay, ...266 DVil 32
POPPY No poppy water half so
good; ....36 NSim 57
POPULATION But now the sounds of
population fail, ...125 DVil 27
PORT Pride in their port, defiance
in their eye, ...327 Trav 16
PORTER No surly porter stands in
guilty state ....105 DVil 26
Here, porter!--this venison with
me to Mile-end; ....55 HofV 97
And the porter and eatables follow'd
behind. ....58 HofV 97
PORTERS At court, the porters,
lacqueys, waiters, ...54 LogR 45
PORTION An equal portion dealt to
all mankind, ...78 Trav 7

eternity; ....III:104 Capt 127
PRAISE$_2$ Yet would the village
praise my wondrous power, ...249 Trav 13
I'll praise her while my life
shall last, ...201 Thrn 81
We scarcely can praise it, or
blame it too much; ....30 Rtal 88
Of praise a mere glutton, he
swallow'd what came, ...109 Rtal 90
Praise but our gods, and every
good is yours. ....II:10 Capt 118
PRAISED Who prais'd me for im-
puted charms, ...107 Ed&A 62
-PRAISED While he was be-
Roscius'd, and you were be-
prais'd! ....118 Rtal 91
PRAISES Yet let them only share
the praises due, ...211 Trav 12
PRANCED Vida, 597
PRANCING Vida, 48, 128
PRANKS Laugh at the jests or
pranks that never fail, ...19 Trav 6
PRAY$_1$ And fools, who came to scoff,
remain'd to pray. ....180 DVil 29
Whene'er he went to pray. ....8 MDog 65
Assist me, I pray, in this woful
attack; ....58 eSSC$_1$ 106
Save us, O Lord! to thee, though
late, we pray, ...III:63 Capt 125
PRAY$_2$ Imprimis, pray observe
his hat, ...15 NSim 56
Pray a slice of your liver, though
may I be curs'd, ...93 HofV 98
'Pray what does Miss Horneck?
take courage, come do,'-- ......17 LetB 132
'Pray, Ma'am, be so good as to give
your advice; ....29 LetB 132
'Pray what are their crimes?'--
'They've been pilfering found.' 48 LetB 133
'But, pray, whom have they pil-
fer'd?'--'A Doctor, I hear.' ...49 LetB 133
PRAYED He watch'd and wept, he
pray'd and felt, for all. ....166 DVil 28
PRAYER My morning prayer, my
evening song, ...200 Thrn 81
PRAYS The Bar-maid now for your
protection prays, ...34 eSSC$_3$ 86
PREACH They always preach best
with a skinful. ....13 "LSm 84
PREACHER'S The village preacher's
modest mansion rose. ....140 DVil 27
PREACHERS When Methodist preachers
come down ....10 "LSm 84
-PREACHING A-preaching that drink-
ing is sinful, ...11 "LSm 84
PRECEDING And e'en the pang preceding death ....II:35 Capt 119
PRECISELY No words--I insist
on't--precisely at three: ....48 HofV 96
PRECISION Have strove to prove with
great precision, ...7 LogR 44
PREGNANT The pregnant quarry team'd
with human form; ....138 Trav 9
PREJUDICE A Scotchman, from pride
and from prejudice free; ....155 Rtal 93
PRELIMINARY Vida, 299
PREPARATION The preparation is the
executioner. ....92 Thrn 77
PREPARE Why this delay? at
length for joy prepare; ....II:41 Capt 119
Vida, 109, 197, 277, 498
PREPARED The good old sire, the
first prepar'd to go ....371 DVil 35
Vida, 30, 74
PREPARES Prepares our monarch's
victories to sing. ....II:70 Capt 121
PREPARING Vida, 51
PRESAGE Lands he could measure,
terms and tides presage, ...209 DVil 30
PRESAGING Every ill presaging, .II:21 Capt 119
PRESENCE Her presence banish'd
all his peace. ....18 DTrn 52
PRESENT Her present face surpass
the old; ....96 DTrn 55
Vida, 572
PRESENTS Love presents the fairest
treasure, ...I:66 Capt 116
PRESS$_1$ Cross-readings, Ship-
news, and Mistakes of the Press. ..170 Rtal 93
PRESS$_2$ Or press the bashful
stranger to his food, ...21 Trav 6
Now press thy fall, ... III:76 Capt 125
PRESSED See also PREST.
Nor the coy maid, half willing
to be press'd, ...249 DVil 31
And gaily press'd, and smil'd; .....50 Ed&A 60
PRESSES Yon patriot, too, who
presses on your sight, ...37 eSis 71
PRESSURE To 'scape the pressure of
contiguous pride? ....304 DVil 33
PREST See also PRESSED.
'Twas Edwin's self that prest. ....148 Ed&A 64
PRESUME No more! when slaves thus
insolent presume, ...II:83 Capt 121
Vida, 156
PRESUMING No more presuming on
her sway, ...101 DTrn 55
PRETENCE Their chief pretence my
flatter'd charms, ...v107 Ed&A 209
But in this parallel my best
pretence is, ...13 eSSC$_2$ 108
PRETEND Who can direct, when all
pretend to know? ....64 Trav 7
Nor dare I pretend to know more
than my betters; ....4 ClRp 100
PRETENDS Pretends to taste, at
Operas cries caro, ...25 eSSC$_3$ 85
PRETTIER A prettier dinner I
never set eyes on; ....92 HofV 98
PRETTY Say, cruel Iris, pretty
rake, ...1 Gift 43
That pretty Bar-maids have done
execution. ....6 eSSC$_3$ 85
I like these here dinners so
pretty and small; ....97 HofV 98
PREVAIL No more the wood-man's
ballad shall prevail; ....244 DVil 31
The whips and angry tortures
shall prevail. ....I:94 Capt 117
Vida, 202, 366
PREVAILED Truth from his lips
prevail'd with double sway, ...179 DVil 29
PREVAILING Still let thy voice,
prevailing over time, ...421 DVil 37

PREVAILS Yet oft a sigh prevails,
and sorrows fall, ...57 Trav 7
And honour sinks where commerce
long prevails. ....92 Trav 8
The foe prevails, the lofty walls
recline-- ....III:53 Capt 124
Cyrus, the conqueror of the
world, prevails, ...III:60 Capt 125
PREVENT Vida, 492
PREVENTIVE And death is your
only preventive: ....63 eSSC$_1$ 106
PREVENTS And shame prevents the
deed, ...192 Thrn 81
PREY$_1$ Ill fares the land, to
hast'ning ills a prey, ...51 DVil 25
Where crouching tigers wait their
hapless prey, ...355 DVil 35
PREY$_2$ Where toads shall pant,
and vultures prey. ....III:82 Capt 126
PRIAM Wak'd Priam in drawing
his curtains by night. ....110 HofV 98
PRIDE The pomp of kings, the
shepherd's humbler pride. ....36 Trav 6
Amidst the store, should thankless
pride repine? ....38 Trav 6
'Twere affectation all, and school-
taught pride, ...v39 Trav 168
Let school-taught pride dissemble
all it can, ...41 Trav 6
Woods over woods in gay theatric
pride; ....108 Trav 8
By arts, the splendid wrecks of
former pride; ....146 Trav 10
Some splendid arts, the wrecks of
former pride; ....v146 Trav 170
Here beggar pride defrauds her
daily cheer, ...277 Trav 14
Lift the tall rampire's artificial
pride. ....286 Trav 14
Where lawns extend that scorn
Arcadian pride, ...319 Trav 15
Pride in their port, defiance in
their eye, ...327 Trav 16
But a bold peasantry, their
country's pride, ...55 DVil 25
And every pang that folly pays to
pride. ....68 DVil 25
I still had hopes, for pride
attends us still, ...89 DVil 26
Thus to relieve the wretched was
his pride, ...163 DVil 28
Not so the loss. The man of
wealth and pride ....275 DVil 32
To 'scape the pressure of
contiguous pride? ....304 DVil 33
My shame in crowds, my solitary
pride; ....412 DVil 37
Than reason-boasting mortals'
pride; ....16 LogR 44
Humility displaces pride; ....98 DTrn 55
Repaid his love with pride. .....v132 Ed&A 210
He left me to my pride; ....134 Ed&A 63
His looks resume their youthful
pride, ...v151 Ed&A 211
Doats upon dancing, and in all
her pride, ...27 eSSC$_3$ 85
A Scotchman, from pride and from
prejudice free; ....155 Rtal 93
But for eating a rasher of what
they take pride in, ...11 HofV 95
My pride forbids it ever should
be said, ...3 epLL 101
Ye fields of Sharon, dress'd in
flow'ry pride, ...I:17 Capt 114
'Tis thus that pride triumphant
rears the head, ...III:13 Capt 123
Like yours, his life began in
pride, ...III:29 Capt 123
Your wealth, your pride, your
kingdom, are no more. ......III:72 Capt 125
Vida, 45, 336, 448, 557
PRIESTS Priests, cannibals, and
hoity-toity queens: ....8 pZob 72
PRIME$_1$ My prime of life in wand'ring
spent and care, ...24 Trav 6
PRIME$_2$ His goods, he hopes, are
prime, and brought from far, ...35 pZob 73
PRIMROSE Sweet as the primrose
peeps beneath the thorn; ....330 DVil 34
On her grave shall the cowslip
and primrose be cast, ...249 Thrn 83
And there shall the cowslip
and primrose be cast, ...257, 261 Thrn 83
PRINCE And brave prince William
show'd his lamp-black face: ....14 DABd 48
Vida, 95
PRINCE'S The beggar's pouch and
prince's purple lie, ...104 Thrn 77
PRINCES Princes and lords may
flourish, or may fade; ....53 DVil 25
PRISON Vida, 405
PRIVATE The dog, to gain some
private ends, ...19 MDog 65
The dog, to gain his private
ends, ...v19 MDog 212
Vida, 586
PRIZE$_1$ Vida, 250, 487
PRIZE$_2$ That independence Britons
prize too high, ...339 Trav 16
Far other aims his heart had
learned to prize, ...147 DVil 28
Say, would the angry fair one
prize ....7 Gift 43
And those who prize the paltry
things, ...71 Ed&A 61
Let us prize death as the best
gift of nature-- ....86 Thrn 77
PRIZED At length his silly head,
so priz'd before, ...43 epLL 102
PROCEED But let us not proceed too
furious, ...9 NSim 56
And now proceed we to our simile. ..14 NSim 56
A just comparison,--proceed. ....22 NSim 56
If I proceed, our bard will be
undone! ....42 eSis 71
And she, whose party's largest,
shall proceed. ....12 eSSC$_1$ 104
Vida, 105, 111, 188
PROCESSIONS Processions form'd
for piety and love, ...151 Trav 10
PROCLAIM The echoes of Thames
shall my sorrows proclaim, ...244 Thrn 83
PROCLAIMS Boldly proclaims that
happiest spot his own, ...66 Trav 7

The clarion's note proclaims the
finish'd war! ....III:84 Capt 126
PROCURE As puffing quacks some
caitiff wretch procure ....1 eGNM 68
PRODUCT No product here the barren
hills afford, ...169 Trav 10
Around the world each needful
product flies, ...283 DVil 32
PRODUCTS That leaves our useful
products still the same. ....274 DVil 32
PROFANE For superstitious rites
and mirth profane? ....I:38 Capt 114
Or join with sounds profane its
sacred mirth! ....I:92 Capt 117
PROFFERS With richest proffers
strove: ....110 Ed&A 63
PROFIT To profit by resembling
thee. ....139 Thrn 79
PROFOUND Where village statesmen
talk'd with looks profound, ...223 DVil 30
A simple song, a sigh profound. ...131 Thrn 78
Vida, 150, 446
PROFUSELY Vida, 347
PROFUSION Ye fields, where summer
spreads profusion round, ...46 Trav 6
To see profusion that he must not
share; ....310 DVil 33
Amidst profusion still I pine; ......2 TrSA 51
And art exhausts profusion round, .129 Thrn 78
PROLOGUES For Epilogues and Pro-
logues on some friend, ...4 eGNM 68
PROLONG My children shall the note
prolong. ....206 Thrn 81
PROMISCUOUS Vida, 359
PROMISCUOUSLY Promiscuously re-
cline; ....102 Thrn 77
Vida, 391
PROMISED Promis'd to hold them on
for life, ...74 DTrn 54
There promised a lover to come--
but, O me! ....245 Thrn 83
Vida, 183
PROMISES$_1$ What! no reply to
promises so ample? ....37 pZob 73
PROMISES$_2$ He promises with equal
air, ...51 LogR 45
PROMPT$_1$ But in his duty prompt at
every call, ...165 DVil 28
PROMPT$_2$ Prompt not their loves:--
the patriot bird pursues ....5 Cati 94
PROMPTER Hold! Prompter, hold!
a word before your nonsense; ....1 epLL 101
PRONE Hence every state to one
lov'd blessing prone, ...93 Trav 8
Both prone to change, no settled
limits fix, ...11 eSSC$_2$ 108
PRONOUNCE But hold--let me pause--
Don't I hear you pronounce ....13 HofV 95
-PRONOUNCING And saw thee fall
with joy-pronouncing eyes: ....10 Queb 46
PROOFS The stress of all my proofs
on him I lay, ...13 NSim 56
PROPER Here for a while my proper
cares resign'd, ...101 Trav 8
Can but pay its proper score. ..II:62 Capt 120
Both are plac'd at the bar, with
all proper decorum, ...43 LetB 133

PROPHET In vain the madd'ning
prophet threatens woe, ...III:3 Capt 122
-PROPHET The master-prophet
grasps his full-ton'd lyre. ....II:64 Capt 120
PROPHETIC See how prophetic
rapture fills his form, ...II:67 Capt 121
PROPHETS Ye prophets, skill'd
in Heaven's eternal truth, ...II:27 Capt 119
PROPORTIONED Is but to lay proportion'd loads on each. ....374 Trav 17
PROSECUTE At law his neighbour
prosecute, ...20 LogR 44
PROSPECT And trace them through
the prospect as it lies: ....100 Trav 8
To Death's great court, the prospect
seems more fair. ....96 Thrn 77
PROSPECTS And, all his prospects
bright'ning to the last, ...111 DVil 27
PROSTRATE Where prostrate error
hails the rising sun? ....I:36 Capt 114
PROTECTION The Bar-maid now for
your protection prays, ...34 eSSC$_3$ 86
PROTECTS Vida, 509
PROTEST But, my Lord, it's no
bounce: I protest in my turn, ...17 HofV 95
PROUD$_1$ Yes! let the rich deride,
the proud disdain, ...251 DVil 31
Here, while the proud their long-
drawn pomps display, ...317 DVil 33
How low the proud, how feeble
are the strong! ....III:62 Capt 125
PROUD$_2$ By proud contempt, or
favour's fostering sun, ...368 Trav 17
The ruin'd spendthrift, now no
longer proud, ...153 DVil 28
Proud swells the tide with loads
of freighted ore, ...269 DVil 32
At proud men's doors they ask a
little bread! ....340 DVil 34
That trade's proud empire hastes
to swift decay, ...427 DVil 37
Too nice for a statesman, too
proud for a wit: ....38 Rtal 88
Of virtues and feelings, that
folly grows proud; ....70 Rtal 89
Vida, 100
PROUDLY That proudly rise, or
humbly court the ground; ....114 Trav 9
When commerce proudly flourish'd
through the state; ....134 Trav 9
PROVE But let them prove it if
they can. ....4 LogR 44
Have strove to prove with great
precision, ...7 LogR 44
Vida, 106
PROVIDENCE Sure 'twas by Providence
design'd, ...1 Byth 42
PROVIDENTLY Then let us,
providently wise, ...II:57 Capt 120
PROVOKE Awake resentment, or
your rage provoke; ....2 GRos 51
But wake thy vengeance and provoke
thy rage. ....75 Thrn 76
PROVOKING In short, so provoking
a devil was Dick, ...57 Rtal 89
PROWLING Vida, 520
PRUDE Comes here at night, and

goes a prude away. ....18 eSSC$_2$ 108
PRUDENCE Vida, 458
PRUDENT Vida, 216, 530
PRUSSIA'S And Prussia's monarch
shew'd his lamp-black face ....v14 DABd 200
PUDDING And Douglas is pudding,
substantial and plain: ....10 Rtal 87
At the sides there was spinach
and pudding made hot; ....83 HofV 98
PUFF And the puff of a dunce he
mistook it for fame; ....110 Rtal 90
PUFFING As puffing quacks some
caitiff wretch procure ....1 eGNM 68
PULLED Then pull'd his breeches
tight, and thus began, ...v(22) DABd 200
PUN Who relish'd a joke, and
rejoic'd in a pun; ....150 Rtal 92
PUNISH The English laws forbid
to punish lunatics. ....42 eSSC$_2$ 109
PUPIL The pupil of impulse, it
forc'd him along, ...45 Rtal 88
PUPPY Both mongrel, puppy, whelp,
and hound, ...15 MDog 65
PURCHASE Pillag'd from slaves to
purchase slaves at home; ....388 Trav 18
PURCHASED And purchas'd strength
from its increasing load. ....33 Thrn 75
PURDON Here lies poor Ned Purdon,
from misery freed, ...1 epEP 100
PURER Vida, 660
PURGED Vida, 661
PURITY Could nought of purity
display, ...123 Ed&A 63
PURLOINED Vida, 404
PURPLE The beggar's pouch and
prince's purple lie, ...104 Thrn 77
PURPOSE To suit my purpose to a
hair; ....8 NSim 56
Vida, 90
PURSUANT He comes pursuant to
divine decree,. ....III:89 Capt 126
PURSUE Impell'd, with steps
unceasing, to pursue ....25 Trav 6
And, as a hare, whom hounds and
horns pursue, ...93 DVil 26
And too fond of the <u>right</u> to pursue
the <u>expedient</u>. ....40 Rtal 88
Hence, intruder! we'll pursue ..II:53 Capt 120
Vida, 9
PURSUED Of fools pursuing, and
of fools pursu'd! ....12 epLL 101
PURSUES As each a different way
pursues, ...72 DTrn 54
Prompt not their loves:--the patriot
bird pursues ....5 Cati 94
PURSUING Quite sick of pursuing
each troublesome elf, ...77 Rtal 89
She that gives all to the false one
pursuing her, ...7 "Amw 94
Of fools pursuing, and of fools
pursu'd! ....12 epLL. 101
PURSUIT Ye gamesters, who, so eager
in pursuit, ...47 eSSC$_1$ 105
PUSHED Vida, 406
PUT When he put on his clothes. ....12 MDog 65
May put off life and be at rest
for ever. ....89 Thrn 77
Then come, put the jorum about, ...19 "LSm 84
I put off being shaved; ....6 Invt 128
Or to put on my duds; ....10 Invt 128
Ah! the Doctor is loo'd! Come,
Doctor, put down.' ....32 LetB 132
PUTRID That caused his <u>putrid</u>
<u>kennel</u> to o'erflow. ....9 GRos 51
PUZZLE Let school-masters puzzle
their brain, ...1 "LSm 84
PUZZLED But in parting with these
I was puzzled again, ...25 HofV 96

QUACK Come, all ye quack bards, and
ye quacking divines, ...81 Rtal 89
QUACKING Come, all ye quack bards,
and ye quacking divines. ....81 Rtal 89
QUACKS As puffing quacks some
caitiff wretch procure ....1 eGNM 68
The scourge of impostors, the terror
of quacks: ....80 Rtal 89
QUADRUPEDS Are known to honest
quadrupeds; ....37 LogR 45
QUAES Their Quis, and their Quaes,
and their Quods, ...7 "LSm 84
QUARRY The pregnant quarry teem'd
with human form; ....138 Trav 9
QUARTER$_1$ How can the piece expect
or hope for quarter? ....38 eSSC$_2$ 109
QUARTER$_2$ Vida, 220
QUARTERS Vida, 484
QUEBEC Quebec in vain shall teach
our breast to glow, ...7 Queb 46
QUEEN As when in Paphian groves the
Queen of Love ....9 MrsX 49
With garlands of beauty the queen
of the May ....251 Thrn 83
Like a tragedy queen he has dizen'd
her out, ...67 Rtal 89
Vida, 65, 73, 132, 195, 248, 255, 276, 281,
292, 294, 315, 334, 369, 382, 429, 493, 500,
516, 525, 550, 553, 573, 583, 589, 600, 606,
618, 643, 650
QUEEN'S Vida, 258
QUEENS Priests, cannibals, and
hoity-toity queens: ....8 pZob 72
On sentimental Queens and Lords in
lace? ....36 eSSC$_2$ 109
Vida, 57, 425
QUELLS And quells the raptures
which from pleasures start. ....4 Queb 46
QUENCH Detection her taper shall
quench to a spark, ...91 Rtal 90
QUICK And by a quick transition,
plainly show ....7 GRos 51
Vida, 567
QUICKLY That quickly they begin to
snore. ....40 NSim 57
But we quickly found out, for who
could mistake her? ....111 HofV 98
QUIET Alas, that such frolic should
now be so quiet! ....52 Rtal 88
QUILL Nor draw the quill to write
for B--b. ....32 LogR 45
QUINTO Is, by quinto Elizabeth,
Death without Clergy. ....40 LetB 133
QUIS Their Quis, and their Quaes,
and their Quods, ...7 "LSm 84

QUIT And e'en the captain quit
the field. ....90 DTrn 55
And quit for Venus, many a
brighter here; '..................4 pZob 72
Vida, 629
QUITE And quite forgot their vices
in their woe; ....160 DVil 28
'Till quite dejected with my scorn, 133 Ed&A 63
Till quite dejected by my scorn, vl33 Ed&A 210
Quite sick of pursuing each
troublesome elf, ...77 Rtal 89
My friend bade me welcome, but struck
me quite dumb, ...69 HofV 97
With looks that quite petrified,
enter'd the maid; ....108 HofV 98
QUITS Who quits a world where
strong temptations try ....101 DVil 26
And quits her Nancy Dawson, for
Che faro, ...26 eSSC$_3$ 85
He quits the woods, and tries the beaten
ways; ....41 epLL 102
Quits the Ballet, and calls for
Nancy Dawson. ....21 eSSC$_2$ 108
QUODS Their Quis, and their Quaes,
and their Quods, ...7 "LSm 84
QUOTH And, 'Madam,' quoth he, 'may
this bit be my poison, ...91 HofV 98
'The tripe,' quoth the Jew, with
his chocolate cheek, ...95 HofV 98
'Your Tripe!' quoth the Jew, 'if
the truth I may speak, ...v95 HofV 242
'O--Oh!' quoth my friend, 'he'll
come on in a trice, ...99 HofV 98
'An't please you,' quoth John, 'I'm
not given to letters, ...3 ClRp 100

RABBLE'S The rabble's rage, and
tyrant's angry steel; ....366 Trav 17
RACE$_1$ Remote from towns he ran his
godly race, ...143 DVil 28
Half naked at a ball or race; ......44 DTrn 53
That still a godly race he ran, ...7 MDog 65
Vida, 486
RACE$_2$ Where rougher climes a nobler
race display, ...166 Trav 10
O there the natives are--a dreadful
race! ....25 pZob 73
A sleek and idle race is all their
care. ....176 Thrn 80
The last remains of Judah's royal
race: ....III:20 Capt 123
RACKED I long had rack'd my
brains to find ....vl NSim 205
RADIANT Vida, 177
RAGE$_1$ Redress the clime, and all its
rage disarm. ....176 Trav 11
The rabble's rage, and tyrant's
angry steel; ....366 Trav 17
Teach erring man to spurn the rage
of gain; ....424 DVil 37
Awake resentment, or your rage
provoke; ....2 GRos 51
Whenever rage or envy rise, ...65 DTrn 54
Denote the rage with which he writes,47 NSim 57
Warm'd up each bustling scene, and
in her rage ....5 eSis 70
And, wondering how their rage was
borne, ...22 Thrn 75
But wake thy vengeance and provoke
thy rage. ....75 Thrn 76
Tremble, ye mortals, at my
rage! ....79,83 Thrn 76,77
Shakespeare himself shall feel my
tragic rage. ....20 epLL 101
Reflect, nor tempt to rage the
royal mind. ....II:14 Capt 118
Vida, 2, 267, 418, 424, 454
RAGE$_2$ Vida, 391
RAGED Vida, 368
RAGING The raging deep, the
whirlwind's roar-- ....218 Thrn 82
Than angry monarch's raging. ...II:24 Capt 119
RAGS Those ill-becoming rags--
that matted hair! ....III:34 Capt 123
RAISE Unknown those powers that
raise the soul to flame, ...219 Trav 12
More skill'd to raise the wretched
than to rise. ....148 DVil 28
More bent to raise the wretched
than to rise. ....v148 DVil 184
Comfort came down the trembling
wretch to raise, ...175 DVil 29
To raise a flame in Cupids of
threescore. ....18 eSis 70
Is this a time to bid us raise the
strain, ...I:87 Capt 117
RAISED How did Grub-street re-echo
the shouts that you rais'd, ...117 Rtal 91
RAKE Say, cruel Iris, pretty rake, ..1 Gift 43
RAKES To this strange spot, Rakes,
Macaronies, Cits, ...15 eSSC$_2$ 108
RALLIES Vida, 361, 461
RALLY But I will rally, and combat
the ruiner: ....5 "Amw 94
RAMBLE O'er plains they ramble
unconfin'd, ...23 LogR 44
RAMPIRE'S Lift the tall rampire's
artificial pride. ....286 Trav 14
RAN Remote from towns he ran his
godly race, ...143 DVil 28
With steady zeal, each honest rustic
ran; ....182 DVil 29
And e'en the story ran that he
could gauge. ....210 DVil 30
That still a godly race he ran, ...7 MDog 65
The wond'ring neighbours ran, ...22 MDog 65
RANDOM Like yon neglected shrub at
random cast, ...103 Trav 8
RANGE Here, as with doubtful, pensive
steps I range, ...v(81) DVil 182
'No flocks that range the valley
free ....21 Ed&A 59
RANGED Amazed the gazing rustics
rang'd around, ...214 DVil 30
Rang'd o'er the chimney, glisten'd
in a row. ....236 DVil 31
Never rang'd in a forest, or smok'd
in a platter; ....2 HofV 95
RANK$_1$ When wealth and rank and noble
blood, ...15 Thrn 74
RANK$_2$ Vida, 24, 644
RANK$_3$ Those pois'nous fields with
rank luxuriance crown'd, ...351 DVil 35
A bloated mass of rank unwieldy

woe; ....392 DVil 36
RANKLING Depriv'd of sight and
rankling in his chain; ....II:89 Capt 121
RANKS Vida, 231, 373, 390, 480,
584
RAPHAELS When they talk'd of
their Raphaels, Correggios, and
stuff, ...145 Rtal 92
RAPTURE She speaks! 'tis rapture
all, and nameless bliss, ...7 MrsX 49
More lasting rapture from his
works shall rise, ...9 epTP 100
Let rapture the minutes em-
ploy; ....I:58 Capt 115
Like the sun, our great monarch
all rapture supplies, ...I:61 Capt 116
Come on, and bid the warbling
rapture rise, ...II:43 Capt 119
See how prophetic rapture fills
his form, ...II:67 Capt 121
RAPTURES Hoards after hoards
his rising raptures fill, ...53 Trav 7
Unfit for raptures, or, if raptures
cheer ....223 Trav 12
And quells the raptures which from
pleasures start. ....4 Queb 46
The raptures of the bridal night? ..22 DTrn 52
Haste to raptures ever rising: ..I:69 Capt 116
RARE Rare compound of oddity,
frolic, and fun! ....149 Rtal 92
RARELY To men remote from power
but rarely known, ...437 Trav 19
RASCALS I'll wager the rascals
a crown ....12 "LSm 84
RASHER But for eating a rasher of
what they take pride in, ...11 HofV 95
RATHER Rather in pity, than in
hate, ...2 Byth 42
Or rather like tragedy giving a
rout. ....68 Rtal 89
No; rather let us triumph still
the more, ...I:41 Capt 115
Or rather, Love's delights
despising, ...I:68 Capt 116
RATIOCINATIONS By ratiocinations
specious, ...6 LogR 44
RATIONAL As rational, the human
kind; ....2 LogR 44
RATIONE Homo est ratione
praeditum,-- ....9 LogR 44
RATTLING The rattling chariots
clash, the torches glare. ....322 DVil 34
The rattling terrors of the
vengeful snake; ....354 DVil 35
RAVAGE To ravage in a country
town! ....12 DTrn 52
RAVAGED Mingling the ravag'd
landscape with the skies. ....358 DVil 35
RAVAGERS Nor did the cruel ravagers
design ....56 Thrn 76
RAVELLED Now, to perplex the
ravell'd noose, ...71 DTrn 54
RAVISHED In vain, to charm thy
ravish'd sight, ...28 Thrn 75
Strephon caught thy ravish'd
eye; ....24 eSSC$_1$ 104
RAY Those blazing suns that dart
a downward ray, ...347 DVil 34
A window, patch'd with paper,
lent a ray, ...7 DABd 48
The window, patch'd with paper,
lent a ray, ...v7 DABd 200
With hospitable ray. ....4 Ed&A 59
Whose ins and outs no ray of
sense discloses, ...13 epLL 101
Emits a brighter ray. ....II:40 Capt 119
RAZOR To eat mutton cold, and cut
blocks with a razor. ....42 Rtal 88
RE- See RE-COUNTS, RE-ECHO, RE-
ECHOED, RE-UNITED
REACH$_1$. Vida, 157
REACH$_2$ And all that freedom's highest
aims can reach, ...373 Trav 17
When truth and virtue reach the
skies, ...3 Thrn 74
Wing all our thoughts to reach the
skies, ...II:4 Capt 118
Vida, 480
READ I read your looks, and see
compliance there. ....II:42 Capt 119
READILY And first I hope, you'll
readily agree ....13 eSSC$_1$ 104
READING Till reading, I forget
what day on, ...5 NSim 56
-READINGS Cross-readings, Ship-news,
and Mistakes of the Press. ....170 Rtal 93
READY And every stranger finds a
ready chair; ....16 Trav 5
His ready smile a parent's warmth
express'd, ...185 DVil 29
But I've eat of your tripe till
I'm ready to burst.' ....94 HofV 98
When you with your bagpipes are
ready to play, ...43 eSSC$_1$ 105
My voice shall be ready to carol
away ....44 eSSC$_1$ 105
Vida, 507, 602
REAL Some spot to real happiness
consign'd, ...60 Trav 7
Honour, that praise which real
merit gains, ...259 Trav 13
Yet, when he deigns his real shape
t' assume, ...35 eSis 71
Vida, 2
REALMS Where'er I roam, whatever
realms to see, ...7 Trav 5
My fortune leads to traverse realms
alone, ...29 Trav 6
Look downward where a hundred realms
appear; ....34 Trav 6
So bless'd a life these thoughtless
realms display, ...255 Trav 13
REAR Sees no contiguous palace rear
its head ....179 Trav 11
REARED Vida, 211
REARS When impious folly rears her
front on high? ....I:40 Capt 115
'Tis thus that pride triumphant
rears the head, ...III:13 Capt 123
REASON$_1$ Stern o'er each bosom reason
holds her state, ...325 Trav 16
Leave reason, faith, and conscience,
all our own. ....438 Trav 19
Reason, they say, belongs to man, ...3 LogR 44

Who mix'd reason with pleasure, and
wisdom with mirth: ....24 Rtal 87
Nature disowns, and reason scorns
thy mirth, ...8 epLL 101
Shall Reason only teach to
weep? ....II:52 Capt 120
REASON- Than reason-boasting
mortals' pride; ....16 LogR 44
REASON$_2$ With no reason on earth to
go out of his way, ...103 Rtal 90
To tell them the reason why asses
had ears? ....2 ClRp 100
REASON'S Or estimate their bliss
on Reason's plan, ...v76 Trav 168
And patriotic boasting reason's
shame! ....v(82) Trav 168
REASSUMES Vida, 452
REBELLION In vain rebellion aims
her secret blow; ....III:4 Capt 122
REBELLIOUS But if, rebellious
to his high command, ...II:11 Capt 118
RECALLED Vida, 324, 423
RECEDING Till earth, receding
from our eyes, ...II:5 Capt 118
RECEIVE May saints with songs
receive thee to their rest; ....109 Thrn 77
Old Shakespeare, receive him, with
praise and with love, ...123 Rtal 91
RECEIVED Receiv'd the harmless
pair. ....44 Ed&A 60
RECKONING An unpaid reck'ning on
the frieze was scor'd, ...v17 DABd 200
Where are we driven? our reck'ning
sure is lost! ....15 pZob 72
RECLINE Promiscuously recline; ....102 Thrn 77
The foe prevails, the lofty
walls recline-- ....III:53 Capt 124
RECLINED On God's supporting
breast reclin'd? ....I:98 Capt 117
Vida, 401
RECLINES Come, and dance on the
spot where your tyrant reclines: ...82 Rtal 89
Here Hickey reclines, a most blunt,
pleasant creature, ...125 Rtal 91
Here Whitefoord reclines, and deny
it who can, ...147 Rtal 92
RECORD Vida, 14
RECOUNT Vida, 3, 386
RE-COUNTS Bends at his treasure,
counts, re-counts it o'er; ....52 Trav 7
RECOVERED The man recover'd of
the bite, ...31 MDog 66
RECTITUDE Unmov'd in conscious
rectitude, ...25 Thrn 75
RECURRING To former joys recurring
ever, ...I:25 Capt 114
RED Where the Red Lion flaring
o'er the way, ...1 DABd 48
And beplaster'd with rouge his own
natural red. ....100 Rtal 90
Grasp the red bolt, and lay the
guilty low? ....III:36 Capt 123
The white was so white, and the
red was so ruddy. ....v4 HofV 238
REDDENING Vida, 115
REDEEM Vida, 153
REDOUBLED Vida, 424

REDRESS Redress the clime, and
all its rage disarm. ....176 Trav 11
Redress the rigours of th'
inclement clime; ....422 DVil 37
REDRESSING Cyrus comes, our
wrongs redressing, ...III:93 Capt 126
Cyrus comes, the world re-
dressing, ...III:95 Capt 126
REDREST Becomes a source of
pleasure when redrest. ....214 Trav 12
RE-ECHO How did Grub-street re-
echo the shouts that you rais'd, ..117 Rtal 91
Vida, 524
RE-ECHOED Who copied his squibs,
and re-echoed his jokes; ....164 Rtal 93
'What the de'il, mon, a pasty!'
re-echoed the Scot, ...103 HofV 98
REFINED The dews of heaven re-
fin'd, ...122 Ed&A 63
REFINEMENT For, as refinement
stops, from sire to son ....229 Trav 12
REFINING Who, too deep for his
hearers, still went on refining, ...35 Rtal 88
REFLECT Left alone to reflect,
having emptied my shelf, ...59 HofV 97
Reflect, nor tempt to rage the
royal mind. ....II:14 Capt 118
REFLECTED Reflected now a
perfect fright: ....82 DTrn 54
REFLECTS No more thy glassy brook
reflects the day, ...41 DVil 24
Reflects new glories on his
breast, ...141 Thrn 79
REFRAIN Vida, 309
REFRESHING In Sleep's refreshing
arms, ...v126 Ed&A 210
Where brooks refreshing
stray; ....III:40 Capt 124
REFUGE A refuge to the
neighbouring poor ....39 Ed&A 60
REFUSE This debt to thy mem'ry
I cannot refuse, ...173 Rtal 93
REFUSING But, neither this nor
that refusing, ...I:75 Capt 116
REGAIN Vida, 407
REGAL Contracting regal power
to stretch their own; ....382 Trav 18
When first ambition struck at
regal power; ....394 Trav 18
REGALE Regale the drabs and bloods
of Drury-lane; ....4 DABd 48
REGARDLESS Vida, 127
REGARDS Or mix in rites that
Heaven regards with pain? ....I:88 Capt 117
I venture at all,--while my
avarice regards ....23 LetB 132
REGRETTING Though my stomach was
sharp, I could scarce help re-
gretting ....5 HofV 95
REHEARSE Say heavenly muse, their
youthful frays rehearse; ....7 Tr 267
REIGN$_1$ A new creation rescu'd from
his reign. ....296 Trav 15
Secure to please while youth
confirms her reign, ...288 DVil 32
The dome where Pleasure holds her
midnight reign ....319 DVil 33

And when a little rest I
sought ....v125 Ed&A 210
Ev'ry passion hush'd to rest, ...37, 45 Thrn 75
May put off life and be at rest
for ever. ....89 Thrn 77
May saints with songs receive thee
to their rest; ....109 Thrn 77
REST$_2$ That either seems destructive
of the rest. ....90 Trav 8
Shall kiss the cup to pass it to the
rest. ....250 DVil 31
The rest of life with anxious
Jack, ...92 DTrn 55
Amongst the rest young Edwin
bow'd, ...111 Ed&A 63
Among the rest young Edwin bow'd, v111 Ed&A 209
With the rest of the crew, ...15 Invt 128
Vida, 449
REST$_3$ A palled corse, and rest
the body there. ....III:18 Capt 123
RESTED Vida, 620
RESTORED Restor'd to love and
thee. ....152 Ed&A 64
RESTORER Cyrus, our great re-
storer, is at hand, ...III:85 Capt 126
RESTRAIN Though tyrant kings,
or tyrant laws restrain, ...428 Trav 19
RESUME His looks resume their
youthful pride, ...v151 Ed&A 211
RETAINED For thus retain'd, as
learned counsel can, ...5 GRos 51
Vida, 448
RETAINS Vida, 626
RETIRE Bless'd be that spot, where
cheerful guests retire ....13 Trav 5
And now, when busy crowds retire ....45 Ed&A 60
And now, when worldly crowds re-
tire ....v45 Ed&A 208
Vida, 103
RETIRED Where grey-beard mirth and
smiling toil retir'd, ...222 DVil 30
Vida, 371
RETIREMENT O blest retirement,
friend to life's decline, ...97 DVil 26
RETIRES Here Douglas retires, from
his toils to relax, ...79 Rtal 89
RETIRING Vida, 218
RETREAT$_1$ 'Tis Nature's kind retreat,
that's always open ....97 Thrn 77
In that secure, serene retreat, ...100 Thrn 77
RETREAT$_2$ Vida, 224
RETREATING Aye, 'twas but a dream,
for now there's no retreating: .....25 epLL 101
Here lesson'd for a while, and
hence retreating, ...29 eSSC$_2$ 109
RETREATS Retreats from care, that
never must be mine, ...98 DVil 26
RETURN$_1$ But alas! that return I
never shall see, ...243 Thrn 83
Vida, 567, 608
RETURN$_2$ What! no return? I find
too late, I fear, ...17 eSSC$_1$ 104
RETURN$_3$ And, many a year elaps'd,
return to view ....79 DVil 25
Here to return--and die at home
at last. ....96 DVil 26
I'll not wear a garland until she
return; ....242 Thrn 83
When she is remov'd, and shall
never return. ....254 Thrn 83
'The younger the worse,' I return
him again, ...57 LetB 133
Vida, 105
RETURNED Return'd and wept, and
still return'd to weep. ....370 DVil 35
'What the de'il, mon, a pasty!'
returned the Scot, ...v103 HofV 242
RETURNING At night returning,
every labour sped, ...191 Trav 11
RE-UNITED Here lies the good Dean,
re-united to earth, ...23 Rtal 87
REVEL While these a constant
revel keep, ...II:51 Capt 120
REVELRY And his long nights
of revelry and ease; ....68 Trav 7
REVELS$_1$ To revels or to rest, ...v46 Ed&A 208
REVELS$_2$ The madd'ning monarch
revels in my veins. ....22 epLL 101
REVENGE Vida, 352, 617
REVERENCE Vida, 150
REVEREND The reverend champion
stood. At his control, ...173 DVil 29
REVERIE While thus I debated, in
reverie centred, ...35 HofV 96
REWARD$_1$ 'What signifies justice?
I want the reward. ....62 LetB 133
Vida, 183, 491
REWARD$_2$ Vida, 672
REYNOLDS That Ridge is anchovy,
and Reynolds is lamb; ....14 Rtal 87
Here Reynolds is laid, and, to
tell you my mind, ...137 Rtal 91
So I cut it, and sent it to
Reynolds undress'd, ...21 HofV 95
REYNOLDS'S But 'tis Reynolds's
way ....39 Invt 129
REYNOLDSES The Reynoldses two, ...16 Invt 128
RHYMING And teas'd each rhyming
friend to help him out. ....8 eGNM 68
RICH$_1$ Yes! let the rich deride,
the proud disdain, ...251 DVil 31
RICH$_2$ The needy sell it, and the
rich man buys; ....308 Trav 15
Laws grind the poor, and rich
men rule the law; ....386 Trav 18
And passing rich with forty
pounds a year; ....142 DVil 28
The rich man's joys increase, the
poor's decay, ...266 DVil 32
And rich men flock from all the
world around. ....272 DVil 32
The pool's very rich--ah! the
Doctor is loo'd!' ....26 LetB 132
RICHARD Here lies honest Richard,
whose fate I must sigh at; ....51 Rtal 88
RICHARD'S Oh! for a Richard's
voice to catch the theme: ....23 epLL 101
RICHES While nought remain'd of
all that riches gave, ...141 Trav 10
And his best riches, ignorance
of wealth. ....62 DVil 25
RICHEST With richest proffers
strove: ....110 Ed&A 63
RICHLY Here, richly deck'd, admits

the gorgeous train; ....320 DVil 33
And though no temple richly
drest, ...I:11 Capt 113
RIDE Patriots, in party-
coloured suits, that ride 'em. .....16 eSis 70
RIDGE That Ridge is anchovy, and
Reynolds is lamb; ....14 Rtal 87
RIDICULE Taught by our art her
ridicule to pause on, ...21 eSSC$_2$ 108
RIFLE We'll rifle the spring of
its earliest bloom, ...256,260 Thrn 83
RIFLING And, rifling ev'ry
youthful grace, ...79 DTrn 54
RIGHT$_1$ True to imagin'd right,
above control, ...332 Trav 16
In vain, to drive thee from the
right, ...30 Thrn 75
To do thy memory right; ....227 Thrn 82
And too fond of the <u>right</u> to
pursue the <u>expedient</u>. ....40 Rtal 88
RIGHT$_2$ A brain of feather! very
right, ...19 NSim 56
His conduct still right, with his
argument wrong; ....46 Rtal 88
Had your senses been right, ...3 Invt 128
Vida, 298
RIGHT$_3$ Far to the right where
Apennine ascends, ...105 Trav 8
Vida, 58, 117, 135, 237, 244, 262,
336, 372, 448
RIGHT- Vida, 280, 487
RIGHTS While e'en the peasant
boasts these rights to scan, ...333 Trav 16
RIGID Vida, 79
RIGOURS Redress the rigours of
th' inclement clime; ....422 DVil 37
RING Ye beaux and belles, that
form this splendid ring, ...5 eSSC$_1$ 103
Vida, 518
RISE$_1$ Thus to my breast alternate
passions rise, ...55 Trav 7
That proudly rise, or humbly court
the ground; ....114 Trav 9
At her command the palace learn'd
to rise, ...135 Trav 9
And e'en those ills, that round
his mansion rise, ...201 Trav 12
It gives their follies also room
to rise; ....268 Trav 14
Calm is my soul, nor apt to rise
in arms, ...379 Trav 17
More skill'd to raise the wretched
than to rise. ....148 DVil 28
More bent to raise the wretched
than to rise. ....v148 DVil 184
But verging to decline, its
splendours rise, ...297 DVil 33
Since from thy tomb a thousand
heroes rise! ....12 Queb 46
Whenever rage or envy rise, ...65 DTrn 54
Surpris'd, he sees new beauties
rise, ...85 Ed&A 62
He sees unnumber'd beauties rise, v85 Ed&A 209
Sink as he sinks, and as he
rises rise; ....28 eGNM 69
More lasting rapture from his
works shall rise, ...9 epTP 100
Whilst from below the trap-door
Demons rise, ...15 epLL 101
Shall make our homage rise. .....I:10 Capt 113
That strain once more; it bids
remembrance rise, ...I:15 Capt 114
Bids expectation rise. ....II:36 Capt 119
Come on, and bid the warbling
rapture rise, ...II:43 Capt 119
Arise, all potent ruler,
rise, ...II:93 Capt 122
Rise to transports past ex-
pressing, ...III:91 Capt 126
Vida, 26
RISE$_2$ Vida, 11
RISES Sink as he sinks, and as
he rises rise; ....28 eGNM 69
Vida, 575
RISING Hoards after hoards his
rising raptures fill, ...53 Trav 7
While the pent ocean rising o'er
the pile, ...291 Trav 15
His rising cares the hermit spied, .61 Ed&A 61
But, while he spoke, a rising
blush ....83 Ed&A 62
The bashful look, the rising
breast, ...89 Ed&A 62
Where prostrate error hails the
rising sun? ....I:36 Capt 114
Haste to raptures ever rising: ..I:69 Capt 116
Vida, 246
RISKS Oft risks his fortune on
one desperate throw, ...24 eSSC$_2$ 108
RITES For superstitious rites and
mirth profane? ....I:38 Capt 114
Or mix in rites that Heaven
regards with pain? ....I:88 Capt 117
RIVAL$_1$ As an actor, confess'd
without rival to shine: ....95 Rtal 90
RIVAL$_2$ 'Twas a neck and a breast--
that might rival M--r--'s: ....24 HofV 95
'Twas a neck and a breast--that
might rival Monroe's: ....v24 HofV 238
RIVALS My rivals give--and let
'em; ....10 Gift 43
RIVER'S There, sorrowing by the
river's glassy bed, ...151 Thrn 79
RIVERS And rivers through the
valley wind, ...III:41 Capt 124
And rivers listen'd as they
flow'd along. ....10 Tr 267
ROAM Where'er I roam, whatever
realms to see, ...7 Trav 5
Such is the patriot's boast,
where'er we roam, ...73 Trav 7
The wealth of climes, where savage
nations roam, ...387 Trav 18
Still aiming at honour, yet fear-
ing to roam, ...47 Rtal 88
ROAR$_1$ So the loud torrent, and the
whirlwind's roar, ...207 Trav 12
Spreads its long arms amidst the
wat'ry roar, ...289 Trav 14
The raging deep, the whirlwind's
roar-- ....218 Thrn 82
Yet content 'if the table he set
on a roar'; ....160 Rtal 93
Vida, 264, 366, 502

ROAR$_2$ Ferments arise, imprison'd
factions roar, ...345 Trav 16
The labouring ship, and hear the
tempest roar, ...67 Thrn 76
ROBBED Has robb'd the neighbour-
ing fields of half their growth, ..280 DVil 32
That very face had robb'd her
mind. ....38 DTrn 53
Who seems to have robb'd his
vizor from the lion; ....28 eSis 71
They robb'd the relic and defac'd
the shrine. ....59 Thrn 76
ROBE The robe that wraps his
limbs in silken sloth ....279 DVil 32
ROBES And trims her robes of
frieze with copper lace; ....276 Trav 14
She left her wheel and robes of
country brown. ....336 DVil 34
ROCKS$_1$ And though rough rocks
or gloomy summits frown, ...v85 Trav 169
These rocks, by custom, turn to
beds of down. ....86 Trav 8
No vernal blooms their torpid
rocks array, ...171 Trav 11
As rocks resist the billows and
the sky. ....430 DVil 37
And rocks forgot their hardness
at the sound. ....12 MrsX 49
Vida, 9
Exulting rocks have crown'd the
power of song! ....9 Tr 267
ROCKS$_2$ Only rocks her to re-
pose. ....43, 51 Thrn 75
ROCKY- And though the rocky-
crested summits frown, ...85 Trav 8
ROD Drove souls to Tart'rus with
his rod, ...52 NSim 57
ROGUE But what vex'd me most was
that d--'d Scottish rogue, ...89 HofV 98
ROGUES That show'd the rogues they
lied: ....30 MDog 66
ROLL Vida, 414
ROLLED Vida, 308
ROLLING Though round its breast
the rolling clouds are spread, ...191 DVil 29
Through rolling worlds, or fields
of liquid light, ...107 Thrn 77
'Wild is the whirlwind rolling ....213 Thrn 82
And fierce the tempest roll-
ing ....II:17 Capt 118
ROLLS Thus idly busy rolls their
world away: ....256 Trav 13
Ye plains where Jordan rolls its
glassy tide, ...I:18 Capt 114
ROME Vida, 677
ROOD When every rood of ground
maintain'd its man; ....58 DVil 25
ROOM It gives their follies also
room to rise; ....268 Trav 14
Those calm desires that ask'd
but little room, ...70 DVil 25
There in a lonely room, from
bailiffs snug, ...5 DABd 48
Swims round the room, the Heinel
of Cheapside; ....28 eSSC$_3$ 85
Vida, 632, 641
-ROOM Have emptied all the
green-room on the stage. ....6 eSis 70
-ROSCIUS'D While he was be-
Roscius'd, and you were be-
prais'd! ....118 Rtal 91
ROSE$_1$ I'll give--but not the full-
blown rose, ...13 Gift 43
ROSE- Or rose-bud more in
fashion; ....14 Gift 43
ROSE$_2$ And over fields where
scatter'd hamlets rose, ...403 Trav 18
Along the lawn, where scatter'd
hamlets rose, ...65 DVil 25
Up yonder hill the village
murmur rose; ....114 DVil 27
The village preacher's modest
mansion rose. ....140 DVil 27
And bless'd the cot where every
pleasure rose ....380 DVil 35
And, just as humour rose or fell, ..41 DTrn 53
ROSES 'What, plant my thistle,
Sir, among his roses! ....16 eGNM 68
ROSINED May rosined lightning
blast me, if I do! ....18 epLL 101
ROUGE And beplaster'd with rouge
his own natural red. ....100 Rtal 90
ROUGH Rough, poor, content, un-
governably bold; ....314 Trav 15
And, though she felt his usage
rough, ...27 DTrn 53
And though rough rocks or gloomy
summits frown, ...v85 Trav 169
ROUGHER Where rougher climes a
nobler race display, ...166 Trav 10
ROUND$_1$ Who frowns, and talks, and
swears, with round parade, ...29 eSis 71
ROUND$_2$ And round his dwelling
guardian saints attend: ....12 Trav 5
Ye fields, where summer spreads
profusion round, ...46 Trav 6
To winnow fragrance round the
smiling land. ....122 Trav 9
Smiles by his cheerful fire, and
round surveys ....193 Trav 11
And e'en those ills, that round
his mansion rise, ...201 Trav 12
It shifts in splendid traffic
round the land: ....262 Trav 14
Repress'd ambition struggles round
her shore, ...346 Trav 16
Have we not seen, round Britain's
peopled shore, ...397 Trav 18
And sleights of art and feats of
strength went round; ....22 DVil 24
While secret laughter titter'd
round the place; ....28 DVil 24
These round thy bowers their cheerful influence shed, ...33 DVil 24
In all my wand'rings round this
world of care, ...83 DVil 26
Though round its breast the rolling
clouds are spread, ...191 DVil 29
Full well the busy whisper,
circling round, ...203 DVil 30
And news much older than their
ale went round. ....224 DVil 30
Careful to see the mantling bliss
go round; ....248 DVil 31

Hung round their bowers, and
fondly look'd their last, ...366 DVil 35
Down, down they sink, and spread
a ruin round. ....394 DVil 36
The serpents round about it
twin'd ....45 NSim 57
He bows, turns round, and whip--
the man's a black! ....40 eSis 71
Her weeping children round ....62 Thrn 76
Fall, round me fall, ye little
things, ...80 Thrn 77
And art exhausts profusion
round, ...129 Thrn 78
Swims round the room, the Heinel
of Cheapside; ....28 eSSC$_3$ 85
While the bacon and liver went
merrily round. ....88 HofV 98
Ah, me! what angry terrors round
us grow; ....II:25 Capt 119
Saps the strong wall, and pours
destruction round; ....III:50 Capt 124
Round and round go the cards,
while I inwardly damn ....5 LetB 131
When uncover'd, a buzz of enquiry
runs round,-- ....47 LetB 133
Then their friends all come round
me with cringing and leering, ..53 LetB 133
Vida, 129, 252, 452, 517, 524
ROUNDS Here as I take my solitary
rounds, ...77 DVil 25
ROUSED Vida, 288
ROUT Or rather like tragedy
giving a rout. ....68 Rtal 89
ROVE Reluctant dost thou rove; .....66 Ed&A 61
Here amidst sylvan bowers we'll
rove, ...v(161) Ed&A 211
ROVED Vida, 233, 337
ROVING Vida, 161
ROW Rang'd o'er the chimney,
glisten'd in a row. ....236 DVil 31
Vida, 645
-ROW To folks at Pater-Noster-
Row; ....34 LogR 45
ROYAL The twelve good rules, the
royal game of goose; ....232 DVil 31
The royal game of goose was there
in view, ...11 DABd 48
And the twelve rules the royal
martyr drew; ....12 DABd 48
Reflect, nor tempt to rage the
royal mind. ....II:14 Capt 118
The last remains of Judah's
royal race: ....III:20 Capt 123
Vida, 339, 430, 472, 499, 510,
558, 587, 619
RUB But how? ay, there's the
rub! --I've got my cue: ....11 eSis 70
RUDDY Where all the ruddy family
around ....18 Trav 6
The fat was so white, and the lean
was so ruddy. ....4 HofV 95
The white was so white, and the
red was so ruddy. ....v4 HofV 238
See the ruddy morning smiling, .II:47 Capt 120
Vida, 624
RUDE Or onward, where the rude
Carinthian boor ....3 Trav 5
'And, ah! forgive a stranger rude, .93 Ed&A 62
RUE Tell each other to rue ....35 Invt 129
RUFFLES It's like sending them
ruffles, when wanting a shirt. .....34 HofV 96
Like sending 'em Ruffles when
wanting a Shirt. ....v34 HofV 239
RUG The Muse found Scroggen
stretch'd beneath a rug; ....6 DABd 48
RUIN$_1$ There in the ruin, heedless
of the dead, ...161 Trav 10
Sunk are thy bowers in shapeless
ruin all, ...47 DVil 24
Down, down they sink, and spread
a ruin round. ....394 DVil 36
Till ruin shakes all; ....III:10 Capt 122
When ruin shakes all, ...III:11 Capt 122
The ruin smokes, destruction
pours along; ....III:51 Capt 124
The ruin smokes, the torrent
pours along; ....III:61 Capt 125
Vida, 97, 614
RUIN$_2$ Its double weight must
ruin all below. ....376 Trav 17
Vida, 634
RUINED Amidst thy tangling walks,
and ruin'd grounds, ...78 DVil 25
The ruin'd spendthrift, now no
longer proud, ...153 DVil 28
RUINER But I will rally, and
combat the ruiner: ....5 "Amw 94
RULE$_1$ That Hickey's a capon, and
by the same rule, ...15 Rtal 87
Vida, 299
RULE$_2$ Laws grind the poor, and rich
men rule the law; ....386 Trav 18
There, in his noisy mansion,
skill'd to rule, ...195 DVil 29
Vida, 181
RULER Arise, all potent ruler,
rise, ...II:93 Capt 122
Vida, 470
RULES The twelve good rules, the
royal game of goose; ....232 DVil 31
And the twelve rules the royal
martyr drew; ....12 DABd 48
RULING And malice is his ruling
passion; ....44 LogR 45
RUMINATES He, only, ruminates his
former food. ....12 Tr 267
RUN Unalter'd, unimprov'd the
manners run; ....230 Trav 12
Yon critic, too--but whither do
I run? ....41 eSis 71
Vida, 118, 187
RUNNING Through ev'ry maze of fancy
running, ...149 Thrn 79
RUNS When uncover'd, a buzz of
enquiry runs round,-- ....47 LetB 133
Vida, 487
RURAL And rural mirth and manners
are no more. ....74 DVil 25
I see the rural virtues leave the
land: ....398 DVil 36
Forlorn, a rural bard complain'd, .152 Thrn 79
RUSH Vida, 106, 153, 222, 356
RUSHED Vida, 343, 428, 529, 620
RUSHY My rushy couch, and frugal

fare, ...19 Ed&A 59
RUSTIC With steady zeal, each honest
rustic ran; ....182 DVil 29
First of the train the patient
rustic came, ...167 Thrn 80
RUSTICS Amazed the gazing rustics
rang'd around, ...214 DVil 30
RUSTY The rusty grate unconscious
of a fire; ....16 DABd 48
A rusty grate unconscious of a
fire. ....v16 DABd 200
RUTHLESS That dire disease, whose
ruthless power ....75 DTrn 54

SABLE Vida, 5, 55, 216, 245, 333,
378, 458, 492, 512, 514, 533, 583,
618, 646
SABLES Groans, weeping friends,
indeed, and gloomy sables, ...90 Thrn 77
SACRED Or join with sounds profane
its sacred mirth! ....I:92 Capt 117
SACRIFICE Nor sacrifice is here; .I:12 Capt 113
SAD The sad historian of the
pensive plain. ....136 DVil 27
Whilst thy sad fate extorts the
heart-wrung tear. ....8 Queb 46
How sad the groves and plains
appear, ...9 DRtH 50
The wound it seem'd both sore and
sad ....25 MDog 66
May oft distract us with their sad
solemnity: ....91 Thrn 77
A visage so sad, and so pale with
affright, ...109 HofV 98
Sad Philomel thus--but let similes
drop-- ....115 HofV 99
Vida, 285, 616
SADDENS And desolation saddens all
thy green: ....38 DVil 24
SADLY These sadly join beside the
murmuring deep, ...159 Thrn 80
But ha! what means yon sadly
plaintive train, ...III:15 Capt 123
SAFE As a safe inn, where weary
travellers, ...87 Thrn 77
Vida, 146, 340, 484
SAFELY Vida, 219
SAFETY I fear'd for your safety,
I fear'd for my own; ....84 Rtal 89
SAFETY'S Vida, 628
SAGE If virtue fail her counsel
sage, ...82 Thrn 77
SAID I'm sure it may be justly
said, ...29 NSim 57
And spurn the sex,' he said: ....82 Ed&A 62
That a Scot may have humour, I had
almost said wit: ....172 Rtal 93
My pride forbids it ever should
be said, ...3 epLL 101
Vida, 38, 305, 317, 573
SAIL Commerce on other shores
display'd her sail; ....140 Trav 10
The willow-tufted bank, the gliding
sail, ...294 Trav 15
Down where yon anchoring vessel
spreads the sail, ...399 DVil 36
Soon Commerce turn'd on other
shores her sail; ....v140 Trav 169
SAINT A mistress or a saint in
every grove. ....152 Trav 10
SAINT- Deign saint-like tenant
of the dale, ...vl Ed&A 208
SAINTS And round his dwelling
guardian saints attend: ....12 Trav 5
May saints with songs receive thee
to their rest; ....109 Thrn 77
SAKE Merry Whitefoord, farewell!
for thy sake I admit ....171 Rtal 93
SALAD Our Garrick's a salad; for
in him we see ....11 Rtal 87
SALLY Vida, 111, 209
SALTNESS Oil, vinegar, sugar, and
saltness agree: ....12 Rtal 87
SALUTE Whatever sweets salute the
northern sky ....117 Trav 9
SAME Find that the bliss of all is
much the same, ...v(81) Trav 168
That leaves our useful products
still the same. ....274 DVil 32
That Hickey's a capon, and by the
same rule, ...15 Rtal 87
'The same.'--'What a pity! how does
it surprise one! ....51 LetB 133
Vida, 44, 444
SAMPLE I'd best step back--and order
up a sample. ....38 pZob 73
SAMPLER Flings down her sampler, and
takes up the woman: ....22 eSis 70
SANDED The white-wash'd wall, the
nicely sanded floor, ...227 DVil 30
The sanded floor that grits beneath
the tread; ....9 DABd 48
SANDS Boasts of his golden sands
and palmy wine, ...70 Trav 7
Vida, 79
SANDY$_1$ O'er Afric's sandy plain, ...214 Thrn 82
O'er Afric's sandy plain, ...II:16 Capt 118
SANDY$_2$ With Sandy, and Sawney,
and Jockey, ...45 eSSC$_1$ 105
SAPPED Till sapp'd their strength,
and every part unsound, ...393 DVil 36
SAPS Saps the strong wall, and
pours destruction round; ......III:50 Capt 124
SAT See also SATE.
Sat by his fire, and talk'd the
night away; ....156 DVil 28
So there I sat stuck, like a
horse in a pound, ...87 HofV 98
Vida, 286
SATE Vida, 29
SATINS At church, in silks and
satins new, ...13 MBlz 47
SATIRE When Satire and Censure
encircl'd his throne, ...83 Rtal 89
SATISFACTION 'I hopes as how to
give you satisfaction.' ....12 eSSC$_3$ 85
SATISFY Could Nature's bounty
satisfy the breast, ...111 Trav 9
The sports of children satisfy the
child; ....154 Trav 10
SAUNTER Comes here to saunter,
having made his bets, ...25 eSSC$_2$ 108
SAVAGE$_1$ And drags the struggling
savage into day. ....190 Trav 11

troubles e'er annoy! ....323 DVil 34
When every bosom swells with
wond'rous scenes, ...7 pZob 72
Ye nodding towers, ye fairy
scenes-- ....164 Thrn 80
No high-life scenes, no sentiment:--
the creature ....39 eSSC$_2$ 109
SCEPTRE Vida, 499
SCHELDT Or by the lazy Scheldt,
or wandering Po; ....2 Trav 5
SCHEME Vida, 90, 152, 278
SCHOLAR A scholar, yet surely no
pedant was he. ....156 Rtal 93
SCHOLARS The land of scholars, and
the nurse of arms, ...356 Trav 17
And scholars, soldiers, kings,
unhonour'd die. ....360 Trav 17
SCHOOL The playful children just
let loose from school; ....120 DVil 27
The village master taught his
little school; ....196 DVil 29
SCHOOL- 'Twere affectation all,
and school-taught pride, ...v39 Trav 168
Let school-taught pride dissemble
all it can, ...41 Trav 6
Let school-masters puzzle their
brain, ...1 "LSm 84
SCIENCE Whence from such lands
each pleasing science flies, ...215 Trav 12
Who perhaps to the summit of
science could soar, ...159 Rtal 93
SCOFF And fools, who came to scoff,
remain'd to pray. ....180 DVil 29
SCOLD 'Tis in vain that at
niggardly caution I scold, ...13 LetB 132
SCOLDS Talks loud, coquets the
guests, and scolds the waiters. ...16 eSSC$_3$ 85
SCOOPS Scoops out an empire, and
usurps the shore; ....290 Trav 14
SCORCHING Vida, 79
SCORE Can but pay its proper
score. ....II:62 Capt 120
SCORED With beer and milk arrears
the frieze was scor'd. ....17 DABd 48
An unpaid reck'ning on the frieze
was scor'd, ...v17 DABd 200
SCORN Where lawns extend that
scorn Arcadian pride, ...319 Trav 15
'Till quite dejected with my
scorn, ...133 Ed&A 63
Till quite dejected by my scorn, v133 Ed&A 210
Bow'd down with chains, the
scorn of all mankind, ...I:85 Capt 117
SCORNING Vida, 417
SCORNS Nature disowns, and reason
scorns thy mirth, ...8 epLL 101
SCORPION Where the dark scorpion
gathers death around; ....352 DVil 35
SCOT That a Scot may have humour,
I had almost said wit: ....172 Rtal 93
'What the de'il, mon, a pasty!'
re-echoed the Scot, ...103 HofV 98
'What the de'il, mon, a pasty!'
returned the Scot, ...v103 HofV 242
Give me my bonny Scot, that
travels from the Tweed. ....38 eSSC$_1$ 105
SCOTCHMAN And Scotchman meet
Scotchman, and cheat in the dark. ..92 Rtal 90
A Scotchman, from pride and from
prejudice free; ....155 Rtal 93
The one is a Scotchman, the other
a Jew, ...75 HofV 97
SCOTTISH But what vex'd me most
was that d--'d Scottish rogue, ...89 HofV 98
SCOUR Vida, 119
SCOURGE The scourge of impostors,
the terror of quacks: ....80 Rtal 89
SCOURGE The one writes the Snarler,
the other the Scourge; ....77 HofV 97
SCOURGED While scourg'd by famine
from the smiling land, ...299 DVil 33
SCREAMING Vida, 409
SCRIBBLING A likeness for the
scribbling kind; ....2 NSim 56
The modern scribbling kind, who
write ....3 NSim 56
With his goosequill the scribbling
elf, ...53 NSim 57
In which our scribling bards
agree, ...v59 NSim 206
Ye news-paper witlings! ye pert
scribbling folks ....163 Rtal 93
SCRIP A scrip with herbs and
fruits supplied, ...27 Ed&A 60
SCROGGEN The Muse found Scroggen
stretch'd beneath a rug; ....6 DABd 48
SCULPTURE And oh! for this! while
sculpture decks thy shrine, ...128 Thrn 78
SCULPTURED Where sculptur'd elegance
and native grace ....144 Thrn 79
Vida, 39
SCURVY For a slice of their scurvy
religion, ...15 "LSm 84
SCYTHE When vice my dart and scythe
supply, ...76 Thrn 76
SCYTHIAN With Scythian stores, and
trinkets deeply laden, ...11 pZob 72
SEA 'And nobody with me at sea but
myself'; ....60 HofV 97
Vida, 36
The sea subsiding spreads a level
plain: ....4 Tr 267
SEA- While sea-born gales their
gelid wings expand ....121 Trav 9
SEAMS To smooth her skin, or hide
its seams; ....86 DTrn 54
SEARCH Vain, very vain, my weary
search to find ....423 Trav 19
SEAS Extols the treasures of his
stormy seas, ...67 Trav 7
SEASONABLE Vida, 292
SEASONS The seasons, fram'd with
listing, found a place, ...13 DABd 48
SEAT His seat, where solitary
sports are seen, ...281 DVil 32
Vida, 177, 619, 651
SEATS$_1$ Seats of my youth, when
every sport could please, ...6 DVil 23
SEATS$_2$ For seats like these beyond
the western main; ....368 DVil 35
The hawthorn bush, with seats be-
neath the shade, ...13 DVil 23
Vida, 184
SECLUDED Secluded from domestic

strife, ...1 DTrn 52
SECOND The second brought its
transports too. ....30 DTrn 53
In book the second, page the
tenth: ....12 NSim 56
Her Second Act displays a livelier
scene-- ....13 eSSC$_3$ 85
Vida, 72, 469, 560, 644
SECRET$_1$ In secret, where he
died. ....136 Ed&A 63
SECRET$_2$ With secret course, which
no loud storms annoy, ...433 Trav 19
While secret laughter titter'd
round the place; ....28 DVil 24
In vain rebellion aims her secret
blow; ....III:4 Capt 122
Vida, 228
SECURE$_1$ Secure to please while
youth confirms her reign, ...288 DVil 32
In that secure, serene retreat, ...100 Thrn 77
Though secure of our hearts, yet
confoundedly sick ....105 Rtal 90
SECURE$_2$ I only would repress them
to secure: ....370 Trav 17
SECURES Compliance with his will
your peace secures, ...II:9 Capt 118
SEDATE Vida, 160
SEDGES But chok'd with sedges,
works its weedy way. ....42 DVil 24
SEDULOUS And, sedulous to stop
the coming tide, ...285 Trav 14
SEE Where'er I roam, whatever
realms to see, ...7 Trav 5
To see the hoard of human bliss so
small; ....58 Trav 7
To see the sum of human bliss so
small; ....v58 Trav 168
May gather bliss to see my fellows
bless'd. ....62 Trav 7
I see the lords of human kind pass
by, ...328 Trav 16
See, though by circling deeps together held, ...v343 Trav 174
Careful to see the mantling
bliss go round; ....248 DVil 31
To see profusion that he must not
share; ....310 DVil 33
To see ten thousand baneful arts
combin'd ....311 DVil 33
To see those joys the sons of
pleasure know ....313 DVil 33
To see each joy the sons of
pleasure know ....v313 DVil 189
I see the rural virtues leave the
land: ....398 DVil 36
See how she moves along with every
grace, ...5 MrsX 49
My charmer, turn to see ....150 Ed&A 64
But alas! that return I never shall
see, ...243 Thrn 83
Our Garrick's a salad; for in him
we see ....11 Rtal 87
Howe'er, from this time I shall
ne'er see your graces, ...5 ClRp 100
At least in many things, I think,
I see ....7 eSSC$_2$ 108
Have we not cause for triumph when
we see ....I:33 Capt 114
Stand fast, and let our tyrants
see ....I:99 Capt 117
I read your looks, and see
compliance there. ....II:42 Capt 119
See the ruddy morning smiling, .II:47 Capt 120
But hush! see, foremost of the
captive choir, ...II:63 Capt 120
See how prophetic rapture fills
his form, ...II:67 Capt 121
See where dethron'd your captive
monarch lies, ...II:88 Capt 121
See where he mourns his friends
and children slain. ....II:90 Capt 121
See yonder tower just nodding
to the fall: ....III:48 Capt 124
See where an army covers all
the ground, ...III:49 Capt 124
'Who, I? let me see, Sir, why
I must pass too.' ....18 LetB 132
To see them so cowardly, lucky,
and civil. ....20 LetB 132
And see how they kneel! Is your
heart made of stone?' ....64 LetB 134
Vida, 30, 37, 45, 81, 163, 477, 539,
657
SEEK Here wretches seek dis-
honourable graves, ...310 Trav 15
To seek a good each government
bestows? ....426 Trav 19
These, far departing, seek a
kinder shore, ...73 DVil 25
To seek her nightly shed, and weep
till morn; ....134 DVil 27
Unpractis'd he to fawn, or seek
for power, ...145 DVil 28
Unskilful he to fawn, or seek
for power, ...v145 DVil 184
I'll seek the solitude he sought, .139 Ed&A 64
I'll seek that less inhospitable
coast, ...223 Thrn 82
Seek the happy and the free: ....I:28 Capt 114
Too late you seek that power
unsought before, ...III:71 Capt 125
-SEEKING The shelter-seeking
peasant builds his shed, ...162 Trav 10
SEEKS Or seeks the den where snow-
tracks mark the way, ...189 Trav 11
Who seeks for rest, but finds
despair ....99 Ed&A 62
That seeks repose, but finds
despair ....v99 Ed&A 209
Vida, 374
SEEM An easy compensation seem to
find. ....148 Trav 10
Till, seeming bless'd, they grow
to what they seem. ....266 Trav 14
Seem length'ning as I go.' ....8 Ed&A 59
Is to seem everything but what they
are. ....26 eSis 70
SEEMED The wound it seem'd both
sore and sad ....25 MDog 66
Vida, 39, 602
SEEMING Till, seeming bless'd, they
grow to what they seem. ....266 Trav 14
SEEMS That either seems destructive
of the rest. ....90 Trav 8

Man seems the only growth that
dwindles here. ....126 Trav 9
The firm-connected bulwark seems
to grow; ....288 Trav 14
Who seems to have robb'd his vizor
from the lion; ....28 eSis 71
And seems to every gazer all in
white, ...38 eSis 71
This seems a barren and a dangerous
coast. ....16 pZob 72
Yon ill foreboding cloud seems big
with thunder. ....18 pZob 72
To Death's great court, the prospect
seems more fair. ....96 Thrn 77
Vida, 513
SEEN Here may be seen, in bloodless
pomp array'd, ...149 Trav 10
Have we not seen, round Britain's
peopled shore, ...397 Trav 18
Seen all her triumphs but
destruction haste, ...399 Trav 18
Seen opulence, her grandeur to
maintain, ...401 Trav 18
Have we not seen, at pleasure's
lordly call, ...405 Trav 18
Amidst thy bowers the tyrant's hand
is seen, ...37 DVil 24
His seat, where solitary sports are
seen, ...281 DVil 32
Fond to be seen, she kept a bevy ...53 DTrn 53
The 'squire himself was seen to
yield, ...89 DTrn 55
For tawdry finery is seen ....99 DTrn 55
There Mangroves spread, and larger
than I've seen 'em-- ....19 pZob 72
While sweetly blending still are
seen ....146 Thrn 79
The pious matron next was seen-- ..182 Thrn 80
At the top a fried liver and bacon
were seen, ...81 HofV 97
Has he not seen how you your favour
place, ...35 $eSSC_2$ 109
Vida, 66, 316, 358, 463
SEES He sees his little lot the
lot of all; ....178 Trav 11
Sees no contiguous palace rear its
head ....179 Trav 11
Sees an amphibious world beneath
him smile; ,,..................292 Trav 15
Surpris'd, he sees new beauties
rise, ...85 Ed&A 62
He sees unnumber'd beauties rise, v85 Ed&A 209
SEIZE Seize the debtor as it
flies. ....II:58 Capt 120
SEIZED For grief had seized his
early age, ...v59 Ed&A 208
Vida, 340, 558, 651
SELDOM The needy seldom pass'd
her door, ...5 MBlz 47
But hang it--to poets who seldom
can eat, ...31 HofV 96
That modern judges seldom enter
here. ....18 $eSSC_1$ 104
For sure I don't wrong you, you
seldom are slack, ...59 $eSSC_1$ 106
SELF 'Twas Edwin's self that
prest. ....148 Ed&A 64
SELF- Nor weighs the solid worth
of self-applause. ....280 Trav 14
The self-dependent lordlings stand
alone, ...341 Trav 16
While self-dependent power can time
defy, ...429 DVil 37
Thy towering mind self-centred
stood, ...26 Thrn 75
SELL The needy sell it, and the rich
man buys; ....308 Trav 15
I have something to sell him; .....20 Invt 128
SEMBLANCE An equal semblance still
to keep, ...49 NSim 57
SEND A thousand gifts would fortune
send; ....29 Thrn 75
To send such good verses to one of
your taste; ....118 HofV 99
Vida, 56, 125, 329, 426
SENDING It's like sending them
ruffles, when wanting a shirt. .....34 HofV 96
Like sending 'em Ruffles when
wanting a Shirt. ....v34 HofV 239
For sending so late ....37 Invt 129
SENSE But small the bliss that
sense alone bestows, ...123 Trav 9
In wit, and sense, and nature's
spite: ....4 NSim 56
I'll leave it to all men of sense, .16 "LSm 84
Whose ins and outs no ray of sense
discloses, ...13 epLL 101
But find no sense--for they had
none to lose. ....32 $eSSC_2$ 109
SENSELESS Are they but senseless
stones and blocks? ....64 NSim 58
SENSES In sweet succession charmed
the senses, ...237 Thrn 82
And they, who lose their senses,
there may find them. ....4 $eSSC_2$ 108
That mortals visit both to find
their senses. ....14 $eSSC_2$ 108
Finds his lost senses out, and pay
his debts. ....26 $eSSC_2$ 108
Had your senses been right, ...3 Invt 128
SENSUAL And sensual bliss is all
the nation knows. ....124 Trav 9
Unknown to them, when sensual
pleasures cloy, ...217 Trav 12
Still first to fly where sensual
joys invade; ....408 DVil 36
SENT From Art more various are the
blessings sent; ....87 Trav 8
So I cut it, and sent it to
Reynolds undress'd, ...21 HofV 95
You'd have sent before night; ......4 Invt 128
Vida, 232, 247, 291, 372, 606, 643
SENTENCE Un-epilogued the Poet
waits his sentence. ....70 $eSSC_1$ 107
SENTIMENT No high-life scenes,
no sentiment:--the creature ......39 $eSSC_2$ 109
SENTIMENTAL On sentimental Queens
and Lords in lace? ....36 $eSSC_2$ 109
SERENE In that secure, serene
retreat, ...100 Thrn 77
SERENELY Serenely gay, and strict
in duty, ...103 DTrn 55
SERIAD Vida, 670
SERIADS Vida, 678

SERIAN Vida, 6, 679
SERIOUS But all his serious thoughts
had rest in Heaven. ....188 DVil 29
Are these thy serious thoughts?--
Ah, turn thine eyes ....325 DVil 34
SERPENTS The serpents round about
it twin'd ....45 NSim 57
I heard a hissing--there are serpents
here! ....24 pZob 73
SERVE Serve her as she hath served
the just! ....II:81 Capt 121
Serve them as they have serv'd
the just, ...III:57 Capt 124
Vida, 403
SERVED They enter'd, and dinner
was serv'd as they came. ....80 HofV 97
Serve her as she hath served the
just! ....II:81 Capt 121
Serve them as they have serv'd
the just, ...III:57 Capt 124
SERVICE The service pass'd,
around the pious man, ...181 DVil 29
SERVILE Not with that face, so
servile and so gay, ...v(19) DABd 200
Ye tame imitators, ye servile
herd, come, ...165 Rtal 93
SERVITUDE And calmly bent, to
servitude conform, ...311 Trav 15
SET$_1$ Besides, a singer in a comic
set!-- ....9 eSSC$_1$ 104
I'm for a different set.--Old men,
whose trade is ....19 eSSC$_1$ 104
SET$_2$ It could not fail, would you
but set about it.' ....10 eGNM 68
Pain met thee like a friend that
set thee free; ....34 Thrn 75
Yet content 'if the table he set
on a roar'; ....160 Rtal 93
A prettier dinner I never set eyes
on; ....92 HofV 98
Whilst his strong limbs conspire
to set him free, ...45 epLL 102
To chain the strong, and set the
captive free. ....III:90 Capt 126
The company set, and the word to
be, Loo; ....2 LetB 131
Two handsomer culprits I never set
eyes on!' ....52 LetB 133
Vida, 298
SETTING Ere yonder setting sun; .II:80 Capt 121
SETTLE 'Some lords, my acquaint-
ance, that settle the nation, ...43 HofV 96
SETTLED Both prone to change, no
settled limits fix, ...11 eSSC$_2$ 108
SETTLES Eternal sunshine settles
on its head. ....192 DVil 29
SEVEN 'I could dine on this tripe
seven days in the week: ....96 HofV 98
I could eat of this Tripe seven
days in the week.' ....v96 HofV 242
SEVERAL And highly fam'd for
several uses. ....34 NSim 57
Vida, 83, 162
SEVERE A man severe he was, and
stern to view; ....197 DVil 29
Yet he was kind; or if severe in
aught, ...205 DVil 30
SEVERER Come ponder his severer
fate, ...III:25 Capt 123
SEX And spurn the sex,' he
said: ....82 Ed&A 62
SEX'S Forgive my sex's fears, for-
give my youth! ....II:28 Capt 119
SHADE The hawthorn bush, with
seats beneath the shade, ...13 DVil 23
While many a pastime circled in
the shade, ...19 DVil 23
These all in sweet confusion
sought the shade, ...123 DVil 27
A shade that follows wealth or
fame, ...75 Ed&A 61
SHADES$_1$ How happy he who crowns
in shades like these, ...99 DVil 26
How blest is he who crowns in
shades like these, ...v99 DVil 183
SHADES$_2$ Vida, 247, 606, 660
SHADES$_3$ That shades the steep,
and sighs at every blast. ....104 Trav 8
SHADING Where shading elms along the
margin grew, ...245 Trav 13
SHADY Ye shady walks, ye waving
greens, ...163 Thrn 80
SHAFT Could Cupid's shaft at
length transfix ....9 DTrn 52
Vida, 431
SHAKE Vida, 50
SHAKES Till ruin shakes all; ..III:10 Capt 122
When ruin shakes all, ...III:11 Capt 122
SHAKESPEARE Old Shakespeare,
receive him, with praise and
with love, ...123 Rtal 91
Shakespeare himself shall feel
my tragic rage. ....20 epLL 101
SHALT 'Thou shalt not thus,' the
Hermit cried, ...v145 Ed&A 211
SHAME$_1$ And patriotic boasting
reason's shame! ....v(82) Trav 168
Unfit in these degenerate times
of shame, ...409 DVil 36
My shame in crowds, my solitary
pride; ....412 DVil 37
Here then at once, I welcome every
shame, ...15 pLab 41
'For shame, fond youth, thy sorrows
hush, ...81 Ed&A 62
To hide her shame from every eye, ...6 "wlw 67
And shame prevents the deed, ...192 Thrn 81
No monster-breed to mark the groves
with shame; ....8 Cati 94
Vida, 541
SHAME$_2$ To shame the meanness of his
humble shed; ....180 Trav 11
SHANKS 'The deuce confound,' he
cries, 'these drumstick shanks, ...31 epLL 102
SHAPE Comes nearest us in human
shape; ....42 LogR 45
Yet, when he deigns his real shape
t' assume, ...35 eSis 71
Vida, 40, 43
SHAPELESS Sunk are thy bowers in
shapeless ruin all, ...47 DVil 24
SHARE$_1$ In all my griefs--and GOD
has given my share-- ....84 DVil 26
-SHARE$_2$ Or drives his vent'rous

plough-share to the steep; ....188 Trav 11
SHARE$_3$ But me, not destin'd such
delights to share, ...23 Trav 6
And estimate the blessings which
they share, ...76 Trav 7
Yet let them only share the praises
due, ...211 Trav 12
And pluck'd his gown, to share the
good man's smile. ....184 DVil 29
To see profusion that he must not
share; ....310 DVil 33
'Then turn to-night, and freely
share ....17 Ed&A 59
'But let a maid thy pity share, ...97 Ed&A 62
Vida, 24, 97, 149
SHARES Nor shares with art the
triumph of her eyes: ....290 DVil 32
SHARON Ye fields of Sharon, dress'd
in flow'ry pride, ...I:17 Capt 114
SHARP Though my stomach was sharp,
I could scarce help regretting ....5 HofV 95
Vida, 347
SHATTER'D The shatter'd veteran, now
first dismay'd; ....158 Thrn 79
SHAVED I put off being shaved; ......6 Invt 128
SHED$_1$ The shelter-seeking peasant
builds his shed, ...162 Trav 10
To shame the meanness of his
humble shed; ....180 Trav 11
He sits him down the monarch of a
shed; ....192 Trav 11
Dear is that shed to which his soul
conforms, ...203 Trav 12
To seek her nightly shed, and weep
till morn; ....134 DVil 27
SHED$_2$ These round thy bowers their
cheerful influence shed, ...33 DVil 24
And fiercely shed intolerable day; ..348 DVil 34
SHEEP And sympathetic sheep; ....10 DRtH 50
SHELF Left alone to reflect, having
emptied my shelf, ...59 HofV 97
SHELTER Vida, 254
SHELTER- The shelter-seeking peasant
builds his shed, ...162 Trav 10
SHELTERED The shelter'd cot, the
cultivated farm, ...10 DVil 23
That only shelter'd thefts of
harmless love. ....362 DVil 35
Far shelter'd in a glade obscure ..v37 Ed&A 208
SHELTERING And there in shelt'ring
thickets hid, ...v141 Ed&A 211
SHELVING Vida, 28
SHELVY On Idra's cliffs as Arno's
shelvy side; ....84 Trav 8
SHEPHERD'S The pomp of kings, the
shepherd's humbler pride. ....36 Trav 6
SHE'S And tries to kill, ere she's
got power to cure. ....24 eSis 70
SHEWED That feebly shew'd the state
in which he lay. ....v8 DABd 200
And Prussia's monarch shew'd his
lamp-black face ....v14 DABd 200
SHIFT Vida, 155
SHIFTED He shifted his trumpet, and
only took snuff. ....146 Rtal 92
SHIFTING The mind still turns where
shifting fashion draws, ...279 Trav 14
SHIFTS It shifts in splendid traffic
round the land: ....262 Trav 14
Next the scene shifts to town, and
there she soars, ...17 eSSC$_3$ 85
Vida, 131
SHINE$_1$ Who can withstand their all-
commanding shine? ....4 MrsX 49
SHINE$_2$ Casts a long look where
England's glories shine, ...421 Trav 19
But pitying his distress, let virtue
shine, ...3 Gros 51
With charms inconstant shine; ......126 Ed&A 63
As an actor, confess'd without rival
to shine: ....95 Rtal 90
Both shine at night, for, but at
Foote's alone, ...9 eSSC$_2$ 108
Vida, 54
SHINES She then shines forth,
solicitous to bless, ...293 DVil 33
SHINING While soul-brought tears
steal down each shining face. ....6 MrsX 49
Vida, 201
SHIP The labouring ship, and hear the
tempest roar, ...67 Thrn 76
SHIP- Cross-readings, Ship-news,
and Mistakes of the Press. ......170 Rtal 93
SHIP'S Our ship's well stor'd;--in
yonder creek we've laid her; ....31 pZob 73
SHIRT It's like sending them ruffles,
when wanting a shirt. ....34 HofV 96
Like sending 'em Ruffles when wanting
a Shirt. ....v34 HofV 239
SHIVERING Where the poor houseless
shiv'ring female lies. ....326 DVil 34
SHOCK$_1$ Ev'ry shock that malice
offers ....42,50 Thrn 75
Vida, 102
SHOCK$_2$ Those eyeless orbs that shock
with ghastly glare, ...III:33 Capt 123
SHOCKS Vida, 389
SHOES Wings grow again from both
his shoes; ....24 NSim 56
SHONE Vida, 175
SHOOK Vida, 555
SHOOTS Vida, 413
SHOP At triumphs in a Fleet-street
shop. ....14 DTrn 52
SHORE Scoops out an empire, and
usurps the shore; ....290 Trav 14
Repress'd ambition struggles round
her shore, ...346 Trav 16
Have we not seen, round Britain's
peopled shore, ...397 Trav 18
These, far departing, seek a kinder
shore, ...73 DVil 25
And shouting Folly hails them from
her shore; ....270 DVil 32
The various terrors of that horrid
shore; ....346 DVil 34
Pass from the shore, and darken all
the strand. ....402 DVil 36
The distant climate and the savage
shore; ....2 pZob 72
To make an observation on the shore. 14 pZob 72
As helpless friends who view from
shore ....66 Thrn 76
Fast by that shore where Thames'

translucent stream ....140 Thrn 79
Vida, 367, 679
SHORES Commerce on other shores
display'd her sail; ....140 Trav 10
Soon Commerce turn'd on other shores
her sail; ....v140 Trav 169
Oswego's dreary shores shall be
my grave; ....222 Thrn 82
Vida, 18
SHORT$_1$ In short, by night, 'twas
fits or fretting; ....51 DTrn 53
In short, 'twas his fate, unemploy'd,
or in place, Sir, ...41 Rtal 88
In short, so provoking a devil was
Dick, ...57 Rtal 89
SHORT$_2$ Cheerful at morn he wakes from
short repose, ...185 Trav 11
And if you find it wond'rous short, ..3 MDog 65
To lengthen a short tail, ...31 Invt 129
SHORT- Such short-liv'd offerings
but disclose ....15 Gift 43
SHORT$_3$ Her hangers-on cut short all; 22 MBlz 47
SHORTLY First let me suppose, what
may shortly be true, ...1 LetB 131
SHOULD Trav, 38, 39, 375; Byth, 3; Gift, 6;
eSis, 3, 30; Thrn, 194; Rtal, 52, 158; HofV, 41;
epLL, 3; Capt, I:32, 39, 77; LetB, 36; Vida,
77, 87, 102, 147, 190, 193, 457, 539
SHOULDERED Shoulder'd his crutch,
and show'd how fields were won. ....158 DVil 28
SHOUT But, whence that shout? Good
heavens! amazement all! ....III:47 Capt 124
SHOUTED Vida, 605
SHOUTING And shouting Folly hails
them from her shore; ....270 DVil 32
The shouting army cry'd with joy
extreme, ...1 Tr 267
SHOUTS How did Grub-street re-echo the
shouts that you rais'd, ...117 Rtal 91
Vida, 293
SHOW$_1$ While broken tea-cups, wisely
kept for show, ...235 DVil 31
One gammon of bacon hangs up for a
show: ....10 HofV 95
Vida, 376, 607
SHOW$_2$ Amidst the swains to show my
book-learn'd skill, ...90 DVil 26
And by a quick transition, plainly
show ....7 GRos 51
Less dreadful show ....II:22 Capt 119
And shall not Heaven for this its
terrors show, ...III:35 Capt 123
Vida, 12, 591, 612
SHOWED See also SHEWED
Shoulder'd his crutch, and show'd
how fields were won. ....158 DVil 28
That dimly show'd the state in which
he lay; ....8 DABd 48
And brave prince William show'd his
lamp-black face: ....14 DABd 48
That show'd the rogues they lied: ...30 MDog 66
SHOWER And, pinch'd with cold, and
shrinking from the shower, ...333 DVil 34
SHOWN Well! since she thus has shown
her want of skill, ...9 eSis 70
To be shown to my friends as a piece
of <u>virtù</u>; ....8 HofV 95
SHOWS He fancies every vice she
shows, ...63 DTrn 54
Death, when unmasked, shows me a
friendly face, ...93 Thrn 77
The First Act shows the simple
country maid, ...9 eSSC$_3$ 85
The Fourth Act shows her wedded to
the 'Squire, ...23 eSSC$_3$ 85
'It shows that their habits are all
dyed in grain.' ....58 LetB 133
SHREDS Arose from powder, shreds,
or lace; ....36 DTrn 53
SHRINE They robb'd the relic and
defac'd the shrine. ....59 Thrn 76
And oh! for this! while sculpture
decks thy shrine, ...128 Thrn 78
And copious libations bestow on his
shrine: ....168 Rtal 93
SHRINKING And trembling, shrinking
from the spoiler's hand, ...49 DVil 24
And, pinch'd with cold, and shrinking
from the shower, ...333 DVil 34
If, shrinking thus, when frowning
power appears, ...II:29 Capt 119
SHRINKS How shrinks my soul to meet
the threaten'd blow! ....II:26 Capt 119
SHRUB Like yon neglected shrub at
random cast, ...103 Trav 8
SHRUBS There, where a few torn
shrubs the place disclose, ...139 DVil 27
SHRUG While oft, with many a smile,
and many a shrug, ...25 eGNM 68
SHUDDERING The shudd'ring tenant of
the frigid zone ....65 Trav 7
And shudd'ring still to face the
distant deep, ...369 DVil 35
SHUN What! no way left to shun th'
inglorious stage, ...1 pLab 41
Vida, 89, 632
SHUT <u>But when she shut her eyes</u>. ....16 MBlz 47
Had shut out the pasty on shutting
his oven ....114 HofV 99
Vida, 630
SHUTTING Had shut out the pasty on
shutting his oven ....114 HofV 99
SHUTS Against the houseless stranger
shuts the door; ....4 Trav 5
SICK Quite sick of pursuing each
troublesome elf, ...77 Rtal 89
Though secure of our hearts, yet
confoundedly sick ....105 Rtal 90
-SICK Vida, 470
SICKENED A relish--a taste--sicken'd
over by learning; ....120 HofV 99
SICKENS The toiling pleasure sickens
into pain; ....262 DVil 32
SICKLY There the pale artist plies
the sickly trade; ....316 DVil 33
Kingdoms, by thee, to sickly greatness
grown, ...389 DVil 36
SIDE On Idra's cliffs as Arno's
shelvy side; ....84 Trav 8
Its uplands sloping deck the mountain's
side, ...107 Trav 8
And e'en his failings lean'd to
Virtue's side; ....164 DVil 28
On Torno's cliffs, or Pambamarca's

side, ...418 DVil 37
Wings upon either side--mark
that. ....16 NSim 56
'But from the mountain's grassy
side ....25 Ed&A 60
I spurn'd him from my side, ...v130 Ed&A 210
Vida, 46, 58, 65, 113, 158, 204,
283, 385, 576
SIDE- The bashful virgin's
side-long looks of love, ...29 DVil 24
SIDES At the sides there was
spinach and pudding made hot; ......83 HofV 98
Thus foil'd in my courage, on all
sides perplex'd, ...27 LetB 132
SIDEWARDS Vida, 123
SIGH$_1$ Yet oft a sigh prevails, and
sorrows fall, ...57 Trav 7
A sigh in suffocating smoke; ....58 DTrn 54
The sigh that rends thy constant
heart ....159 Ed&A 64
And the last sigh that rends thy
heart, ...**v159 Ed&A 211**
A simple song, a sigh profound. ...131 Thrn 78
With many a tear and many a sigh
between; ....170 Thrn 80
SIGH$_2$ Or sigh with pity at some
mournful tale, ...20 Trav 6
How sigh for such a friend! .....v124 Ed&A 210
Here lies honest Richard, whose
fate I must sigh at; ....51 Rtal 88
Yet still I sit snug, and continue
to sigh on, ...21 LetB 132
SIGHED Vida, 238, **434**
SIGHING Sighing we pay, and think
e'en conquest dear; ....6 Queb 46
SIGHS Yet still he sighs, for
hoards are **wanting** still: ....54 Trav 7
That shades the steep, and sighs
at every blast. ....104 Trav 8
Who sighs for operas, and dotes
on dancing, ...20 eSSC$_2$ 108
Vida, 278
SIGHT Need we expose to vulgar
sight ....21 DTrn 52
The glass, grown hateful to her
sight, ...81 DTrn 54
Yon patriot, too, who presses on
your sight, ...37 eSis 71
In vain, to charm thy ravish'd
sight, ...28 Thrn 75
The hardy veteran after struck
the sight, ...207 Thrn 81
Depriv'd of sight and rankling in
his chain; ....II:89 Capt 121
Vida, 31, 432, 515, 627
SIGN- 'When once the sign-post
caught the passing eye, ...220 DVil 30
SIGNIFIES 'What signifies handsome,
when people are thieves?' ....60 LetB 133
'What signifies justice? I want
the reward. ....62 LetB 133
SILENCE Vida, 537
SILENT But silent bats in drowsy
clusters cling; ....350 DVil 34
Silent went next, neglectful of
her charms, ...377 DVil 35
In all the silent manliness of
grief. ....384 DVil 36
Vida, 33
SILENTLY Vida, 170
SILKEN The robe that wraps his
limbs in silken sloth ....279 DVil 32
SILKS At church, in silks and
satins new, ...13 MBlz 47
SILLY At length his silly head,
so priz'd before, ...43 epLL 102
SILVER$_1$ Vida, 674
SILVER$_2$ Vida, 56, 669
SIMILAR Both similar blessings
bestow; ....I:62 Capt 116
SIMILE And now proceed we to
our simile. ....14 NSim 56
And here my simile unites, ...27 NSim 57
And here my simile almost tript, ...55 NSim 57
Shall lend my simile assistance. ...62 NSim 58
SIMILES Sad Philomel thus--but let
similes drop-- ....115 HofV 99
SIMPERING His simp'ring friends,
with pleasure in their eyes, ...27 eGNM 69
SIMPLE Bless'd be those feasts with
simple plenty crown'd, ...17 Trav 5
These simple blessings of the lowly
train; ....252 DVil 31
A simple song, a sigh profound. ...131 Thrn 78
The First Act shows the simple
country maid, ...9 eSSC$_3$ 85
On the stage he was natural, simple,
affecting; ....101 Rtal 90
The simple plumage, or the glossy
down ....4 Cati 94
SIMPLEST In nature's simplest charms
at first array'd; ....296 DVil 33
'In humble, simplest habit clad, ..113 Ed&A 63
SIMPLING Forsake the fair, and
patiently--go simpling; ....6 pZob 72
SIMPLY The dancing pair that simply
sought renown, ...25 DVil 24
SINCE And, since 'tis hard to
combat, learns to fly! ....102 DVil 26
Since from thy tomb a thousand
heroes rise! ....12 Queb 46
Since none implor'd relief in
vain!-- ....15 DRtH 50
Then since he perish'd by my
fault, ...v137 Ed&A 210
Since then, unhelp'd, our bard
must now conform ....31 eGNM 69
Well! since she thus has shown her
want of skill, ...9 eSis 70
Well then a truce, since she re-
quests it too: ....43 eSis 71
Vida, 144, 164, 258
SINCERE Not less sincere, than
civil: ....18 Gift 43
Myra, too sincere for feigning, ...3 Sonn 46
Whose temper was generous, open,
sincere; ....151 Rtal 93
SINFUL A-preaching that drinking
is sinful, ...11 "LSm 84
SING Those matted woods where birds
forget to sing, ...349 DVil 34
And tune my feeble voice to sing
thy praise. ....2 MrsX 49
Excuse me, Ma'am. The Author bid

me sing it. ....4 eSSC$_1$ 103
Suspend your conversation while
I sing. ....6 eSSC$_1$ 103
I'll sing to amuse you by night and
by day, ...41 eSSC$_1$ 105
The day demands it; sing us Sion's
song. ....I:82 Capt 116
Prepares our monarch's victories
to sing. ....II:70 Capt 121
SINGER Besides, a singer in a
comic set!-- ....9 eSSC$_1$ 104
SINGING Why, sure the girl's beside
herself: an Epilogue of singing, 7 eSSC$_1$ 103
SINGLE No single brute his fellow
leads. ....38 LogR 45
Vida, 102, 108, 505
SINGS Sings to its mate, and nightly
charms the nest; ....12 Cati 94
There is a place, so Ariosto sings, 1 eSSC$_2$ 108
SINK$_1$ One sink of level avarice
shall lie, ...359 Trav 17
SINK$_2$ They sink at last, or feebly
man the soul; ....v156 Trav 171
Down, down they sink, and spread
a ruin round. ....394 DVil 36
Sink as he sinks, and as he rises
rise; ....28 eGNM 69
Till all my companions sink under
the table; ....20 Rtal 87
And sink thee lowest of the low.III:77 Capt 125
SINKING And save from infamy my
sinking age! ....2 pLab 41
My life on't, this had kept her play
from sinking; ....7 eSis 70
Vida, 457
SINKS And honour sinks where
commerce long prevails. ....92 Trav 8
When struggling Virtue sinks by
long controul, ...v155 Trav 170
Now sinks at last, or feebly mans
the soul; ....156 Trav 10
And talent sinks, and merit weeps
unknown; ....354 Trav 17
Sinks to the grave with unperceiv'd
decay, ...v109 DVil 183
Obscure it sinks, nor shall it
more impart ....239 DVil 31
And while he sinks, without one arm
to save, ...301 DVil 33
Sink as he sinks, and as he rises
rise; ....28 eGNM 69
And as our fortune sinks, our wishes
soar, ...I:42 Capt 115
She sinks, she groans, she dies. II:78 Capt 121
SINNER And now that I think on't,
as I am a sinner! ....51 HofV 96
SINNING Unless when she was sinning. 12 MBlz 47
SINS And e'en in penance planning
sins anew. ....130 Trav 9
Vida, 661
SION Give, give your songs of Sion
to the wind, ...III:87 Capt 126
SION'S The day demands it; sing
us Sion's song. ....I:82 Capt 116
SIR 'What I? dear Sir,' the
Doctor interposes; ....15 eGNM 68
'What, plant my thistle, Sir, among
his roses! ....16 eGNM 68
In short, 'twas his fate,
unemploy'd or in place, Sir, ...41 Rtal 88
As 'D-- --, Sir,' and 'Sir, I
wear a sword'; ....28 eSSC$_2$ 109
'What does Mrs. Bunbury?' 'I, Sir?
I pass.' ....16 LetB 132
'Who, I? let me see, Sir, why I
must pass too.' ....18 LetB 132
SIR First Sir Charles advances with
phrases well strung, ...55 LetB 133
SIRE For, as refinement stops,
from sire to son ....229 Trav 12
Beheld the duteous son, the sire
decay'd, ...407 Trav 18
The good old sire, the first
prepar'd to go ....371 DVil 35
The good old sire, unconscious of
decay, ...155 Thrn 79
SIRES Heavens! how unlike their
Belgic sires of old! ....313 Trav 15
SISTER'S Vida, 14
SIT I sit me down a pensive hour
to spend; ....32 Trav 6
Here let me sit in sorrow for
mankind, ...102 Trav 8
May sit, like falcons cow'ring on
the nest; ....234 Trav 13
He eyes the centre, where his friends
sit snug; ....26 eGNM 68
Here, waiter! more wine, let me sit
while I'm able, ...19 Rtal 87
Yet still they sit snug, not a creature
will aim ....11 LetB 132
Yet still I sit snug, and continue
to sigh on, ...21 LetB 132
SITE Vida, 497
SITS He sits him down the monarch
of a shed; ....192 Trav 11
She sits all night at cards, and
ogles at spadille. ....31 eSSC$_3$ 86
Mark where he sits, with executing
art, ...II:65 Capt 120
SIX At least, in six weeks, I could
not find 'em out; ....26 Rtal 87
-SIX Our swain, arriv'd at thirty-
six? ....10 DTrn 32
SIXTEEN Vida, 42
SIXTY- Vida, 23
SIZE With hoop of monstrous size, ..14 MBlz 47
Here trees of stately size--and
turtles in 'em-- ....20 pZob 72
SKIES A weary waste expanding to
the skies: ....6 Trav 5
That, like the circle bounding earth
and skies, ...27 Trav 6
Again the long-fall'n column sought
the skies; ....136 Trav 9
To kinder skies, where gentler
manners reign, ...239 Trav 13
To tempt its new-fledg'd offspring
to the skies, ...168 DVil 28
Mingling the ravag'd landscape with
the skies. ....358 DVil 35
Like colours o'er the morning skies, 87 Ed&A 62
Like clouds that deck the morning
skies, ...v87 Ed&A 209

When truth and virtue reach the
skies, ...3 Thrn 74
Her soul was fitting to its kindred
skies: ....121 Thrn 78
To act as an angel, and mix with
the skies: ....120 Rtal 91
While converts thank their poet
in the skies. ....10 epTP 100
The sun with his splendour illumines
the skies, ...I:63 Capt 116
Wing all our thoughts to reach the
skies, ...II:4 Capt 118
Vida, 513
SKILL And late the nation found,
with fruitless skill, ...143 Trav 10
But mock'd all tune, and marr'd the
dancer's skill; ....248 Trav 13
Amidst the swains to show my book-
learn'd skill, ...90 DVil 26
In arguing too, the parson own'd his
skill, ...211 DVil 30
Well! since she thus has shown her
want of skill, ...9 eSis 70
Ogles and leers with artificial
skill, ...29 $eSSC_3$ 86
Those poets, who owe their best fame
to his skill, ...121 Rtal 91
When they judg'd without skill he
was still hard of hearing: .....144 Rtal 92
SKILLED And the gay grandsire, skill'd
in gestic lore, ...253 Trav 13
More skill'd to raise the wretched
than to rise. ....148 DVil 28
There, in his noisy mansion, skill'd
to rule, ...195 DVil 29
Skill'd in no other arts was she ...39 DTrn 53
And, skill'd in legendary lore, ...51 Ed&A 60
Ye prophets, skill'd in Heaven's
eternal truth, ...II:27 Capt 119
Skilled in every peaceful art; III:100 Capt 127
Now, ladies, I ask, if law-matters
you're skill'd in, ...35 LetB 132
SKIN To smooth her skin, or hide its
seams; ....86 DTrn 54
SKINFUL They always preach best with
a skinful. ....13 "LSm 84
SKIRTS Beside yon straggling fence
that skirts the way, ...193 DVil 29
SKY Whatever sweets salute the
northern sky ....117 Trav 9
To sport and flutter in a kinder
sky. ....238 Trav 13
As rocks resist the billows and
the sky. ....430 DVil 37
To crown the favourites of the sky--115 Thrn 78
To rend the sky, ...II:20 Capt 118
Vida, 625
SLACK For sure I don't wrong you,
you seldom are slack, ...59 $eSSC_1$ 106
SLAIN See where he mourns his friends
and children slain. ....II:90 Capt 121
Vida, 351, 371, 435, 440, 473, 623
SLANDER And slander itself must
allow him good nature: ....126 Rtal 91
SLANTING Vida, 113, 553
SLATTERN By turns a slattern or a
belle: ....42 DTrn 53

SLAUGHTER To slaughter I condemn: ..22 Ed&A 59
Vida, 386
SLAVE But towns unmann'd, and lords
without a slave; ....142 Trav 10
SLAVER His frothy slaver, venom'd
bites; ....48 NSim 57
SLAVES A land of tyrants, and a den
of slaves, ...309 Trav 15
Pillag'd from slaves to purchase
slaves at home; ....388 Trav 18
Insulting slaves! if gentler methods
fail, ...I:93 Capt 117
No more! when slaves thus
insolent presume, ...II:83 Capt 121
Yet know, ye slaves, that still
remain behind ....II:91 Capt 122
SLAY Vida, 551, 600
SLAYS Vida, 212
SLEEK A sleek and idle race is all
their care. ....176 Thrn 80
How piercing is that eye! how sleek
that brow! ....35 epLL 102
SLEEP Alike too both conduce to
sleep. ....50 NSim 57
A charm that lulls to sleep; ....74 Ed&A 61
Vida, 664
SLEEPING For who like you can wake
the sleeping lyre? ....I:84 Capt 117
SLEEP'S In Sleep's refreshing
arms, ...v126 Ed&A 210
SLEEPS In thy black aspect every
passion sleeps, ...9 epLL 101
SLEIGHTS And sleights of art and
feats of strength went round; ......22 DVil 24
Vida, 320
SLENDER Vida, 277
SLEW Vida, 429, 545, 620, 654
SLICE For a slice of their scurvy
religion, ...15 "LSm 84
Pray a slice of your liver, though
may I be curs'd, ...93 HofV 98
SLIGHT My acquaintance is slight, or
I'd ask my Lord Clare. ....50 HofV 96
SLIGHT Vida, 208
SLIGHTED Aid slighted truth; with
thy persuasive strain ....423 DVil 37
SLIGHTLY That you think very slightly
of all that's your own: ....122 HofV 99
You may make a mistake, and think
slightly of this. ....124 HofV 99
SLIGHTS Slights every borrow'd
charm that dress supplies, ...289 DVil 32
The gift, who slights the giver? ....8 Gift 43
SLIPPED Vida, 530
SLIPPING Vida, 399
SLOPES While Resignation gently
slopes the way; ....110 DVil 26
SLOPING Its uplands sloping deck the
mountain's side, ...107 Trav 8
The wavy lawn, the sloping green-- 147 Thrn 79
SLOTH The robe that wraps his limbs
in silken sloth ....279 DVil 32
Vida, 542
SLOVEN And so it fell out, for that
negligent sloven ....113 HofV 99
SLOW$_1$ Remote, unfriended, melancholy,
slow, ...1 Trav 5

Onward, methinks, and diligently
slow, ...287 Trav 14
The slow canal, the yellow-
blossom'd vale, ...293 Trav 15
There, as I pass'd with careless
steps and slow, ...115 DVil 27
With fainting steps and slow; ....6 Ed&A 59
But, mischievously slow, ...58 Thrn 76
Vida, 458, 495, 540
SLOW$_2$ Vida, 150, 218
SLOWLY That this way slowly bend along
the plain? ....III:16 Capt 123
Vida, 274
SLUMBER Dull as their lakes that
slumber in the storm. ....312 Trav 15
SLUMBERED She never slumber'd
in her pew,-- ....15 MBlz 47
SLY I fret in my gizzard, yet,
cautious and sly, ...9 LetB 132
Vida, 228, 328
SLY- That sly-boots was cursedly
cunning to hide 'em. ....28 Rtal 88
SLYER Vida, 273
SLYLY Vida, 406
SMALL To see the hoard of human
bliss so small; ....58 Trav 7
To see the sum of human bliss so
small; ....v58 Trav 168
But small the bliss that sense alone
bestows, ...123 Trav 9
Though poor the peasant's hut,
his feasts though small, ...177 Trav 11
How small, of all that human hearts
endure, ...429 Trav 19
That one small head could carry
all he knew. ....216 DVil 30
Thus at the court both great and
small ....57 LogR 45
This, I believe, between us great
or small, ...3 GCRL 51
I like these here dinners so pretty
and small; ....97 HofV 98
SMALL- Lo! the small-pox, whose
horrid glare ....77 DTrn 54
SMALLEST When titles are the
smallest claim-- ....14 Thrn 74
SMIGLECIUS Wise Aristotle and
Smiglecius, ...5 LogR 44
SMILE$_1$ Exults, and owns his cottage
with a smile. ....164 Trav 10
And pluck'd his gown, to share the
good man's smile. ....184 DVil 29
His ready smile a parent's warmth
express'd, ...185 DVil 29
While oft, with many a smile, and
many a shrug, ...25 eGNM 68
Not a look, not a smile shall my
passion discover: ....6 "Amw 94
SMILE$_2$ Sees an amphibious world
beneath him smile; ....292 Trav 15
SMILED Near yonder copse, where once
the garden smil'd, ...137 DVil 27
And gaily press'd, and smil'd; .....50 Ed&A 60
And he smil'd as he look'd at the
venison and me. ....38 HofV 96
Who smil'd as he gaz'd on the
Ven'son and me. ....v38 HofV 239
Vida, 317
SMILES$_1$ While Botanists, all cold
to smiles and dimpling, ...5 pZob 72
With his long-winded speeches, his
smiles and his brogue; ....90 HofV 98
Thy smiles increase the wretch's
woe; ....vI:28 Capt 250
SMILES$_2$ Smiles by his cheerful fire,
and round surveys ....193 Trav 11
The little urchin smiles, and
spreads her lure, ...23 eSis 70
And as she smiles, her triumphs to
complete, ...21 eSSC$_3$ 85
SMILING To winnow fragrance round
the smiling land. ....122 Trav 9
The smiling long-frequented village
fall? ....406 Trav 18
Where smiling spring its earliest
visit paid, ...3 DVil 23
Sweet smiling village, loveliest
of the lawn, ...35 DVil 24
And half a tillage stints thy
smiling plain: ....40 DVil 24
Where grey-beard mirth and smiling
toil retir'd, ...222 DVil 30
While scourg'd by famine from the
smiling land, ...299 DVil 33
Who mump their passion, and who,
grimly smiling, ...21 eSSC$_1$ 104
The smiling looks of each bewitching
bairn. ....40 eSSC$_1$ 105
See the ruddy morning smiling, II:47 Capt 120
With smiling hopes and chilling
fears, ...14 Tr 267
SMIRKING All smirking, and pleasant,
and big with adventure, ...3 LetB 131
SMIT Vida, 3
SMITH No more the smith his dusky
brow shall clear, ...245 DVil 31
SMOKE A sigh in suffocating smoke; 58 DTrn 54
SMOKED With sulky eye he smoak'd the
patient man, ...v(21) DABd 200
Never rang'd in a forest, or
smok'd in a platter; ....2 HofV 95
SMOKES The ruin smokes, destruction
pours along; ....III:51 Capt 124
The ruin smokes, the torrent pours
along; ....III:61 Capt 125
SMOOTH Glides the smooth current
of domestic joy. ....434 Trav 19
To smooth her skin, or hide its
seams; ....86 DTrn 54
SMOULDERING Their level life is
but a smould'ring fire, ...221 Trav 12
SMUTTED The swain mistrustless of
his smutted face, ...27 DVil 24
SNAKE The rattling terrors of the
vengeful snake; ....354 DVil 35
SNAKE- Filled with a snake-
encircl'd wand; ....32 NSim 57
SNARE Vida, 276
SNARLER The one writes the Snarler,
the other the Scourge; ....77 HofV 97
SNATCH Again they snatch the gleamy
steel, ...229 Thrn 82
SNATCHED For Pollio snatch'd away; ..2 DRtH 50
Vida, 244, 431, 515

SNATCHING Thus snatching his hat,
he brush'd off like the wind, ...57 HofV 97
SNEERED Vida, 657
SNORE That quickly they begin to
snore. ....40 NSim 57
SNORT Vida, 68
SNORTING Vida, 141
SNOW Or winter wraps the polar world
in snow, ...420 DVil 37
Vida, 42, 78
SNOW- Or seeks the den where
snow-tracks mark the way, ...189 Trav 11
The snow-white vesture, and the
glittering crown, ...3 Cati 94
SNOWY Vida, 369, 501
SNOWY- Vida, 61
SNUFF He shifted his trumpet, and
only took snuff. ....146 Rtal 92
SNUG There in a lonely room, from
bailiffs snug, ...5 DABd 48
He eyes the centre, where his friends
sit snug; ....26 eGNM 68
Yet still they sit snug, not a
creature will aim ....11 LetB 132
Yet still I sit snug, and continue
to sigh on, ...21 LetB 132
SO Trav, 58, v58, 89, 207, 255; DVil, 275, 414; DABd, v(19); DTrn, 19, 47, 50, 67; NSim, 36, 39; Ed&A, 143, 144, 158; MDog, 24; pZob, 27, 37; Thrn, 177; Rtal, 17, 52, 57, 66, 69, 115, 134, 157, 158; HofV, 4, v4, 9, 21, 65, 87, 97, 109, 113, 123; epLL, 43; $eSSC_1$, 25, 47, 51; $eSSC_2$, 1; Invt, 11, 26, 37; LetB, 20, 29, 34, 59, 65; Vida, 33, 75, 91, 104, 265, 409, 451, 519, 615
SOAR Who perhaps to the summit of
science could soar, ...159 Rtal 93
And as our fortune sinks, our wishes
soar. ....I:42 Capt 115
Shall vanish as we soar. ....II:6 Capt 118
SOARS Next the scene shifts to
town, and there she soars, ...17 $eSSC_3$ 85
SOBER The sober herd that low'd to
meet their young; ....118 DVil 27
SOCIAL Gay sprightly land of mirth
and social ease, ...241 Trav 13
For honour forms the social temper
here: ....258 Trav 13
Keeps man from man, and breaks the
social tie; ....340 Trav 16
Nor this the worst. As social bonds
decay, ...v349 Trav 174
SOFT$_1$ Yet, why this killing soft
dejection? ....v5 Sonn 196
Soft as the dew from heav'n descends,33 Ed&A 60
Thou soft companion of the breast!II:2 Capt 118
Thus, when soft love subdues the
heart ....13 Tr 267
SOFT$_2$ 'Give me another horse! bind
up my wounds!--soft--'twas but a
dream,' ....24 epLL 101
SOFTEN Comes to soften every
pain. ....III:98 Capt 126
To melt me to pity, and soften
my swearing. ....54 LetB 133
SOFTENED The mingling notes came
soften'd from below; ....116 DVil 27
SOFTER But while this softer art
their bliss supplies, ...267 Trav 14
Vida, 173
SOIL These here disporting own the
kindred soil, ...119 Trav 9
And force a churlish soil for
scanty bread; ....168 Trav 10
Each wish contracting, fits him to
the soil. ....184 Trav 11
Thus, while around the wave-subjected
soil ....297 Trav 15
For just experience tells, in every
soil, ...371 Trav 17
SOLDIER But man and steel, the
soldier and his sword; ....170 Trav 10
The broken soldier, kindly bade to
stay, ...155 DVil 28
-SOLDIER Vida, 404
SOLDIERS And scholars, soldiers, kings,
unhonour'd die. ....360 Trav 17
Vida, 205
SOLE Vida, 622
SOLEMN Vida, 171
SOLEMN- 'What, yon solemn-faced,
odd-looking man that stands
near!' ....50 LetB 133
SOLEMNITY May oft distract us with
their sad solemnity: ....91 Thrn 77
SOLICITOUS She then shines forth,
solicitous to bless, ...293 DVil 33
SOLID Nor weighs the solid worth of
self-applause. ....280 Trav 14
SOLITARY in barren solitary pomp
repose? ....404 Trav 18
Along thy glades, a solitary guest, 43 DVil 24
Here as I take my solitary rounds, 77 DVil 25
All but yon widow'd, solitary thing 129 DVil 27
His seat, where solitary sports
are seen, ...281 DVil 32
My shame in crowds, my solitary
pride; ....412 DVil 37
SOLITUDE And sought a solitude
forlorn, ...135 Ed&A 63
I'll seek the solitude he sought, 139 Ed&A 64
SOLITUDES E'en now, where Alpine
solitudes ascend, ...31 Trav 6
SOME Trav, 20, 26, 51, 60, 109, v146, 197, 224, 233, 413; DVil, 189, 287, 305; MDog, 19; eGNM, 1, 4, 23; Thrn, 32, 41, 49; "LSm, 23; Rtal, 27; HofV, 9, 43, 78, 112; $eSSC_2$, 41; Capt, II:56; Vida, 152, 229, 233, 271, 327, 441, 527
SOMETHING I'll give thee something
yet unpaid, ...17 Gift 43
I think I met with something there, 7 NSim 56
He's keeping a corner for something
that's nice: ....100 HofV 98
You've got an odd something--a kind
of discerning-- ....119 HofV 99
Yet something vain, like one that
shall be nameless, ...28 epLL 102
I have something to sell him; .....20 Invt 128
SON For, as refinement stops, from
sire to son ....229 Trav 12
Beheld the duteous son, the sire
decay'd, ...407 Trav 18
'Forbear, my son,' the hermit cries, 9 Ed&A 59

O Lucifer, thou son of morn, ..III:73 Capt 125
Vida, 293, 322
SONG Give ear unto my song; ....2 MDog 65
A simple song, a sigh profound. ...131 Thrn 78
My morning prayer, my evening song, 200 Thrn 81
My morning and my evening song; ...204 Thrn 81
The day demands it; sing us Sion's
song. ....I:82 Capt 116
Exulting rocks have crown'd the
power of song! ....9 Tr 267
SONGS May saints with songs receive
thee to their rest; ....109 Thrn 77
Give, give your songs of Sion to
the wind, ...III:87 Capt 126
SONGSTERS Blest as the songsters
of the grove, ...v(163) Ed&A 211
SONS The sons of Italy were surely
blest. ....112 Trav 9
Methinks her patient sons before
me stand, ...283 Trav 14
How much unlike the sons of Britain
now! ....316 Trav 15
Her useful sons exchang'd for useless
ore? ....398 Trav 18
Those fenceless fields the sons of
wealth divide, ...307 DVil 33
To see those joys the sons of
pleasure know ....313 DVil 33
To see each joy the sons of pleasure
know ....v313 DVil 189
In these bold times, when Learning's
sons explore ....1 pZob 72
Arise, ye sons of worth, arise, ...1 Thrn 74
Old Edward's sons, unknown to
yield, ...225 Thrn 82
Here come the sons of scandal and
of news, ...31 $eSSC_2$ 109
But hush, my sons, our tyrant
lords are near; ....I:51 Capt 115
Desist, my sons, nor mix the strain
with theirs. ....I:56 Capt 115
Haste, ye sprightly sons of
pleasure; ....I:65 Capt 116
Ye sons of Judah, why the lute
unstrung? ....I:79 Capt 116
SOON Soon Commerce turn'd on other
shores her sail; ....v140 Trav 169
View him soon after to inferiors, ..49 LogR 45
Jack soon was dazzl'd to behold ....95 DTrn 55
But soon a wonder came to light, ...29 MDog 66
They'd as soon think of eating the
pan it is fried in. ....12 HofV 95
Vida, 430, 666
SOONER 'I wish I'd been called in
a little sooner:' ....54 $eSSC_1$ 106
Vida, 94
SOOTHE To soothe the stranger's
woe; ....58 Ed&A 61
What charm can soothe her melancholy, 3 "wlw 67
SOPORIFIC Its soporific virtue's
such, ...38 NSim 57
SORE Let us lament in sorrow sore, 25 MBlz 47
The wound it seem'd both sore and
sad ....25 MDog 66
Those streams which cheer the sore
oppress, ...III:45 Capt 124
SORROW Here let me sit in sorrow
for mankind, ...102 Trav 8
Wept o'er his wounds, or tales of
sorrow done, ...157 DVil 28
And sorrow, guilt, and pain, by
turns dismay'd, ...172 DVil 29
And clasp'd them close, in sorrow
doubly dear; ....382 DVil 36
Let us lament in sorrow sore, ...25 MBlz 47
'But mine the sorrow, mine the
fault, ...137 Ed&A 64
Where modest want and patient
sorrow dwell; ....123 Thrn 78
Bending at once with sorrow and
with age, ...169 Thrn 80
At last the impetuous sorrow fir'd
his breast. ....212 Thrn 82
In want and sorrow groan; ....III:24 Capt 123
Behold his wretched corse with
sorrow worn, ...III:31 Capt 123
SORROWING There, sorrowing by the
river's glassy bed, ...151 Thrn 79
SORROWS Yet oft a sigh prevails, and
sorrows fall, ...57 Trav 7
Good heaven! what sorrows gloom'd
that parting day, ...363 DVil 35
'The sorrows of thy breast? ....64 Ed&A 61
'For shame, fond youth, thy sorrows
hush, ...81 Ed&A 62
A thousand sorrows urg'd thy end: ..31 Thrn 75
The echoes of Thames shall my sorrows
proclaim, ...244 Thrn 83
SORT Good people all, of every sort, 1 MDog 65
SOUGHT Again the long-fall'n column
sought the skies; ....136 Trav 9
For praise too dearly lov'd, or
warmly sought, ...269 Trav 14
The dancing pair that simply sought
renown, ...25 DVil 24
These all in sweet confusion sought
the shade, ...123 DVil 27
Her love was sought, I do aver, ...17 MBlz 47
Long had I sought in vain to find ...1 NSim 56
And when a little rest I sought v125 Ed&A 210
And sought a solitude forlorn, ...135 Ed&A 63
I'll seek the solitude he sought, 139 Ed&A 64
She still reliev'd, nor sought my
praise, ...197 Thrn 81
Vida, 370
SOUL Where my worn soul, each
wand'ring hope at rest, ...61 Trav 7
Now sinks at last, or feebly mans the
soul; ....156 Trav 10
She leaves at last, or feebly mans
the soul; ....v156 Trav 170
They sink at last, or feebly man the
soul; ....v156 Trav 171
My soul, turn from them; turn we
to survey ....165 Trav 10
Dear is that shed to which his soul
conforms, ...203 Trav 12
Unknown those powers that raise the
soul to flame, ...219 Trav 12
And the weak soul, within itself
unblest, ...271 Trav 14
Fierce in their native hardiness of
soul, ...331 Trav 16
Ye powers of truth, that bid my soul

aspire, ...363 Trav 17
Calm is my soul, nor apt to rise
in arms, ...379 Trav 17
Despair and anguish fled the
struggling soul; ....174 DVil 29
The soul adopts, and owns their
first-born sway; ....256 DVil 31
But for my soul I cannot credit
'em; ....10 LogR 44
But not a soul will budge to give
him place. ....30 eGNM 69
Her soul was fitting to its kindred
skies: ....121 Thrn 78
Every glance that warms the soul, 236 Thrn 82
How shrinks my soul to meet the
threaten'd blow! ....II:26 Capt 119
Vida, 413
The soul rejects the aid of art, ...15 Tr 267
SOUL- Grief dares to mingle her
soul-piercing voice, ...3 Queb 46
While soul-brought tears steal down
each shining face. ....6 MrsX 49
SOULS With this he drives men's
souls to hell. ....42 NSim 57
Drove souls to Tart'rus with his rod,52 NSim 57
SOUND Fir'd at the sound, my genius
spreads her wing, ...317 Trav 15
And Niagara stuns with thund'ring
sound? ....412 Trav 19
Sweet was the sound, when oft at
evening's close ....113 DVil 27
While words of learned length and
thund'ring sound ....213 DVil 30
And rocks forgot their hardness
at the sound. ....12 MrsX 49
'And love is still an emptier sound, 77 Ed&A 61
The growing sound their swift
approach declares;-- ....I:55 Capt 115
Vida, 18, 354, 523
-SOUNDING The hollow-sounding
bittern guards its nest; ....44 DVil 24
SOUNDS And as a child, when scaring
sounds molest, ...205 Trav 12
But now the sounds of population
fail, ...125 DVil 27
The sounds of barb'rous pleasure
strike mine ear: ....I:52 Capt 115
Or join with sounds profane its
sacred mirth! ....I:92 Capt 117
SOURCE Becomes a source of pleasure
when redrest. ....214 Trav 12
And thus polluting honour in its
source, ...395 Trav 18
Thou source of all my bliss, and
all my woe, ...413 DVil 37
SOUTH From north, from south, from
east, from west, ...II:71 Capt 121
SOUTHERN Till, more unsteady than
the southern gale, ...139 Trav 9
But, more unsteady than the southern
gale, ...v139 Trav 169
SOVEREIGN Vida, 153
SPACE Takes up a space that many
poor supplied; ....276 DVil 32
Space for his lake, his park's
extended bounds, ...277 DVil 32
Space for his horses, equipage, and
hounds; ....278 DVil 32
Vida, 53, 130, 638, 647
SPACES Vida, 23
SPADILLE She sits all night at cards,
and ogles at spadille. ....31 $eSSC_3$ 86
SPARE Do you spare her, and I'll
for once spare you. ....44 eSis 71
SPARK$_1$ Yon broad, bold, angry spark,
I fix my eye on, ...27 eSis 71
SPARK$_2$ Detection her taper shall
quench to a spark, ...91 Rtal 90
SPARRING Well, Madam, what if, after
all this sparring, ...65 $eSSC_1$ 106
SPEAK But let us be candid, and
speak out our mind, ...113 Rtal 91
'Your Tripe!' quoth the Jew, 'if
the truth I may speak, ...v95 HofV 242
May speak our gratitude, but not
his fame. ....2 epTP 100
I'd speak a word or two, to ease my
conscience. ....2 epLL 101
SPEAKING Her moral play a speaking
masquerade; ....4 eSis 70
SPEAKS She speaks! 'tis rapture all,
and nameless bliss, ...7 MrsX 49
Vida, 415
And speaks in moments more than years.16 Tr 267
SPEAR Vida, 422, 609
SPEARS Vida, 372, 426, 631
SPECIAL He was, could he help it?--
a special attorney. ....136 Rtal 91
SPECIOUS By ratiocinations specious, 6 LogR 44
SPED At night returning, every labour
sped, ...191 Trav 11
If to the city sped--What waits
him there? ....309 DVil 33
SPEECHES Our Townshend make speeches,
and I shall compile; ....88 Rtal 90
The one with his speeches, and t'other
with Thrale; ....72 HofV 97
With his long-winded speeches, his
smiles and his brogue; ....90 HofV 98
SPEED Vida, 380
SPEEDS That speeds the power of
music to the heart, ...I:90 Capt 117
Feels for each tone, and speeds
it to the heart; ....II:66 Capt 120
SPEEDY Vida, 476
SPEND I sit me down a pensive
hour to spend; ....32 Trav 6
SPENDTHRIFT The ruin'd spendthrift,
now no longer proud, ...153 DVil 28
SPENT My prime of life in wand'ring
spent and care, ...24 Trav 6
For ten pounds in hand, and ten
pounds to be spent. ....66 LetB 134
SPHERE Vida, 124
SPICY No spicy fragrance while
they grow; ....I:48 Capt 115
SPIED His rising cares the hermit
spied, ...61 Ed&A 61
SPIES Vida, 274
SPINACH At the sides there was
spinach and pudding made hot; ......83 HofV 98
SPIRIT Our bard into the general
spirit enters, ...9 pZob 72
Bless'd spirit thou, whose fame,

just born to bloom ....18 Thrn 74
And ah! bless'd spirit, wheresoe'er
thy flight, ...106 Thrn 77
But peace to his spirit, wherever
it flies, ...119 Rtal 91
Give me the young, the gay, the
men of spirit. ....30 $eSSC_1$ 105
SPIRITS What spirits were his!
what wit and what whim! ....53 Rtal 88
SPITE And must in spite of them
maintain, ...11 LogR 44
In wit, and sense, and nature's
spite: ....4 NSim 56
Vida, 565
SPLEEN Insulting repartee or
spleen. ....60 DTrn 54
SPLENDID To spurn the splendid
things by heaven supply'd. ....v40 Trav 168
By arts, the splendid wrecks of
former pride; ....146 Trav 10
Some splendid arts, the wrecks of
former pride; ....v146 Trav 170
It shifts in splendid traffic
round the land: ....262 Trav 14
To boast one splendid banquet once
a year; ....278 Trav 14
Between a splendid and a happy
land. ....268 DVil 32
Where, splendid as the youthful
poet's dream, ...142 Thrn 79
Ye beaux and belles, that form
this splendid ring, ...5 $eSSC_1$ 103
SPLENDOUR Ye glitt'ring towns,
with wealth and splendour crown'd, ..45 Trav 6
In barren splendour feebly waits
the fall. ....286 DVil 32
So next day, in due splendour to
make my approach, ...65 HofV 97
The sun with his splendour illumines the skies, ...I:63 Capt 116
SPLENDOURS The parlour splendours
of that festive place; ....226 DVil 30
Vain, transitory splendours! Could
not all ....237 DVil 31
But verging to decline, its
splendours rise, ...297 DVil 33
SPLITTING 'Though splitting, I'll
still keep a corner for thot.' ....104 HofV 98
SPOIL Or you may chance to spoil
a thriving trade. ....34 pZob 73
To spoil such a delicate picture
by eating; ....6 HofV 95
SPOILED When both have been spoil'd
in to-day's <u>Advertiser</u>? ....44 Invt 129
SPOILER'S And trembling, shrinking
from the spoiler's hand, ...49 DVil 24
SPOILS Vida, 541, 430, 607
SPOKE And the loud laugh that spoke
the vacant mind; ....122 DVil 27
With louder plaints the mother
spoke her woes, ...379 DVil 35
<u>From those who spoke her praise</u>. ....4 MBlz 47
And freshmen wonder'd as he spoke. ..6 DTrn 52
But, while he spoke, a rising
blush ....83 Ed&A 62
Whene'er he spoke amidst the
train, ...v121 Ed&A 210
But all my wants, before I spoke, ..195 Thrn 81
Whilst thus he spoke, astonish'd,
to his view, ...37 epLL 102
-SPOKEN An under-bred, fine-spoken
fellow was he, ...37 HofV 96
A fine-spoken Custom-house Officer
he, ...v37 HofV 239
SPONTANEOUS Spontaneous joys, where
Nature has its play, ...255 DVil 31
What was good was spontaneous, his
faults were his own. ....50 Rtal 88
$SPORT_1$ Seats of my youth, when every
sport could please, ...6 DVil 23
They eat their meals, and take their
sport, ...25 LogR 44
Vida, 13
$SPORT_2$ To sport and flutter in a
kinder sky. ....238 Trav 13
SPORTIVE How often have I led thy
sportive choir, ...243 Trav 13
Vida, 181, 207, 297
SPORTIVELY Vida, 1
SPORTS By sports like these are all
their cares beguil'd, ...153 Trav 10
The sports of children satisfy the
child; ....154 Trav 10
At sports like these, while foreign
arms advance, ...v(155) Trav 170
Led up their sports beneath the
spreading tree; ....18 DVil 23
Succeeding sports the mirthful band
inspir'd; ....24 DVil 24
These were thy charms, sweet village;
sports like these, ...31 DVil 24
Thy sports are fled, and all thy
charms withdrawn; ....36 DVil 24
Those healthful sports that grac'd
the peaceful scene, ...71 DVil 25
His seat, where solitary sports are
seen, ...281 DVil 32
SPOT Bless'd be that spot, where
cheerful guests retire ....13 Trav 5
And find no spot of all the world
my own. ....30 Trav 6
Some spot to real happiness consign'd, 60 Trav 7
But where to find that happiest
spot below, ...63 Trav 7
Boldly proclaims that happiest spot
his own, ...66 Trav 7
But past is all his fame. The very
spot ....217 DVil 30
Come, and dance on the spot where
your tyrant reclines: ....82 Rtal 89
To this strange spot, Rakes,
Macaronies, Cits, ...15 $eSSC_2$ 108
Vida, 558, 599
SPOUSES False wits, false wives,
false virgins, and false spouses! ..14 eSis 70
SPRAY There gentle music melts on
ev'ry spray; ....322 Trav 16
SPREAD Yet still, e'en here, content
can spread a charm, ...175 Trav 11
For him light labour spread her
wholesome store, ...59 DVil 25
To strip the brook with mantling
cresses spread, ...132 DVil 27
Though round its breast the rolling

clouds are spread, ...191 DVil 29
Down, down they sink, and spread
a ruin round. ....394 DVil 36
The humid wall with paltry pictures
spread: ....10 DABd 48
Where wilds immeasurably spread, ...7 Ed&A 59
And spread his vegetable store, ...49 Ed&A 60
Alternate spread alarms: ....90 Ed&A 62
There Mangroves spread, and larger
than I've seen 'em-- ....19 pZob 72
Shall spread and flourish from
the tomb, ...19 Thrn 74
Like an ill-judging beauty, his
colours he spread, ...99 Rtal 90
Still shall our fame and growing
power be spread, ...III:5 Capt 122
Vida, 337, 511, 583
SPREADING Led up their sports
beneath the spreading tree; ....18 DVil 23
SPREADS Ye fields, where summer
spreads profusion round, ...46 Trav 6
Spreads its long arms amidst the
wat'ry roar, ...289 Trav 14
Fir'd at the sound, my genius
spreads her wing, ...317 Trav 15
Where wild Oswego spreads her
swamps around, ...411 Trav 19
Down where yon anchoring vessel
spreads the sail, ...399 DVil 36
The little urchin smiles, and
spreads her lure, ...23 eSis 70
Vida, 134, 249
The sea subsiding spreads a level
plain: ....4 Tr 267
SPRIGHTLY Gay sprightly land of
mirth and social ease, ...241 Trav 13
Haste, ye sprightly sons of
pleasure; ....I:65 Capt 116
SPRING$_1$ And flies where Britain
courts the western spring; ....318 Trav 15
Where smiling spring its earliest
visit paid, ...3 DVil 23
I'll strip all the spring of its
earliest bloom: ....248 Thrn 83
We'll rifle the spring of its
earliest bloom, ...256,260 Thrn 83
SPRING$_2$ That feebly bends beside
the plashy spring; ....130 DVil 27
And water from the spring. ....28 Ed&A 60
SPRINGS Hence all the good from
opulence that springs, ...301 Trav 15
And every virtue springs from
pain: ....I:46 Capt 115
Vida, 245, 315
SPURN To spurn the splendid things
by heaven supply'd. ....v40 Trav 168
To spurn imploring famine from the
gate; ....106 DVil 26
Teach erring man to spurn the
rage of gain; ....424 DVil 37
And spurn the sex,' he said: ....82 Ed&A 62
To spurn the venal gifts as
flattery. ....11 Thrn 74
You spurn the favours offer'd from
his hand, ...II:12 Capt 118
SPURNED 'From better habitations
spurn'd, ...65 Ed&A 61

I spurn'd him from my side, ...v130 Ed&A 210
SPURNS And spurns the plan that
aims at other ends; ....96 Trav 8
Indignant spurns the cottage from
the green; ....282 DVil 32
Oh, let me fly a land that spurns
the brave, ...221 Thrn 82
Vida, 213
SPURS Vida, 539
SPY Vida, 214
SQUALID His squalid limbs with
pond'rous fetters torn; ....III:32 Capt 123
SQUARE Tumultuous grandeur crowds
the blazing square, ...321 DVil 34
Vida, 23, 108, 217, 243, 531
SQUIBS Who copied his squibs, and
re-echoed his jokes; ....164 Rtal 93
'SQUIRE The 'squire and captain
took their stations, ...55 DTrn 53
The 'squire himself was seen to
yield, ...89 DTrn 55
The Fourth Act shows her wedded to
the 'Squire, ...23 eSSC$_3$ 85
'SQUIRES On 'Squires and Cits she
there displays her arts, ...19 eSSC$_3$ 85
STAG 'Twas thus that Aesop's stag,
a creature blameless, ...27 epLL 102
STAGE What! no way left to shun th'
inglorious stage, ...1 pLab 41
Thus on the stage, our play-wrights
still depend ....3 eGNM 68
Have emptied all the green-room on
the stage. ....6 eSis 70
On the stage he was natural, simple,
affecting; ....101 Rtal 90
No--I will act. I'll vindicate the
stage: ....19 epLL 101
The Moon, says he:--but I affirm
the Stage: ....6 eSSC$_2$ 108
STAIN Vida, 206
STAINS To-morrow's tears may wash
our stains away. ....II:32 Capt 119
Vida, 27
STAKE And ogling the stake which
is fix'd in the centre. ....4 LetB 131
I lay down my stake, apparently
cool, ...7 LetB 131
STAMP Unite to stamp the beauties
of the place, ...145 Thrn 79
STAND$_1$ Determin'd took their stand: 55 Thrn 76
STAND$_2$ Methinks her patient sons
before me stand, ...283 Trav 14
The self-dependent lordlings stand
alone, ...341 Trav 16
'Tis yours to judge, how wide the
limits stand ....267 DVil 32
E'en now, methinks, as pond'ring
here I stand, ...397 DVil 36
Stand fast, and let our tyrants
see ....I:99 Capt 117
Vida, 185
STANDARDS Vida, 78
STANDS No surly porter stands in
guilty state ....105 DVil 26
The lovely stranger stands con-
fess'd ....91 Ed&A 62
At the Pit door stands elbowing a

way, ...24 eGNM 68
'What, yon solemn-faced, odd-looking
man that stands near!' ....50 LetB 133
Vida, 55
STAR Without a star, a coronet or
garter, ...37 $eSSC_2$ 109
Vida, 626
STARS Vida, 625
START Fear, pity, justice, indig-
nation start, ...389 Trav 18
And quells the raptures which from
pleasures start. ....4 Queb 46
STARTS He starts, he pants, he takes
the circling maze. ....42 epLL 102
STARVES To thrive by flattery, though
he starves by wit. ....72 $eSSC_1$ 107
$STATE_1$ Hence every state to one
lov'd blessing prone, ...93 Trav 8
When commerce proudly flourish'd
through the state; ....134 Trav 9
Upon a minister of state; ....48 LogR 45
Perhaps, to vulgar eyes, bestrides
the state; ....34 eSis 71
Vida, 266, 457, 593
$STATE_2$ Stern o'er each bosom reason
holds her state, ...325 Trav 16
Yet think not, thus when Freedom's
ills I state, ...361 Trav 17
Vida, 142, 533, 634
$STATE_3$ No surly porter stands in
guilty state ....105 DVil 26
That dimly show'd the state in which
he lay; ....8 DABd 48
That feebly shew'd the state in
which he lay. ....v8 DABd 200
To one of my state. ....38 Invt 129
Vida, 241, 469
STATED Vida, 84
STATELY Here trees of stately size--
and turtles in 'em-- ....20 pZob 72
Vida, 276, 442
STATES Such are the charms to barren
states assign'd; ....209 Trav 12
And yet, perhaps, if states with
states we scan, ...v75 Trav 168
Teach him, that states of native
strength possess'd, ...425 DVil 37
STATESMAN Too nice for a statesman,
too proud for a wit: ....38 Rtal 88
STATESMEN Where village statesmen
talk'd with looks profound, ...223 DVil 30
Ye friends to truth, ye statesmen,
who survey ....265 DVil 32
Statesmen with bridles on; and,
close beside 'em, ...15 eSis 70
Ye statesmen, warriors, poets, kings;81 Thrn 77
STATION Whose talents to fill any
station were fit, ...161 Rtal 93
Vida, 217, 235
STATIONS The 'squire and captain
took their stations, ...55 DTrn 53
STATUTES Each wanton judge new penal
statutes draw, ...385 Trav 18
STAUNCH I thought of a friend that
was trusty and staunch; ....20 HofV 95
STAY The broken soldier, kindly bade
to stay, ...155 DVil 28

Vida, 541
STEADY With steady zeal, each
honest rustic ran; ....182 DVil 29
And steady loyalty, and faithful
love. ....406 DVil 36
STEAL While soul-brought tears
steal down each shining face. ....6 MrsX 49
STEALING Well! what of that? out
with it--stealing; ....58 NSim 58
STEDFAST Vida, 400
STEED Vida, 127, 141
STEEDS Vida, 68, 270
STEEL But man and steel, the soldier
and his sword; ....170 Trav 10
The rabble's rage, and tyrant's
angry steel; ....366 Trav 17
Luke's iron crown, and Damiens' bed
of steel, ...436 Trav 19
Again they snatch the gleamy steel, 229 Thrn 82
Vida, 347
STEEP That shades the steep, and
sighs at every blast. ....104 Trav 8
Or drives his vent'rous plough-
share to the steep; ....188 Trav 11
STEER When wise Astronomers to India
steer, ...3 pZob 72
STEERING To coxcombs averse, yet
most civilly steering, ...143 Rtal 92
STEERS He this way steers his course,
in hopes of trading-- ....12 pZob 72
STEMS Basks in the glare, or stems
the tepid wave, ...71 Trav 7
Where noble stems transmit the
patriot flame, ...357 Trav 17
$STEP_1$ Where at each step the stranger
fears to wake ....353 DVil 35
Vida, 160, 196, 279, 495, 505
$STEP_2$ I'd best step back--and order
up a sample. ....38 pZob 73
STEPPED Vida, 549
STEPS Impell'd, with steps unceasing,
to pursue ....25 Trav 6
Here, as with doubtful, pensive
steps I range, ...v(81) DVil 182
There, as I pass'd with careless
steps and slow, ...115 DVil 27
No busy steps the grass-grown
foot-way tread, ...127 DVil 27
Through torrid tracts with fainting
steps they go, ...343 DVil 34
Nor force nor fraud could turn my
steps aside; ....6 pLab 41
With fainting steps and slow; ....6 Ed&A 59
Vida, 111
STERN Stern o'er each bosom reason
holds her state, ...325 Trav 16
Lead stern depopulation in her
train, ...402 Trav 18
A man severe he was, and stern to
view; ....197 DVil 29
Vida, 146, 198, 251, 261
STERNER Some sterner virtues o'er
the mountain's breast ....233 Trav 13
STICK Who'd not be a glutton, and
stick to the last? ....18 Rtal 87
STILL Trav, 9, 54, 77, v78, 82, 145,
v145, 175, 247, 279, 352, 369, 431;

DVil, 23, 85, 89, 95, 138, 212, 215,
274, 356, 369, 370, 408, 421, 426;
LogR, 55; DRtH, 19; TrSA, 2; DTrn,
37; NSim, 49; Ed&A, 14, 72, 77, 129,
v129, v131, v158; MDog, 7; eGNM, 3;
Thrn, 35, 146, 197; eSSC$_3$, 3, 33;
Rtal, 35, 46, 47, 122, 141, 144,
166; HofV, 104; eSSC$_1$, 20, 22, 62;
eSSC$_2$, 40; Capt, I:22, 24, 41, 54,
vII:34, 39, 91, III:5, 6; LetB,
11, 21, 33; Vida, 443, 611, 626

STIMULATES For every want that
stimulates the breast, ...213 Trav 12

STINTS And half a tillage stints
thy smiling plain: ....40 DVil 24

STIRRING No stirring--I beg--my
dear friend--my dear friend! ....56 HofV 97

STOCK Ye jockey tribe, whose stock
of words are few, ...49 eSSC$_1$ 106

STOCKING A cap by night--a stocking
all the day! ....20 DABd 48

STOLE Vida, 586

STOMACH Though my stomach was sharp,
I could scarce help regretting ....5 HofV 95

STONE And see how they kneel! Is
your heart made of stone?' ....64 LetB 134

STONES Are they but senseless
stones and blocks? ....64 NSim 58

STOOD Where once the cottage stood,
the hawthorn grew, ...80 DVil 25
The reverend champion stood. At
his control, ...173 DVil 29
Thy towering mind self-centred
stood, ...26 Thrn 75
Like some well-fashion'd arch thy
patience stood, ...32 Thrn 75
They stood, while hope and comfort
fail, ...69 Thrn 76
Once on the margin of a fountain
stood, ...29 epLL 102
Vida, 195, 234, 334, 507, 518, 598,
622, 648

STOOPED Well, having stoop'd to
conquer with success, ...1 eSSC$_3$ 85

STOOPS Imagination fondly stoops
to trace ....225 DVil 30
When lovely woman stoops to
folly, ...1 "wlw 67
Still stoops among the low to
copy nature. ....40 eSSC$_2$ 109

STOP And, sedulous to stop the
coming tide, ...285 Trav 14
Its motions stop, or frenzy fire
the wheels. ....348 Trav 16
To stop too fearful, and too faint
to go, ...420 Trav 19
Or Flavia been content to stop ......13 DTrn 52
And now that I think on't, the
story may stop. ....116 HofV 99
That stop the hunter's way: ....III:42 Capt 124

STOPPED Vida, 552

STOPS For, as refinement stops,
from sire to son ....229 Trav 12

STORE Amidst the store, should
thankless pride repine? ....38 Trav 6
Amidst the store, 'twere thank-
less to repine. ....v38 Trav 168
As some lone miser visiting his
store, ...51 Trav 7
For him light labour spread her
wholesome store, ...59 DVil 25
But this vile hour disperses all
my store, ...9 pLab 41
And spread his vegetable store, ...49 Ed&A 60
Dispense thy balmy store. ....II:3 Capt 118
To-morrow's most unbounded store II:61 Capt 120
Vida, 491

STORED Our ship's well stor'd;--in
yonder creek we've laid her; ....31 pZob 73
The Mohawk too--with angry phrases
stored, ...27 eSSC$_2$ 109

STOREHOUSE But where's this place,
this storehouse of the age? ....5 eSSC$_2$ 108

STORES For me your tributary stores
combine; ....49 Trav 7
No stores beneath its humble thatch 41 Ed&A 60
With Scythian stores, and trinkets
deeply laden, ...11 pZob 72

STORM Dull as their lakes that
slumber in the storm. ....312 Trav 15
Swells from the vale, and midway
leaves the storm, ...190 DVil 29
'To 'bide the pelting of this
pitiless storm'-- ....32 eGNM 69
Awful as clouds that nurse the
growing storm; ....II:68 Capt 121
Vida, 51, 577

STORM'S And, plac'd on high above
the storm's career, ...33 Trav 6

STORMS And dear that hill which lifts
him to the storms; ....204 Trav 12
With secret course, which no loud
storms annoy, ...433 Trav 19
But storms that fly, ...II:19 Capt 118

STORMY Extols the treasures of
his stormy seas, ...67 Trav 7
Where the bleak Swiss their stormy
mansions tread, ...167 Trav 10
But meteors glare, and stormy
glooms invest. ....174 Trav 11
Vida, 438

STORY And e'en the story ran that
he could gauge. ....210 DVil 30
And now that I think on't, the
story may stop. ....116 HofV 99

STOUT Our hearts and our liquors
are stout; ....19 "LSm 84
For the foot guards so stout ......26 Invt 128

STOUTLY Good liquor, I stoutly
maintain, ...3 "LSm 84

STRAGGLING Beside yon straggling
fence that skirts the way, ...193 DVil 29
Vida, 453, 463, 519

STRAIGHT$_1$ Vida, 123, 134

STRAIGHT$_2$ Vida, 423

STRAIGHTWAY Vida, 38

STRAIN Aid slighted truth; with thy
persuasive strain ....423 DVil 37
His bounty in exalted strain ....13 DRtH 50
Desist, my sons, nor mix the strain
with theirs. ....I:56 Capt 115
Come, take the lyre, and pour the
strain along, ...I:81 Capt 116
Is this a time to bid us raise the

strain, ...I:87 Capt 117
That strain once more; it bids
remembrance rise, ...I:15 Capt 114
STRAINING Though fraught with all
learning, yet straining his
throat ....33 Rtal 88
STRAITENED Vida, 239
STRAND Pass from the shore, and
darken all the strand. ....402 DVil 36
STRANGE To this strange spot,
Rakes, Macaronies, Cits, ...15 $eSSC_2$ 108
Vida, 307, 462, 542
STRANGER Against the houseless
stranger shuts the door; ....4 Trav 5
And every stranger finds a ready
chair; ....16 Trav 5
Or press the bashful stranger to
his food, ...21 Trav 6
Where at each step the stranger
fears to wake ....353 DVil 35
Invites each passing stranger that
can pay; ....2 DABd 48
That welcomes every stranger that
can pay, ...v(20) DABd 200
The modest stranger lowly bends ....35 Ed&A 60
The grateful stranger lowly
bends. ....v35 Ed&A 208
The lovely stranger stands con-
fess'd ....91 Ed&A 62
'And, ah! forgive a stranger rude, .93 Ed&A 62
A stranger to flatt'ry, a stranger
to fear; ....152 Rtal 93
STRANGER'S To soothe the stranger's
woe; ....58 Ed&A 61
The pensive stranger's woe; ......v58 Ed&A 208
STRANGERS And strangers led astray. 40 Ed&A 60
STRAW Let boys play tricks, and
kick the straw; not I: ....13 eGNM 68
For giving advice that is not worth
a straw, ...37 LetB 133
STRAY There all around the gentlest
breezes stray, ...321 Trav 16
Whom love has taught to stray; .....98 Ed&A 62
From lawn to woodland stray; ..v(162) Ed&A 211
Where brooks refreshing stray; III:40 Capt 124
Thus stray from my text? ....34 Invt 129
From wisdom to stray, ...40 Invt 129
Vida, 7, 138
STRAYED Why have I stray'd from
pleasure and repose, ...425 Trav 19
If to some common's fenceless
limits stray'd, ...305 DVil 33
Vida, 617, 671
STRAYING Streams along the valley
straying. ....II:50 Capt 120
STRAYS From courts, to camps, to
cottages it strays, ...263 Trav 14
E'en now, perhaps, as there some
pilgrim strays ....413 Trav 19
STREAM Fast by that shore where
Thames' translucent stream ....140 Thrn 79
STREAMING O Wolfe! to thee a stream-
ing flood of woe, ...5 Queb 46
STREAMS And brighter streams than
fam'd Hydaspes glide. ....320 Trav 15
Streams along the valley stray-
ing. ....II:50 Capt 120

For streams of mercy long; ....III:44 Capt 124
Those streams which cheer the
sore opprest, ...III:45 Capt 124
-STREET For Kent-street well may
say, ...26 MBlz 47
At triumphs in a Fleet-street shop. 14 DTrn 52
How did Grub-street re-echo the
shouts that you rais'd, ...117 Rtal 91
STREETS Around from all the
neighbouring streets ....21 MDog 65
Thy streets forlorn ....III:80 Capt 126
STRENGTH Its former strength
was but plethoric ill. ....144 Trav 10
Enfeebles all internal strength of
thought; ....270 Trav 14
Still gather strength, and force
unwilling awe. ....352 Trav 17
And sleights of art and feats of
strength went round; ....22 DVil 24
Relax his pond'rous strength, and
lean to hear; ....246 DVil 31
Till sapp'd their strength, and
every part unsound, ...393 DVil 36
Teach him, that states of native
strength possess'd, ...425 DVil 37
And purchas'd strength from its
increasing load, ...33 Thrn 75
Nor can my strength perform what
they require; ....174 Thrn 80
And as my strength decay'd, her
bounty grew.' ....180 Thrn 80
Vida, 41, 44, 133, 478, 559, 603
STREPHON Strephon caught thy
ravish'd eye; ....24 $eSSC_1$ 104
STRESS The stress of all my proofs
on him I lay, ...13 NSim 56
STRETCH Contracting regal power to
stretch their own; ....382 Trav 18
And stretch me where he lay. ......140 Ed&A 64
STRETCHED The Muse found Scroggen
stretch'd beneath a rug; ....6 DABd 48
STREW And apples, bitter apples
strew the ground. ....22 pZob 73
Then strew all around it (you can
do no less) ....169 Rtal 93
STRICT Serenely gay, and strict
in duty, ...103 DTrn 55
STRIFE Secluded from domestic
strife, ...1 DTrn 52
While sullen or loquacious strife, .73 DTrn 54
Vida, 394, 456
STRIKE Its vistas strike, its
palaces surprise; ....298 DVil 33
To catch the heart, or strike for
honest fame; ....410 DVil 36
They're perfectly disgraceful!
strike me dead! ....33 epLL 102
The sounds of barb'rous pleasure
strike mine ear; ....I:52 Capt 115
Begin, ye captive bands, and
strike the lyre, ...II:45 Capt 120
STRIKING His pencil was striking,
resistless, and grand; ....139 Rtal 91
STRING And now his voice,
accordant to the string, ...II:69 Capt 121
STRIP To strip the brook with
mantling cresses spread, ...132 DVil 27

Strip but his vizor off, and sure
I am ....31 eSis 71
I'll strip all the spring of its
earliest bloom; ....248 Thrn 83
STRIPPED Till time may come, when
stripp'd of all her charms, ...355 Trav 17
STROKE Let not the hungry Bavius'
angry stroke ....1 GRos 51
STRONG$_1$ And overwhelm the
strong. ....III:46 Capt 124
How low the great, how feeble are
the strong! ....III:52 Capt 124
How low the proud, how feeble are
the strong! ....III:62 Capt 125
To chain the strong, and set
the captive free. ....III:90 Capt 126
STRONG$_2$ Unquench'd by want, unfann'd by strong desire; ....222 Trav 12
Who quits a world where strong
temptations try ....101 DVil 26
Whilst his strong limbs conspire
to set him free, ...45 epLL 102
Saps the strong wall, and pours
destruction round; .... III:50 Capt 124
Vida, 205, 364, 449
STRONG$_3$ Yet these each other's
power so strong contest, ...89 Trav 8
STROVE Whilst her fond husband
strove to lend relief ....383 DVil 36
Have strove to prove with great
precision, ...7 LogR 44
She strove the neighbourhood to
please, ...9 MBlz 47
With richest proffers strove: .....110 Ed&A 63
What first to hide he strove; ...v150 Ed&A 211
STRUCK When first ambition struck
at regal power; ....394 Trav 18
The hardy veteran after struck the
sight, ...207 Thrn 81
Less dreadful struck me with dis-
may, ...219 Thrn 82
My friend bade me welcome, but
struck me quite dumb, ...69 HofV 97
Vida, 432, 554
STRUGGLES Repress'd ambition
struggles round her shore, ...346 Trav 16
STRUGGLING When struggling Virtue
sinks by long controul, ...v155 Trav 170
And drags the struggling savage
into day. ....190 Trav 11
Despair and anguish fled the
struggling soul; ....174 DVil 29
STRUNG First Sir Charles advances
with phrases well strung, ...55 LetB 133
STUBBORN Condemn the stubborn fool
who can't submit ....71 eSSC$_1$ 107
Vida, 122, 167
STUCK So there I sat stuck, like
a horse in a pound, ...87 HofV 98
STUDIES Vida, 467
STUDIOUS Vida, 13, 282
STUDY The haunch was a picture for
painters to study, ...3 HofV 95
STUFF When they talk'd of their
Raphaels, Correggios, and stuff, ..145 Rtal 92
STUNS And Niagara stuns with
thund'ring sound? ....412 Trav 19

STYGIANS Their Lethes, their Styxes,
and Stygians: ....6 "LSm 84
STYLE Macpherson write bombast, and
call it a style, ...87 Rtal 90
STYXES Their Lethes, their Styxes,
and Stygians: ....6 "LSm 84
SUBDUES Thus, when soft love sub-
dues the heart ....13 Tr 267
-SUBJECTED Thus, while around the
wave-subjected soil ....297 Trav 15
SUBMISSION Caesar persuades, sub-
mission must be mine; ....12 pLab 41
SUBMISSIVE Though poor, luxurious;
though submissive, vain; ....128 Trav 9
SUBMIT Condemn the stubborn fool
who can't submit ....71 eSSC$_1$ 107
SUBSIDING The sea subsiding spreads
a level plain: ....4 Tr 267
SUBSTANTIAL And Douglas is pudding,
substantial and plain: ....10 Rtal 87
SUBTLE Vida, 92, 173, 416, 456, 538
SUBTLY Vida, 112
SUCCEED Vida, 275
SUCCEEDING While low delights,
succeeding fast behind, ...157 Trav 10
Succeeding sports the mirthful
band inspir'd; ....24 DVil 24
SUCCESS Well, having stoop'd to
conquer with success, ...1 eSSC$_3$ 85
Vida, 267, 556
SUCCESSFUL Vida, 431
SUCCESSION Whose bright succession
decks the varied year; ....116 Trav 9
With sweet succession, taught e'en
toil to please; ....32 DVil 24
In sweet succession charmed the
senses, ...237 Thrn 82
SUCCOUR$_1$ And beg the succour of the
lordly bull; ....522 Vida 151
SUCCOUR$_2$ To succour, should I
need. ....194 Thrn 81
SUCH Trav, 23, 73, 209, 215, 235,
337; Gift, 15; DTrn, 7; NSim, 21,
38; Ed&A, v124; eSSC$_3$, 32; Rtal,
17, 29, 52; HofV, 6, 33, v33,
118; epEP, 3; eSSC$_1$, 8; Capt,
III:83; LetB, 36; Vida, 27, 249,
279, 301, 417, 616
SUCKED Jack suck'd his pipe, and
often broke ....57 DTrn 54
SUDDEN Vida, 147, 290, 328, 485, 547,
600
SUDS To meddle in suds, ...9 Invt 128
SUES No Zephyr fondly sues the
mountain's breast, ...173 Trav 11
SUFFER Teach us to estimate what
all must suffer; ....85 Thrn 77
SUFFERED When noble aims have
suffer'd long controul, ...v155 Trav 171
SUFFERS Ev'ry added pang she
suffers ....40, 48 Thrn 75
The good man suffers but to
gain, ...I:45 Capt 115
SUFFICE Let it suffice, that each
had charms; ....25 DTrn 52
SUFFOCATING A sigh in suffocating
smoke; ....58 DTrn 54

Why, sure the girl's beside her-
self: an Epilogue of singing, .7 eSSC$_1$ 103
For sure I don't wrong you, you
seldom are slack, ...59 eSSC$_1$ 106
And sure the folks of both are
lunatics. ....12 eSSC$_2$ 108
Vida, 343
He sure must conquer, who himself
can tame! ....2 Tr 267
SURELY The sons of Italy were surely
blest. ....112 Trav 9
A scholar, yet surely no pedant was
he. ....156 Rtal 93
SURER That instinct is a surer
guide ....15 LogR 44
SUREST Who pepper'd the highest was
surest to please. ....112 Rtal 90
SURFACE The parting surface leaves
his brazen axle dry. ....6 Tr 267
SURLY No surly porter stands in
guilty state ....105 DVil 26
SURPASS Her present face surpass
the old; ....96 DTrn 55
SURPASSES A courtier any ape sur-
passes. ....46 LogR 45
SURPRISE$_1$ Vida, 33, 307, 319, 432,
604
SURPRISE$_2$ Its vistas strike, its
palaces surprise; ....298 DVil 33
'The same.'--'What a pity! how
does it surprise one! ....51 LetB 133
Vida, 556
SURPRISED Surpris'd, he sees new
beauties rise, ...85 Ed&A 62
SURROUND Vida, 66
SURROUNDING Vida, 482
SURROUNDS Vida, 436, 619
SURVEY My soul, turn from them;
turn we to survey ....165 Trav 10
Ye friends to truth, ye statesmen,
who survey ....265 DVil 32
SURVEYED The young contending as
the old survey'd; ....20 DVil 23
Vida, 170
SURVEYS Smiles by his cheerful fire,
and round surveys ....193 Trav 11
Vida, 471
SUSPEND Suspend your conversation
while I sing. ....6 eSSC$_1$ 103
Suspend awhile the task, the tear
suspend, ...I:3 Capt 113
Awhile the bliss suspend; .....III:28 Capt 123
We still shall find uncertainty
suspend; ....v78 Trav 168
SUSTAIN Vida, 49, 114, 393
SUSTAINED All whom her clemency
sustain'd; ....154 Thrn 79
SWAIN Where health and plenty
cheer'd the labouring swain, ...2 DVil 23
The swain mistrustless of his
smutted face, ...27 DVil 24
Usurp the land and dispossess the
swain; ....64 DVil 25
The swain responsive as the milk-
maid sung, ...117 DVil 27
Our swain, arriv'd at thirty-
six? ....10 DTrn 52

Pity take on your swain so
clever, ...25 eSSC$_1$ 104
SWAINS Ye bending swains, that
dress the flow'ry vale, ...48 Trav 6
Amidst the swains to show my book-
learn'd skill, ...90 DVil 26
SWALLOWED Of praise a mere glutton,
he swallow'd what came, ...109 Rtal 90
SWAMPS Where wild Oswego spreads
her swamps around; ....411 Trav 19
SWARMING Vida, 517
SWARTHY Vida, 55, 80, 210, 429, 504,
589
SWAY$_1$ As in those domes, where
Caesars once bore sway, ...159 Trav 10
Truth from his lips prevail'd with
double sway, ...179 DVil 29
The soul adopts, and owns their
first-born sway; ....256 DVil 31
No more presuming on her sway, ...101 DTrn 55
SWAY$_2$ As duty, love and honour
fail to sway, ...350 Trav 16
Gave wealth to sway the mind with
double force. ....396 Trav 18
SWEAR To swear the pill, or drop,
has wrought a cure; ....2 eGNM 68
SWEARING To melt me to pity, and
soften my swearing. ....54 LetB 133
SWEARS Who frowns, and talks, and
swears, with round parade, ...29 eSis 71
SWEEP$_1$ Vida, 364
SWEEP$_2$ Vida, 137
SWEEPS As ocean sweeps the labour'd
mole away; ....428 DVil 37
SWEET Sweet Auburn! loveliest
village of the plain, ...1 DVil 23
These were thy charms, sweet village;
sports like these, ...31 DVil 24
With sweet succession, taught e'en
toil to please; ....32 DVil 24
Sweet smiling village, loveliest of
the lawn, ...35 DVil 24
Sweet Auburn! parent of the bliss-
ful hour, ...75 DVil 25
Sweet was the sound, when oft at
evening's close ....113 DVil 27
These all in sweet confusion
sought the shade, ...123 DVil 27
To sweet oblivion of his daily
care; ....242 DVil 31
Sweet as the primrose peeps be-
neath the thorn; ....330 DVil 34
Do thine, sweet AUBURN, thine, the
loveliest train, ...337 DVil 34
And thou, sweet Poetry, thou
loveliest maid, ...407 DVil 36
In sweet succession charmed the
senses, ...237 Thrn 82
These hills how sweet! those
plains how wond'rous fair, ...I:21 Capt 114
Vida, 33
SWEET- Our Cumberland's sweet-
bread its place shall obtain, ...9 Rtal 87
SWEETEN All claims that bind and
sweeten life unknown; ....342 Trav 16
SWEETER But sweeter still, when
Heaven was with us there! ....I:22 Capt 114

Sweeter from remember'd woes; .III:92 Capt 126
SWEETLY While sweetly blending
still are seen ....146 Thrn 79
SWEETLY- What heart but feels
his sweetly-moral lay, ...3 epTP 100
SWEETS Whatever sweets salute the
northern sky ....117 Trav 9
Diffuse their balmy sweets
around. ....I:50 Capt 115
SWELLING Tear off reserve, and
bare my swelling heart; ....390 Trav 18
SWELLS Swells at my breast, and
turns the past to pain. ....82 DVil 26
Swells from the vale, and midway
leaves the storm, ...190 DVil 29
Proud swells the tide with loads of
freighted ore, ...269 DVil 32
When every bosom swells with
wond'rous scenes, ...7 pZob 72
SWEPT Whose beard descending swept
his aged breast; ....152 DVil 28
Vida, 449
$SWIFT_1$ That trade's proud empire
hastes to swift decay, ...427 DVil 37
The growing sound their swift
approach declares;-- ....I:55 Capt 115
Vida, 126, 490, 575
$SWIFT_2$ Swift mantling to the
view; ....86 Ed&A 62
SWIMS Swims round the room, the
Heinel of Cheapside; ....28 $eSSC_3$ 85
SWING Vida, 516
SWINGING At the bottom was tripe
in a swinging tureen; ....82 HofV 97
SWISS Where the bleak Swiss their
stormy mansions tread, ...167 Trav 10
SWORD But man and steel, the
soldier and his sword; ....170 Trav 10
As 'D-- --, Sir,' and 'Sir, I wear
a sword'; ....28 $eSSC_2$ 109
Vida, 246, 344, 653
SWORDS Vida, 96, 112, 631
SWORE And swore the dog had lost
his wits, ...23 MDog 65
And while they swore the dog was
mad, ...27 MDog 66
They swore the man would die. ......28 MDog 66
SYLVAN Here amidst sylvan
bowers we'll rove, ...v(161) Ed&A 211
SYMPATHETIC And wiser he, whose
sympathetic mind ....43 Trav 6
And sympathetic sheep; ....10 DRtH 50
Around in sympathetic mirth ....53 Ed&A 61
SYMPATHISE And bids his bosom
sympathise with mine. ....422 Trav 19
SYRIAN All, all is lost. The
Syrian army fails, ...III:59 Capt 125
SYSTEM Till over-wrought, the
general system feels ....347 Trav 16

TABLE Till all my companions sink
under the table; ....20 Rtal 87
Yet content 'if the table he set
on a roar'; ....160 Rtal 93
Vida, 22
TAIL To measure each tail, ...30 Invt 129
To lengthen a short tail, ...31 Invt 129

TAILS The men have tails, the
women paint the face! ....26 pZob 73
To wear tails in high taste, ...27 Invt 129
TAKE Here as I take my solitary
rounds, ...77 DVil 25
They eat their meals, and take
their sport, ...25 LogR 44
To take their evening rest, ...46 Ed&A 60
To take us in when we have drained
the cup ....98 Thrn 77
No lord will take me now, my vigour
fled, ...173 Thrn 80
But for eating a rasher of what
they take pride in, ...11 HofV 95
To-morrow you take a poor dinner
with me; ....47 HofV 96
I'll take no denial--you shall, and
you must, ...v53 HofV 240
Pity take on your swain so
clever, ...25 $eSSC_1$ 104
Who take a trip to Paris once
a year ....33 $eSSC_1$ 105
Ay, take your travellers,
travellers indeed! ....37 $eSSC_1$ 105
Come, take the lyre, and pour
the strain along, ...I:81 Capt 116
'Pray what does Miss Horneck?
take courage, come do,'-- ......17 LetB 132
But the judge bids them, angrily,
take off their hat. ....46 LetB 133
Vida, 642
TAKEN Then first, at last even
Jove was taken in, ...13 MrsX 49
'I'm glad I have taken this house
in my way. ....46 HofV 96
TAKES In wild excess the vulgar
breast takes fire, ...225 Trav 12
And the brown Indian takes a
deadly aim; ....v416 Trav 175
Takes up a space that many poor
supplied; ....276 DVil 32
And to perform takes equal care. ...52 LogR 45
Flings down her sampler, and takes
up the woman: ....22 eSis 70
He starts, he pants, he takes the
circling maze. ....42 epLL 102
Goes out, affronts his man, and
takes a beating. ....30 $eSSC_2$ 109
Vida, 100, 213
TALE Or sigh with pity at some
mournful tale, ...20 Trav 6
With many a tale repays the nightly
bed. ....198 Trav 11
No more the farmer's news, the
barber's tale, ...243 DVil 31
This tale of the bacon a damnable
bounce? ....14 HofV 95
To go on with my tale--as I gaz'd
on the haunch, ...19 HofV 95
TALENT And talent sinks, and merit
weeps unknown; ....354 Trav 17
TALENTS Yet, with talents like
these, and an excellent heart, ...97 Rtal 90
Whose talents to fill any station
were fit, ...161 Rtal 93
TALES Wept o'er his wounds, or
tales of sorrow done, ...157 DVil 28

Has wept at tales of innocence
distress'd; ....328 DVil 34
TALKED Sat by his fire, and talk'd
the night away; ....156 DVil 28
Where village statesmen talk'd with
looks profound, ...223 DVil 30
But never talk'd of love. ....112 Ed&A 63
When they talk'd of their Raphaels,
Correggios, and stuff, ...145 Rtal 92
TALKING For talking age and
whisp'ring lovers made; ....14 DVil 23
TALKS Who frowns, and talks, and
swears, with round parade, ...29 eSis 71
Talks loud, coquets the guests, and
scolds the waiters. ....16 eSSC$_3$ 85
TALL Lift the tall rampire's
artificial pride. ....286 Trav 14
As some tall cliff, that lifts its
awful form, ...189 DVil 29
TAME Ye tame imitators, ye servile
herd come, ...165 Rtal 93
He sure must conquer, who himself
can tame! ....2 Tr 267
TANGLED Through tangled forests,
and through dangerous ways; ....414 Trav 19
TANGLING Amidst thy tangling walks,
and ruin'd grounds, ...78 DVil 25
TAPER To husband out life's taper
at the close, ...87 DVil 26
To where yon taper cheers the vale ..3 Ed&A 59
Detection her taper shall quench to
a spark, ...91 Rtal 90
TAPER'S Hope, like the gleaming
taper's light, ...II:37 Capt 119
Hope, like the glim'ring taper's
light, ...vII:37 Capt 250
TAPERS Like flaring tapers
bright'ning as they waste; ....400 Trav 18
TARDY And tardy, tardy are the
times ....193 Thrn 81
TARTARUS Drove souls to Tart'rus
with his rod, ...52 NSim 57
TASK Suspend awhile the task, the
tear suspend, ...I:3 Capt 113
Vida, 9
TASTE To send such good verses to
one of your taste; ....118 HofV 99
A relish--a taste--sicken'd over
by learning; ....120 HofV 99
To wear tails in high taste, ...27 Invt 129
Pretends to taste, at Operas
cries <u>caro</u>, ...25 eSSC$_3$ 85
TAUGHT And all are taught an
avarice of praise; ....264 Trav 14
And thou, fair Freedom, taught
alike to feel ....365 Trav 17
With sweet succession, taught e'en
toil to please; ....32 DVil 24
The village master taught his little
school; ....196 DVil 29
Taught by that power that pities
me, ...23 Ed&A 59
Whom love has taught to stray; .....98 Ed&A 62
How have I mended what he
taught, ...v127 Ed&A 210
Is taught his former folly to
deplore; ....44 epLL 102
Taught by our art her ridicule
to pause on, ...21 eSSC$_2$ 108
Vida, 667, 675
-TAUGHT 'Twere affectation all,
and school-taught pride, ...v39 Trav 168
Let school-taught pride dissemble
all it can, ...41 Trav 6
TAUNTS Vida, 566
TAWDRY Hence ostentation here, with
tawdry art, ...273 Trav 14
For tawdry finery is seen ....99 DTrn 55
TEA- See also TEACUPS.
While broken tea-cups, wisely kept
for show, ...235 DVil 31
TEACH Teach erring man to spurn
the rage of gain; ....424 DVil 37
Teach him, that states of native
strength possess'd, ...425 DVil 37
Quebec in vain shall teach our
breast to glow, ...7 Queb 46
Teach us to estimate what all must
suffer; ....85 Thrn 77
Shall Reason only teach to
weep? ....II:52 Capt 120
TEACUPS See also TEA-.
And five crack'd teacups dress'd
the chimney board; ....18 DABd 48
TEAR$_1$ And kiss'd her thoughtless
babes with many a tear, ...381 DVil 36
Or dim thy beauty with a tear? ......6 Sonn 46
Whilst thy sad fate extorts the
heart-wrung tear. ....8 Queb 46
Ye Muses, pour the pitying tear .....1 DRtH 50
Even pitying hills would drop a
tear!-- ....11 DRtH 50
The tribute of a tear be mine, ...130 Thrn 78
With many a tear and many a sigh
between; ....170 Thrn 80
Suspend awhile the task, the
tear suspend, ...I:3 Capt 113
And offer up a tear. ....I:14 Capt 113
Why dim thy beauty with a tear? ...v6 Sonn 196
TEAR$_2$ Tear off reserve, and bare
my swelling heart; ....390 Trav 18
TEARS His lovely daughter, lovelier
in her tears, ...375 DVil 35
While soul-brought tears steal
down each shining face. ....6 MrsX 49
And tears began to flow. ....60 Ed&A 61
And tears would often flow. ......v60 Ed&A 208
And the tears of her country shall
water her tomb. ....262 Thrn 83
To-morrow's tears may wash our
stains away. ....II:32 Capt 119
Vida, 433, 502, 601
TEASED And teas'd each rhyming
friend to help him out. ....8 eGNM 68
TEASING Now teasing and vexing,
yet laughing at all! ....56 Rtal 89
TEEMED The pregnant quarry teem'd
with human form; ....138 Trav 9
TELL And tell of all I felt, and
all I saw; ....92 DVil 26
No more my titles shall my children
tell, ...17 pLab 41
Add too, what certain writers tell, 41 NSim 57
Let me ponder, and tell what I think

of the dead. ....22 Rtal 87
Then what was his failing? come,
tell it, and, burn ye! ....135 Rtal 91
Here Reynolds is laid, and, to tell
you my mind, ...137 Rtal 91
To tell them the reason why asses
had ears? ....2 ClRp 100
Lend me your hands.--Oh! fatal
news to tell: ....35 $eSSC_1$ 105
So tell Horneck and Nesbitt, ...11 Invt 128
(By-the-bye you may tell him, ...19 Invt 128
Tell each other to rue ....35 Invt 129
TELLS For just experience tells,
in every soil, ...371 Trav 17
TEMPER For honour forms the social
temper here: ....258 Trav 13
Whose temper was generous, open,
sincere; ....151 Rtal 93
At least, it's your temper, as very
well known, ...121 HofV 99
At least, it's your temper, 'tis
very well known, ...v121 HofV 242
TEMPEST There, while above the
giddy tempest flies, ...417 Trav 19
The labouring ship, and hear the
tempest roar, ...67 Thrn 76
And wild the tempest howling ......215 Thrn 82
And fierce the tempest rolling .II:17 Capt 118
The tempest gathers all around, II:75 Capt 121
TEMPESTUOUS Vida, 363
TEMPLE And though no temple
richly drest, ...I:11 Capt 113
We'll make his temple in our
breast, ...I:13 Capt 113
TEMPLE'S While oft some temple's
mould'ring tops between ....109 Trav 9
TEMPLES 'No more shall my crook or
my temples adorn, ...240 Thrn 83
No more will her crook or her
temples adorn; ....252 Thrn 83
TEMPT Explore the mine, or tempt
the dangerous deep; ....104 DVil 26
To tempt its new-fledg'd offspring
to the skies, ...168 DVil 28
'To tempt the dangerous gloom; .....10 Ed&A 59
Reflect, nor tempt to rage the
royal mind. ....II:14 Capt 118
TEMPTATIONS Who quits a world
where strong temptations try ......101 DVil 26
TEMPTS No foreign beauty tempts
to false desire; ....2 Cati 94
TEN To see ten thousand baneful
arts combin'd ....311 DVil 33
That we wish'd him full ten times
a day at Old Nick; ....58 Rtal 89
He turn'd and he varied full ten
times a day. ....104 Rtal 90
With two full as clever, and ten
times as hearty. ....74 HofV 97
For ten pounds in hand, and ten
pounds to be spent. ....66 LetB 134
TENANT The shudd'ring tenant of the
frigid zone ....65 Trav 7
Its panting tenant is not mine. .....4 TrSA 51
Deign saint-like tenant of the
dale, ...v1 Ed&A 208
TENDER 'To win me from his tender
arms ....105 Ed&A 62
Vida, 284, 468
TENDERNESS And kind connubial
tenderness, are there; ....404 DVil 36
TENT Vida, 91, 638
TENTH In book the second, page
the tenth: ....12 NSim 56
TENTS Vida, 464
TEPID Basks in the glare, or stems
the tepid wave, ...71 Trav 7
TERENCE The Terence of England, the
mender of hearts; ....62 Rtal 89
TERM This day beyond its term my
fate extends, ...19 pLab 41
TERMED By classic authors term'd
caduceus, ...33 NSim 57
TERMS Lands he could measure, terms
and tides presage, ...209 DVil 30
TERRIBLE That she came with some
terrible news from the baker: .....112 HofV 98
TERROR And is a terror only at a
distance; ....94 Thrn 77
The scourge of impostors, the
terror of quacks: ....80 Rtal 89
Vida, 107, 116, 133, 158, 249, 511,
578, 583
TERRORS In every government, though
terrors reign, ...427 Trav 19
The various terrors of that horrid
shore; ....346 DVil 34
The rattling terrors of the venge-
ful snake; ....354 DVil 35
Levell'd its terrors at the fair; ..78 DTrn 54
Yet, ah! what terrors frowned up-
on her fate-- ....52 Thrn 76
How great a king of terrors I! .....77 Thrn 76
Think, timely think, what terrors
are behind; ....II:13 Capt 118
Ah, me! what angry terrors round
us grow; ....II:25 Capt 119
And shall not Heaven for this
its terrors show, ...III:35 Capt 123
Vida, 337
TEXT Thus stray from my text? .....34 Invt 129
THAMES The echoes of Thames shall
my sorrows proclaim, ...244 Thrn 83
THAMES' Fast by that shore where
Thames' translucent stream ....140 Thrn 79
THAN Trav, 139, 320; DVil, 148, 224,
254, 356; Byth, 2; Gift, 18; LogR,
16; Ed&A, 72; pZob, 19; Thrn, 220;
ClRp, 4; Capt, II:24, 54; LetB, 10;
Vida, 645
THANK While converts thank their
poet in the skies. ....10 epTP 100
THANKLESS Amidst the store, should
thankless pride repine? ....38 Trav 6
Amidst the store, 'twere thankless
to repine. ....v38 Trav 168
$THANKS_1$ Thanks, my Lord, for your
venison, for finer or fatter ....1 HofV 95
They never have my gratitude nor
thanks; ....32 epLL 102
$THANKS_2$ And thanks his gods for
all the good they gave. ....72 Trav 7
THATCH No stores beneath its humble
thatch ....41 Ed&A 60

THAT'S NSim, 20; Ed&A, 156, v156;
Thrn, 97; HofV, 100, 122; LetB, 25,
28; Vida, 183
THEATRIC Woods over woods in gay
theatric pride; ....108 Trav 8
THEE Trav, 8; DVil, 386, 389, 416;
Gift, 17, 19, 20; Queb, 5, 10; Ed&A,
12, 152, 153; Thrn, 30, 34, 109,
137, 139; Capt, I:30, vI:30, III:63,
77, 103, 106
THEFTS That only shelter'd thefts
of harmless love. ....362 DVil 35
THEIRS For wealth was theirs, not
far remov'd the date, ...133 Trav 9
Theirs are those arts that mind to
mind endear, ...257 Trav 13
Desist, my sons, nor mix the
strain with theirs. ....I:56 Capt 115
THEME Oh! for a Richard's voice
to catch the theme: ....23 epLL 101
Our monarch's fame the noblest
theme supplies. ....II:44 Capt 119
The time, the theme, the place,
and all conspire. ....II:46 Capt 120
THEMES Celestial themes confess'd
his tuneful aid; ....5 epTP 100
THEMSELVES To call it freedom when
themselves are free; ....384 Trav 18
Heroes themselves had fallen be-
hind!-- ....7 DRtH 50
Vida, 165
THEN Trav, 216, 377; DVil, 293, 303;
pLab, 15; DABd, v(22); MrsX, 13; DTrn,
20; NSim, 43; Ed&A, 17, 29, v137;
eGNM, 31; eSis, 43; Thrn, 17, 127;
"LSm, 19; Rtal, 21, 135, 169; HofV,
16, 45; Capt, II:57, III:12; LetB,
53, 59; Vida, 19, 29, 61, 71, 81,
103, 172, 188, 194, 220, 280, 311,
336, 420, 427, 477, 498, 548, 551,
557, 561, 570, 587, 637, 642, 646,
672
THENCE Well! what is it from thence
we gather? ....17 NSim 56
Vida, 56, 535
THERE Trav, 161, 321, 322, 323,
413, 417; DVil, 57, 115, 139, 154,
195, 309, 316, 318, 345, 404;
pLab, 5; DABd, 5, 11, v11; NSim,
7; Ed&A, 141, v141; MDog, 5, 14;
eGNM, 14; eSis, 17; pZob, 19,
24, 25; Thrn, 132, 135, 151, 245,
257, 261; $eSSC_3$, 17, 19; HofV, 49,
83, 87, 98; $eSSC_2$, 1, 3, 4; Capt,
I:22, II:42, III:18; Vida, 17,
45, 48, 92, 101, 200, 219, 256,
337, 398, 463, 529, 532, 620,
648
THEREFORE Vida, 494, 638
THERE'S eSis, 11; HofV, 27, v27,
29, 101; epLL, 25
THEY'D They'd as soon think of
eating the pan it is fried in. ......12 HofV 95
THEY'RE pZob, 27; "LSm, 8; epLL, 33;
LetB, 59; HofV, 76
THEY'VE 'Pray what are their
crimes?'--'They've been pilfering
found.' ....48 LetB 133
THICK Vida, 356, 482
THICKETS And there in shelt'ring
thickets hid, ...v141 Ed&A 211
THIEF Being each as great a thief
as he: ....60 NSim 58
THIEVES 'What signifies handsome,
when people are thieves?' ....60 LetB 133
THIN To pamper luxury, and thin
mankind; ....312 DVil 33
THINE Trav, 335, 336; DVil, 325,
337; Gift, 5; Thrn, 105, 111, 228;
Capt, III:54
THING All but yon widow'd, solitary
thing ....129 DVil 27
To decency so fine a thing? ....50 DTrn 53
Harmless and young, of ev'ry
thing afraid; ....10 $eSSC_3$ 85
THINGS To spurn the splendid
things by heaven supply'd. ....v40 Trav 168
These little things are great to
little man; ....42 Trav 6
How ill exchang'd are things like
these for thee! ....386 DVil 36
So with decorum all things carried; 19 DTrn 52
And those who prize the paltry
things, ...71 Ed&A 61
'An Epilogue--things can't go on
without it; ....9 eGNM 68
Those things are not our forte at
Covent Garden.' ....20 eGNM 68
Mere transitory things! ....9 Thrn 74
Fall, round me fall, ye little
things, ...80 Thrn 77
Though equal to all things, for all
things unfit, ...37 Rtal 88
As in some Irish houses, where
things are so so, ...9 HofV 95
'I get these things often;'--but
that was a bounce: ....42 HofV 96
Were things that I never dislik'd
in my life, ...63 HofV 97
A treasury for lost and missing
things; ....2 $eSSC_2$ 108
At least in many things, I think,
I see ....7 $eSSC_2$ 108
THINK Yet think not, thus when
Freedom's ills I state, ...361 Trav 17
That those who think must govern
those that toil; ....372 Trav 17
Who think it freedom when a part
aspires! ....378 Trav 17
Sighing we pay, and think e'en
conquest dear; ....6 Queb 46
I think I met with something there, 7 NSim 56
To blend their virtues while they
think of thee. ....137 Thrn 78
Let me ponder, and tell what I
think of the dead. ....22 Rtal 87
They'd as soon think of eating the
pan it is fried in. ....12 HofV 95

I think they love venison--I know
they love beef; ....28 HofV 96
And now that I think on't, as I am
a sinner! ....51 HofV 96
Some think he writes Cinna--he owns
to Panurge.' ....78 HofV 97
And now that I think on't, the story
may stop. ....116 HofV 99
That you think very slightly of all
that's your own: ....122 HofV 99
You may make a mistake, and think
slightly of this. ....124 HofV 99
I don't think he'll wish to come
back. ....4 epEP 100
At least in many things, I think,
I see ....7 eSSC$_2$ 108
Think, timely think, what terrors
are behind; ....II:13 Capt 118
Think not to-morrow can repay ..II:59 Capt 120
All play their own way, and they
think me an ass,-- ....15 LetB 132
Don't you think the best way is to
venture for't twice?' ....30 LetB 132
THINKING Have pleas'd our eyes,
and sav'd the pain of thinking. .....8 eSis 70
Though I could not help thinking
my gentleman hasty, ...61 HofV 97
So, perhaps, in your habits of
thinking amiss, ...123 HofV 99
As I hope to be saved! without
thinking on asses.' ....6 ClRp 100
THINKS He thinks her features
coarser grown; ....62 DTrn 54
He thinks her ugly as the devil. ...70 DTrn 54
Thinks black alone is beauty's
favourite hue. ....10 Cati 94
THINS Or thins her lip, or points
her nose: ....64 DTrn 54
Vida, 98
THIRD A third, a fourth, were not
amiss, ...31 DTrn 53
Vida, 487
THIRST$_1$ Vida, 19, 64
THIRST$_2$ Vida, 476
THIRSTY Vida, 426
THIRTY-SIX Our swain, arriv'd at
thirty-six? ....10 DTrn 52
THISTLE 'What, plant my thistle,
Sir, among his roses! ....16 eGNM 68
THITHER And haply too some pilgrim,
thither led, ...197 Trav 11
Thither no more the peasant shall
repair ....241 DVil 31
THORN To pick her wintry faggot
from the thorn, ...133 DVil 27
Near yonder thorn, that lifts its
head on high, ...219 DVil 30
Sweet as the primrose peeps be-
neath the thorn; ....330 DVil 34
And the new-blossomed thorn
shall whiten her tomb.' ...250, 258 Thrn 83
THOSE Trav, 17, v17, v80, 159,
201, 219, 257, 302, 336, 372;
DVil, 30, 69, 70, 71, 291, 307,
313, 347, 349, 351; MBlz, 4;
Ed&A, 71; eGNM, 20; Rtal, 121;
Capt, I:21, 35, 80, III:33, 34,
45; Vida, 27, 121, 141
THOT 'Though splitting, I'll still
keep a corner for thot.' ....104 HofV 98
THOU Trav, 365, 367; DVil, 385, 407,
413, 415, 416; Queb, 11; Ed&A, 66,
v145, v156; Thrn, 18, 20, 117;
Rtal, 174; epLL, 7, 11; Capt,
I:23, vI:27, II:2, 73, III:73,
78, 105
THOUGH Trav, 77, v77, 85, v85, 128,
129, v145, 177, 247, v343, 427, 428;
DVil, 191, 212, 426; Queb, 11;
TrSA, 3; DTrn, 27, 69; NSim, 39;
Ed&A, 15; pZob, 28; Thrn, 179;
Rtal, 33, 37, 105, 148; HofV, 5,
61, 64, 93, 104; eSSC$_1$, 72; Capt,
I:11, 31, III:63; LetB, 42; Vida,
318, 344, 467, 561
THOUGHT$_1$ Enfeebles all internal
strength of thought; ....270 Trav 14
I'll waste no longer thought in
choosing; ....I:74 Capt 116
By the gods, I'll enjoy it: though
'tis but in thought! ....42 LetB 133
Vida, 21, 282, 485
THOUGHT$_2$ My noble mistress thought
not so: ....177 Thrn 80
And thought of convincing, while
they thought of dining; ....36 Rtal 88
I thought of a friend that was
trusty and staunch; ....20 HofV 95
Or ever thought that jumping was a
jest. ....6 epLL 101
Vida, 272, 340
THOUGHTFUL Intent on high designs,
a thoughtful band, ...329 Trav 16
THOUGHTLESS So bless'd a life these
thoughtless realms display, ...255 Trav 13
And kiss'd her thoughtless babes
with many a tear, ...381 DVil 36
THOUGHTS But all his serious
thoughts had rest in Heaven. ......188 DVil 29
Are these thy serious thoughts?--
Ah, turn thine eyes ....325 DVil 34
I had thoughts, in my chambers, to
place it in view, ...7 HofV 95
Wing all our thoughts to reach
the skies, ...II:4 Capt 118
Vida, 242, 263, 355, 466, 540, 614
THOUSAND To see ten thousand
baneful arts combin'd ....311 DVil 33
Since from thy tomb a thousand
heroes rise! ....12 Queb 46
A thousand gifts would fortune
send; ....29 Thrn 75
A thousand sorrows urg'd thy end: ..31 Thrn 75
THRACIAN Vida, 400
THRALE The one with his speeches,
and t'other with Thrale; ....72 HofV 97
The one at the House, and the
other with THRALE. ....v72 HofV 241
THREAT$_1$ Vida, 618
THREAT$_2$ Vida, 119, 272, 513
THREATEN Shall wrath vindictive
threaten ere it fall! ....III:38 Capt 124
THREATENED How shrinks my soul
to meet the threaten'd blow! ...II:26 Capt 119

While self-dependent power can
time defy, ...429 DVil 37
A time there was, when glory was
my guide, ...5 pLab 41
Howe'er, from this time I shall
ne'er see your graces, ...5 ClRp 100
Is this a time to bid us raise the
strain, ...I:87 Capt 117
The time, the theme, the place,
and all conspire. ....II:46 Capt 120
Now, now's our time! ye wretches
bold and blind, ...III:69 Capt 125
TIMELY Think, timely think, what
terrors are behind: ....II:13 Capt 118
TIMES$_1$ But times are alter'd;
trade's unfeeling train ....63 DVil 25
Unfit in these degenerate times of
shame, ...409 DVil 36
In virtuous times of yore, ...6 DRtH 50
In these bold times, when Learning's
sons explore ....1 pZob 72
And tardy, tardy are the times ....193 Thrn 81
TIMES$_2$ That we wish'd him full ten
times a day at Old Nick; ....58 Rtal 89
He turn'd and he varied full ten
times a day. ....104 Rtal 90
With two full as clever, and ten
times as hearty. ....74 HofV 97
TIMOROUS These far dispers'd, on
timorous pinions fly, ...237 Trav 13
TINCTURES Vida, 207
TINTS His well acquainted tints,
and kindred hues. ....6 Cati 94
TIPSY The coachman was tipsy, the
chariot drove home; ....48 Rtal 88
TIRE By holding out to tire each
other down; ....26 DVil 24
TIRED And still as each repeated
pleasure tir'd, ...23 DVil 24
TIRES And tires their echoes with
unvaried cries. ....46 DVil 24
'TIS DVil, 102, 267; MrsX, 7; DTrn, 43; eSis,
25; pZob, 27, 29; Thrn, 4, 97, 239; HofV, v121;
Capt, II:82; III:13; Invt, 39; LetB, 13, 14,
42; Vida, 140, 676
TITLES No more my titles shall
my children tell, ...17 pLab 41
When titles are the smallest claim-- 14 Thrn 74
TITTERED While secret laughter
titter'd round the place; ....28 DVil 24
TO- See TO-DAY, TO-DAY'S, TO-MORROW,
TO-MORROW'S, TO-NIGHT
TOADS Where toads shall pant, and
vultures prey. ....III:82 Capt 126
TOAST The chop-house toast of
ogling connoisseurs. ....18 eSSC$_3$ 85
TO-DAY She had not died to-day. ....28 MBlz 47
He had not died to-day. ....4 DRtH 50
The pleasures that we lose to-day;II:60 Capt 120
TO-DAY'S When both have been spoil'd
in to-day's Advertiser? ....44 Invt 129
TOGETHER See, though by circling
deeps together held, ...v343 Trav 174
'Twas you, or I, or he, or all
together, ...1 GCRL 51
I'll make them both together mine. I:76 Capt 116
Vida, 521

TOIL$_1$ To pause from toil, and trim
their ev'ning fire; ....14 Trav 5
Nor ask luxuriance from the planter's
toil; ....120 Trav 9
But calm, and bred in ignorance and
toil, ...183 Trav 11
Impels the native to repeated toil, 298 Trav 15
When toil remitting lent its turn
to play, ...16 DVil 23
With sweet succession, taught e'en
toil to please; ....32 DVil 24
Where grey-beard mirth and smiling
toil retir'd, ...222 DVil 30
Contented toil, and hospitable care,403 DVil 36
To want, to toil, and every ill
consign'd, ...I:86 Capt 117
Vida, 532, 635
TOIL$_2$ And monarchs toil, and poets
pant for fame, ...v358 Trav 174
That those who think must govern
those that toil; ....372 Trav 17
TOILED Where kings have toil'd, and
poets wrote for fame, ...358 Trav 17
TOILING The toiling pleasure sickens
into pain; ....262 DVil 32
TOILS$_1$ Here Douglas retires, from his
toils to relax, ...79 Rtal 89
TOILS$_2$ Vida, 431
-TOITY Priests, cannibals, and
hoity-toity queens: ....8 pZob 72
TOLD My horns! I'm told horns are the
fashion now.' ....36 epLL 102
Vida, 678
TOMB Since from thy tomb a thousand
heroes rise! ....12 Queb 46
Shall spread and flourish from the
tomb, ...19 Thrn 74
To bless the tomb that wraps thy
clay; ....133 Thrn 78
And the new-blossomed thorn shall
whiten her tomb.' ....250 Thrn 83
And the new-blossom'd thorn shall
whiten her tomb. ....258 Thrn 83
And the tears of her country shall
water her tomb. ....262 Thrn 83
Still follow your master. and visit
his tomb: ....166 Rtal 93
This tomb, inscrib'd to gentle
Parnell's name, ...1 epTP 100
TOMMY To persuade Tommy Townshend to
lend him a vote; ....34 Rtal 88
TO-MORROW To-morrow you take a poor
dinner with me; ....47 HofV 96
Think not to-morrow can repay ...II:59 Capt 120
TO-MORROW'S To-morrow's tears may wash
our stains away. ....II:32 Capt 119
To-morrow's most unbounded store II:61 Capt 120
TONE Feels for each tone, and speeds
it to the heart; ....II:66 Capt 120
-TONED The master-prophet grasps his
full-ton'd lyre. ....II:64 Capt 120
TONGUE Our Burke shall be tongue,
with a garnish of brains; ....6 Rtal 87
Till every tongue in every land II:95 Capt 122
TO-NIGHT 'Then turn to-night, and
freely share ....17 Ed&A 59
To-night I head our troops at Warwick

Lane: ....18 eGNM 68
TOOK And took a long farewell, and
wish'd in vain ....367 DVil 35
The 'squire and captain took their
stations, ...55 DTrn 53
Determin'd took their stand: ....55 Thrn 76
He shifted his trumpet, and only took
snuff. ....146 Rtal 92
Vida, 184, 196, 587, 671
TOOKE'S A chapter out of Tooke's
Pantheon, ...6 NSim 56
TOP At the top a fried liver and
bacon were seen, ...81 HofV 97
TOPPED The decent church that
topp'd the neighbouring hill, ...12 DVil 23
TOPS While oft some temple's
mould'ring tops between ....109 Trav 9
TORCHES The rattling chariots clash,
the torches glare. ....322 DVil 34
TORE Vida, 503
TORN There, where a few torn shrubs
the place disclose, ...139 DVil 27
His squalid limbs with pond'rous
fetters torn; ....III:32 Capt 123
TORNADO While oft in whirls the
mad tornado flies, ...357 DVil 35
TORNO'S On Torno's cliffs, or
Pambamarca's side, ...418 DVil 37
TORODDLE Toroddle, toroddle,
toroll. ....9,18,27 "LSm 84
TOROLL Toroddle, toroddle,
toroll. ....9,18,27 "LSm 84
TORPID No vernal blooms their
torpid rocks array, ...171 Trav 11
TORRENT So the loud torrent, and
the whirlwind's roar, ...207 Trav 12
The ruin smokes, the torrent pours
along; ....III:61 Capt 125
TORRID Whatever blooms in torrid
tracts appear, ...115 Trav 9
Through torrid tracts with fainting
steps they go, ...343 DVil 34
TORTOISES Vida, 28
TORTURES The whips and angry tortures
shall prevail. ....I:94 Capt 117
Can whips or tortures hurt the
mind ....I:97 Capt 117
TOTTERING Defac'd by time and
tottering in decay, ...160 Trav 10
Reprieve the tottering mansion from
its fall! ....238 DVil 31
TOTTERS Vida, 348
TOUCH And haply, though my harsh
touch falt'ring still, ...247 Trav 13
For let folks only get a touch, ...37 NSim 57
TOUCHED And while his passion touch'd
my heart, ...131 Ed&A 63
TOUGH Vida, 62, 333
TOUTE Make but of all your fortune
one va toute; ....48 $eSSC_1$ 105
TOWER See yonder tower just nodding
to the fall: ....III:48 Capt 124
Vida, 442, 445
TOWERED Vida, 506
TOWERING Thy towering mind self-
centred stood, ...26 Thrn 75
TOWERS The towers of Kew, ...161 Thrn 80
Ye nodding towers, ye fairy scenes--164 Thrn 80
Vida, 50, 260, 353
TOWN When idly first, ambitious
of the town, ...335 DVil 34
To ravage in a country town! ....12 DTrn 52
And in that town a dog was found, ..13 MDog 65
Who knows each art of coaxing up
the town, ...5 eGNM 68
Next the scene shifts to town, and
there she soars, ...17 $eSSC_3$ 85
TOWNS Ye glitt'ring towns, with
wealth and splendour crown'd, ...45 Trav 6
But towns unmann'd, and lords without
a slave; ....142 Trav 10
Remote from towns he ran his godly
race, ...143 DVil 28
TOWNSHEND To persuade Tommy
Townshend to lend him a vote; ......34 Rtal 88
Our Townshend make speeches, and
I shall compile; ....88 Rtal 90
TOY A bill, a jewel, watch, or
toy, ...9 Gift 43
TRACE And trace them through the
prospect as it lies: ....100 Trav 8
Trace every scene, and wonder at
the change, ...v(82) DVil 182
Well had the boding tremblers
learn'd to trace ....199 DVil 29
Imagination fondly stoops to
trace ....225 DVil 30
Alas! too well mine eyes
indignant trace ....III:19 Capt 123
-TRACKS Or seeks the den where
snow-tracks mark the way, ...189 Trav 11
TRACTS Whatever blooms in torrid
tracts appear, ...115 Trav 9
Through torrid tracts with faint-
ing steps they go, ...343 DVil 34
TRADE There the pale artist plies
the sickly trade; ....316 DVil 33
Or you may chance to spoil a
thriving trade. ....34 pZob 73
While thus he describ'd them by
trade, and by name, ...79 HofV 97
I'm for a different set.--Old men,
whose trade is ....19 $eSSC_1$ 104
Vida, 318
TRADER His honour is no mercenary
trader; ....32 pZob 73
TRADE'S But times are alter'd;
trade's unfeeling train ....63 DVil 25
That trade's proud empire hastes
to swift decay, ...427 DVil 37
TRADING He this way steers his
course, in hopes of trading-- ......12 pZob 72
TRAFFIC It shifts in splendid
traffic round the land: ....262 Trav 14
TRAGEDY Like a tragedy queen he
has dizen'd her out, ...67 Rtal 89
Or rather like tragedy giving a
rout. ....68 Rtal 89
TRAGIC Shakespeare himself shall
feel my tragic rage. ....20 epLL 101
TRAIN Lead stern depopulation in
her train, ...402 Trav 18
Forc'd from their homes, a
melancholy train, ...409 Trav 18

And all the village train, from labour free, ...17 DVil 23
But times are alter'd; trade's unfeeling train ....63 DVil 25
Remembrance wakes with all her busy train, ...81 DVil 26
She only left of all the harmless train, ...135 DVil 27
His house was known to all the vagrant train, ...149 DVil 28
These simple blessings of the lowly train; ....252 DVil 31
Here, richly deck'd, admits the gorgeous train; ....320 DVil 33
Do thine, sweet AUBURN, thine, the loveliest train, ...337 DVil 34
Whene'er he spoke amidst the train, ...v121 Ed&A 210
First of the train the patient rustic came, ...167 Thrn 80
Ye travell'd tribe, ye macaroni train, ...31 eSSC$_1$ 105
But ha! what means yon sadly plaintive train, ...III:15 Capt 123
Love and pleasure in his train; ....III:96 Capt 126
Vida, 168, 192, 296, 434

TRAITOR'S And still our vengeance crush the traitor's head. ....III:6 Capt 122

TRANSFIX Could Cupid's shaft at length transfix ....9 DTrn 52

TRANSIENT Withers the beauty's transient flower: ....76 DTrn 54
As bright, as transient too. ......88 Ed&A 62

TRANSITION And by a quick transition, plainly show ....7 GRos 51

TRANSITORY Thou transitory flower, alike undone ....367 Trav 17
Vain, transitory splendours! Could not all ....237 DVil 31
A transitory passion. ....16 Gift 43
Mere transitory things! ....9 Thrn 74
The transitory breath of fame below: ....8 epTP 100

TRANSLUCENT Fast by that shore where Thames' translucent stream .140 Thrn 79

TRANSMIT Where noble stems transmit the patriot flame, ...357 Trav 17

TRANSPORT Ye gods! what transport e'er compared to this. ....8 MrsX 49

TRANSPORTS The second brought its transports too. ....30 DTrn 53
Rise to transports past expressing, ...III:91 Capt 126

TRAP- Whilst from below the trap-door Demons rise, ...15 epLL 101

TRAPPINGS Are but the trappings of an hour-- ....8 Thrn 74
Off! off! vile trappings! a new passion reigns! ....21 epLL 101

TRAVELLED Ye travell'd tribe, ye macaroni train, ...31 eSSC$_1$ 105

TRAVELLERS As a safe inn, where weary travellers, ...87 Thrn 77
Ay, take your travellers, travellers indeed! ....37 eSSC$_1$ 105

TRAVELS Give me my bonny Scot, that travels from the Tweed. .....38 eSSC$_1$ 105

TRAVERSE My fortune leads to traverse realms alone, ...29 Trav 6
To traverse climes beyond the western main; ....410 Trav 18

TREAD$_1$ The sanded floor that grits beneath the tread; ....9 DABd 48

TREAD$_2$ Where the bleak Swiss their stormy mansions tread, ...167 Trav 10
No busy steps the grass-grown footway tread, ...127 DVil 27
'For here, forlorn and lost I tread, ...5 Ed&A 59
Vida, 37

TREASURE Bends at his treasure, counts, re-counts it o'er; ....52 Trav 7
With all those ills superfluous treasure brings, ...302 Trav 15
Love presents the fairest treasure, ...I:66 Capt 116

TREASURES Extols the treasures of his stormy seas, ...67 Trav 7

TREASURY A treasury for lost and missing things; ....2 eSSC$_2$ 108

TREAT$_1$ Your very good mutton's a very good treat; ....32 HofV 96

TREAT$_2$ To treat as dearest friend, a foe; ....28 LogR 45

TREE Led up their sports beneath the spreading tree; ....18 DVil 23
'The dew, the blossom on the tree, 125 Ed&A 63

TREES Here trees of stately size-- and turtles in 'em-- ....20 pZob 72

TREMBLE Tremble, ye mortals, at my rage! ....79,83 Thrn 76,77
Tremble, thou vice-polluted breast; ....II:73 Capt 121

TREMBLED And trembled as he frown'd. ....65 Thrn 76

TREMBLERS Well had the boding tremblers learn'd to trace ....199 DVil 29

TREMBLING And trembling, shrinking from the spoiler's hand, ...49 DVil 24
Comfort came down the trembling wretch to raise, ...175 DVil 29
Vida, 221, 231, 244, 253, 292, 517

TREMENDOUS Vida, 411

TRIBE Ye travell'd tribe, ye macaroni train, ...31 eSSC$_1$ 105
Ye jockey tribe, whose stock of words are few, ...49 eSSC$_1$ 106
Of all the tribe here wanting an adviser ....33 eSSC$_2$ 109

TRIBES Do thy fair tribes participate her pain? ....338 DVil 34
Hence through their tribes no mix'd polluted flame, ...7 Cati 94
Ye captive tribes, that hourly work and weep ....I:1 Capt 113

TRIBUTARY For me your tributary stores combine; ....49 Trav 7

TRIBUTE The tribute of a tear be mine, ...130 Thrn 78
Needless to him the tribute we bestow-- ....7 epTP 100

TRICE '0--Oh!' quoth my friend,

'he'll come on in a trice, ...99 HofV 98
TRICK₁ If they were not his own
by finessing and trick, ...106 Rtal 90
Vida, 327
TRICK₂ Vida, 319
TRICKS Its tricks the kitten tries; 54 Ed&A 61
Let boys play tricks, and kick the
straw; not I: ....13 eGNM 68
No countryman living their tricks
to discover; ....90 Rtal 90
Vida, 312
TRIED He tried each art, reprov'd
each dull delay, ...169 DVil 28
Farewell, and Oh! where'er thy
voice be tried, ...417 DVil 37
'For still I tried each fickle
art, ...129 Ed&A 63
Vida, 474, 630
TRIES And, as a bird each fond
endearment tries ....167 DVil 28
Each former art she vainly tries ...83 DTrn 54
In vain she tries her paste and
creams, ...85 DTrn 54
Its tricks the kitten tries; ....54 Ed&A 61
And tries to kill, ere she's got
power to cure. ....24 eSis 70
He quits the woods, and tries the
beaten ways; ....41 epLL 102
Vida, 555, 581
TRIFLERS In these, ere triflers
half their wish obtain, ...261 DVil 32
TRIFLING Though grave, yet trifling;
zealous, yet untrue; ....129 Trav 9
Are trifling, and decay; ....70 Ed&A 61
More trifling still than they. .....72 Ed&A 61
TRIM To pause from toil, and trim
their ev'ning fire; ....14 Trav 5
TRIMMED The hermit trimm'd his
little fire, ...47 Ed&A 60
TRIMS And trims her robes of frieze
with copper lace; ....276 Trav 14
TRINKETS With Scythian stores,
and trinkets deeply laden, ...11 pZob 72
TRIP Who take a trip to Paris once
a year ....33 eSSC₁ 105
TRIPE At the bottom was tripe in
a swinging tureen; ....82 HofV 97
Now, my Lord, as for tripe, it's
my utter aversion, ...85 HofV 98
But I've eat of your tripe till
I'm ready to burst.' ....94 HofV 98
'The tripe,' quoth the Jew, with
his chocolate cheek, ...95 HofV 98
'Your Tripe!' quoth the Jew, 'if
the truth I may speak, ...v95 HofV 242
'I could dine on this tripe seven
days in the week: ....96 HofV 98
I could eat of this Tripe seven
days in the week.' ....v96 HofV 242
TRIPT And here my simile almost
tript, ...55 NSim 57
TRIUMPH₁ The paste-board triumph
and the cavalcade; ....150 Trav 10
Nor shares with art the triumph
of her eyes: ....290 DVil 32
Which triumph forces from the
patriot heart, ...2 Queb 46

Have we not cause for triumph when
we see ....I:33 Capt 114
Come on, my companions, the
triumph display; ....I:57 Capt 115
TRIUMPH₂ No; rather let us
triumph still the more, ...I:41 Capt 115
Vida, 569, 637
TRIUMPHANT Triumphant music
floats along the vale; ....I:53 Capt 115
'Tis thus that pride triumphant
rears the head, ...III:13 Capt 123
Vida, 361, 607
TRIUMPHED Where many a time he
triumph'd, is forgot. ....218 DVil 30
I triumph'd in his pain. ....132 Ed&A 63
Vida, 215, 373
TRIUMPHS Seen all her triumphs
but destruction haste, ...399 Trav 18
At triumphs in a Fleet-street
shop. ....14 DTrn 52
And as she smiles, her triumphs
to complete, ...21 eSSC₃ 85
The triumphs that on vice attend I:43 Capt 115
TRODDEN But crush'd, or trodden
to the ground, ...I:49 Capt 115
TROLLS With patient angle trolls
the finny deep, ...187 Trav 11
TROOP Vida, 436
TROOPS To-night I head our troops
at Warwick Lane: ....18 eGNM 68
Vida, 82, 151, 219, 268, 270, 289,
330, 369, 458, 501, 512, 514,
565
TROPHIES Then all their trophies
last; and flattery turns to fame. ..17 Thrn 74
TROTT John Trott was desired by
two witty peers ....1 ClRp 100
TROUBLES Sure scenes like these no
troubles e'er annoy! ....323 DVil 34
TROUBLESOME Quite sick of pursuing
each troublesome elf, ...77 Rtal 89
TRUANT I knew him well, and every
truant knew; ....198 DVil 29
TRUCE Well then a truce, since
she requests it too: ....43 eSis 71
TRUE True to imagin'd right, above
control, ...332 Trav 16
'Tis true she dress'd with modern
grace, ...43 DTrn 53
We'll live and love so true; ......158 Ed&A 64
But the chaste blackbird, to its
partner true, ...9 Cati 94
First let me suppose, what may
shortly be true, ...1 LetB 131
TRUMPET He shifted his trumpet, and
only took snuff. ....146 Rtal 92
TRUSTY I thought of a friend that
was trusty and staunch; ....20 HofV 95
TRUTH Ye powers of truth, that bid
my soul aspire, ...363 Trav 17
O then how blind to all that truth
requires, ...377 Trav 17
Truth from his lips prevail'd
with double sway, ...179 DVil 29
Ye friends to truth, ye statesmen,
who survey ....265 DVil 32
Aid slighted truth; with thy

UNERRING Vida, 10, 125
UNFANNED Unquench'd by want, un-
fann'd by strong desire; ....222 Trav 12
UNFASHIONED By forms unfashion'd,
fresh from Nature's hand; ....330 Trav 16
UNFEELING But times are alter'd;
trade's unfeeling train ....63 DVil 25
UNFEIGNED Shall offer up un-
feign'd applause. ....II:96 Capt 122
UNFIT Unfit for raptures, or, if
raptures cheer ....223 Trav 12
Unfit in these degenerate times
of shame, ...409 DVil 36
Though equal to all things, for
all things unfit, ...37 Rtal 88
UNFRIENDED Remote, unfriended,
melancholy, slow, ...1 Trav 5
UNGOVERNABLY Rough, poor, content,
ungovernably bold; ....314 Trav 15
UNHALLOWED 'Whose feet unhallow'd
thus intrude ....95 Ed&A 62
And shall I mix in this unhallow'd
crew? ....17 epLL 101
UNHAPPY 'And whence, unhappy youth,'
he cried, ...63 Ed&A 61
As some unhappy wight, at some new
play, ...23 eGNM 68
Unhappy Zedekiah is no more! ..III:22 Capt 123
Vida, 214, 652
UNHELPED Since then, unhelp'd,
our bard must now conform ....31 eGNM 69
UNHONOURED And scholars, soldiers,
kings, unhonour'd die. ....360 Trav 17
UNHURT Vida, 631
UNIMPROVED Unalter'd, unimprov'd
the manners run; ....230 Trav 12
UNINHABITED The place is un-
inhabited, I fear! ....23 pZob 73
UNITE Unite to stamp the beauties
of the place, ...145 Thrn 79
UNITED Each guest brought his dish,
and the feast was united; ....2 Rtal 87
-UNITED Here lies the good Dean,
re-united to earth, ...23 Rtal 87
UNITES And here my simile unites, ..27 NSim 57
UNIVERSAL Sure these denote one
universal joy! ....324 DVil 34
UNIVERSE Who, born for the Universe,
narrow'd his mind, ...31 Rtal 88
UNKNOWN Unknown to them, when
sensual pleasures cloy, ...217 Trav 12
Unknown those powers that raise
the soul to flame, ...219 Trav 12
All claims that bind and sweeten
life unknown; ....342 Trav 16
And talent sinks, and merit
weeps unknown; ....354 Trav 17
Old Edward's sons, unknown to
yield, ...225 Thrn 82
UNLESS <u>Unless when she was sinning</u>. 12 MBlz 47
Vida, 331
UNLIKE Heavens! how unlike their
Belgic sires of old! ....313 Trav 15
How much unlike the sons of Britain
now! ....316 Trav 15
UNMANNED But towns unmann'd, and
lords without a slave; ....142 Trav 10
UNMARKED Vida, 307
UNMASKED Death, when unmasked, shows
me a friendly face, ...93 Thrn 77
UNMEANING Blushes when hir'd, and,
with unmeaning action, ...11 $eSSC_3$ 85
UNMOLESTED Unenvied, unmolested,
unconfin'd: ....258 DVil 31
UNMOVED Unmov'd in conscious
rectitude, ...25 Thrn 75
UNNUMBERED He sees unnumber'd
beauties rise, ...v85 Ed&A 209
Unnumber'd suitors came; ....106 Ed&A 62
UNPAID I'll give thee something
yet unpaid, ...17 Gift 43
An unpaid reck'ning on the frieze
was scor'd, ...v17 DABd 200
UNPERCEIVED Bends to the grave
with unperceiv'd decay, ...109 DVil 26
Sinks to the grave with un-
perceiv'd decay, ...v109 DVil 183
UNPLEASED Vida, 257
UNPRACTISED Unpractis'd he to
fawn, or seek for power, ...145 DVil 28
UNPROFITABLY With blossom'd furze
unprofitably gay, ...194 DVil 29
UNPUNISHED Vida, 250
UNQUENCHED Unquench'd by want,
unfann'd by strong desire; ....222 Trav 12
UNREGARDED Or unregarded love? .....68 Ed&A 61
UNRETURNED Or grieve for friendship
unreturn'd, ...67 Ed&A 61
UNSEEN On earth unseen, or only
found ....79 Ed&A 61
Unseen the modest were supplied, ..125 Thrn 78
Unseen, though constant, used to
flow; ....179 Thrn 80
Vida, 282, 428
UNSKILFUL Unskilful he to fawn,
or seek for power, ...v145 DVil 184
UNSPOILED By flattery un-
spoiled-- ....v(147) Rtal 232
UNSPOKEN What if we leave the
Epilogue unspoken? ....68 $eSSC_1$ 106
UNSOUGHT Too late you seek that
power unsought before, ...III:71 Capt 125
UNSOUND Till sapp'd their
strength, and every part un-
sound, ...393 DVil 36
UNSTEADY Till, more unsteady than
the southern gale, ...139 Trav 9
But, more unsteady than the
southern gale, ...v139 Trav 169
UNSTRUNG Ye sons of Judah, why
the lute unstrung? ....I:79 Capt 116
UNTHINKING Unthinking wretches!
have not you, and all, ...II:85 Capt 121
UNTIL Thrn, 242; Vida, 598, 632
UNTO Give ear unto my song; ....2 MDog 65
Vida, 652
UNTRAVELLED My heart untravell'd
fondly turns to thee; ....8 Trav 5
UNTRUE Though grave, yet trifling;
zealous, yet untrue; ....129 Trav 9
UNVARIED And tires their echoes
with unvaried cries. ....46 DVil 24
UNWIELDY Unwieldy wealth, and
cumbrous pomp repose; ....66 DVil 25

A bloated mass of rank unwieldy
woe; ....392 DVil 36
UNWILLING Still gather strength,
and force unwilling awe. ....352 Trav 17
UPLANDS Its uplands sloping deck
the mountain's side, ...107 Trav 8
UPON LogR, 48; NSim, 16; Thrn, 52;
eSSC$_3$, 27; Vida, 233, 286, 508, 560
URCHIN The little urchin smiles, and
spreads her lure, ...23 eSis 70
URGED A thousand sorrows urg'd thy
end: ....31 Thrn 75
Yet let that wisdom, urged by her
example, ...84 Thrn 77
URN Vida, 38
USAGE And, though she felt his
usage rough, ...27 DTrn 53
USE The pictures plac'd for
ornament and use, ...231 DVil 31
By use and daily meditation worn; .184 Thrn 81
Of use I insist, ...21 Invt 128
USED Unseen, though constant, used
to flow; ....179 Thrn 80
Vida, 34
USEFUL Her useful sons exchang'd
for useless ore? ....398 Trav 18
That leaves our useful products
still the same. ....274 DVil 32
His feet are useful as his head. ...30 NSim 57
USELESS Her useful sons exchang'd
for useless ore? ....398 Trav 18
USES And highly fam'd for several
uses. ....34 NSim 57
USURP Usurp the land and dispossess
the swain; ....64 DVil 25
USURPS Scoops out an empire, and
usurps the shore; ....290 Trav 14
UTMOST Vida, 332, 443
UTTER Now, my Lord, as for tripe,
it's my utter aversion, ...85 HofV 98

VA Make but of all your fortune
one va toute; ....48 eSSC$_1$ 105
VACANT And the loud laugh that
spoke the vacant mind; ....122 DVil 27
Lightly they frolic o'er the vacant
mind, ...257 DVil 31
VAGRANT His house was known to all
the vagrant train, ...149 DVil 28
VAIN$_1$ You vain, whom youth and
pleasure guide, ...III:27 Capt 123
VAIN$_2$ That good, which makes
each humbler bosom vain? ....40 Trav 6
Though poor, luxurious; though
submissive, vain; ....128 Trav 9
Vain, very vain, my weary search to
find ....423 Trav 19
Vain, transitory splendours! Could
not all ....237 DVil 31
And took a long farewell, and wish'd
in vain ....367 DVil 35
That man and all his ways are vain; 12 LogR 44
Quebec in vain shall teach our
breast to glow, ...7 Queb 46
Since none implor'd relief in
vain!-- ....15 DRtH 50
In vain she tries her paste and
creams, ...85 DTrn 54
Long had I sought in vain to find ...1 NSim 56
Importunate and vain: ....130 Ed&A 63
In vain, to charm thy ravish'd
sight, ...28 Thrn 75
In vain, to drive thee from the
right, ...30 Thrn 75
Yet something vain, like one that
shall be nameless, ...28 epLL 102
Of French friseurs, and nosegays,
justly vain, ...32 eSSC$_1$ 105
Still importunate and vain; .....I:24 Capt 114
In vain the madd'ning prophet
threatens woe, ...III:3 Capt 122
In vain rebellion aims her secret
blow; ....III:4 Capt 122
'Tis in vain that at niggardly
caution I scold, ...13 LetB 132
'Tis in vain that I flatter the
brave and the bold: ....14 LetB 132
Vida, 202, 474, 572, 635, 636
VAINLY Each former art she vainly
tries ....83 DTrn 54
Say, was it that vainly directing
his view ....75 Rtal 89
VALE Ye bending swains, that dress
the flow'ry vale, ...48 Trav 6
The slow canal, the yellow-blossom'd
vale, ...293 Trav 15
Swells from the vale, and midway
leaves the storm, ...190 DVil 29
To where yon taper cheers the vale ..3 Ed&A 59
To yonder fire, that cheers the
vale ....v3 Ed&A 208
Triumphant music floats along the
vale; ....I:53 Capt 115
VALIANT Vida, 518
VALLEY 'No flocks that range the
valley free ....21 Ed&A 59
Streams along the valley stray-
ing. ....II:50 Capt 120
And rivers through the valley
wind, ...III:41 Capt 124
VALOUR Vida, 359
VANGUARD Vida, 73
VANISH Shall vanish as we soar. .II:6 Capt 118
VANITY Here vanity assumes her
pert grimace, ...275 Trav 14
VANQUISHED For e'en though
vanquish'd, he could argue still; .212 DVil 30
Vida, 534, 629
VARIED Whose bright succession
decks the varied year; ....116 Trav 9
He turn'd and he varied full ten
times a day. ....104 Rtal 90
VARIES Vida, 43
VARIOUS From Art more various are
the blessings sent; ....87 Trav 8
The various terrors of that horrid
shore; ....346 DVil 34
At a dinner so various, at such a
repast, ...17 Rtal 87
Vida, 27, 43, 639
VARNISHED The varnish'd clock that
click'd behind the door; ....228 DVil 30
VARYING By doctrines fashion'd to
the varying hour; ....146 DVil 28

victories to sing. ....II:70 Capt 121
VICTORIOUS Vida, 360, 525
VICTORS Vida, 222
VICTORY That fortitude is
victory. ....I:100 Capt 117
O God of hosts, the victory is
thine! ....III:54 Capt 124
VIEW$_1$ Some fleeting good, that
mocks me with the view; ....26 Trav 6
A man severe he was, and stern to
view; ....197 DVil 29
The royal game of goose was there
in view, ...11 DABd 48
The game of goose was there expos'd
to view ....v11 DABd 200
Swift mantling to the view; ....86 Ed&A 62
Expanding to the view; ....v86 Ed&A 209
Say, was it that vainly directing
his view ....75 Rtal 89
I had thoughts, in my chambers, to
place it in view, ...7 HofV 95
Whilst thus he spoke, astonish'd,
to his view, ...37 epLL 102
Vida, 280, 546, 651
VIEW$_2$ But view them closer, craft
and fraud appear, ...305 Trav 15
And, many a year elaps'd, return
to view ....79 DVil 25
View him soon after to inferiors, ..49 LogR 45
And view with favour, the 'Good-
natur'd Man.' ....v34 eGNM 215
As helpless friends who view
from shore ....66 Thrn 76
And, as they view ....160 Thrn 80
Vida, 226, 289
VIEWED Vida, 241
VIEWING Vida, 285
VIEWS$_1$ Vida, 561
VIEWS$_2$ The morn was cold, he views
with keen desire ....15 DABd 48
VIGOROUS Vida, 441
VIGOUR Boast of a florid vigour
not their own; ....390 DVil 36
Alive, the foe thy dreadful vigour
fled, ...9 Queb 46
No lord will take me now, my vigour
fled, ...173 Thrn 80
Should bonds repress the vigour of
the mind? ....I:32 Capt 114
VILE But this vile hour disperses
all my store, ...9 pLab 41
Off! off! vile trappings! a new
passion reigns! ....21 epLL 101
VILLAGE$_1$ Yet would the village praise
my wondrous power, ...249 Trav 13
The smiling long-frequented village
fall? ....406 Trav 18
Sweet Auburn! loveliest village of
the plain, ...1 DVil 23
These were thy charms, sweet village;
sports like these, ...31 DVil 24
Sweet smiling village, loveliest of
the lawn, ...35 DVil 24
The village all declar'd how much
he knew; ....207 DVil 30
VILLAGE$_2$ And all the village train,
from labour free, ...17 DVil 23
Up yonder hill the village murmur
rose; ....114 DVil 27
The village preacher's modest
mansion rose. ....140 DVil 27
The village master taught his
little school; ....196 DVil 29
Where village statesmen talk'd
with looks profound, ...223 DVil 30
She once, perhaps, in village plenty
bless'd, ...327 DVil 34
VINDICATE No--I will act. I'll
vindicate the stage: ....19 epLL 101
And vindicate thy people's cause;II:94 Capt 122
VINDICTIVE Shall wrath vindictive
threaten ere it fall! ....III:38 Capt 124
Vida, 258
VINE To deck it, bring with you
festoons of the vine, ...167 Rtal 93
VINEGAR Oil, vinegar, sugar, and
saltness agree: ....12 Rtal 87
VIRGIN'S The bashful virgin's side-
long looks of love, ...29 DVil 24
VIRGINS False wits, false wives,
false virgins, and false spouses! ..40 eSis 70
VIRTU To be shown to my friends as
a piece of <u>virtu</u>; ....8 HofV 95
VIRTUE When struggling Virtue sinks
by long controul, ...v155 Trav 170
Now lost to all; her friends, her
virtue fled, ...331 DVil 34
But for himself, in conscious
virtue brave, ...373 DVil 35
Thou nurse of every virtue, fare
thee well! ....416 DVil 37
But pitying his distress, let
virtue shine, ...3 GRos 51
When truth and virtue reach the
skies, ...3,5 Thrn 74
Virtue, on herself relying, ...36,44 Thrn 75
If virtue fail her counsel sage, ...82 Thrn 77
And should we mourn? should coward
virtue fly, ...I:39 Capt 115
And every virtue springs from
pain: ....I:46 Capt 115
Vida, 672
VIRTUE'S$_1$ Angels around befriending
Virtue's friend; ....108 DVil 26
And e'en his failings lean'd to
Virtue's side; ....164 DVil 28
Affliction still is virtue's
opportunity! ....35 Thrn 75
VIRTUE'S Its soporific virtue's such,38 NSim 57
VIRTUES Some sterner virtues o'er
the mountain's breast ....253 Trav 13
I see the rural virtues leave the
land: ....398 DVil 36
To blend their virtues while they
think of thee. ....137 Thrn 78
Of virtues and feelings, that folly
grows proud; ....70 Rtal 89
To find out men's virtues, and
finding them few, ...76 Rtal 89
VIRTUOUS In virtuous times of yore, 6 DRtH 50
How do the good, the virtuous fall! 73 Thrn 76
VISAGE A visage so sad, and so pale
with affright, ...109 HofV 98
VISIONARY Whence, and what art thou,

WATCHFUL Vida, 508
WATER$_1$ No poppy water half so good; 36 NSim 57
And water from the spring. ....28 Ed&A 60
WATER$_2$ And the tears of her country shall water her tomb. ....262 Thrn 83
WATERY Spreads its long arms amidst the wat'ry roar, ...289 Trav 14
WAVE Basks in the glare, or stems the tepid wave, ...71 Trav 7
And freshen'd from the wave the Zephyr flew; ....246 Trav 13
WAVE- Thus, while around the wave-subjected soil ....297 Trav 15
WAVES While winds and waves their wishes cross-- ....68 Thrn 76
Vida, 367
The curling waves before his coursers fly: ....5 Tr 267
WAVING Ye shady walks, ye waving greens, ...163 Thrn 80
WAVY The wavy lawn, the sloping green-- ....147 Thrn 79
WAY Or seeks the den where snow-tracks mark the way, ...189 Trav 11
Through life's more cultur'd walks, and charm the way, ...236 Trav 13
But chok'd with sedges, works its weedy way. ....42 DVil 24
While Resignation gently slopes the way; ....110 DVil 26
Allur'd to brighter worlds, and led the way. ....170 DVil 28
Beside yon straggling fence that skirts the way, ...193 DVil 29
There the black gibbet glooms beside the way. ....318 DVil 33
What! no way left to shun th' inglorious stage, ...1 pLab 41
Where the Red Lion flaring o'er the way, ...1 DABd 48
As each a different way pursues, ...72 DTrn 54
Yet grant a word by way of post-script. ....56 NSim 57
And guide my lonely way, ...2 Ed&A 59
To guide my nightly way, ...v2 Ed&A 208
Companion of her way. ....100 Ed&A 62
Companion of the way. ....v100 Ed&A 209
At the Pit door stands elbowing a way, ...24 eGNM 68
He this way steers his course, in hopes of trading-- ....12 pZob 72
With no reason on earth to go out of his way, ...103 Rtal 90
'I'm glad I have taken this house in my way. ....46 HofV 96
That leads to truth through pleasure's flowery way! ....4 epTP 100
Adorns and cheers our way; .....II:38 Capt 119
Adorns and chears the way; ....vII:38 Capt 250
That this way slowly bend along the plain? ....III:16 Capt 123
That stop the hunter's way: ...III:42 Capt 124
And this way leads his formidable band. ....III:86 Capt 126
But 'tis Reynolds s way ....39 Invt 129
All play their own way, and they think me an ass,-- ....15 LetB 132
Don't you think the best way is to venture for't twice?' ....30 LetB 132
Vida, 8, 139, 255, 484, 552
-WAY No busy steps the grass-grown foot-way tread, ...127 DVil 27
WAYS$_1$ Through tangled forests, and through dangerous ways; ....414 Trav 19
He quits the woods, and tries the beaten ways; ....41 epLL 102
WAYS$_2$ That man and all his ways are vain; ....12 LogR 44
And never follow'd wicked ways,-- ..11 MBlz 47
WEAK And the weak soul, within itself unblest, ...271 Trav 14
Is both a weak and erring creature; 14 LogR 44
Vida, 474, 623
WEALTH Ye glitt'ring towns, with wealth and splendour crown'd, ...45 Trav 6
Wealth, commerce, honour, liberty, content. ....88 Trav 8
Where wealth and freedom reign, contentment fails, ...91 Trav 8
For wealth was theirs, not far remov'd the date, ...133 Trav 9
Yet still the loss of wealth is here supplied ....145 Trav 10
Are here displayed. Their much-lov'd wealth imparts ....303 Trav 15
Fictitious bonds, the bonds of wealth and law, ...351 Trav 17
The wealth of climes, where savage nations roam, ...387 Trav 18
Gave wealth to sway the mind with double force. ....396 Trav 18
Where wealth accumulates, and men decay: ....52 DVil 25
And his best riches, ignorance of wealth. ....62 DVil 25
Unwieldy wealth, and cumbrous pomp repose; ....66 DVil 25
With all the freaks of wanton wealth array'd, ...260 DVil 31
Yet count our gains. This wealth is but a name ....273 DVil 32
Not so the loss. The man of wealth and pride ....275 DVil 32
Those fenceless fields the sons of wealth divide, ...307 DVil 33
But now her wealth and finery fled, 21 MBlz 47
A shade that follows wealth or fame, ...75 Ed&A 61
And all his wealth was mark'd as mine, ...103 Ed&A 62
My wealth perhaps their aim. ....v108 Ed&A 209
No wealth nor power had he; ....114 Ed&A 63
When wealth and rank and noble blood, ...15 Thrn 74
Your wealth, your pride, your kingdom, are no more. ......III:72 Capt 125
WEALTHY A wealthy lord was he; ....102 Ed&A 62
WEAR I'll not wear a garland--Augusta's away, ...241 Thrn 83
I'll not wear a garland until she return; ....242 Thrn 83
For who'd wear a garland when she is away, ...253 Thrn 83
As 'D-- --, Sir,' and 'Sir, I

wear a sword'; ....28 $eSSC_2$ 109
To wear tails in high taste, ...27 Invt 129
WEARY A weary waste expanding to the skies: ....6 Trav 5
Vain, very vain, my weary search to find ....423 Trav 19
As a safe inn, where weary travellers, ...87 Thrn 77
WEDDED The Fourth Act shows her wedded to the 'Squire, ...23 $eSSC_3$ 85
WEDGED Vida, 252
WEEDY But chok'd with sedges, works its weedy way. ....42 DVil 24
WEEK 'I could dine on this tripe seven days in the week: ....96 HofV 98
I could eat of this Tripe seven days in the week.' ....v96 HofV 242
WEEKS At least, in six weeks, I could not find 'em out; ....26 Rtal 87
WEEP For him no wretches, born to work and weep, ...103 DVil 26
To seek her nightly shed, and weep till morn; ....134 DVil 27
Return'd and wept, and still return'd to weep. ....370 DVil 35
If hills could learn to weep. ......12 DRtH 50
But leaves the wretch to weep? .....76 Ed&A 61
'Tis ours to weep the want below! ...4 Thrn 74
Call on their mistress--now no more--and weep. ....162 Thrn 80
Ye captive tribes, that hourly work and weep ....I:1 Capt 113
Shall Reason only teach to weep? ....II:52 Capt 120
Vida, 657
WEEPING Weeping, murmuring, complaining, ...1 Sonn 46
Her weeping children round ....62 Thrn 76
Groans, weeping friends, indeed, and gloomy sables, ...90 Thrn 77
To dwell a weeping hermit there. ..135 Thrn 78
Oh! where shall weeping want repair, ...189 Thrn 81
WEEPS And talent sinks, and merit weeps unknown; ....354 Trav 17
The joy that dimples, and the woe that weeps. ....10 epLL 101
WEIGHS Nor weighs the solid worth of self-applause. ....280 Trav 14
WEIGHT Its double weight must ruin all below. ....376 Trav 17
And every added weight of woe ....I:9 Capt 113
WELCOME Here then at once, I welcome every shame, ...15 pLab 41
May cherubs welcome their expected guest; ....108 Thrn 77
My friend bade me welcome, but struck me quite dumb, ...69 HofV 97
WELCOMES That welcomes every stranger that can pay, ...v(20) DABd 200
WELFARE Their welfare pleas'd him, and their cares distress'd; ....186 DVil 29
$WELL_1$ With food as well the peasant is supplied ....83 Trav 8
I knew him well, and every truant knew; ....198 DVil 29
Well had the boding tremblers learn'd to trace ....199 DVil 29
Full well they laugh'd, with counterfeited glee, ...201 DVil 30
Full well the busy whisper, circling round, ...203 DVil 30
Thou nurse of every virtue, fare thee well! ....416 DVil 37
The old buffoon will fit my name as well; ....18 pLab 41
For Kent-street well may say, ...26 MBlz 47
Each bard might well display; ......14 DRtH 50
And well my life shall pay; ....138 Ed&A 64
Our ship's well stor'd;--in yonder creek we've laid her; ....31 pZob 73
Augusta's care had well supplied. 186 Thrn 81
His well acquainted tints, and kindred hues. ....6 Cati 94
At least, it's your temper, as very well known, ...121 HofV 99
At least, it's your temper, 'tis very well known, ...v121 HofV 242
Where are the chiels? Ah! Ah, I well discern ....39 $eSSC_1$ 105
Alas! too well mine eyes indignant trace ....III:19 Capt 123
'Well done!' cry the ladies; 'Ah, Doctor, that's good! ....25 LetB 132
May well be call'd picking of pockets in law; ....38 LetB 133
First Sir Charles advances with phrases well strung, ...55 LetB 133
WELL- Like some well-fashion'd arch thy patience stood, ...32 Thrn 75
$WELL_2$ Well! what is it from thence we gather? ....17 NSim 56
Well! what of that? out with it--stealing; ....58 NSim 58
Well! since she thus has shown her want of skill, ...9 eSis 70
Well then a truce, since she requests it too: ....43 eSis 71
Well, having stoop'd to conquer with success, ...1 $eSSC_3$ 85
Well, suppose it a bounce--sure a poet may try, ...15 HofV 95
Well, Madam, what if, after all this sparring, ...65 $eSSC_1$ 106
$WELL_3$ Yet in a man 'twas well enough. ....28 DTrn 53
WE'LL Ed&A, 158, v(161), v(168); Thrn, 256, 260; HofV, 49, 73, 105, 106; Capt, I:13; II:53
WENT And sleights of art and feats of strength went round; ....22 DVil 24
And news much older than their ale went round. ....224 DVil 30
Silent went next, neglectful of her charms, ...377 DVil 35
Whene'er he went before. ....8 DRtH 50
That went reliev'd away. ....16 DRtH 50
Whene'er he went to pray. ....8 MDog 65
Went mad and bit the man. ....20 MDog 65
Who, too deep for his hearers, still went on refining, ...35 Rtal 88
While the bacon and liver went merrily round. ....88 HofV 98
An order went out, ...25 Invt 128
Vida, 16, 373, 583

WEPT Wept o'er his wounds, or
tales of sorrow done, ...157 DVil 28
He watch'd and wept, he pray'd
and felt, for all. ....166 DVil 28
Has wept at tales of innocence
distress'd; ....328 DVil 34
Return'd and wept, and still
return'd to weep. ....370 DVil 35
To new-found worlds, and wept for
others' woe; ....372 DVil 35
Vida, 434

WEST From north, from south, from
east, from west, ...II:71 Capt 121

WESTERN And flies where Britain
courts the western spring; ....318 Trav 15
To traverse climes beyond the
western main; ....410 Trav 18
For seats like these beyond the
western main; ....368 DVil 35

WE'VE Our ship's well stor'd;--in
yonder creek we've laid her; ....31 pZob 73

WHAT See also WHAT'S
Trav, 266; DVil, 60, 309, 363; pLab, 1, 4;
Gift, 3; MrsX, 8; NSim, 5, 17, 41, 58, 63;
Ed&A, 73, v127, v150; "wlw, 3, 4; eGNM, 15,
16; eSis, 1, 10, 13, 26; pZob, 17, 37;
Thrn, 52, 85, 174, 188, 220; Rtal, 22, 32,
50, 53, 109, 116, 135, 157; HofV, 11, 39,
53, 89, 103, v103; epTP, 3; epLL, 7; eSSC$_1$,
11, 17, 65, 68; Capt, I:31; II:13, 25; III:
15; LetB, 1, 16, 17, 41, 48, 50, 51, 60, 62;
Vida, 6, 82, 272, 275, 296, 297, 462, 542,
544

WHATE'ER Whate'er my cell bestows; ..18 Ed&A 59
Whate'er he had was mine. ....v104 Ed&A 209

WHATEVER See also WHATE'ER
Where'er I roam, whatever realms
to see, ...7 Trav 5
Whatever fruits in different climes
were found, ...113 Trav 9
Whatever blooms in torrid tracts
appear, ...115 Trav 9
Whatever sweets salute the northern
sky ....117 Trav 9

WHAT'S Hold, ma'am, your pardon.
What's your business here? ....1 eSSC$_1$ 103

WHEEL$_1$ The lifted axe, the agonising
wheel, ...435 Trav 19
She left her wheel and robes of
country brown. ....336 DVil 34

WHEEL$_2$ Vida, 314

WHEELING Vida, 129

WHEELS Its motions stop, or frenzy
fire the wheels. ....348 Trav 16

WHELP Both mongrel, puppy, whelp,
and hound, ...15 MDog 65

WHEN Trav, 37, 64, 134, v155, v155, 205, 214,
217, 355, 361, 378, 380, 381, 383, 384, 394;
DVil, 6, 16, 56, 58, 113, 204, 233, 291,
292, 335, 365; pLab, 5, 20; Gift, 12; MBlz,
12, 16, 20, 23; MrsX, 9; DTrn, 33, 45;
Ed&A, 45, v45, 117, v125, v(167); MDog, 12,
18; "wlw, 1; eSis, 35; pZob, 1, 3, 7; Thrn,
3, 5, 12, 14, 15, 76, 88, 93, 98, 205, 253,
254; "LSm, 10, 14; eSSC$_3$, 11; Rtal, 1, 83,
102, 108, 144, 145; "Amw, 1; HofV, 26, 34,
v34, 67; eSSC$_1$, 42, 43, 60; Capt, I:22, 33,
40, 77; II:29, 83; III:11; Invt, 22, 33, 44;
LetB, 41, 47, 60; Vida, 15, 19, 36, 105,
109, 112, 115, 159, 187, 261, 265, 299,
340, 363, 473, 507, 520, 571, 624, 642,
661, 679; Tr, 13

WHENCE Whence from such lands each
pleasing science flies, ...215 Trav 12
Pants to the place from whence at
first she flew, ...94 DVil 26
'And whence, unhappy youth,' he
cried, ...63 Ed&A 61
Whence, and what art thou, visionary
birth? ....7 epLL 101
But whence, when joy should
brighten o'er the land, ...I:77 Capt 116
But, whence that shout? Good
heavens! amazement all! ....III:47 Capt 124
Vida, 599

WHENE'ER <u>Whene'er he went be-
fore</u>. ....8 DRtH 50
Whene'er he went to pray. ....8 MDog 65
Whene'er he spoke amidst the
train, ...v121 Ed&A 210
Vida, 164

WHENEVER See also WHENE'ER
Whenever rage or envy rise, ...65 DTrn 54

WHERE Trav, 3, 5, 13, 15, v17, 18,
31, 34, 46, 61, 63, 91, 92, 105,
159, 166, 167, 189, 239, 245, 279,
282, 284, 318, 319, 357, 358, 387,
403, 411, 415, 421; DVil, 2, 3, 8,
52, 65, 80, 101, 137, 138, 139, 171,
218, 220, 221, 222, 223, 255, 281,
303, 319, 326, 342, 344, 349, 352,
353, 355, 380, 399, 408, 419; DABd,
1, 3; Ed&A, 3, 7, 96, 136, 140;
eGNM, 26, 33; pZob, 15; Thrn, 87,
101, 103, 123, 140, 142, 144, 171,
189, 224; Rtal, 73, 82, 122; HofV,
9, 26, 67, 84, v84; eSSC$_1$, 39; Capt,
I:2, 18, 36, II:65, 88, 90, III:40,
49, 82; LetB, 61; Vida, 8, 59, 154,
334, 518

WHERE'ER Where'er I roam, whatever
realms to see, ...7 Trav 5
Such is the patriot's boast, where'er
we roam, ...73 Trav 7
Farewell, and Oh! where'er thy
voice be tried, ...417 DVil 37
Vida, 617

WHEREFORE Or, wherefore his
characters thus without fault? .....74 Rtal 89

WHERE'S But where's this place,
this storehouse of the age? ....5 eSSC$_2$ 108

WHERESOE'ER And ah! bless'd spirit,
wheresoe'er thy flight, ...106 Thrn 77

WHEREVER See also WHERE'ER
But peace to his spirit, wherever
it flies, ...119 Rtal 91

WHETHER Whether where equinoctial
fervours glow, ...419 DVil 37
'Twas one, both, three of them,
they know not whether; ....2 GCRL 51
Whether crimes such as yours should
not come before Fielding? ......36 LetB 132

WHILE$_1$ Here for a while my proper
cares resign'd, ...101 Trav 8

Mute for a while, and sullenly
distress'd, ...211 Thrn 82
Here lesson'd for a while, and
hence retreating, ...29 eSSC$_2$ 109
A little while, and all their
power is fled; ....III:14 Capt 123
WHILE$_2$ Trav, 109, 121, 141,
v(155), 157, 195, 267, 291, 297,
333, 417; DVil, 19, 28, 110,
213, 235, 263, 285, 288, 299,
301, 315, 317, 357, 429; MrsX,
6; DTrn, 59, 73; Ed&A, 83, 131;
MDog, 27; eGNM, 25; pZob, 5;
Thrn, 68, 69, 110, 128, 137, 146,
148, 201, 238; Rtal, 19, 36, 44,
116, 118; Cati, 13; HofV, 35, 79,
88, 107; epTP, 10; eSSC$_1$, 6; Capt,
I:48, II:51; Invt, 8; LetB, 5, 8,
23; Vida, 9, 146, 154, 203, 226,
269, 555
WHILST Whilst her fond husband
strove to lend relief ....383 DVil 36
Whilst thy sad fate extorts the
heart-wrung tear. ....8 Queb 46
Whilst from below the trap-door
Demons rise, ...15 epLL 101
Whilst thus he spoke, astonish'd,
to his view, ...37 epLL 102
Whilst his strong limbs conspire
to set him free, ...45 epLL 102
WHIM What spirits were his! what
wit and what whim! ....53 Rtal 88
And Angelica's whim ....41 Invt 129
WHIP He bows, turns round, and
whip--the man's a black! ....40 eSis 71
WHIPS The whips and angry tortures
shall prevail. ....I:94 Capt 117
Can whips or tortures hurt the
mind ....I:97 Capt 117
WHIRLS While oft in whirls the
mad tornado flies, ...357 DVil 35
WHIRLWIND 'Wild is the whirlwind
rolling ....213 Thrn 82
Fierce is the whirlwind howling II:15 Capt 118
WHIRLWIND'S So the loud torrent,
and the whirlwind's roar, ...207 Trav 12
The raging deep, the whirlwind's
roar-- ....218 Thrn 82
WHISKS Who whisks about the house,
at market caters, ...15 eSSC$_3$ 85
WHISPER Full well the busy whisper,
circling round, ...203 DVil 30
WHISPERED And his last falt'ring
accents whisper'd praise. ....176 DVil 29
WHISPERING For talking age and
whisp'ring lovers made; ....14 DVil 23
The watchdog's voice that bay'd.
the whisp'ring wind, ...121 DVil 27
WHISTLE For he knew when he pleas'd
he could whistle them back. ....108 Rtal 90
WHISTLING Vida, 346
WHITE$_1$ And seems to every gazer all
in white, ...38 eSis 71
The white was so white, and the red
was so ruddy. ....v4 HofV 238
Vida, 5, 125, 131, 190, 303, 428,
496, 566
WHITE$_2$ The fat was so white, and
the lean was so ruddy. ....4 HofV 95
The white was so white, and the red
was so ruddy. ....v4 HofV 238
Vida, 27, 55, 78, 88, 332, 531
WHITE- The white-wash'd wall, the
nicely sanded floor, ...227 DVil 30
-WHITE The snow-white vesture,
and the glittering crown, ...3 Cati 94
Vida, 61
WHITEFOORD Here Whitefoord reclines,
and deny it who can, ...147 Rtal 92
Merry Whitefoord, farewell! for
<u>thy</u> sake I admit ....171 Rtal 93
WHITEN And the new-blossomed
thorn shall whiten her tomb.' 250, 258 Thrn 83
WHITENED Vida, 259, 621
WHITES Vida, 383
WHITHER Yon critic, too--but
whither do I run? ....41 eSis 71
Whither shall my choice incline? I:73 Capt 116
WHO Trav, 64, 372, 378; DVil, 99,
v99, 101, 180, 265; Gift, 8; LogR,
19; MBlz, 3, 4, 8; MrsX, 4; NSim,
3; Ed&A, 71, 99, 107, v112; eGNM,
5, 19; eSis, 28, 29, 30, 37;
Thrn, 66, 166; eSSC$_3$, 15; Rtal,
24, 31, 35, 63, 93, 112, 121, 147,
151, 153, 159, 164; HofV, 26, 31,
v38, v76, 111; epEP, 2; eSSC$_1$, 21,
26, 33, 47, 53, 71; eSSC$_2$, 4, 17,
20; Capt, I:29, vI:29, 84, III:23,
65, 101; LetB, 18; Vida, 122, 141,
188, 282, 307, 382, 386, 445, 477,
482, 549; Tr, 2
WHO'D For who'd wear a garland when
she is away, ...253 Thrn 83
Who'd not be a glutton, and stick
to the last? ....18 Rtal 87
WHOLE$_1$ While pity harmonized the
whole. ....238 Thrn 82
Vida, 415, 508
WHOLE$_2$ One only master grasps the
whole domain, ...39 DVil 24
The whole pool as my own--'Come,
give me five cards.' ....24 LetB 132
WHOLESOME For him light labour
spread her wholesome store, ...59 DVil 25
WHOM Trav, 242; DVil, 93; pLab, 13;
Ed&A, 98; MDog, 6; Thrn, 153, 154;
Capt, III:27; LetB, 49; Vida, 86,
122, 132, 173, 243, 567
WHO'S Nor know who's in or out at
court; ....26 LogR 44
Looking, as who should say, D-- --!
who's afraid? ....30 eSis 71
WHOSE Trav, 43, 47, 116; DVil, 152;
DTrn, 75, 77; Ed&A, 95; Thrn, 18, 168;
Rtal, 29, 43, 51, 151, 154, 161;
HofV, 41; epLL, 13, 14; eSSC$_1$, 12,
19, 49; eSSC$_2$, 23; Vida, 114
WHOSOEVER Vida, 96, 302
WHY$_1$ Why have I stray'd from
pleasure and repose, ...425 Trav 19
Yet, why impair thy bright per-
fection? ....5 Sonn 46
Yet, why this killing soft

dejection? ....v5 Sonn 196
Why dim thy beauty with a tear? ...v6 Sonn 196
Why these denote a brain of
feather. ....18 NSim 56
To tell them the reason why asses
had ears? ....2 ClRp 100
Yet, why complain? What, though
by bonds confin'd, ...I:31 Capt 114
Ye sons of Judah, why the lute
unstrung? ....I:79 Capt 116
Or why those harps on yonder
willows hung? ....I:80 Capt 116
Why this delay? at length for
joy prepare; ....II:41 Capt 119
WHY$_2$ Our modern bards! why what
a pox ....63 NSim 58
'What have we got here?--Why, this
is good eating! ....39 HofV 96
'Why, whose should it be?' cried
I with a flounce, ...41 HofV 96
Why, sure the girl's beside her-
self: an Epilogue of singing, 7 eSSC$_1$ 103
Why, let them come, one good
remains to cheer; ....I:95 Capt 117
'Who, I? let me see, Sir, why I
must pass too.' ....18 LetB 132
WICKED And never follow'd wicked
ways,-- ....11 MBlz 47
WICKET The wicket, opening with
a latch, ...43 Ed&A 60
WIDE Lakes, forests, cities, plains,
extending wide, ...35 Trav 6
'Tis yours to judge, how wide the
limits stand ....267 DVil 32
How wide her mouth, how wild her
eyes! ....66 DTrn 54
Vida, 134, 337, 503, 511
WIDENS Vida, 99
WIDGEONS Your bustards, your ducks,
and your widgeons; ....24 "LSm 84
WIDOWED All but yon widow'd,
solitary thing ....129 DVil 27
WIELD Vida, 201
WIFE Jack finds his wife a perfect
beauty. ....104 DTrn 55
And my wife, little Kitty, is
famous for crust. ....54 HofV 97
Though clogg'd with a coxcomb, and
Kitty his wife. ....64 HofV 97
Vida, 471
WIGHT As some unhappy wight, at
some new play, ...23 eGNM 68
WILD In wild excess the vulgar
breast takes fire, ...225 Trav 12
Where wild Oswego spreads her
swamps around, ...411 Trav 19
And still where many a garden flower
grows wild; ....138 DVil 27
Where wild Altama murmurs to their
woe. ....344 DVil 34
How wide her mouth, how wild her
eyes! ....66 DTrn 54
'Wild is the whirlwind rolling ....213 Thrn 82
And wild the tempest howling ......215 Thrn 82
Vida, 269, 409, 432, 514
WILD- Our Will shall be wild-
fowl of excellent flavour, ...6 Rtal 87
WILDERNESS Far in a wilderness
obscure ....37 Ed&A 60
WILDLY Where wildly huddled to the
eye, ...103 Thrn 77
WILDS Thus every good his native
wilds impart, ...199 Trav 11
Where wilds immeasurably spread, ...7 Ed&A 59
To wilds shall turn, ...III:81 Capt 126
WILE Even children follow'd
with endearing wile, ...183 DVil 29
WILES Vida, 456, 483
WILL I give it with good will. .....16 Ed&A 59
Who scatter'd around wit and
humour at will; ....153 Rtal 93
Compliance with his will your
peace secures, ...II:9 Capt 118
And let thy will be done. .....III:58 Capt 124
WILL Our Will shall be wild-
fowl, of excellent flavour, ...7 Rtal 87
WILLIAM And brave prince William
show'd his lamp-black face: ....14 DABd 48
Here lies honest William, whose
heart was a mint, ...43 Rtal 88
WILLIAMS There's COLEY, and
WILLIAMS, and HOWARD, and HIFF, ..v27 HofV 238
WILLING Nor the coy maid, half
willing to be press'd, ...249 DVil 31
Only binds the willing heart. III:102 Capt 127
Vida, 475
WILLOW- The willow-tufted bank,
the gliding sail, ...294 Trav 15
WILLOWS Or why those harps on
yonder willows hung? ....I:80 Capt 116
WIN 'To win me from his tender
arms ....105 Ed&A 62
WIND$_1$ The watchdog's voice that
bay'd the whisp'ring wind, ...121 DVil 27
Thus snatching his hat, he brush'd
off like the wind, ...57 HofV 97
He bounds aloft, outstrips the
fleeting wind: ....40 epLL 102
Give, give your songs of Sion to
the wind, ...III:87 Capt 126
Vida, 76
WIND$_2$ And rivers through the
valley wind, ...III:41 Capt 124
-WINDED With his long-winded
speeches, his smiles and his
brogue; ....90 HofV 98
WINDOW A window, patch'd with paper,
lent a ray, ...7 DABd 48
The window, patch'd with paper,
lent a ray, ...v7 DABd 200
WINDS While winds and waves their
wishes cross-- ....68 Thrn 76
Vida, 36, 364
WINE Boasts of his golden sands and
palmy wine, ...70 Trav 7
Here, waiter! more wine, let me sit
while I'm able, ...19 Rtal 87
Wine shall bless the brave and
free. ....I:70 Capt 116
Wine and beauty thus inviting, ..I:71 Capt 116
WING$_1$ Fir'd at the sound, my
genius spreads her wing, ...317 Trav 15
WING$_2$ Vida, 69, 237
WING$_3$ Wing all our thoughts to

reach the skies, ...II:4 Capt 118
WINGED Vida, 126, 176
WINGS While sea-born gales their
gelid wings expand ....121 Trav 9
Wings upon either side--mark that. .16 NSim 56
Wings grow again from both his
shoes; ....24 NSim 56
Vida, 491
WINKED Vida, 286
WINNING With manners wond'rous
winning, ...10 MBlz 47
WINNOW To winnow fragrance round
the smiling land. ....122 Trav 9
WINTER But winter ling'ring chills
the lap of May; ....172 Trav 11
The hearth, except when winter
chill'd the day, ...233 DVil 31
Or winter wraps the polar world in
snow, ...420 DVil 37
WINTRY To pick her wintry faggot
from the thorn, ...133 DVil 27
WISDOM Though patriots flatter,
still shall wisdom find ....77 Trav 7
Wisdom and worth were all he had, .115 Ed&A 63
Yet let that wisdom, urged by her
example, ...84 Thrn 77
Who mix'd reason with pleasure, and
wisdom with mirth: ....24 Rtal 87
From wisdom to stray, ...40 Invt 129
WISE Wise Aristotle and Smiglecius, .5 LogR 44
When wise Astronomers to India
steer, ...3 pZob 72
Then let us, providently wise, .II:57 Capt 120
WISELY While broken tea-cups,
wisely kept for show, ...235 DVil 31
Vida, 417
WISER And wiser he, whose sympathetic
mind ....43 Trav 6
What! five long acts--and all to
make us wiser! ....1 eSis 70
I answer, no, no, for he always
was wiser: ....130 Rtal 91
He has not left a better or wiser
behind: ....138 Rtal 91
Our Author's the least likely to
grow wiser; ....34 eSSC$_2$ 109
But, alas! your good worships,
how could they be wiser, ...43 Invt 129
WISH$_1$ Each wish contracting, fits
him to the soil. ....184 Trav 11
In these, ere triflers half their
wish obtain, ...261 DVil 32
Hoards, e'en beyond the miser's
wish abound, ...271 DVil 32
WISH$_2$ And oft I wish, amidst the
scene, to find ....59 Trav 7
And wish the avenging fight. ......230 Thrn 82
Still, as a Bar-maid, I could wish
it too, ...3 eSSC$_3$ 85
I don't think he'll wish to come
back. ....4 epEP 100
'I wish I'd been called in a little
sooner:' ....54 eSSC$_1$ 106
I wish for life, and yield me to
my fears. ....II:30 Capt 119
I wish all my friends may be
bolder than I: ....10 LetB 132

Vida, 515
WISHED Nor e'er had chang'd, nor
wished to change his place; ....144 DVil 28
And took a long farewell, and
wish'd in vain ....367 DVil 35
He only wish'd for worlds beyond
the grave. ....374 DVil 35
That we wish'd him full ten times
a day at Old Nick; ....58 Rtal 89
As often we wish'd to have Dick
back again. ....60 Rtal 89
Vida, 497
-WISHED- Vida, 599
WISHES Their wants but few, their
wishes all confin'd. ....210 Trav 12
And piety, with wishes plac'd
above, ...405 DVil 36
While winds and waves their wishes
cross-- ....68 Thrn 76
And as our fortune sinks, our
wishes soar. ....I:42 Capt 115
WIT$_1$ In wit, and sense, and
nature's spite: ....4 NSim 56
With wit that's flighty, learning
light; ....20 NSim 56
What spirits were his! what wit and
what whim! ....53 Rtal 88
Who scatter'd around wit and humour
at will; ....153 Rtal 93
That a Scot may have humour, I had
almost said wit: ....172 Rtal 93
To thrive by flattery, though he
starves by wit. ....72 eSSC$_1$ 107
WIT$_2$ Too nice for a statesman,
too proud for a wit: ....38 Rtal 88
As a wit, if not first, in the very
first line: ....96 Rtal 90
Yet happy if Woodfall confess'd
him a wit. ....162 Rtal 93
WIT$_3$ To wit--most wond'rously
endu'd, ...35 NSim 57
WITHDRAWN Thy sports are fled, and
all thy charms withdrawn; ....36 DVil 24
WITHDREW Vida, 291
WITHERED Vida, 603
WITHERS Withers the beauty's
transient flower: ....76 DTrn 54
WITHIN Trav, 271; MrsX, 14; Vida, 91,
157, 464
WITHOUT Trav, 142, 337; DVil, 301;
MrsX, 14; eGNM, 9; eSSC$_3$, 2; Rtal,
74, 95, 144; ClRp, 6; eSSC$_1$, 26;
eSSC$_2$, 37; Capt, III:105; LetB,
40; Vida, 232, 556
WITHSTAND Who can withstand their
all-commanding shine? ....4 MrsX 49
WITLINGS Ye news-paper witlings! ye
pert scribbling folks ....163 Rtal 93
WIT'S The Gamester too, whose wit's
all high or low, ...23 eSSC$_2$ 108
WITS$_1$ And swore the dog had lost
his wits, ...23 MDog 65
Lost human wits have places there
assign'd them, ...3 eSSC$_2$ 108
Come thronging to collect their
scatter'd wits. ....16 eSSC$_2$ 108
WITS$_2$ False wits, false wives,

false virgins, and false spouses! ..14 eSis 70
We'll have Johnson, and Burke; all
the wits will be there; ....49 **HofV 96**
I've all the critics and the wits
for me. ....14 eSSC$_1$ 104
WITTY John Trott was desired by
two witty peers ....1 ClRp 100
WIVES False wits, false wives,
false virgins, and false spouses! ..14 eSis 70
Vida, 560
WOE The pensive exile, bending with
his woe, ...419 Trav 19
And quite forgot their vices in
their woe; ....160 DVil 28
Extorted from his fellow creature's
woe. ....314 DVil 33
Where wild Altama murmurs to their
woe. ....344 DVil 34
To new-found worlds, and wept for
others' woe; ....372 DVil 35
A bloated mass of rank unwieldy
woe; ....392 DVil 36
Thou source of all my bliss, and
all my woe, ...413 DVil 37
O Wolfe! to thee a streaming flood
of woe, ...5 Queb 46
To soothe the stranger's woe; ......58 Ed&A 61
The pensive stranger's woe; ......v58 Ed&A 208
Their charms were his, but woe to
me! ....127 Ed&A 63
Yet still (and woe betide the
hour!) ....v129 Ed&A 210
And waken every note of woe; ....2 Thrn 74
Comforter of every woe, ...113 Thrn 78
The joy that dimples, and the woe
that weeps. ....10 epLL 101
And every added weight of woe ....I:9 Capt 113
Thy smiles increase the wretch's
woe; ....vI:28 Capt 250
In vain the madd'ning prophet
threatens woe, ...III:3 Capt 122
WOE- 'And ah!' she cries, all
woe-begone, ...187 Thrn 81
WOEFUL See WOFUL
WOES With louder plaints the mother
spoke her woes, ...379 DVil 35
Sweeter from remember'd woes; .III:92 Capt 126
WOFUL Assist me, I pray, in this
woful attack; ....58 eSSC$_1$ 106
WOLF Vida, 520
WOLFE O Wolfe! to thee a stream-
ing flood of woe, ...5 Queb 46
WOMAN When lovely woman stoops to
folly, ...1 "wlw 67
Flings down her sampler, and takes
up the woman: ....22 eSis 70
He turns old woman, and bestrides
a broom. ....36 eSis 71
WOMEN The men have tails, the women
paint the face! ....26 pZob 73
His gallants are all faultless, his
women divine, ...65 Rtal 89
WON Shoulder'd his crutch, and
show'd how fields were won. ....158 DVil 28
WONDER$_1$ And still they gaz'd, and
still the wonder grew, ...215 DVil 30
But soon a wonder came to light, ...29 MDog 66
WONDER$_2$ Trace every scene, and
wonder at the change, ...v(82) DVil 182
WONDERED And freshmen wonder'd
as he spoke. ....6 DTrn 52
WONDERING And, wond'ring man could
want the larger pile, ...163 Trav 10
The wondering fair one turn'd to
chide, ...147 Ed&A 64
The wond'ring neighbours ran, ...22 MDog 65
And, wondering how their rage was
borne, ...22 Thrn 75
Vida, 29
WONDERS And comedy wonders at being
so fine; ....66 Rtal 89
WONDROUS Yet would the village
praise my wondrous power, ...249 Trav 13
With manners wond'rous winning, ...10 MBlz 47
And, though her fops are wond'rous
civil, ...69 DTrn 54
And if you find it wond'rous short, .3 MDog 65
When every bosom swells with
wond'rous scenes, ...7 pZob 72
These hills how sweet! those plains
how wond'rous fair, ...I:21 Capt 114
WOND'ROUSLY To wit--most
wond'rously endu'd, ...35 NSim 57
WOOD- No more the wood-man's ballad
shall prevail; ....244 DVil 31
WOODCOCK Let some cry up woodcock
or hare, ...23 "LSm 84
WOODFALL Yet happy if Woodfall
confess'd him a wit. ....162 Rtal 93
WOODFALLS Ye Kenricks, ye Kellys,
and Woodfalls so grave, ...115 Rtal 91
WOODLAND From lawn to woodland
stray; ....v(162) Ed&A 211
Zephyrs through the woodland
playing, ...II:49 Capt 120
WOODS Woods over woods in gay
theatric pride; ....108 Trav 8
Those matted woods where birds for-
get to sing, ...349 DVil 34
He quits the woods, and tries the
beaten ways; ....41 epLL 102
Vida, 264
WORD Who never wanted a good word-- .3 MBlz 47
Yet grant a word by way of post-
script. ....56 NSim 57
Hold! Prompter, hold! a word be-
fore your nonsense; ....1 epLL 101
I'd speak a word or two, to ease
my conscience. ....2 epLL 101
The company set, and the word to
be, Loo; ....2 LetB 131
WORDS While words of learned length
and thund'ring sound ....213 DVil 30
Give him good words indeed, but no
assistance. ....22 eGNM 68
No words--I insist on't--precisely
at three: ....48 HofV 96
No words, my dear GOLDSMITH! my
very good Friend! ....v56 HofV 240
Ye jockey tribe, whose stock of
words are few, ...49 eSSC$_1$ 106
Vida, 570
WORK For him no wretches, born to
work and weep, ...103 DVil 26

Ye captive tribes, that hourly work
and weep ....I:1 Capt 113
WORKS₁   More lasting rapture from
his works shall rise, ...9 epTP 100
WORKS₂   But chok'd with sedges, works
its weedy way. ....42 DVil 24
WORLD   And find no spot of all the
world my own. ....30 Trav 6
Creation's heir, the world, the
world is mine! ....50 Trav 7
In passive ease they leave the
world to chance. ....v(156) Trav 170
Pleas'd with thyself, whom all
the world can please, ...242 Trav 13
Thus idly busy rolls their world
away: ....256 Trav 13
Sees an amphibious world beneath
him smile; ....292 Trav 15
In all my wand'rings round this
world of care, ...83 DVil 26
Who quits a world where strong
temptations try ....101 DVil 26
His Heaven commences ere the world
be pass'd! ....112 DVil 27
And rich men flock from all the
world around. ....272 DVil 32
Around the world each needful
product flies, ...283 DVil 32
For all the luxuries the world
supplies: ....284 DVil 32
Where half the convex world in-
trudes between, ...342 DVil 34
Or winter wraps the polar world
in snow, ...420 DVil 37
Of whom the world might say, ...6 MDog 65
When they have journeyed through a
world of cares, ...88 Thrn 77
This world itself, if thou art
here, ...117 Thrn 78
Let us, let all the world agree, ..138 Thrn 79
He led such a damnable life in
this world,-- ....3 epEP 100
His lunar, and our mimic world
agree. ....8 eSSC₂ 108
Insulted, chain'd, and all the
world a foe, ...I:5 Capt 113
Thou, like the world, th'
opprest oppressing, ...vI:27 Capt 250
Cyrus, the conqueror of the
world, prevails, ...III:60 Capt 125
Comes to give the world re-
pose. ....III:94 Capt 126
Cyrus comes, the world re-
dressing, ...III:95 Capt 126
Vida, 677
WORLDLY   And now, when worldly
crowds retire ....v45 Ed&A 208
WORLD'S   The world's a masquerade!
the maskers, you, you, you. ....12 eSis 70
WORLDS   Allur'd to brighter worlds,
and led the way. ....170 DVil 28
To new-found worlds, and wept for
others' woe; ....372 DVil 35
He only wish'd for worlds beyond
the grave. ....374 DVil 35
Through rolling worlds, or fields
of liquid light, ...107 Thrn 77

To worlds below ....II:23 Capt 119
-WORM   Jack Book-worm led a
college life; ....2 DTrn 52
WORN   Where my worn soul, each
wand'ring hope at rest, ...61 Trav 7
Of life, or worn our days to
wretchedness. ....99 Thrn 77
By use and daily meditation worn; .184 Thrn 81
Behold his wretched corse with
sorrow worn, ...III:31 Capt 123
-WORN   And e'en the bare-worn
common is denied. ....308 DVil 33
WORSE   'The younger the worse,' I
return him again, ...57 LetB 133
Vida, 594
-WORSHIP   Ourselves alone from idol-
worship free? ....I:34 Capt 114
WORSHIPS   Your worships must
know ....23 Invt 128
But, alas! your good worships, how
could they be wiser, ...43 Invt 129
WORST₁   Nor this the worst. As
nature's ties decay, ...349 Trav 16
Nor this the worst. As social bonds
decay, ...v349 Trav 174
But still the worst remain'd behind, 37 DTrn 53
WORST₂   His very worst foe can't
accuse him of that: ....132 Rtal 91
'Thou best humour'd man with the
worst humour'd muse.' ....174 Rtal 93
WORTH₁   Or e'en imaginary worth
obtains, ...260 Trav 13
Nor weighs the solid worth of
self-applause. ....280 Trav 14
Wisdom and worth were all he had, 115 Ed&A 63
Arise, ye sons of worth, arise, ...1 Thrn 74
Truth, beauty, worth, and all that
most engage, ...74 Thrn 76
WORTH₂   For giving advice that is not
worth a straw, ...37 LetB 132
Vida, 183
WOULD   Trav, 249, 370; DVil, 30; Gift, 7; DRtH,
11; Ed&A, v60, v122; MDog, 28; eGNM, 10; Thrn,
29, 239; Rtal, 49; HofV, v33, 70; Vida,
235, 276, 279, 300, 328, 492, 541, 544, 637
WOUND₁   The wound it seem'd both
sore and sad ....25 MDog 66
Vida, 349, 447
WOUND₂   Vida, 112, 154
WOUNDS   Wept o'er his wounds, or
tales of sorrow done, ...157 DVil 28
'Give me another horse! bind up my
wounds!--soft--'twas but a dream,'24 epLL 101
WRANGLING   Now wrangling and grumbling to keep up the ball, ...55 Rtal 89
WRAPPED   Five greasy nightcaps wrapp'd
her head. ....46 DTrn 53
WRAPS   The robe that wraps his limbs
in silken sloth ....279 DVil 32
Or winter wraps the polar world in
snow, ...420 DVil 37
To bless the tomb that wraps thy
clay; ....133 Thrn 78
WRATH   Shall wrath vindictive
threaten ere it fall! ....III:38 Capt 124
WRECKS   By arts, the splendid wrecks
of former pride; ....146 Trav 10

Some splendid arts, the wrecks
of former pride; ....v146 Trav 170
WRETCH Comfort came down the
trembling wretch to raise, ...175 DVil 29
But leaves the wretch to weep? ......76 Ed&A 61
A wretch forlorn,' she cried; ....94 Ed&A 62
As puffing quacks some caitiff
wretch procure ....1 eGNM 68
The wretch who wants each other
blessing, ...I:29 Capt 114
On hope the wretch relies; ......II:34 Capt 119
The Wretch condemn'd with life to
part, ...vII:33 Capt 250
WRETCHED$_1$ More skill'd to raise
the wretched than to rise. ....148 DVil 28
More bent to raise the wretched
than to rise. ....v148 DVil 184
Thus to relieve the wretched was
his pride, ...163 DVil 28
WRETCHED$_2$ She, wretched matron,
forc'd, in age, for bread, ...131 DVil 27
Behold his wretched corse with
sorrow worn, ...III:31 Capt 123
WRETCHEDNESS Of life, or worn our
days to wretchedness. ....99 Thrn 77
WRETCHES Here wretches seek dishonourable graves, ...310 Trav 15
For him no wretches, born to work
and weep, ...103 DVil 26
Unthinking wretches! have not you,
and all, ...II:85 Capt 121
Ye wretches who, by fortune's
hate, ...III:23 Capt 123
Now, now's our time! ye wretches
bold and blind, ...III:69 Capt 125
WRETCH'S Thy smiles increase the
wretch's woe; ....vI:28 Capt 250
-WRIGHTS Thus on the stage, our
play-wrights still depend ....3 eGNM 68
WRING And wring his bosom, is--to
die. ....8 "wlw 67
WRITE 'Twas certain he could write,
and cypher too; ....208 DVil 30
Nor draw the quill to write for
B--b. ....32 LogR 45
The modern scribbling kind, who write 3 NSim 56
Macpherson write bombast, and call
it a style, ...87 Rtal 90
Who dabble and write in the Papers--
like you; ....v76 HofV 241
WRITERS Add too, what certain writers
tell, ...41 NSim 57
WRITES Denote the rage with which
he writes, ...47 NSim 57
The one writes the Snarler, the other the
Scourge; ....77 HofV 97
Some think he writes Cinna--he owns
to Panurge.' ....78 HofV 97
WRITING 'Alas, young man, my writing
days are over; ....12 eGNM 68
WRONG$_1$ All earth-born cares are
wrong: ....30 Ed&A 60
For earth-born cares are wrong: ...v30 Ed&A 208
His conduct still right, with his
argument wrong; ....46 Rtal 88
Vida, 279
WRONG$_2$ For sure I don't wrong you,
you seldom are slack, ...59 eSSC$_1$ 106
WRONGS For thine and Britain's
wrongs they feel, ...228 Thrn 82
Cyrus comes, our wrongs
redressing, ...III:93 Capt 126
WROTE Where kings have toil'd,
and poets wrote for fame, ...358 Trav 17
You, I, he, wrote it not--'twas
Churchill's all. ....4 GCRL 51
WROUGHT To swear the pill, or drop,
has wrought a cure; ....2 eGNM 68
-WROUGHT Till over-wrought, the
general system feels ....347 Trav 16
-WRUNG Whilst thy sad fate extorts
the heart-wrung tear. ....8 Queb 46

YE Trav, 45, 46, 47, 48, 363; DVil, 265; MrsX,
8; DRtH, 1; Thrn, 1, 79, 80, 81, 83, 163, 164;
Rtal, 81, 115, 135, 163, 165; eSSC$_1$, 5, 16,
31, 47, 49, 51, 57; Capt, I:1, 17, 18, 19,
20, 65, 79; II:27, 45, 91; III:23, 69; LetB,
39; Vida, 6, 10; Tr, 8
YEAR Whose bright succession decks
the varied year; ....116 Trav 9
On some high festival of once a year,224 Trav 12
To boast one splendid banquet once
a year; ....278 Trav 14
And, many a year elaps'd, return to
view ....79 DVil 25
And passing rich with forty pounds
a year; ....142 DVil 28
Scarce half alive, oppress'd with
many a year, ...3 pLab 41
O! had he liv'd another year!-- .....3 DRtH 50
Who take a trip to Paris once a
year ....33 eSSC$_1$ 105
YEARS The fond companion of his
helpless years, ...376 DVil 35
And speaks in moments more than
years. ....16 Tr 267
YELL Vida, 411
YELLOW And owns its offspring in
their yellow eyes. ....14 Cati 94
YELLOW- The slow canal, the yellow-
blossom'd vale, ...293 Trav 15
YELLS And all around distressful
yells arise, ...418 Trav 19
YES Yes, brother, curse with me
that baleful hour, ...393 Trav 18
Yes! let the rich deride, the proud
disdain, ...251 DVil 31
No doubt they're all barbarians.--
Yes, 'tis so, ...27 pZob 73
But for a head, yes, yes, I have
a head. ....34 epLL 102
The Epilogue. The Epilogue? Yes, the
Epilogue, my dear. ....2 eSSC$_1$ 103
Yes, I shall die, hu, hu, hu, hu! 27 eSSC$_1$ 105
Yes, I must die, ho, ho, ho, ho! 28 eSSC$_1$ 105
Yes, he's far gone:--and yet some
pity fix, ...41 eSSC$_2$ 109
Yes, my companions, Heaven's
decrees are past, ...III:1 Capt 122
YET Trav, 28, 54, 57, 75, v75, 89, 129, 145,
v145, 175, 211, 249, 361; DVil, 205, 273; pLab,
14; Gift, 17; Sonn, 5, v5; Queb, 11; DTrn,
28; NSim, 56; Ed&A, v129; eSis, 21, 35;

pZob, 13; Thrn, 52, 84; Rtal, 27, 33, 47, 56, 97, 105, 128, 143, 156, 160, 162; HofV, 62; epLL, 28; $eSSC_2$, 41; Capt, I:31; II:91; Invt, 33; LetB, 9, 11, 21, 63; Vida, 7, 109, 120, 124, 136, 176, 177, 202, 250, 257, 430, 441, 452, 464, 526, 562, 568, 610, 629

YEW Vida, 62

YIELD The 'squire himself was seen to yield, ...89 DTrn 55
Old Edward's sons, unknown to yield, 225 Thrn 82
I wish for life, and yield me to my fears. ....II:30 Capt 119
Vida, 99, 148, 222, 361, 395

YON Like yon neglected shrub at random cast, ...103 Trav 8
All but yon widow'd, solitary thing 129 DVil 27
Beside yon straggling fence that skirts the way, ...193 DVil 29
Down where yon anchoring vessel spreads the sail, ...399 DVil 36
To where yon taper cheers the vale ...3 Ed&A 59
Yon broad, bold, angry spark, I fix my eye on, ...27 eSis 71
Yon politician, famous in debate, ...33 eSis 71
Yon patriot, too, who presses on your sight, ...37 eSis 71
Yon critic, too--but whither do I run? ....41 eSis 71
Yon ill foreboding cloud seems big with thunder. ....18 pZob 72
But ha! what means yon sadly plaintive train, ...III:15 Capt 123
'What, yon solemn-faced, odd-looking man that stands near!' ....50 LetB 133

YONDER Up yonder hill the village murmur rose; ....114 DVil 27
Near yonder copse, where once the garden smil'd, ...137 DVil 27
Near yonder thorn, that lifts its head on high, ...219 DVil 30
To yonder fire, that cheers the vale v3 Ed&A 208
For yonder faithless phantom flies ..11 Ed&A 59
For yonder phantom only flies .....v11 Ed&A 208
Our ship's well stor'd;--in yonder creek we've laid her; ....31 pZob 73
Or why those harps on yonder willows hung? ....I:80 Capt 116
Ere yonder setting sun; ....II:80 Capt 121
To yonder gloomy dungeon turn your eyes; ....II:87 Capt 121
And now, methinks, to yonder bank they bear ....III:17 Capt 123
See yonder tower just nodding to the fall: ....III:48 Capt 124

YORE In virtuous times of yore, ...6 DRtH 50

YOU'D You'd have sent before night; 4 Invt 128

YOU'LL NSim, 11; eSis, 32; $eSSC_1$, 13

YOUNG$_1$ The young contending as the old survey'd; ....20 DVil 23
The sober herd that low'd to meet their young; ....118 DVil 27
Give me the young, the gay, the men of spirit. ....30 $eSSC_1$ 105

YOUNG$_2$ Amongst the rest young Edwin bow'd, ...111 Ed&A 63
Among the rest young Edwin bow'd, v111 Ed&A 209
'Young man,' cries one--a bard laid up in clover-- ....11 eGNM 68
'Alas, young man, my writing days are over; ....12 eGNM 68
Harmless and young, of ev'ry thing afraid; ....10 $eSSC_3$ 85
'Consider, dear Doctor, the girls are but young.' ....56 LetB 133
Vida, 61, 226, 288, 342, 547, 563

YOUNGER 'The younger the worse,' I return him again, ...57 LetB 133

YOU'RE For you're always polite and attentive, ...61 $eSSC_1$ 106
Now, ladies, I ask, if law-matters you're skill'd in, ...35 LetB 132

YOUTH$_1$ 'And whence, unhappy youth,' he cried, ...63 Ed&A 61
'For shame, fond youth, thy sorrows hush, ...81 Ed&A 62
He, fond youth, that could carry me, ...3 "Amw 94
Vida, 214

YOUTH$_2$ A youth of labour with an age of ease; ....100 DVil 26
Seats of my youth, when every sport could please, ...6 DVil 23
Secure to please while youth confirms her reign, ...288 DVil 32
In innocence and youth complaining, 231 Thrn 82
Forgive my sex's fears, forgive my youth! ....II:28 Capt 119
You vain, whom youth and pleasure guide, ...III:27 Capt 123
Vida, 8, 174, 440

YOUTHFUL And, rifling ev'ry youthful grace, ...79 DTrn 54
His looks resume their youthful pride, ...v151 Ed&A 211
Where, splendid as the youthful poet's dream, ...142 Thrn 79
Say heavenly muse, their youthful frays rehearse; ....7 Tr 267

YOU'VE You've got an odd something-- a kind of discerning-- ....119 HofV 99

ZEAL With steady zeal, each honest rustic ran; ....182 DVil 29
Vida, 356

ZEALOUS Though grave, yet trifling; zealous, yet untrue; ....129 Trav 9
Vida, 145

ZEDEKIAH Unhappy Zedekiah is no more! ....III:22 Capt 123

ZEDEKIAH'S Beheld our power in Zedekiah's fall? ....II:86 Capt 121

ZEPHYR No Zephyr fondly sues the mountain's breast, ...173 Trav 11
And freshen'd from the wave the Zephyr flew; ....246 Trav 13

ZEPHYRS Zephyrs through the woodland playing, ...II:49 Capt 120

ZONE The shudd'ring tenant of the frigid zone ....65 Trav 7